High and Dry

High and Dry

GARDENING WITH COLD-HARDY DRYLAND PLANTS

Robert Nold

Timber Press

Frontispiece: *Townsendia condensata* and velvet ant. *Pages 6–7*: *Purshia stansburiana* and two-tailed swallowtail (*Papilio multicaudata*). All illustrations—photographs and watercolors—are by Cindy Nelson-Nold.

Published in 2008 by
Timber Press, Inc.
The Haseltine Building
133 S.W. Second Avenue, Suite 450
Portland, Oregon 97204-3527, U.S.A.
www.timberpress.com

For contact information regarding editorial, marketing, sales, and distribution in the United Kingdom, see www.timberpress.co.uk.

Designed by Susan Applegate.
Printed in China.

Library of Congress Cataloging-in-Publication Data

Nold, Robert.
High and dry: gardening with cold-hardy dryland plants/Robert Nold.
p. cm.
Includes bibliographical references and index.
ISBN-13: 978-0-88192-872-3
1. High altitude gardening—Rocky Mountains. 2. Drought-tolerant plants—Rocky Mountains. I. Title. II. Title: Gardening with cold-hardy dryland plants.
SB458.94.N65 2008
635.9′528—dc22 2007023509

A catalog record for this book is also available from the British Library.

To the memory of
Homer Hill,
master propagator
of native plants

Contents

Foreword

I suspect there will always be glossy seed catalogs stuffing mailboxes in January, and no end of coffee table books of lush borders brimming with roses and giant delphiniums. But let us hope we will still have that other sort of book, books like Claude Barr's *Jewels of the Plains*, or any one of Elizabeth Lawrence's classics—beautifully written accounts of plants and gardens written by real gardeners who can wield a mighty pen as well as trowel.

As I read and reread Bob Nold's account of our western native Great Plains plants, the tousled wildflowers of the Great Basin badlands and alpine ridges, I could almost feel the prairie wind whistling in my ears, see the paintbrush poking up through the sagebrush, catch the scent of the fragrant rose-red matted phlox I saw once on a camping trip at Bryce, dewy at dawn. The Rocky Mountain and Intermountain regions contain the lion's share of America's national parks and public lands. This area is renowned for wildflower displays and scenic grandeur. It is astonishing to think that the great American Interior West—one of the fastest-growing regions in the world, burgeoning with high-tech enterprises and vast metropolises—has never had a gardening book dedicated to the proposition that one might actually grow within the city what grows beyond the city limits. I doubt that there is anywhere on the globe where urban and suburban gardens are so utterly different from the natural environment they replace. And yet we Westerners claim we love our mountains and plains and live here because of them. (If I hear one more SUV-driving hypocrite who lives in a McMansion use the word "sustainable," or "environmental," or "conservation" . . .)

Anyone who tries to create a truly native garden filled with penstemons and buckwheats and all the other treasures that Bob Nold describes so beautifully is too apt to apply the same cultural techniques required by lawns, hybrid tea roses, and our other alien garden phantasms. One is almost guaranteed failure—unless one is lucky enough to stumble upon and buy and read this book. And even if you live in Boise, Boston, or Bordeaux, Bob has shown you how to condense the Big Sky and towering western buttes and their attendant minion wildflowers into a trough on your balcony or into a xeriscape along your street.

The volume you hold in your hands is one of the very few books I know of that are executed with verbal artistry, with utterly novel content, charm, humor, and wisdom, all while providing a fascinating, detailed roadmap to profound stewardship in gardens. As more and more pristine prairie is busted and paved for shopping malls and oil rigs, this book is nothing less than an act of grace. Amen.

Panayoti Kelaidis
Denver, Colorado

Introduction

This book is the product of a gardener, who, after forty-five years of living in what he has always loudly proclaimed to be the most awful gardening climate on the planet, finally came to his senses and decided things were not as bad as that. True, trying to garden in a semi-arid climate that also features brutally cold winters does not sound like the most pleasant situation to be in, but there is a wide variety, in fact an almost endless variety, of native plants that are not only beautiful but provide highly satisfactory choices for the garden.

The gardener is, of course, me, and although I blush easily, this book is probably as much about me as it is about gardening. There will still be wailing and groaning, plenty of whining, mixed in with a few boastful proclamations. More than once a trowel will be hurled to the ground in fury, and my long-suffering spouse will once again be told to expect the house to be put up for sale, in anticipation of a move to any climate where it rains more than once a year, preferably one where temperatures rarely, instead of continually, go below freezing.

I am wary of gardening books written by people who purport to have knowledge of how to garden in climates dissimilar to the ones in which they garden. I have none. I have absolutely no idea what gardening is like anywhere else, although I have visited gardens on both coasts of North

Penstemon angustifolius var. *caudatus* and pepsis wasp

America, and have even experienced rain in the middle of January, a bizarre and unbelievably wonderful experience.

This book is directed toward gardeners living west of the 100th meridian in North America, north of the low deserts of Arizona, and east of the Cascades and Sierra Nevada. I do assume, possibly wrongly, that gardening in climates similar to Denver's (those of Salt Lake City, Cheyenne, Boise, Helena, Flagstaff, and Spokane, to name just a few cities) has more or less the same set of joys and frustrations. I invite other gardeners interested in growing some of the plants I describe to listen in on my monologue: many of these plants have been successfully grown in other climates by providing the plants with a more porous soil and protection from excessive moisture in winter. The chief factor in successful cultivation seems to be providing the plants with a sufficient amount of sun during the growing season. Denver is one of the sunniest cities in North America, with light intensity, expressed in calories received, equivalent to Cairo, and thirty-three percent more ultraviolet light than cities on the coasts. The glare from the sun here is considerable; I wear sunglasses every day.

I feel I have an advantage living in Denver. Thanks to the irrepressible efforts of the practically omniscient Panayoti Kelaidis, the Rock Alpine Garden at Denver Botanic Gardens has become a shrine that attracts worshipful pilgrims in every month of the year, not only rock gardeners but all gardeners interested in seeing the available selection of winter-hardy plants capable of enduring intense sunlight and low humidity. After a prolonged bout of despair, which this climate occasionally encourages, a visit to the Rock Alpine Garden made everything seem better. As the years passed, the plantings at the Gardens expanded in sophistication and beauty, with more and more plants growing happily in a climate where, forty years ago, we thought nothing would grow. I and everyone else gardening in the region owe an enormous debt to the efforts of Panayoti, who, more than anyone else, has turned Denver and the Rocky Mountain region into a paradise for gardeners.

The plants described in this book are all, with a very few exceptions, plants I have grown in my garden. Some are actually still alive. My comments on drought tolerance are based on observation, particularly during 2002, the horrific year when the garden received one inch (2.5cm) of precipitation in eleven months. (An additional four inches, 10 cm, came in the month of September.)

My preference is for selecting plants that will do well in a "normal" year (for me, that would be about ten inches, 25 cm, of precipitation, much of that falling as snow), without any supplemental irrigation once the plants are established, and winter hardy to –10F (–23C). I hope that readers will not think I try to make a religion out of this; it is acceptable to water from time to time, and to protect prized plants from cold now and then.

I also don't have very much patience with horticultural information derived from guessing the climatic conditions of a plant's natural habitat; the criterion here must always be the observed garden performance of the plant over a period of years. This is the only way that I can impart helpful information and advice.

Readers hoping to find information on how to relate the growing of these plants to one of the seemingly endless series of trademarked landscaping styles like Xeriscape™ will be disappointed. Many of the plants designated as "low-water" in the nursery industry have failed repeatedly in the garden here, so I have to focus on my own experience.

These are harsh climates that gardeners in our region must deal with from week to week. I would argue that the climates in our region offer exponentially more difficult gardening than any of those found on either coast of North America, but at the same time many plants are more easily grown here than elsewhere. I see my purpose here as being, to paraphrase Allen Ginsberg, to ease the pain of gardening, and direct gardeners to more amenable and suitable plants so that going out into the garden is as much of a dream as it is anywhere else on earth.

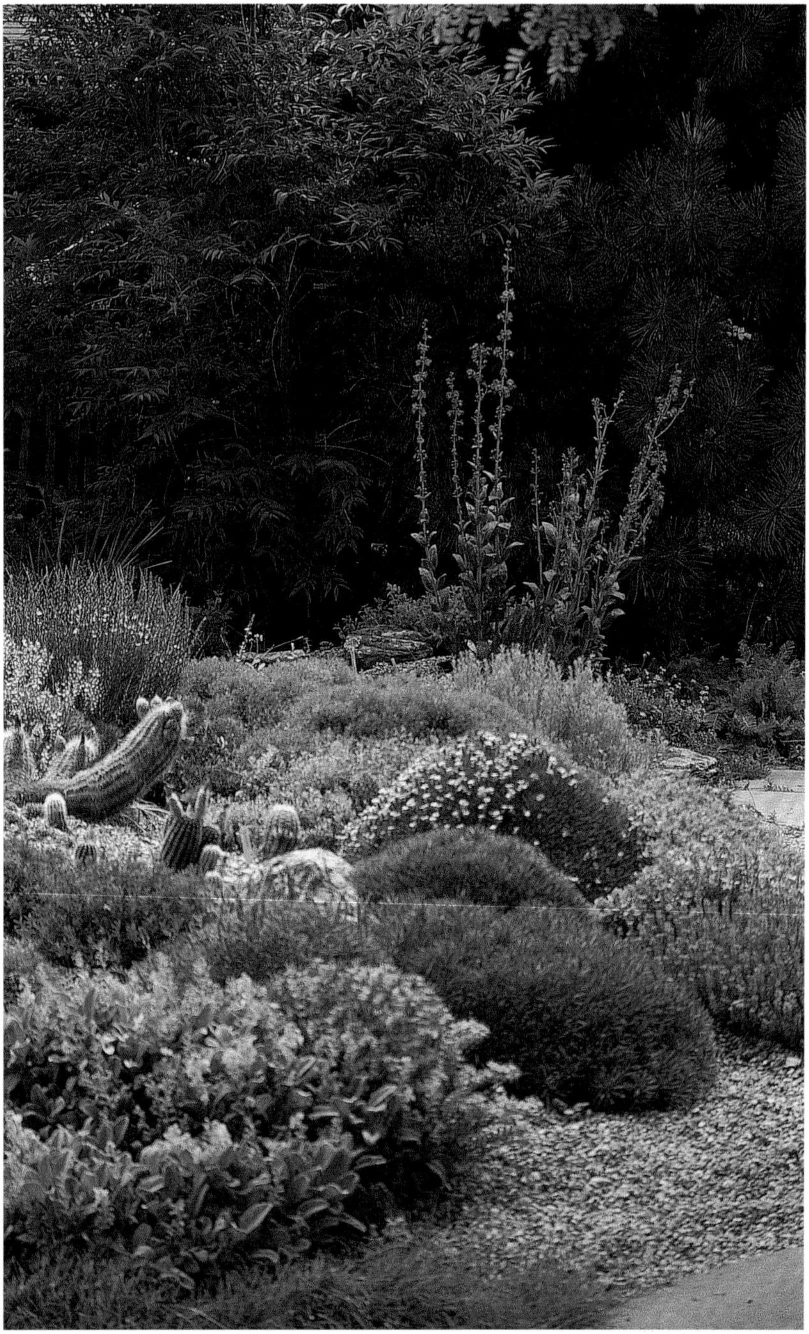

CHAPTER ONE

The High Plains Garden

If the Pilgrims Had Landed at La Jolla

I once attended a lecture on growing native drought-tolerant plants given by someone who did not actually grow native drought-tolerant plants—they'd just heard of them. The lecturer was well known in American horticulture and had acquired a considerable reputation east of the Mississippi River.

The lecture, before my attention began to wander as it almost always does, focused on the proper cultivation of these plants, which included soil preparation (such as the addition of organic matter), mulching, watering techniques, fertilizing, pest control, and so forth. In other words, it was a catalog of the usual good gardening practices.

These practices actually originate in farming, not in ornamental gardening; heavy soil is made lighter by adding organic matter so that the fine roots of vegetables can move more quickly through the friable soil, and organic matter supplies nutrients as it breaks down into the soil. A lighter, more porous soil allows rain to enter the soil, and maintaining soil like this without it drying out instantly is possible since rain is common in areas where this technique is practiced. Mulching keeps down weeds and prevents the sun from heating up the soil excessively.

Making the change from farming to ornamental gardening via veg-

Dry garden with *Penstemon superbus* in back

etable gardening is fairly effortless, since most garden plants originate in climates with regular rainfall and require a soil similar to that recommended for vegetable gardening. Woodland plants in particular demand an extremely light soil, preferably enriched by centuries of rotting leaves, for their thread-fine roots.

Since, rightly or wrongly, horticulture has assumed that the conditions and climate of a plant's native habitat dictate how it should be grown, most garden plants suited to temperate climates are native to climates with relatively high rainfall. At the same time, living in a climate with high rainfall is conducive to a great deal of gardening, since there are plenty of plants from which to choose. It is like having an empty stomach and going to an all-you-can-eat buffet.

The staggeringly high quality of gardening in Great Britain and the vast assortment of plants grown there is mirrored, with the constraints imposed by colder winters and more "sun," in eastern North American gardening (to say nothing of the west coast, which, given the climates there, has developed almost an independent style of horticulture). There are good reasons why American horticulture is so heavily influenced by east-coast gardening; all you have to do is visit the innumerable ravishingly beautiful public and private gardens there to see why this is so.

I sat there half-listening to the lecture, thinking that the speaker was just about as clueless as a person could possibly be. Why on earth would anyone think that plants native to an area that gets ten inches (25 cm) of precipitation a year have the same cultivation requirements as plants—any plants—native to eastern North America? and why did the audience approve of this?

For a variety of reasons, including the obvious one featuring covered wagons, the exact same style of gardening practiced in eastern North America is practiced in the Rocky Mountain and Intermountain regions. ("Anglos from temperate climates suddenly confronted with vast, treeless, arid spaces," in Gary Snyder's words.) It's odd to think that gardening styles are the result of a sort of horticultural Manifest Destiny. Cities are planted with trees native to eastern North America; parks and gardens are planted with the same plants grown in eastern North America. All this is accomplished with massive irrigation to compensate for the region's much lower rainfall (not to mention low humidity, high light intensity, and wind). Jack Kerouac called Salt Lake City "a city of sprinklers." So is Denver, where I live.

What if the Pilgrims had landed at La Jolla instead of Plymouth Rock? Our standards of beauty in horticulture might resemble an imitation of California coastal chaparral instead of a green garden half-smothered with trees. Gardening techniques would have evolved from trying to cultivate plants from climates radically different from those of Great Britain—and by extension, eastern North America—and the standards of beauty and plant performance might be equally different. Imagine a gardening style where any (any!) plant needing summer watering would be automatically rejected . . .

Some attempts have been made, since the mid 1980s, to create at least the idea of regional gardening styles in the gardening literature, but these almost always focus only on plant choices instead of advocating new gardening techniques that are appropriate to growing dryland plants. Writing on this subject is usually populated with phrases like "signature plants" that create "a sense of place," so much so that these have become platitudes, and mystifying ones at that. Obviously these are only notions in the mind of the writer. If by "signature plants" it is meant plantings of plants uniquely grown in a particular region, and by a "sense of place" it is meant (as it usually does) plants native to that particular area, then signs would have to be employed all over the garden indicating which are the unique plants and which are the native ones.

Even botanists do not always recognize unusual plants that would create a sense of place, or that would definitely suggest that this is a garden closer to Oz than something straight out of a gardening magazine. I have had occasion to explain, when someone with a considerable knowledge of the flora of Arizona, doubted that the desert willow (*Chilopsis linearis*) was hardy in Denver, that the small tree they walked under before knocking on our front door was the desert willow itself. (In fact the only person I recall even noticing this plant, which is the largest thing in the front yard, was a non-gardener who had previously lived in Arizona and recognized it immediately. Everyone else who has visited the garden, when the subject came up, has suggested the desert willow is not hardy. "But," I have to say, "you walked right under it . . .")

So much for the sense of place.

Chilopsis linearis

The long journey across the Great Plains must have destroyed, or subdued, any desire for immersion in new experiences that could not be translated from ones that had their origins further east on the continent, since even when you see gardens planted with native dryland plants there is heavy irrigation; this is especially true in public gardens. (I admit that this is slightly puritanical of me.) The theory here is that well-watered gardens look better, which is of course true, but is it realistic to think that this is a sustainable type of gardening in times of drought and perpetual water shortages?

Dryland gardening has no history in the cold-winter regions of western North America, except for the examples of a brave few like Claude Barr. Elsewhere it is called dryland gardening but with irrigation, either obvious or clandestine. It is hard for people to accept the idea that a garden does not have to be watered.

I would argue that successful dryland gardening requires a rejection of much of the accepted wisdom of traditional horticulture, a whole new catalog of plants, a new gardening technique, and a wholesale acceptance, without reservation, of the realities of the climates of the west.

Drought and Watering

Though some garden writers, not to mention those who write plant descriptions in nursery catalogs, tend to use the word "drought" with utter abandon, making it difficult to know exactly how much water a plant really requires, I will stick with the most rigid and easily understood definition of drought. "Drought" means absence of rain.

Drought-tolerant plants will grow and flower even when enduring prolonged drought, causing the gardener little or no concern during summers when watering restrictions are imposed, during years of normal precipitation, or, sometimes, during severe drought.

How a plant behaves in the wild does not always translate into the same behavior in the garden. In fact it's no exaggeration to claim that the conditions a plant finds in the wild only offer a very generalized idea of what to expect once the plant is in a garden, the garden being a much different sort of place, even if there is an overt effort to replicate natural conditions. Thus the only real way a garden plant can be truly characterized as drought-tolerant is by its performance in the garden. Until it has been planted and grown for several years in a dry garden, it should be considered an unknown quantity, though it is reasonable to assume that plants native to the same area as your garden will survive perfectly well without supplemental irrigation.

A few clarifications must be made at this point. Some species are drought-tolerant only if they receive expected moisture at a certain period of the year. Penstemons are a classic example of this; if the spring is suitably wet, following the pattern of natural rainfall they have adapted to, they will endure months of total summer drought with aplomb. If the spring is dry, they will spend too much energy trying to grow leaves and may die by the onset of autumn. This is a common, observable phenomenon in our dry garden.

Other species may be adapted to drought in their native habitats but perform poorly in cold-winter gardens. I think that the reason for this

Dry garden

is that plants native to areas with milder winters find their development in cold-winter gardens arrested by unseasonably late frosts and are forced to spend energy recouping in June instead of settling in for a dry summer. So, the less cold-hardy a plant is, especially in spring, the less drought-tolerant it will be. This is a maxim that should be kept in mind when reading about plants whose cultivation is extrapolated from what must be a passing knowledge of a plant's habitat. Typically, the hardier Californians fall in this category. Many Californian species whose cultural notes are accompanied by a dire warning against summer watering actually do require it, and sometimes a lot of it, in cold-winter climates.

The only area in North America where plants are adapted to total summer drought is west of the Sierra Nevada. Since plants native to the Intermountain and Rocky Mountain regions, and the Great Plains, grow during the summer (with some exceptions), when it rains, the often-repeated claim that some of these plants can be negatively affected (i.e., killed) by summer watering can be dismissed as fiction.

In fact the plants described in this book can be watered regularly, will not die during the rare rainy summer, and respond to heavy watering by more robust growth and more profuse flowering. True, some of the rock garden plants may rot if the humidity is too high, but these are exceptions.

I suspect that one reason for the notion that native dryland plants can't be watered is derived from an unconscious (or conscious) puritanical attitude that reacts to any form of pleasure, including garden watering and especially (or, more specifically) lawn watering. The various landscape practices aimed at water conservation (or something) developed by water providers, usually identified with a trademark, seem to me to verge more on a religion than a practical approach to gardening. The characteristic fervor can be detected by the constant attacks on Kentucky bluegrass lawns, and the comparison of the amount of water "required" (usually the amount recommended for optimum performance, not the amount actually needed to keep the lawn green) by these lawns versus "low-water" plants. The water given these plants is often two or three times the amount I give my lawn, but of course, the actual amount of watering is rarely specified. (The late Henry Mitchell's comment that "the duplicity of some garden writers is breathtaking" is apropos here.) Anyway, at the risk of incurring the undying enmity of practically everyone, I am purposely ignoring the existence of all these landscaping practices . . . none of which was invented by gardeners.

I have no objection if you decide you want to water your plants every week. Your garden can't then be called a dry garden, of course, though most people (sigh . . .) still insist they can use this to describe a heavily watered garden. (In this case it's dry, I suppose, like dry champagne.)

Drip irrigation is favored by some gardeners as a way to conserve water. It is certainly vastly more efficient than setting a sprinkler and walking away, but it is still watering. I am aware of the current belief in some gardening circles that drip irrigation is not actually irrigation. Gardens on drip irrigation are just as much watered gardens as those where the sprinklers run day and night; they just use much less water. Some native plant experts advise against drip for reasons that I do not quite understand, but their alternative, no irrigation, is something I do understand.

The dry garden, or the no-water garden if you like, is simply an alternative way of doing things. There are a few things you need to know, or possibly I should say you need to think about accepting, before you jump into a commitment to maintaining a dry garden. And it is a commitment.

The native plants mentioned in this book will tolerate drought, but they rebel against total drought lasting for months on end. Some of the plants do have unknown boundaries of drought tolerance, but a planting of nothing but native plants may begin to fail in a year that brings less than one inch (2.5cm) of precipitation. There is nothing morally wrong with watering the garden in times of extreme duress, though I don't do this. I do lose plants, which is something you may want to think about if you decide not to water too.

At the height of summer, large cracks may appear in the soil (I think these add character), and some of the more particular plants may be shrunken, shriveled clumps. The neighbors may talk. (They're the ones with the high water bills.)

Once the garden has been planted, it is extremely difficult to introduce new plants into the garden, unless the summer is a rainy one, or you make a conscious effort to water your new acquisitions regularly.

Soil

Soil is a controversial subject; once we have decided to abandon irrigation as a gardening resource it would seem to make sense that we abandon traditional ideas about soil, but few people have been willing to do this.

So, "well-drained soil." This is the first and last time this phrase, all too often parroted in gardening literature, will appear in this book. In climates where rain is a rare event to be celebrated and danced in, drainage is not a concern, and soil that retains no moisture at all is a recipe for disaster. We will take our clay soils as they come, modify them with some serious digging, maybe make berms or raised beds here and there, and let excess moisture—in hopes that such a thing will occur—run off into dry wells or onto the lawn.

Sandy soils may require adding some clay or loam in order to prevent excessive drying out, unless there is a layer of clay not too far beneath the surface, but still there are plants that grow in pure, deep sand throughout the west, and if you have a very sandy soil maybe some area of the garden should be reserved for these treasures, since no one else will be able to grow them well. One caveat, though: these plants will need extra watering until their roots have reached into moisture-retaining clay.

Some deep-sand plants to be considered are *Ipomoea leptophylla* (bush morning-glory) and various penstemons, like *Penstemon ambiguus*, though these can be grown with some degree of success in very dry clay soil, too.

Soil amendments using organic matter are for vegetable gardeners.

The facts are straightforward: in the wild, drought-tolerant plants never grow in soil with any amount of organic matter in them, and as garden plants they do not need organic matter incorporated into the soil. Organic matter comes from trees and shrubs, and a persistent layer of leaves on the soil surface implies a high-rainfall climate. Plants that prefer soils with high organic content do so because their roots are small and adapted to threading their way through the loose, leafy soils that high-rainfall woodland habitats provide. When organic matter is incorporated into heavy clay soils in dry regions an alien element is introduced that may lead to the accumulation of soil-borne pathogens. In any case it is simply not necessary since our plants will do perfectly well in heavy, dry soils, their roots delving deep for necessary moisture, or snaking just below the surface in the case of cactus.

At first, I did add organic matter to the clay soil in the garden. Little did I realize that this was an activity that needed to be done every year, just as in vegetable gardening. There was no trace of organic matter within just a few years, and the soil so treated is just as rock-hard as soil left on its own.

It's a good practice to dig over the area you want to plant, preferably before the soil freezes solid, if such a thing happens in your garden. This digging is a lot of work. I like a spading fork, though a regular spade will do. Buy a good tool; good gardening tools will last for ever, which is more than you can say for your back if the spade breaks while you are digging. Double-digging isn't really necessary; digging to the depth of the blades is usually sufficient. The clods can be left to the action of frost for the winter, and by spring the soil will be much easier to work.

This soil preparation is, as they say, a one-time thing. When the garden is planted there is no opportunity to dig the garden again. Clay is sometimes said to seize up, years after it's been dug, but I have never noticed any problems in this way. I do detect a certain difficulty in digging holes for new plants in an established dry garden. This is an understatement.

My digging tools of choice in this situation (the sheriff's department has some peculiar aversion to use of dynamite in the garden) are a Model 1945 U.S. Army entrenching tool that saw action in Korea and has been my gardening companion most of my life, and an incredible trowel made by Yeoman and Company, of Monticello, Iowa. The Yo-Ho is about a foot (30 cm) long, with a heavy, sharp blade that allows me to dig in the hardest soil without spraining my wrist, though sometimes it's still an effort that requires careful moderation in the use of language.

For some reason, weeds find summer-dry soil a congenial place in which to germinate and grow. There is apparently no end to life's mysteries.

Planning the Garden

This is the obligatory section on planning the garden. Every gardening book seems to have one, so here it is.

People often ask me for help in designing their garden, or want me to tell them what to plant. I never plan anything, have no talent whatsoever for designing anything, and stopped telling people what to plant when I realized they didn't really want the advice of someone as utterly inept as I am. I start digging and see what happens. Most of the design work here, such as it is, was done by border collies running back and forth and around and around in the yard, establishing paths even though I might have wanted paths elsewhere. And the garden itself has evolved over the years, plants added here, ripped out there, and so the lack of an overall design scheme is readily apparent to visitors who expect to find one.

The main objection to garden design, as I see it, is that it implies a certain amount of ready cash and a thing called "spare time." Quite a few gardening books seem to have been written by people with the resources that allow them to have nothing else to do but garden. (In more than a few cases it is actually true.) I've always wondered if people reading these books feel slightly put off by this.

The photographs of gardens you see in magazines, especially, are almost all of very young gardens. Your garden will look like this in two or three years if you plant everything at once. If you plant over a period of years, it will take time to look lush and billowing. Never mind what you hear: anyone can have a beautiful garden, all it takes is time.

So, if you want an instant garden and can afford it, hire a garden designer. Otherwise, go to the nursery and pick out your plants, start digging, and don't worry about what people will think. Your garden should make you happy above all, and though the comments of visitors will be welcome (sometimes), the rule should be, do what you like.

Right away you will find that quite a few of the plants I recommend are not available anywhere. I feel your pain.

The Wild Garden

A wild garden is just my term for an unplanned garden in which plants grow chaotically but happily. It's what you might call a garden designer's nightmare and probably would not get you much coverage in the gardening section of your local newspaper. No, you will probably be ignored completely, in favor of heavily watered gardens. Such is life.

We have a garden like this in the front yard, of all places. A tactful visitor once remarked, "The back yard is nice, but what are you going to do in the front yard?" I imagine it will make the house difficult to sell in the future. Even though some neighborhood children came up to the

Front yard, view of the manor house

front door and were surprised to find it answered, thinking the house was abandoned, the neighbors seem to tolerate the front yard. There have been no torch-carrying crowds banging on the door at one o'clock in the morning, demanding we change the front yard to conform to the All-American ideal landscape.

In fact a lot of writing has been done about converting the front yard into something more individualistic than lawn, junipers, and driveway; as a result, front gardens are much more common than they used to be but are still rare in suburbs, where homeowners' covenants often forbid them. Probably the biggest difference between the average front garden and ours is that the garden in our front yard is never watered, which means that by the end of July after weeks of drought it can look a little tired.

Anyway, to get back to creating the garden, you start with a space, make a few paths (mine are dirt) so that you can get around once your plants are burgeoning, buy plants, and start planting. As a general rule shrubs and small trees go at the back of an area that only has one side (which in a designed garden would be called a border since it borders something, like a crumbling wall built during the reign of Henry IV), or more or less in the center of a circular or square area. As you get closer to the paths, or the front of the area you're planting, the plants should get shorter, though you can mix it up a little and plant some taller plants where the shorter ones ordinarily would be. Cacti should be kept well away from the edges of paths.

You may well say that this sounds an awful lot like planning. But nothing is drawn up on paper, and keeping cacti away from the edges of paths is based not on aesthetics, but on practicality. One of the paths in the front garden here is now blocked by an enormous opuntia that used to jab visitors in the ankle when they passed by, and I was unwilling to move the thing.

If you breeze through the plant descriptions and ignore my warning about planting whiplash daisy (*Erigeron flagellaris*), you will have an instant, ineradicable ground cover. At least it will be a native ground cover. Buffalograss, especially, and galleta grass are worth considering as ground covers too. Pea gravel, intermixed with other similarly colored gravel of a larger size (just pea gravel is less attractive than gravel

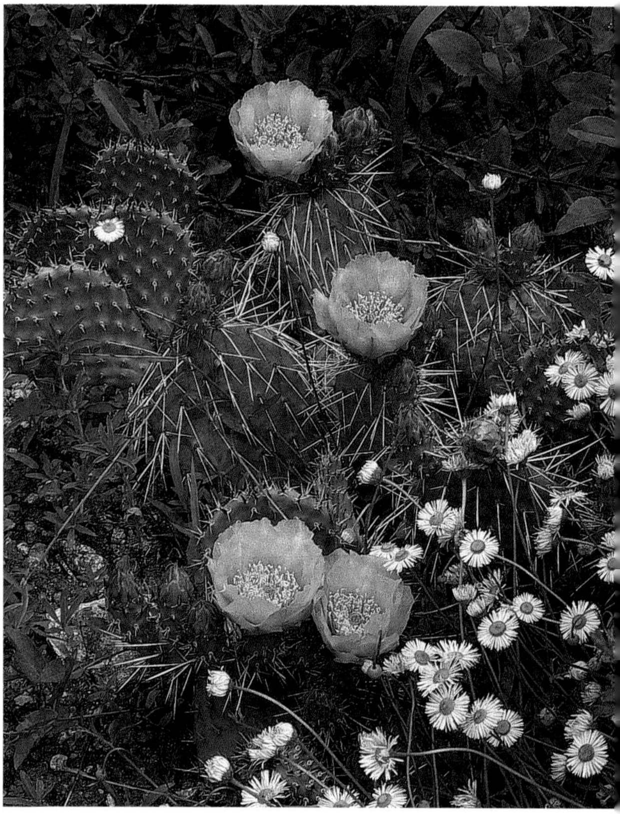

Opuntia polyacantha and *Erigeron flagellaris*

of varying sizes), makes a good mulch if you don't want a ground cover. Or you can just have dirt if you don't mind pulling weeds. (If you decide to plant opuntias and provide no ground cover, guess who will be weeding amongst them?)

The only real difference between a wild garden and a dryland perennial border is that the latter is more organized, or the plantings are a bit more controlled. I admit the distinction is arbitrary. I find that native dryland plants look better in a less controlled design, in a more or less naturalistic setting, or in rock gardens, but this is only my personal preference. Since the design of a garden is only controlled at the outset and as the years pass the plants take more and more control, the initial design—the design in plants, that is—no longer exists. Even the architecture of the garden changes over time, as raised beds sink, paths have to be altered, and so on.

The wild garden offers an excuse for artless design. The ultimate, unconscious goal (though now that I've said it, it can hardly be unconscious any more) is serendipity; plants are allowed to seed where they will, and every year brings some new change, as some plants die and others replace them.

Rock Gardens

The most complete and triumphant expression of the potential of cold-winter dryland gardening is found in the rock garden. Nothing else even comes close. Rock gardens give us almost limitless plant choices and a protracted blooming season unequaled by any other type of garden. The foliage of most of these plants is evergreen, so there is something to look at during open periods in winter; many dryland plants take advantage of the hot winter sun and flower before spring officially arrives. The plants are, with a few exceptions, thoroughly adapted to cold; wide temperature fluctuations; hot winter sun; winds that would shrivel other plants to nothing in a matter of hours; and, should you happen to live in an area where this might happen, frost at any time of the year.

One of the things that immediately turns most people off rock gardening is the notion that in order to have a successful rock garden you have to have a large quantity of rock placed in a "natural" manner, in a way that resembles a rock outcrop in nature. This large quantity of rock, to most people, means buying rock (or "stone": one does not buy rock, one buys stone—I keep forgetting) and having it shipped. The rock itself is usually not inexpensive, and most purveyors insist on charging you by weight, so you may have to lay out a considerable amount of cash just to get started.

The truth is, that while purchased lichen-covered rock, laid out in a naturalistic manner, can be very beautiful, rocks collected from the side of the road or a field (you may need permission to do this) can also be satisfactory; roadside rocks may need to be washed several times to ensure that no road salt remains on them. The lichen (sometimes incorrectly called moss) usually dies in a city garden, either from being watered with treated drinking water or from air pollution, so this is something to keep in mind when contemplating buying rocks just because they have fancy lichens on them. Various remedies to keep the lichen alive (washing them with stale beer, buttermilk, molasses, or manure tea) are rarely effective in city gardens. Buttermilk is a really poor idea if you have dogs; why it rarely lasts on the troughs for more than a few minutes I will leave to your imagination.

Large rocks, ones requiring a forklift or a crane, are often preferred by serious builders of artistic rock gardens. Adding large rocks here and there definitely adds to the beauty of the garden, though it does take away room for more plants. I strongly recommend buying rocks in this situation instead of trying to drag or push them home from the side of the road; these really ought to be all the same kind of rock. Most dealers in ornamental stone (i.e., rock) will let you select the rocks you want, at least in the larger sizes. Even though you can arrange for these to be delivered, do remember that large rocks are heavy. I have a metal pry bar that I can use to sort of ease the rocks along. And you could always get help (the same people who offered to help you move house the day after you actually did move could be called to help move rocks).

How you place the rocks is again a personal choice; visiting public and private rock gardens may be inspirational, but since most gardeners in our region live within easy driving distance of the mountains, probably the best place to study rock formations is in the mountains themselves.

When placing the rocks, beware of a myth that stalks rock gardening (usually promulgated by those who have never had a rock garden); that is, that you should bury the rocks to two-thirds of their depth. The rocks can be buried only as deep as they need to be to prevent them from moving if stepped on. After they're placed, step on them to see if they move.

Even in the relatively dry Rocky Mountain region, standing water may be an important consideration in winter or early spring. There may be occasions when large amounts of melting snow, or, less frequently, rain, may saturate the soil in the rock garden, and so constructing the garden on a slope is the best method. A typical technique is to create raised beds or berms, and then stick the rocks in here and there. Even if you find yourself unable to duplicate a natural rock formation, the plants will not notice the difference.

Besides the advantage of having fast-draining slopes, the berms can be oriented to receive more or less sun, or more or less wind. Larger rocks placed on the north side of an east-west oriented berm may provide a little shade and shelter for rock ferns and other choice plants.

The height of the berm is closely proportionate to its length. You can imagine what the effect of a six-foot-high (1.8m) berm is in a small garden; the vaguely ludicrous impression of a huge gumdrop made of earth and rocks can be nullified by making a high berm like this about twice as long as it is high. Really, though, a berm three to four feet (90 to 120cm) high looks less unnatural, and will do the drainage job just as well as a taller one.

In order not to look ridiculous, a berm can be sculpted to be of varying heights, lower in some places, higher in others, with the sides sloping at different angles here and there.

One thing you probably don't want to do is just pile up dirt until you achieve the height you want. The berm will sink, sooner or later—usually just about the time it looks its best, but eventually, without fail, it will sink. The best method, to ensure that your berm retains at least most of its planned height, is to build it around a core of nonsinking material—flat tires, used carpet, last month's computers, old refrigerators, water heaters, wrecked cars, whatever. Organic matter that will decay over time, such as wood, is not recommended, for obvious reasons. I use cinder blocks. The cavities in the blocks need to be carefully filled with soil to avoid air pockets.

The best filler soil is the heaviest, stickiest clay you can find, which for most gardeners means the soil they have in their gardens. This is packed into the crevices around the blocks, and then mounded up to give the desired general outline. Rocks can be sunk into this clay and will not move much, if at all, once they have gone through a winter or two. Areas between the rocks can be filled with gravel, to a depth of six inches (15cm) or so. The original skeleton will then be invisible to all.

It is not at all necessary to buy rock for the rock garden, and, in fact, if you feel like it, you can omit the rock altogether and just grow the plants in raised beds. While the idea of a rockless rock garden may seem like a contradiction to some, many plants can be grown perfectly well without the aid or support of rocks. Gardeners who want a lot of plants instead of a lot of rocks have my complete sympathy. Most "rock garden plants" do not grow in rock outcrops in nature, and so omitting rocks is a perfectly natural way to grow them.

Rockless rock gardens can be constructed in the same way, with berms. The soil of choice here is again heavy clay. The rockless rock garden is an ideal home for many dryland rock garden plants that do not need the protection (whether from wind, drought, or winter sun) of a rock; such gardens will essentially be berms planted with various plants that revel in the exposed, sunny, dry location.

Dryland plants suitable for the rock garden have very different soil requirements from those traditionally associated with rock gardens. None of these plants—eriogonums, penstemons, townsendias, physarias, and so forth—grow in soils with high organic content. Humus is the result of decomposed organic matter found in regions of high rainfall; in dry areas, the cover of trees and shrubs which provides this organic matter is practically nonexistent, and the resulting soils may be pure clay, pure sand, or various combinations of decomposed rock, clay, and sand. Soil for the dryland rock garden can be ordinary clay soil. Dryland gardens, by definition, are never watered, so once the plants have been established, they can be left alone, unwatered. The clay soil may absorb like a sponge the occasional soaking by rain or heavy snowfall, but overall dry conditions in our region will dry out the soil adequately to save the plants from rot.

Both irrigated and dryland rock gardens can be mulched. The main purpose of the mulch, aside from being attractive (ideally), is to keep the plants' crowns dry. Gravel mulch an inch or two (2.5 to 5cm) thick is perfect. Again, a mulch composed of uniformly sized gravel has a certain look about it that some find slightly unattractive; I use pea gravel, but the uniformity of shape might be broken up with larger rocks, as it is in nature. Organic matter, such as shredded bark, is never used; this is perhaps the one inviolable rule of rock gardening. Organic mulches will absorb water and rot plant crowns in no time, not to mention their propensity for blowing away, or harboring the odd slug or two. Rocky Mountain gardeners who can claim both rotting plants and slugs must live in doubled humiliation, with the stone of shame about their necks.

Siting the Rock Garden

If you took my suggestion before building your own rock garden and went up into the mountains to look at rock outcrops, the first thing you may have noticed was that the word "timberline" has a definite meaning: there are no trees where these plants grow. Likewise, in dry areas in the wild where you might find plants suitable for your dry rock gardens, there are no trees.

Rock garden plants, are, as a rule, creatures of the sun, and so the rock garden is sited to receive as much sun as possible.

The moral of this—unfortunately for Americans, who are undoubtedly the most tree-crazed people on earth (except when it comes to saving old-growth forests, of course)—is that the typical excess of trees in yards (Christopher Lloyd believed that the majority of American gardens were "too heavily treed") needs reevaluation, with a chain saw. Trees and rock gardens are incompatible, so you may need to cut down a few of them to let some light into the garden.

Very few rock garden plants will tolerate anything more than the filtered shade of a honey locust (*Gleditsia triacanthos*) for more than a few hours every day, and the tree's incessant need for water and the resulting desert created by tree roots is an unhealthy site for rock garden plants. Failure to remove fallen leaves in autumn can suffocate alpine plants, so this extra work is another consideration. A leaf blower can be a big help; it is more effective than raking and causes less damage to the plants.

A few plants, often those that haunt shady ledges in mountains, will tolerate almost no direct sunlight in our region, and these need a different treatment. Unlike woodland plants, they still may insist on being provided with gritty soil and sometimes the protection of a rock or two. For these plants, the shady location could be either on a north-facing slope (particularly on one of those six-foot-high berms) or on the north side of the house.

Pots and Troughs

Now that growing plants in pots (or, to use that gross utilitarian word, "containers") has become fashionable, it's nice to know that dryland plants are just as suited to this type of culture as are petunias. Typically the pots are the beautiful glazed ones coming out of Southeast Asia, not too expensive and safe to keep outdoors all winter. Ordinary flower pots are good too, though after a few winters these will start to flake and eventually fall apart.

Cacti are perhaps the ultimate container plants, especially the smaller ones that might disappear in a larger garden setting; when combined with tender succulents or other plants that can be lifted from the pots and overwintered indoors, they create a very pleasant impression.

The growing medium can be pretty much anything you want. I generally make my own out of whatever I have on hand—equal parts perlite, scoria, and sand, with some handfuls of potting soil or peat moss thrown in. This should be well watered in the pot for a day or two, or longer, before actually planting anything in it, to avoid having it sink later. As the mix sinks with watering, you can firm it with your hand, then plant on top of it, filling in the gaps with additional mix. The finished product can be mulched, or surfaced, with stone, mainly for looks.

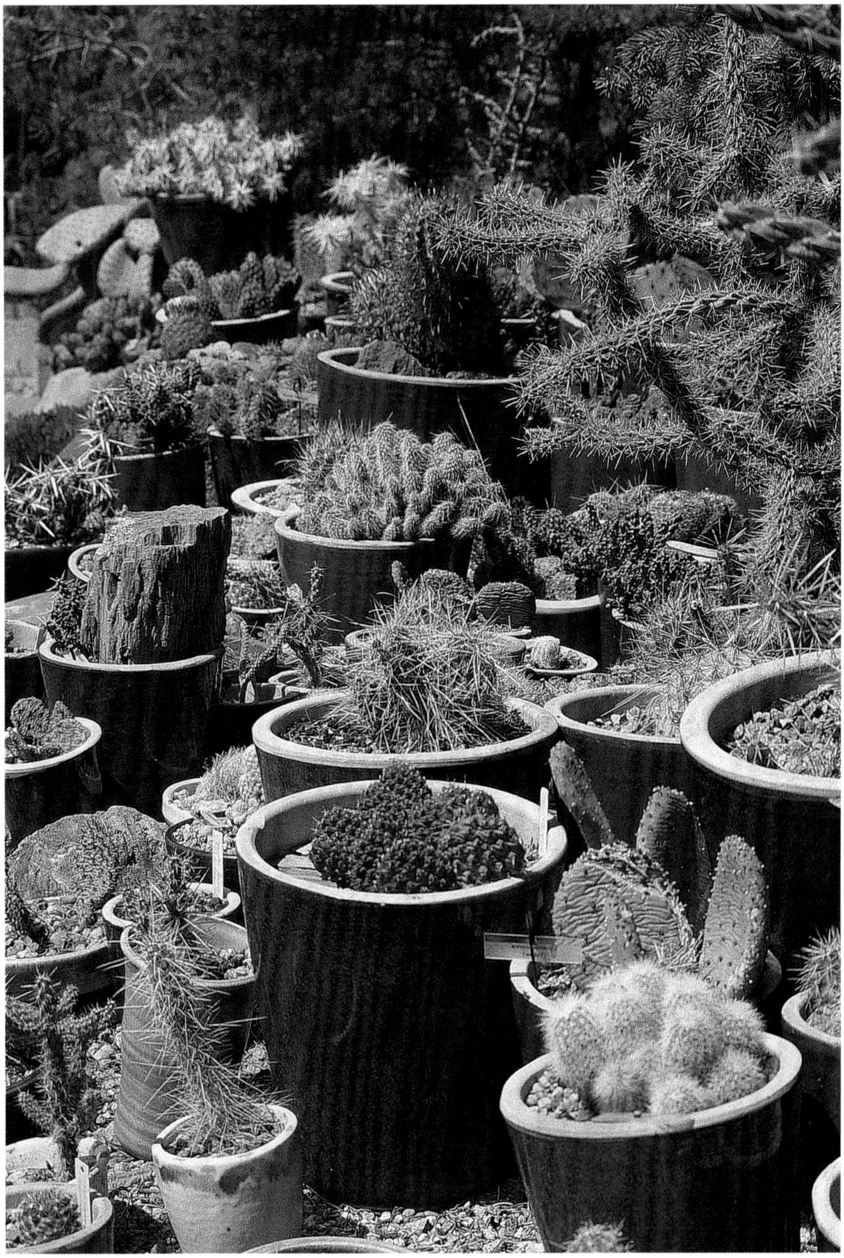

Potted cacti,
Kelaidis garden

You can also use plain dirt to fill the pot; if you enjoy lifting objects that can weigh as much as a small car, then dirt should be your choice.

Just as in the garden, the more porous the mix, the more watering will be required. Containers of dryland rock garden plants will dry out just as fast as containers of anything else, and the plants will die. Some of these containers may actually require daily watering.

There is a surprising amount of controversy about drainage in pots. The old-fashioned method of placing a few shards of old flower pots over the drainage holes has come under criticism in the last decade or so, the claim being that the capillary action of the shards (or crocks, as they're sometimes called) draws moisture away from the roots, or some such thing. The other claim has to do with a buildup of salts on the inside walls of the pot due to the water-absorbent properties of clay, causing root corrosion; and so painting the inside surface of the pots with a waterproofing agent is recommended, thus causing moisture to be drawn down to the drainage holes, where the salts can be safely flushed from the pot by watering. Before filling the pot, a paper towel is placed over the drainage hole; this will eventually disappear, and the whole pot will be filled with soilless mix and roots.

As a gardener who still paints the wounds on pruned tree branches, I was not inclined to pay much attention to things like this. When I remarked on these pot theories in an online discussion with rock gardeners, the comments from transatlantic gardeners (who have been growing alpine plants in pots the old-fashioned way for decades, and who have achieved a degree of successful cultivation rarely experienced elsewhere) were enough to convince me that theory does not always translate into practice. You can treat your pots as you like.

Troughs, at least here, are containers that you make, or buy; it isn't too likely that you will be able to find old stone drinking troughs like those found in Great Britain. Troughs are made out of hypertufa, and the recipes for troughs vary as much as those for chili.

My own recipe, like most everything else I do, is based on laziness and expediency, so I use whatever I have on hand. My spouse made a plywood mold with an inner, removable section, so all the troughs made here look alike. The mold is covered with plastic sheeting, which is stapled on, so it can be removed when it gets too grimy. I read articles that suggested a release agent, like linseed oil, was not necessary; I had to throw away the trough I made without a release agent since there was no release.

The mixture itself is equal parts peat moss, perlite, and Portland cement. I add enough water to make the mixture the consistency of cottage cheese, add a handful of fiberglass reinforcing fibers, and sometimes a little liquid acrylic bonding agent, pack the resulting slop into the mold (with the central section in place), jiggle it a little to help it settle, poke it here and there to help force air bubbles out of the mix, cover the whole thing with plastic to keep it from drying out too quickly, and let it sit around in the garage or shed for a few weeks.

A few days after making the trough I sometimes try to get the central section out of the mold by gently rocking it out of its place; if this is done too soon after making the trough, the trough will collapse. The trough is then covered again, and the concrete mixture is left to cure slowly.

After three or four weeks have passed (I write this knowing that I have sometimes only waited a week or so before unmolding the trough), the new trough can be dragged out into the open and left there until you are ready to plant. But just before you do plant the trough, there are two things that need to be taken care of. One is drainage holes; I have never had anything but dismal results trying to poke holes in the bottom of troughs during the construction process, so I drill holes in the bottom using a carbide-tipped bit. (This is also necessary if you accidentally buy a glazed pot without a drainage hole. If you let the drill bit do the work, rather than trying to force it by leaning into the drill with all your weight, the bit will drill the hole without cracking the pot.)

The next thing is removal of fiberglass fibers sticking out all over the surface of the trough like a sweater coming out of the dryer. A butane torch will burn these off quite effectively, though you want to be careful of water-filled air pockets bursting when the flame hits them. There is a lot to be said for gardening with a blowtorch.

The troughs can be planted with the same porous mix used for pots. I stick slabs of styrofoam at angles in the trough partly as filler, and partly to balance rocks on top of them. I think that stylized miniature rock formations are extremely attractive in troughs; you can arrange these the way you want, though the adage that all rocks should be of the same type really does hold true here. Once the rocks are arranged, the plants can be placed and a gritty mixture of your soilless mix plus small stones ("squeegee," in my part of the world) about the thickness of a dime arranged around them. Then a mulch is spread over all, preferably of the same color as the rocks, but again this is according to your taste.

The grit, or squeegee (or gravel dug from abandoned anthills), is crucial to plant health here simply because it keeps the crowns of the plants dry. Most of these dryland rock garden plants are unaccustomed to having moisture in the soil just below the surface, so this grit can literally mean the difference between life and death.

The troughs will leach calcium carbonate. White deposits will form on the outsides of the troughs. This is said to be horrible, and leaving the troughs out in the rain is the solution. I have had troughs out in the garden for almost twenty years, and there has never been enough rain to leach out the calcium carbonate, and its presence has never affected the plants in the troughs in any visible way. Calcium carbonate deposits, which are admittedly unattractive (you see similarly colored deposits on old flowerpots if your tap water is alkaline), can be washed off with a hose.

In my garden, troughs are left outside, sitting on their cinder blocks, all winter, and no protection is required.

Troughs, and pots, their more elegant counterparts, make a nice addition to the garden, and if you think of them as a sort of outsized bonsai, still to be fussed over if you like, your gardening experience will be enhanced in ways you might not have suspected. We have acquired several more glazed pots in the past few years, and now I can't imagine the garden without them.

Shade

There is a lot to be said for shade, especially in climates with hot summers. There is also a lot to be said for the truth, and the two concepts, shade and truth, are uneasy companions when it comes to gardening. Shade, that is, the shade cast by trees, is a product of regular rainfall; there is no shade on the moon.

In regions where the rainfall is high, there are a lot of trees, and in regions where the rainfall is low, there are few trees. It is as simple as that. When deciduous trees are established in cold-winter dry-climate gardens, they are quite drought-tolerant, simply because their roots suck all the moisture out of the ground as far as their roots can reach. The roots of most trees grow just under the soil, like those of cactus.

There is a tiny handful of plants (cyclamen, ivy) that will do well without irrigation under trees, but, to quote Henry Mitchell, "Most flowers will not grow in dry shade no matter how much you water."

If you insist on having a garden smothered with trees, you will have to water constantly, no matter what anyone says. Shade lovers are directed to *The Complete Shade Gardener* by George Schenk, which also happens to be one of the best gardening books I've ever read.

Companion Plants

Even though the plants listed in this book are limited to those with which I have had experience in the garden, I see this as evidence of the enormous potential of dryland gardening in cold-winter climates. There are even more plants to consider should you wish not to restrict yourself to native plants.

One good reason to allow nonnatives into your dry garden is that you can go to almost any nursery and actually buy the plants, instead of leaving empty spaces in your garden for years waiting for that special plant you read about and can't find.

Some plants that are conventionally believed to be drought-tolerant, like lilacs and peonies, are anything but, so beware. The list of plants that follows barely covers the possibilities; so many plants from the deserts of Central Asia have yet to reach our gardens.

To start with shrubs, there are some familiar plants that will take severe prolonged drought in stride, much more so than even native plants. *Buddleia alternifolia*, in its silver-leafed cultivar 'Argentea', has been in the garden for almost twenty years and has never been watered. This small tree (as it is here) was broken almost to the ground in the blizzard of '03 but turned right around and grew right back to its former height within the year; all plants should be this tough.

The peashrub *Caragana arborescens* is good, though not exciting; it is deciduous in periods of severe drought, which makes it slightly less than desirable as a hedge. There are other species of peashrub that are sort of on the extreme outer orbit of horticulture and, should you develop a taste for them, are worth looking for.

Cotoneasters (particularly *Cotoneaster apiculatus* and *C. multiflorus*) and pyracanthas (*Pyracantha coccinea*) are also good. Pyracanthas are said to be borderline hardy in the Rocky Mountain region, yet there is a neighborhood just to the south of where I live that was planted with nothing but pyracanthas during what must have been a landscaping craze back in the early 1970s.

Roses are often described as being drought-tolerant, which is true to a point (the plants won't die), but there is a fairly broad line between neglect and good gardening practices. I recommend only four nonnative roses. Rose species with yellow flowers, like *Rosa hugonis* (sometimes considered a subspecies of *R. xanthina*) and *R. foetida*, are extremely drought-tolerant but are of course happier with more moisture. The *R. spinosissima* hybrid 'Frühlingsgold' is another good choice. *Rosa fedtschenkoana*, a gray-leafed rose with single white flowers, is probably only available from seed collectors. There are other species, from Central Asia, not in the nursery trade, like *R. ecae* and *R. kokanica*, that might do well too.

The brooms, members of the genera *Cytisus*, *Genista*, and *Chamaecytisus* (you won't come across this last one unless you order seed from Czech collectors), are very reliable performers in sunny dry gardens. *Cytisus scoparius* (Scotch broom) can be killed at temperatures below −20F (−29C)—in this climate anyway—so I don't recommend it (if it isn't killed, the resulting damage is so hideous that you wish the plant had been killed), but the white broom, *C. albus*, is extremely durable. *Cytisus* ×*kewensis* and *C. purgans* are good too. *Genista pilosa* and *G. tinctoria* are good, but *G. lydia*, which gets enormous (in the lateral dimension), can also be killed in a sunny, cold, windy winter.

Lavenders are okay, but I find them highly vulnerable to cold winter winds. All the cultivars of *Lavandula angustifolia* and *L.* ×*intermedia* are good, as is *L. lanata*, though it can suddenly disappear when you least expect it.

Rosemary, if you can grow it, is good, though if damaged by too much cold (wind, rather than low temperatures, being the agent of destruction here), it does not sprout from the base of winter-killed branches. *Rosma-*

rinus 'Arp', with grayish green leaves, and *R.* 'Madeleine Hill' (or 'Hill's Hardy') are your best bets. They benefit from a burlap wrap in their first winter.

There are a number of perennials, some of them really subshrubs, that do well in the dry garden, though it pays to be suspicious of plants that readily grow in what most gardeners would call harsh conditions. The last thing you want is to have the garden overrun by invasive weeds. Most of these are herbs; hyssop is an example. I still grow it, but seemingly every single seed, out of ten trillion produced, germinates, even in years of extreme drought.

Snapdragons, ordinary garden snapdragons, believe it or not, are an excellent choice for a mind-numbingly dry garden. The plants are perennials, grown as annuals, and here they last three or four years before passing on, leaving another generation—of different colors—to carry on. They are less prone to rust when grown very dry.

Rock garden plants contribute an almost endless list of plants that you can grow without any supplemental irrigation once the plants are established. Acantholimons are a superior choice; these form enormous spiky mounds of blue, blue-silver, or green linear leaves. The pink flowers on twisting, woody stalks, opening at the same time as the papery faded flowers, are an added attraction. Good choices are *Acantholimon acerosum*, *A. androsaceum*, *A. halophilum*—a monster, three feet (90 cm) across and high in as many years)—*A. litwinowii*, *A. venustum*, and so on. Contrary to what some rock gardening books claim, they set fertile seed, and little acantholimon seedlings are common in the rock garden. Not so much fun to kneel on.

Aurinia saxatilis, the basket of gold alyssum sold everywhere, is the most drought-tolerant plant I have ever grown, including cacti. Only a stone is more drought-tolerant. It will seed freely and form attractive clumps of gray-green leaves that look nice under shrubs. I have not tried the variegated form or the other color forms ('Dudley Nevill', for instance) under dry conditions.

Foxtail lilies (*Eremurus* spp.) are so well adapted to Denver's climate (and possibly by extension, to other cities in our region) that some gardeners find them seeding all over the place. They haven't done this with me. In general, these plants like a generous amount of moisture in spring, which is not an unusual thing to expect, and then will tolerate drought for the rest of the year. *Eremurus stenophyllus* (*E. bungei*) is the most commonly available one, though some named varieties are now almost as common in the trade.

The spreading *Helichrysum tianshanicum* has been in the front garden here for ages. It has woolly, blue-gray leaves, forming a small mound about three inches (7.5cm) high, with clusters of small yellow daisy flowers in early summer. It fairly reeks of curry, a pleasant smell to me.

Irises are often considered drought-tolerant; I don't find the cultivars of *Iris germanica* to be especially so, and my taste does not incline toward the modern cultivars anyway. I think plants with unnaturally ruffled flowers look pretty ridiculous. The oncocyclus irises are good choices for the dry garden, though, despite their reputation for being ungrowable (a reputation gained by being grown in wet climates). The trouble with these, as with so many other plants, is finding them. I know of no source for any of the species other than growing them from wild-collected seed, an expensive undertaking that requires years of patience. If you are lucky enough to find some plants, they do benefit from division after a few years in the garden.

Arilbred irises (hybrids between oncocyclus irises and other bearded irises) have various percentages of oncocyclus genetic material in them and even more varied attractiveness. These plants were bred, it has been said, to be more growable for the "average gardener." The only ones I have come across were mostly of *Iris germanica* ancestry, and I have thrown away every single one of these that bloomed in the garden.

Matthiola longipetala (*M. bicornis*; night-scented stock) is an annual whose seed can be sown any time from October onward. The almost leafless, unimpressive plants that result from this sowing have a disgustingly acrid smell when handled, but the pink and white flowers, blooming all summer, waft an intensely fragrant scent of cloves and vanilla through the night air. They too will reseed.

Ptilotrichum spinosum (spiny alyssum), in its cultivar 'Roseum', offers a half-basketball-sized mound of not-terribly-threatening spines and tiny green leaves with sprays of pink alyssum flowers in spring. As the plant ages it offers a slightly disheveled, yet pleasant, combination of dead twigs and living branches—an oddly effective look. The crucifer

Vella spinosa is similar, except the leaves are slightly larger and it has the typical four-parted yellow mustard flowers.

Several of the Turkish salvias offer even better drought resistance than the native ones. The best are *Salvia dumetorum*, a three-foot (90cm) smelly thing with spires of smallish blue-purple flowers all summer, and *S. recognita*, even taller, with large, incised, oily-sticky leaves and inch-long (2.5cm) pink flowers in spring. The seed of the latter is like black buckshot and almost never germinates, until plants are established in the garden, and then you will have plenty.

The cold-winter semi-arid regions of western North America are possibly the world's most perfect environment for growing temperate-climate bulbs. An almost endless variety can (and should) be grown in the dry clay soils in the company of most of the plants described in this book. (Daffodils and snowdrops must be excluded, however; snowdrops continue growing throughout the summer and require some supplemental irrigation.) Several species of wild onion, including *Allium flavum* subsp. *tauricum* (alliophile Mark McDonough gave me a number of gorgeous color forms—pale pink, pink, yellow, butterscotch, and so on—with long-lasting sprays of flowers), are well-suited to these conditions, though some species do have a will of their own when it comes to self-perpetuation.

Chionodoxa luciliae is easy, and beautiful growing through the straw-colored blades of last year's blue grama; various crocus species, both spring- and autumn-flowering, are perfectly content with a dry garden as their home.

Cyclamen, especially *Cyclamen coum*, are astonishingly well-adapted to dry gardens. I would not have thought this was the case until I discovered dozens of seedlings in the dry rock garden, the seed carried across the path by ants. The plants grow more slowly than they do in an irrigated garden, but eventually they do flower. The leaves appear in late autumn and remain all winter, only to wither after flowering, which, if the plants are in sun, can be any time after mid-January.

The Iranian fritillaries, *Fritillaria imperialis* and *F. persica*, are the largest and most spectacular bulbs you can grow in a dry garden. Bulbs of both of these are pricey, reek of skunk, and have a large cavity in the center left by last year's flower stalk. Conventional wisdom claims that in order to avoid rotting from moisture collecting in this cavity, the bulbs should be planted at an angle, or even almost sideways. I have seen no reason not to do this, considering the amount of money you have to shell out for a good drift of either of these plants.

Bulbous irises, like *Iris danfordiae* and *I. reticulata*, are also good choices. Both of these, including the dozen or so color forms of the latter, bloom before the vernal equinox and multiply readily. The age-old prejudice against *I. danfordiae* not blooming the second year because it breaks down into nonflowering bulblets must come from wetter climates, since it is a regular and dependable bloomer in the garden here. Both the straight species of *I. reticulata*, which is scented of violets, and its color forms are ravishing when grown in dormant blue grama and buffalograss lawns.

Tulips of all kinds can be grown in the dry garden. Even the common garden-variety (sorry) do well, though most of my bulbs have succumbed to various accidents involving a trowel. *Tulipa tarda* is one of the best, and reseeds itself like no other.

Winter

In high, lonely mountain valleys the sun rises late in the morning and sets early in the evening, and the temperature falls to −40 or −50F (−40 to −45.5C) at night on occasion, but the major cities in our area are rarely snowbound and rarely, in fact, very cold. You would think, listening to the ecstatic weather reports on television or reading pamphlets aimed at drawing skiers to the various states, that city dwellers only get to work in the winter by skiing cross-country or in a one-horse open sleigh. I have never been on skis, and have never seen an ice storm, sleet, freezing drizzle, or snow lying on the ground longer than a few days (until the winter of 2006–07, that is). Sunny, dry, "open" winters—sometimes blessed with hurricane-force winds, at other times gently bathed in thick smog—are the rule.

Warm winds blowing in an easterly direction often succeed periods of bitter cold, melting snow faster than the sun can, and creating a disconcerting impression, especially at night, that winter is just a figment of the imagination. These chinooks, as they are known, are generally associated with the eastern slopes of the Rocky Mountains, though I suppose they occur elsewhere.

It's true that Denver, where I live, can have bitterly cold weather, cold air streaming down from the Arctic unimpeded by any east-west mountain range (this galls me no end, of course), but the periods of cold are brief, sometimes lasting only one night, and the effect this has on plants is, with reservations, surprisingly negligible. I once had occasion to go out on a night when the thermometer reached −27F (−33C); aside from the stunning difficulty in breathing, I noticed that pine needles shattered like glass when touched and . . . it was cold. The cold, though, departed the next day, and the following spring, despite some prolonged wailing and groaning, little damage was evident.

The real trouble here is that cold weather (meaning temperatures below about 10F, −12C) can strike any time between October and April, and plants may not be ready for the sudden drop in temperature. Though I have no scientific evidence to back this up, there seems to be a complex relationship between hardiness to cold based not only on low temperatures but the duration of the cold, wind speed, and the time of the year that the cold strikes. Damage or death after a hard winter is sometimes attributed to the winter itself when the real cause is too quick a drop in temperature before winter has really begun.

Plants enter dormancy at different times in autumn and early winter, and some species may be completely resistant to very low temperatures in January, when they are completely dormant, but be killed outright by less cold temperatures coming too early, say in October or November. Other plants may tolerate very cold temperatures, if only for one night. It is difficult to predict how a plant will perform in a garden.

You can protect your plants, if you want to, in various ways. Covering plants with mulching material is effective, but choose something that will not pack down after several snowfalls and rot the plants with heavy, wet organic matter (straw is a disaster here); pine needles are probably the best, and less likely to blow away. For small shrubs I use nursery peat pots, turned upside down with the bottom removed, held in place by large nails used for staking tents, and filled with styrofoam peanuts. A little duct tape over the top holds the peanuts in place. You will see that beauty is not the principal aim here.

Wind, not low temperature, is the greatest killer of plants in my winter garden. Combined with hot sun, plants can dry out to shriveled sticks in a few days, regardless of the temperature. An antidesiccant spray is effective for some plants, but others need to be planted out of the full force of winter winds. When the wind brings freezing temperatures, which fortunately is rare, it can kill plants that otherwise would endure much colder temperatures.

Excessive watering in autumn, especially coupled with warm weather, may keep a plant in growth at a time when it should be entering dormancy, and this may have an adverse effect on the plant's ability to survive the winter. Likewise, lack of adequate moisture at the same time of the year can weaken a plant so that it dies at the earliest possible opportunity.

Obviously there are no set rules for these situations. Each garden is different, and weather is so unpredictable that there isn't any point in making even the broadest generalizations. Keeping new plants slightly but evenly moist is probably the best prescription for success. If the plants are established they can often be left to fend for themselves.

Gardeners, especially rock gardeners, are frequently warned about protecting plants from "winter wet." I only vaguely know what this means. Where I live, rain in winter is about as common as snow in July; winter is the dry season, and the average precipitation for December, January, and February is half an inch (1.25cm) per month.

It is commonly recommended that this lack of winter rainfall be compensated for by watering. This is a recommendation that I have totally ignored for forty-five years. Dormant plants are dormant plants, and they don't benefit from watering in the middle of January. If the soil is frozen, no water is taken up by the plants; if the soil is dry and the plants are dormant, nothing happens if you water them. I have yet to lose a plant from lack of water in winter. It may be apparent that native plants, in the wild, do not require supplemental irrigation in winter, and get along with what little moisture there is.

Snow cover does protect plants from extreme cold, but the idea that winter snow (as opposed to autumn or spring snow) is a form of moisture that plants can use is a myth so pervasive, in and out of horticulture, that debunking it is as difficult as observation of the actual fact is simple. Snow falling in January does not melt, it evaporates. If it melted, then winter-brown lawns would turn green, which they don't. Yet if you water the lawn with a sprinkler for fifteen minutes in January, it begins to turn green within a few days. (Not golf-course green, just greener than before.)

Snow evaporates because at higher elevations, particularly in our area, "west of the treeline" (Gary Snyder's definition of "west," meaning past the end of the forested areas of North America, discounting the mountains), the sunlight is always intense, twelve months of the year, and in winter its heat is more than palpable, even on a cold winter's day. There is no dim pale yellow ball in a humid, hazy sky as there is in the east. In winter, the sun is always present, always in your eyes, especially in the afternoon.

The absence of cloud cover has both negative and positive effects on the winter garden. Traditional broad-leafed evergreens find winter rough going unless they are in shade (and even then the wind and low humidity usually does them in), and other plants object to the hot winter sun. The mountain dryad, *Dryas octopetala*, is rated hardy to –50F (–45.5C), yet here it was killed right down to the roots one snowless winter where the temperature never dropped below 20F (–6.5C).

On the other hand, sunny, dry winters allow many plants that would be marginally hardy to survive temperatures they never experience in the wild; the dry soil probably prevents a layer of moisture from surrounding a plant's crown and causing rot. Hundreds of species of plants continue to photosynthesize throughout a sunny winter and, even though not in flower, they will continue to look attractive all through the winter. This is particularly true in the rock garden, where most of the herbaceous plants maintain rosettes of leaves or are completely evergreen. Especially when combined with suitable exotic plants, such as lavenders, horehounds, and others, the sunny winter garden can be quite beautiful, and there is a slow, quiet, suspended quality to this time of year, with its comparatively settled weather, that, to me, almost equals the excitement of spring or the fullness of summer.

Spring

Ah, spring! Here in Denver, I spend most of the spring with the shades drawn, as heavy, wet snow falls, weekend after weekend. In the rock gardens and troughs, plants start to bloom around mid-January, and there is a constant succession of flowers, always spoiled by snow, until late

May when the whole garden bursts into bloom, the day before a record snowfall.

On those days when it isn't snowing (invariably weekdays), plants such as *Townsendia hookeri* will be in flower, sometimes in early February on a south-facing site. *Mahonia repens*, if it didn't start blooming in January, may open its clusters of sweet-scented flowers. *Aquilegia jonesii* blooms in March; physarias and *Penstemon nitidus* will be in bloom in April.

The first seedlings will appear in the seed pots, though the big flush may come later.

There is not a whole lot of work that needs to be done in the spring, since of course you did all the necessary work before cold weather set in a few months ago. March and April are excellent months in which to plant out plants. Mail-order nurseries will send your order when you specify, and I've always had greater success with shipments that arrive in April: a week or so spent gradually exposing your new acquisitions to cool weather and your garden conditions, and the plants can be set out in the garden. Some of the more tender plants, especially cacti and other succulents, should probably wait until the last frost, but not much later than that. If the plants have been grown outdoors, then plants purchased locally, or from local mail-order nurseries, can safely be planted the day they arrive in your garden. (Since it starts to snow the day I decide to plant, I usually have to wait until a weekday, take a sick day from work, and plant like a crazy person.)

On the Great Plains, anyway, sudden drops in temperature are quite common in late April and May. The inevitable snow that results is good for the garden; the cold temperatures are not. New transplants should be protected from cold; established plants that might be considered borderline hardy can be set back to the point that their ability to endure summer drought is compromised. There is not much you can do about this except to hope for additional moisture in the weeks to come.

Eventually, of course, it does stop snowing. And then it starts to hail.

Summer

Summer, to me, is the smell of water from sprinklers falling on dry grass, an endless succession of hot, dry days and cool, breezy nights, with the scent of ponderosa pine wafting down from the mountains and thunderstorms flickering in the distance. Some summers are not like that, of course, and at least one year we had daily thunderstorms, bringing no rain, driving from the mountains east across the plains, sometimes so many during the day that we had the lights on in the house at eleven o'clock in the morning.

So, as they say, you never can tell.

If the garden is visited by a hailstorm (if you haven't had to call your insurance agent after a hailstorm, you haven't really had hail: the hailstorm that hit our garden completely defoliated every plant except two, destroyed the roof, and totaled the car parked in the driveway), you can spend the summer doing something else, instead of gardening. Though some plants may be killed, the garden will recover. Nonnative woody plants, especially trees, will carry the scars for decades, and you should expect branches to die for at least fifteen years after the event.

At this point there is a strong temptation to give in to despair. It is no use telling people who have been visited by a devastating hailstorm that things will be better the next year, even though they will be.

Someone, possibly Sartre or Groucho Marx, said that life begins on the other side of despair. I don't know about this; true gardening certainly begins this way and every garden, no matter where it is, is visited by some climatic horror at one time or another. You get over it.

Gardeners seem to be possessed by the delusion that planting is done for the ages, that a garden will last forever. From my perspective, nothing could be less true. Like humans, plants grow, age, and die. I love Christopher Lloyd's perceptive characterization of the garden at Great Dixter as "a happy, if impermanent, microcosm." Gardens change by the hour, plants growing and flowering, as they gradually (or sometimes, in my case, quickly) age toward death. Gardeners, especially in supremely difficult gardening climates, need to learn to revel in the opening of a new flower, the scent of the garden at high noon on a blistering hot day in late July, or the sight of hawkmoths visiting the garden at twilight.

Autumn

By mid-September it may have stopped hailing, and snow has already fallen once, or maybe twice. There are few things more depressing than snow in September, but it melts the next day. A cold snap can ruin autumn too, with nothing but dead brown leaves rustling in the trees and shrubs until hurricane-force winds blow them into the next state, but autumn can of course also be gorgeous. Typically this is a very dry season (sometimes wetter as you go further south, owing to the effects of the Mexican monsoon), day after day bringing cooler temperatures, bright slanting sunlight, low humidity, with everything drenched in gold from the cottonwood leaves falling. Both cottonwood and aspen leaves (and the wood, too) have an exquisite aroma that wafts through the garden after a thundershower or when snow melts.

Rabbitbrushes (*Chrysothamnus* spp.) are the main native plant show, contributing to the golden impression, and these can continue well into late November. *Hesperaloe parviflora* is still going, into November, *Salvia azurea* is peaking, and other plants may take advantage of the cooler weather to bloom again.

Where I live, October can be as good as, or better than, April and May.

Left Out in the Sun, to Die

Growing drought-tolerant plants is the easiest type of gardening there is. Nothing else even approaches dryland gardening when it comes to the amount of work that does not have to be done: take away the initial planting, and what do you have? Lying in a hammock on a summer's day, watching clouds pass by, lifting a cold Gardener's Beverage to the lips . . .

The plants were carefully watered just two days ago and were in fine fettle when inspected. But yesterday, while the gardener was at work, or napping, the temperature rose to 100F (38C), the humidity dropped to five percent, and a gentle thirty mile-per-hour (48kph) breeze blew all day. And now, when the gardener finally gets out of the hammock and wanders over to look at all the new plants, he or she sees that most of the leaves are dried to a crisp. Though a considerable amount of panicked watering takes place, within a week all the plants are dead; no amount of watering, even with tears, will bring back the little plants.

This is by no means an imaginary scenario, except for the hammock. Once the plants are transported out into the garden, their pampered life ends and the realities of outdoor life, hot sun, drying winds, sudden cold, and a heavier soil grip the plants in paroxysmal death wishes that are too often fulfilled. I have personally overseen the deaths of hundreds, if not thousands, of tiny, helpless plants brought into my garden and sent to their doom in the sun-drenched soil.

There are a few ways you can prevent these little tragedies.

Consider any new plant as hopelessly tender until it makes it through the first winter, no matter how native it might be. Even nursery-grown plants of species native to the empty lot next to your house can die if you don't pay any attention to them.

As a rule, nursery-grown plants, grown "hard" (in relatively poor soil and left outdoors all summer), are the easiest to keep alive during the summer and autumn, but any plant accustomed to the outdoor life regardless of soil will generally be less susceptible to drying by sun and wind than plants grown indoors.

Plants can be planted any time the soil is not frozen, but the first principle in planting must be Plant Early. Plants set out in earliest spring are easier to establish while days are still relatively cool, and they take months of summer drought much more agreeably than plants stuck in the ground at the end of July. Plants set out in March or April can sometimes even be left to their own devices, without additional watering, if you're lucky. I do not recommend this method. Plants that are in the process of becoming established are still susceptible to being killed by drought in July, August, September, and October.

Autumn is another excellent time of the year for planting, but it should be remembered, if you live in my part of the world, that this is the beginning of the dry season and plants will need extra watering. (This extra watering is beneficial anyway, since some plants need to grow basal leaves in autumn in order to overwinter.)

I usually leave newly purchased plants in partial shade for a few days before setting them out into the garden; they need close attention paid to watering at this time, and also shelter from wind. It may be a good idea to repot the plants in larger pots to allow the greater volume of soilless mix to accommodate the regular watering the plants need at this time. If no noticeable changes take place in these few days, the plants may be planted.

Wilting at this time, or after the plants have been transplanted, is usually a sign that the soilless mix has dried out, although it can also be the result of damage from wind or low humidity. Wilted plants are often weakened to the point that they never fully recover, so this situation should be avoided by careful watering. Wilting of new transplants can be avoided by shading the plants (I used to cut out a gallon nursery container and fashion a sort of tent out of it, but the tents always fell over onto the plants; Claude Barr's method of setting a coffee can over a plant during the day works, but is far too labor-intensive), or by using one of the antidesiccant sprays available from nurseries. These have yielded spectacular results for me in prevention of wilt, and at present I have nothing but complete faith in them. (Make sure you read the manufacturer's recommendations and cautions before you start spraying.)

Roots

Day after day, all through the year, roots are pushing downward and outward through the soil in search of water and minerals for growth. This vaguely creepy business goes on unnoticed and undisturbed until one day when the indecisive gardener, having planted without thinking too hard about how large a plant can really get, suddenly decides to move the plant to a better place, and, with one twist of the spading fork, an agonizing series of snaps is heard. Not only heard but felt, deeply, within the gardener's suddenly repentant psyche. It is just as well that we cannot hear plants scream. Gardeners, of course, can scream.

The roots of young dryland plants may grow to a depth of six feet (1.8m) before the visible green part of the plant is even six inches (15cm) tall. This adaptation to survival in dry climates means that once a plant has been established, transplanting it is killing it. The old adage "think before you plant" holds well here. If only I had paid attention to it, I would not have had the deaths of hundreds of plants on my conscience.

There are exceptions to the deep-root rule just like there are exceptions to everything. Cacti are notoriously shallow-rooted, their roots snaking just below the soil surface to catch moisture from even the briefest of thundershowers, and agaves can be dug up fairly easily, even though the remaining roots will produce new plants for years to come.

Generally, though, once a plant has gone through one winter, it is probably better to consider it established and therefore immovable.

Every now and then a smaller plant can be moved (this book is nothing if not a book of exceptions to rules) in late winter or early spring, when still dormant or just at the point of emerging from dormancy, by gently (. . . gently . . .) digging it up and moving it to the new location. I prefer to do this as quickly and as silently as possible; it is as though the plant were still under the anesthetic of winter, and by the time it wakes up, spring, and a new growing season, has started.

Many alpine plants do most of their root growth in early spring, so moving these is not much of a risk, but again, smaller plants take to this operation much better than larger ones.

It should be understood by now that digging up plants in the wild is almost never successful. I removed some irises from the middle of a dirt road several years ago and they did survive, but that is an exception. Cacti are especially subject to predatory collectors, and in some instances populations of exceptionally rare cacti have been wiped out within a few weeks of their discovery. I believe Arizona is the only state in which cacti are protected by law; other states should follow this example. There are plenty of nurseries and seed catalogs that pander to people like us, anyway.

In this book, then, the word "transplant" almost always refers to moving a plant, either nursery-grown or one grown by you, from a pot to the garden. There is an art to this. I'm not exactly sure what it is, but it is an art.

Nursery-grown plants are grown in a soilless mix that allows the roots to grow quickly in a porous soil that can be heavily watered and fertilized, and at the same time not remain waterlogged. A porous soil, as has been reiterated many times, dries out instantly and requires almost daily watering. If the soil in the pot is planted directly into the garden, there is a difference between this soil and the garden soil in the way the two take up moisture, and as a result the clump of soilless mix either dries out or stays too wet. Death is almost always the result.

The trick is to get plants established (meaning that their roots are growing into the surrounding soil) as quickly as possible. Plants set out in their little soilless pots often heave out of the ground with the action of freezing and thawing in midwinter; this is something you want to avoid since usually you don't see the plant flung out of the ground until it's too late.

One remedy for this is to make all the garden soil a porous soil like that of the potted plant. You can do this; you can buy specially mixed soil from companies dealing in landscaping materials, but the amount of water needed to keep plants alive in a highly porous soil, in a sunny, dry climate, is even more staggering than the expense of the soil.

Since my aim here is to present practical solutions to gardening in a dry climate, and not a book written by someone born to wealth with endless amounts of spare time, my current approach is to remove as much of the soilless mix as possible either right before planting or as the plants are set into the ground. I say "current approach" because I change my mind constantly. I admit that sometimes I do just jam a plant into the ground, and the plant lives.

Experienced gardeners will note, possibly with alarm or contempt, that I am deliberately ignoring the accepted rules of planting; there will be no five-dollar plants in fifty-dollar holes for me. I think digging huge holes for little plants is a complete waste of time.

The first way to plant is to remove the plant from the pot and set it in a dishpan full of water, so that the soilless mix is washed away. This is pretty effective though of course not all the mix will be removed, which is not critical. Soilless mix that clings to fine feeder roots should not be disturbed, either. After the plant has spent its time in the bath, it can be planted directly into the garden soil (clay), with the dug-out soil gently pushed back into the hole and then watered in.

The second way is similar, but a hole is dug (not too big), the plant set in the hole, and then the hole (what's left of it) is filled with water, two or three times. This helps wash away the soilless mix too, and is less work. Do remember to backfill the hole once the water has drained away for the last time. You can then firm the plant in, in the traditional method, either with your feet or your fists, if you like.

Some plants, though, dislike this treatment. There isn't very much we can do about this; it's in the nature of some plants to have roots that are easily damaged by the act of planting, no matter how gently we may set our little green treasure into the ground. *Silene hookeri* is an example. For plants like this the best solution, sometimes, is to sow seed directly into the ground.

When plants should be set out into the garden is a matter of concern to some people, but not so much for me. Where I live plants can be planted almost any time of the year (the soil doesn't freeze very deeply here), though of course plants can't be moved from a greenhouse out into the garden in the middle of winter.

Some other plants (zauschnerias, marginally hardy succulents) seem to do best when planted immediately after the last frost (I know this is a conundrum: the only way you know that the frost is the last frost is if there aren't any others, until suddenly it's the middle of June and it may be too late to plant some things), but others do fine planted any time. Zauschnerias seem to need time, preferably a whole summer, to get their roots down into the garden soil before they are completely winter hardy.

There is also some anecdotal theory, especially prevalent in the world of serious rock gardeners, that certain plants react badly to being transplanted because of the complexities of their roots systems. A corollary to this is that certain plants (sometimes the same plants, sometimes other plants) are less drought-tolerant when transplanted as opposed to having their seed sown directly into the ground, either by you or by the plant itself. Both of these ideas seem perfectly plausible to me. Plants with sensitive root systems may spend too much energy trying to get their roots growing in an acceptable way, and have less energy to withstand either drought or cold winters.

If these plants set seed and it germinates, then all is well. Otherwise, you will have to spend a little extra time with your plants, watering them before they start to wilt, and possibly giving them some winter protection.

Pot- or root-bound plants are occasionally a problem, now that container-grown plants have almost entirely replaced field-grown plants. Since you can plant container-grown plants almost any time of the year their advantages are considerable, but this is one area where they can fall down flat. I find ornamental grasses to be particularly prone to becoming root-bound; usually what comes out of the pot is nothing but a mass of roots wound into a tight pot-shaped ball.

In watered gardens, establishing root-bound plants can be tricky since the roots need to be encouraged to move out into the garden soil before winter comes, otherwise the roots may shrivel to nothing when the surrounding soil dries out. In dry gardens, establishing these plants is even more difficult, unless you are totally committed to regular watering. One way to assist the roots is first to soak them in a dishpan to make them more flexible (this doesn't always work), and then pry at least a few of the growing roots (generally white-tipped) apart from the root ball, rather like untangling a ball of twine. The plant, with its now-frizzy root ball, can be planted in the way suggested earlier, with the surrounding soil filled into the hole by repeated visits with the watering can.

Propagation

Since this book mentions more than a few plants that are not readily available from nurseries, it seems only fair to describe methods of growing plants from seed. This is an almost effortless activity, but waiting for some species to germinate requires patience, sometimes an awful lot of patience.

As a rule, private collectors and rock garden societies send out their lists in autumn or early winter, which just happens to be the ideal time to sow most seed. One of the most exciting things about gardening, for me, is anticipating the seedlists and spending chilly evenings poring over the lists, and, really, doing some vicarious traveling.

It may come as a surprise to learn that winter sowing, outdoors, is recommended for a wide variety of species. The purpose of this, besides imitating what happens in nature, is to use the alternate freezing and thawing periods to help break down germination inhibitors, or to crack a hard seed coat that would otherwise only crack by natural means (fire, or being passed through an animal's digestive system).

There is an endless amount of tiresome debate concerning the "correct" method for germinating seed. It may be true that certain species germinate a higher percentage of seed when subjected to some other method, like being treated with gibberellic acid or hydrogen peroxide. These treatments are impractical for the home gardener, and since the germination "requirements" for some seeds do not replicate conditions the species finds in the wild, the insistence on the absolute necessity of these methods need not be taken too seriously. After sowing seed of some three thousand species outdoors, I have never found one that did not germinate this way. You might only get one seedling out of all this, but maybe one is all you need. If you get ten thousand seedlings, you might want to think twice about planting a plant that yields so many seedlings from a small packet of seed.

Species with peculiar requirements for germination are discussed in the plant descriptions; the basic method for winter sowing is described here.

Seeds are sown about the first or second week of January. It can be earlier or later, so long as there will be sufficient cold after the seeds are sown. Ordinary plastic pots you buy from a nursery are perfectly suitable, though they will last only a few years before becoming brittle. I use the B.E.F. growers' pots, made out of polypropylene, that I got years ago; they cost twenty-five cents apiece and have been left outside for over a decade. I don't know of any current source in North America for these pots, which are small and allow the soilless mix to dry out a little too easily.

Whatever kind of plastic pot you use, you will need to reserve an area for them, a place where the pots can sit around for a while (meaning, possibly, for years). An open frame, say a rectangle of boards, is ideal. The ground should be covered with something impermeable; a sheet of plastic works, but shingles are even better. If you live in hail country you will have a steady supply of these. You can also use tar paper.

The frame should be filled with about four inches (10 cm) of sand. The sand will keep the soilless mix inside the pots moist, and should roots grow through the bottom of the pot, the plastic (or whatever you used) will prevent the roots from growing into the soil below. Once roots have grown into the soil, moving a plant in a pot is hopeless. The smug satisfaction derived from avoiding this minor disaster is worth going to all this trouble.

The soilless mix you use can be anything you want; you can buy a commercial mix (but add one-third sand to this), or make your own. Equal parts peat moss, perlite, and sand are good, as are equal parts vermiculite, perlite, and sand. The sand makes the pots heavier and keeps them from tipping over or blowing away.

Some people prefer wetting the mixture first, before filling the pots, but I prefer using a dry mixture, and filling pots as though I were on an assembly line. The pots go into dishpans, and, with the dry method, hot water is poured on them with a watering can. Peat moss is easier to wet with hot water. After the pots cool (did I forget to say I was working outside in January?), the seeds are sprinkled on the surface, lightly pressed down into the mix with a special spoon (just an ordinary spoon, but only used for this), and then the surface is sprinkled with coating of gravel. Sandblasting gravel, or even gravel collected from red ant hills, is perfect. The gravel covering should not be deeper than the width of the gravel itself. This keeps the soilless mix moist and prevents rain from washing away the seed.

Then a plastic label is stuck in the pot, labeled in pencil. Pencil is the only writing medium that will remain legible after a year in the sun in my garden. Everything else fades.

The pots are left in the dishpans until the soilless mix has fully absorbed the water, maybe for an hour, then they're arranged in plastic flats that have been tested for leaks. New flats, which you can get at any nursery, usually have no holes in them. The flats sit on shelves, in shade, and the pots are left where they are until March or April, when they are more or less carefully inspected for signs of germination. Periodically, the flats are filled with water. If the water freezes and the pots are encased in ice, no harm is done, but allowing the soilless mix to dry out can kill some seeds, especially after they have absorbed water, or it can plunge them into a deep dormancy that may take years to overcome.

Once the seeds have germinated the pots are moved into the light, but not full blazing sun. After a few weeks of this the pots are exposed to full sun and kept watered, but not soaking, until August or September, when the difficult decision of moving them out into the garden can be made. If you have my kind of luck most of your seedlings will die, but some will live, and next year you may even have flowers on your new plants.

If you have frames, or even just an area where the pots are out in the sun, then none of this is necessary. The seeds germinate, the seedlings are immediately exposed to sun and the garden environment, and plants can be transplanted into the garden in August or September with ease.

As I said earlier, sometimes patience is needed, because certain species, or even just some packets of seed, may take more than one year to germinate. Or there can be successive germination over a period of years, which means that care must be taken when pricking out older, more fully developed seedlings, in order not to disturb younger seedlings. (You can also plant the whole potful, which saves a lot of worry, though you will have a dozen or a hundred plants in a space the diameter of your pot.)

Of course not every single species on the planet needs, or even accepts, this kind of treatment, and there are some that you can start like you would tomatoes. Seed of agaves and yuccas, and species of their ilk, can be germinated by sowing in pots under lights.

I do not recommend growing herbaceous plants under lights. It can be done, of course, but getting the tender little plants out from under the lights into a sun-drenched windswept garden is a task I find hopeless. Plants grown in a nursery greenhouse are an entirely different story.

Other seed has such a brief viability that it's best sown immediately after it's collected off the plant. Rabbitbrush is an example of this kind of seed, though no one ever offers it.

A more obscure category is those seeds that require some special treatment owing to an extremely hard seed coat that cold can't crack. These are usually attacked with sandpaper or even a file. I use a jeweler's loupe when I do this, so I don't rip into the embryo and kill the seed. Seeds so treated should be sown immediately, under lights, and watered.

Hydrochloric acid treatment is sometimes recommended for hard seed coats. This of course should be left to professionals. I suppose if you had a really bad case of indigestion . . . well, never mind.

Then again, the lazy method (the one I turn to first) dictates that some seeds can be sown simply by throwing them on the ground. If you have paid a lot of money for the seed packet this might not seem like such a bright idea, but with inexpensive seed, or older seed, this works fairly well. I do this with California poppies, some penstemons, and other things.

My final method is the easiest of all. I buy seed, give it to friends who are professional propagators, and get a few plants in return. This is the best way of all, since professionals can grow better plants than I can, and they get new species to try, and possibly new plants to add to their catalogs.

There are other ways to propagate plants besides growing them from seed. Division is one common method, though dryland plants offer almost no opportunities for this. Irises are an obvious example of plants that can be divided. Plants with running roots can also be divided, though maybe this exercise would be closer to taking cuttings.

Growing plants from cuttings (except cacti) is something other people do. I tried it once or twice, and that was that. My belief is that you need at least a greenhouse (for humidity and protection from wind), luck, and possibly a staff of dedicated gardeners for this to work.

I should add—to get back to seed propagation for a minute—that obtaining plants of species listed as endangered or threatened can only be done legally by purchasing seed from a firm that has a federal permit for trafficking in endangered species. The seed is always, I believe, collected from stock plants at the nursery, not from plants in the wild. You can sometimes purchase plants grown from such seed as well. If you are concerned about acquiring seed or plants, you can ask the nursery if they have the permit.

Bugs

Many years ago, it seems, our neighbor, who has no garden, leaned over the fence and asked us what it was that we sprayed on the garden to kill bugs. The answer was nothing. Apparently people who don't have gardens assume that people who do are constantly drenching the garden with some kind of toxic spray. In the first place, it would take a person far less lazy than I am to be able to spray at the right time, and in the second place, we have dogs, so for me the case is closed.

Nowhere am I more useless to people asking for help than on the subject of pests and diseases. I generally do nothing, which is not the answer people want. "How can you possibly do nothing when my prize aspidistra is at stake?" My reply is usually, "Grow something else."

I don't kill aphids, flea beetles, ants, grasshoppers, or anything else. (I let my wife, who likes spiders, transport black widows away from the house, out to the field that abuts the garden.) I am completely useless.

Back in the days when I did kill things (actions for which I am now extremely sorry), I used diatomaceous earth for ants, and Dr. Bronner's castile soap (a capful to a quart/liter of water) will do in aphids, slugs (not that you should see any in your garden), both gray and black blister beetles, pear psylla, earwigs, and even yellow jackets.

The larvae, pinkish red and about half an inch (1.25cm) long, of the flea beetle that attacks penstemons and paintbrushes can be dispatched with a spray containing pyrethrin.

A soap spray, applied on leaf surfaces as a preventative, can be used for powdery mildew and blackspot on roses, both of which are common even in dry climates.

Other fungal diseases are fairly rare in my climate, though gardeners are always getting something they shouldn't and then asking me what to do about it (my response is almost always to stop watering so much), when they really should be asking someone else. County agricultural extension agents can help you better than I can.

Native plants can get diseases more often associated with traditional garden plants. Fireblight on rosaceous plants is fairly common; I don't spray for this but know I should. Maybe next year.

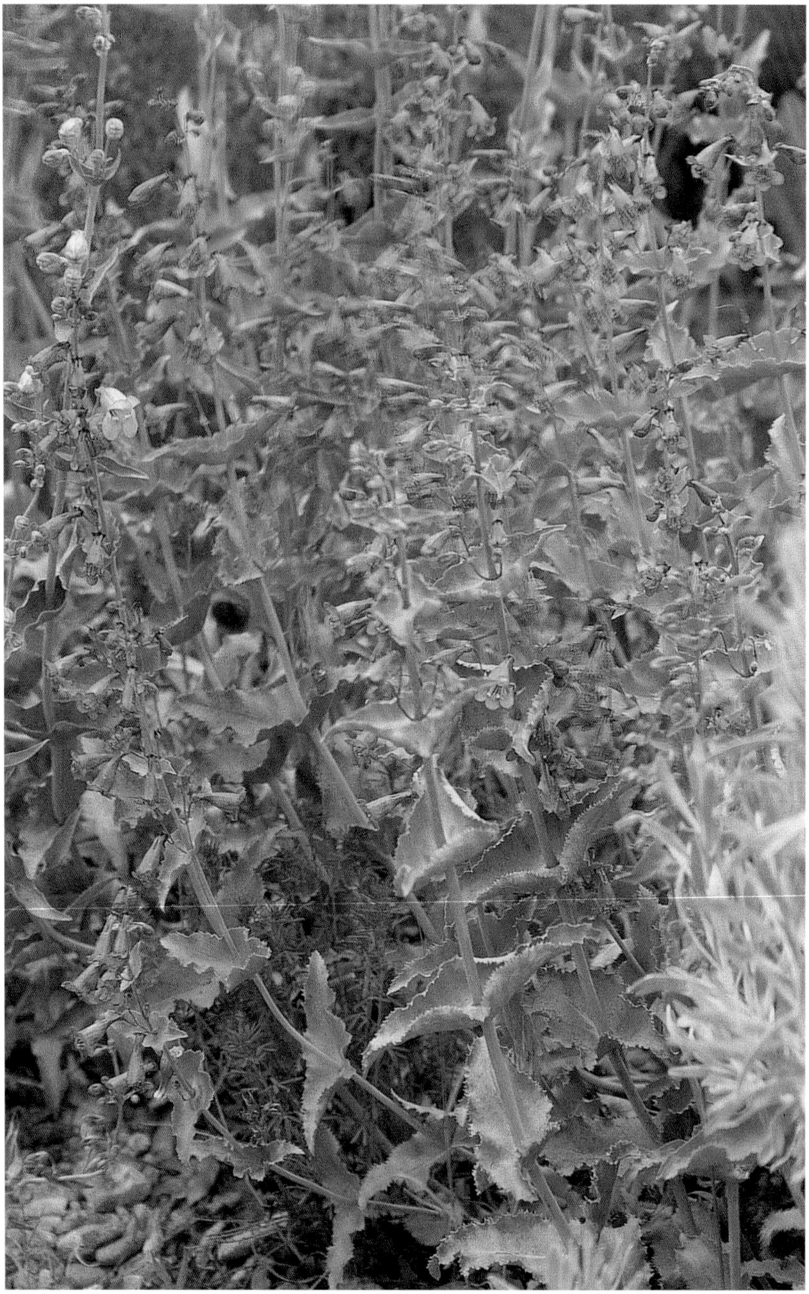

INTERLUDE

The Plants

The descriptions of plants in the chapters that follow are a mixture of personal observation and extensive consultation with the various floras and plant books listed in the bibliography. The descriptions in the floras do not always agree with each other; where there is disagreement, I have come to my own conclusions based on the plants grown in my garden or from my limited experience with the plants growing in the wild.

Plants in the nursery trade sometimes acquire an incorrect or misleading name through mistakes in labeling; the error rate is surprisingly low considering the huge number of plants now available, but wrong names do still persist. The most obvious example is *Penstemon caespitosus* 'Claude Barr'. It isn't the end of the world that the plant is consistently mislabeled, though it does give a wrong impression of *P. caespitosus*.

I have a feeling that some people will page through the plant descriptions that follow and decide that the author has become completely carried away with the idea of listing as many plants as possible. This could be true. There is a strong temptation to become a collector of plants, especially rock garden plants, which can lead, in Graham Stuart Thomas's words, to a garden that is a "meaningless jumble of disparate plants." We still want some cohesiveness in the garden; fortunately, the obsessive collector has recourse to growing many of the tinier treasures in pots or troughs, which makes the jumble less apparent.

There are a lot of plants here. Any time you make extensive lists of plants there will always be someone who gleefully points out plants you forgot to mention. After having spent a couple of years racking my poor brain trying to think of plants that I could possibly have forgotten, I decided to give up and convince myself that the lists here are about as inclusive as I could make them. Few things are more terrifying to authors than imagining they've left out whole sections of whatever it is they're writing about, and that these omissions are revealed to them only the day the book is published, or, worse, the day the first reader opens the book.

One way I tried to avoid omissions was by using the indexes of the various floras as alphabetical checklists; the catalog of slides was another way. Walking through the garden and reminiscing about what used to be growing in this or that now-bare space was yet another way. Still, there are probably plants I have left out, and possibly some I should not have included.

Names

The botanical names (i.e., the nomenclature) used in this book are the ones I feel like using. Nomenclatural changes are proposed every so often, and it's difficult to keep up with the latest changes. In any case it's important to remember that nomenclatural changes are proposals and nothing more. Until the new names find acceptance in the taxonomic community, there is little point in using them in a gardening book, except to help you look for plants that might get relabeled by someone who is excessively concerned about the latest proposed nomenclature.

Cacti are an exception, and I believe you could not find two articles or books that agree on any cacti names at all. This is symptomatic of something, but I don't know what it is.

Sometimes gardeners get overly attached to plant names. Changes of nomenclature usually reflect the results of scientific observation, and there is no point in getting hysterical, like the horticultural community did when botanists tried to slip *Zauschneria* into *Epilobium* some years ago. (I call them zauschnerias to avoid more hysteria.) Conservatism here is just hopeless. The plants are still the same plants.

Rock gardeners are particularly subject to dwelling on the importance of retaining plant names they are used to. When a variety or subspecies is subsumed into the main species, an outcry is heard across several continents. I suspect this is due to the tendency to collect names as much as plants. The chapter on rock garden plants does relentlessly dispense botanical names; the acquisitive instinct here, as I know well, is equally relentless.

Botanical names (often wrongly called Latin names) are based on Latin (and usually use the Latin method of gender agreement: a feminine generic name means a feminine ending to the specific name) but are often derived from the Greek, or from an indigenous language. (*Camassia quamash* is but one example.)

People new to gardening sometimes find the botanical names daunting, not only because so many sophisticated gardeners use these names instead of common names (if the plants even have them), but because when they try to pronounce the names, looking for plants at a nursery or attending plant society meetings, they find their pronunciation corrected.

While some people advocate trying to pronounce the names based on what might be called standard Latin pronunciation (e.g., pronouncing the masculine genitive ending *–ii* as "ee-ee"), in order to effect a kind of botanical Esperanto, it only works when used by people speaking English. This is the exact opposite of what was intended. Aside from the aural experience of hearing groups of learned people crying "ee-ee" constantly, imagine what non-English-speaking botanists would make of specific epithets like *wrightii* or *jonesii*. The ee-ee would be understood, but nothing else.

It still becomes necessary to adapt your pronunciation when in the company of gardeners whose first language is not English, because they don't accept any kind of universal pronunciation either. (They might say they do, but they don't.) Once you find a way to communicate that skirts around the most improbable English pronunciations (like *wrightii*), you can concentrate on enjoying the plants and the garden.

For English speakers, then, botanical names should be pronounced as though they were English words. There is no need to try to pronounce plants names as though you were Marcus Aurelius inspecting the perennial borders. *Acer* rhymes with "racer," *Pinus* with "sinus," and dictionaries support this. The masculine genitive ending is pronounced "ee-eye" (as is the feminine, *–iae*), and only a few people will look at you askance.

Believe it or not, the English language has rules for pronouncing some words, rules that are followed even in daily conversation. Botanical names of Greek origin have a fairly regular pronunciation. I forget what the exact rule is, but basically, words are accentuated on the antepenultimate (next to the next to the last) syllable. Think of apostrophe, catastrophe, or Penelope. Plant examples are chrysanthemum, astragalus, and agastache. The last one is so commonly mispronounced ("a-*gas*-ta-kee" is correct) that maybe you will have to resort to carrying this book around. (Well, maybe not, since I recommend none of them.)

Penstemon barbatus and horse lubber grasshopper (*Taeniopoda eques*)

CHAPTER TWO

Perennials and Annuals

My favorite definition of a perennial is a plant that, had it lived, would have come back the next year. This is not so far from the truth in some cases; there are plants that can be defined as perennial but, in times of serious drought, these same plants end their life cycle after only a few years. The behavior of some penstemons, both in the wild and in the garden, illustrates this perfectly. If the summer is exceedingly dry, the plants will flower, set seed, and not have enough energy to grow their new basal leaves, which are essential for their long-term survival. So you make a note to collect at least a little seed, for sowing directly in early winter, or hope nature does this for you, or sow seeds in pots, which gives you a little more control.

There are more perennials here than annuals, hence the reversal of the usual order in the chapter title. Most annuals are completely unsuited to growing in the dry garden, but some do quite well if seed is sown in early winter or early spring.

As a generalization, the plants included in this chapter are over a foot (30 cm) tall and would not be considered suitable for the rock garden, though of course this is just personal taste, and I don't go outside with a ruler, measure the plants, and trim them down to size.

Penstemon cardinalis and *Berlandiera lyrata*

I'm afraid that some of my comments, especially those that seem to contradict accepted opinion, may distress some readers, but the comments do reflect forty-five years of gardening in a dry climate, and almost twenty years maintaining an unirrigated garden (though I should mention again that more than a few passers-by in our neighborhood, and not just children, have wondered out loud if the house wasn't abandoned) in which these plants were tested. Perennials have been the subject of so much hyperbole in reference to their drought tolerance that I can only wonder what gardeners new to dryland gardening think when they purchase a plant claimed to grow with no irrigation and the plant dies of drought within a week of being planted. I suppose that drought tolerance is just another of those characteristics, like winter hardiness, that tend to become exaggerated when the time comes to print the next year's plant catalog.

Limiting myself to dryland plants of western North America means that some plants will be excluded. *Gaura lindheimeri*, for instance, is not from the southwestern United States as so often claimed (it's from eastern Texas, along the Gulf Coast, and Louisiana), is no more drought-tolerant than any other plant, and, besides, is not reliably hardy. I grow this as an annual in an irrigated garden.

The number of native dryland perennials available in the nursery trade has increased dramatically in the last decade, and seed collectors offer a comparatively huge selection, so have at it.

Agastache (giant hyssop). These are, mostly, plants of the Mexican monsoon, accustomed (like other plants where this phenomenon occurs) to receiving relatively large amounts of rainfall in late July, August, and September. As the species hybridize readily, more and more named selections appear every year, so much so that it's impossible to keep up with the new names. Almost all are extremely beautiful plants and valuable additions to the autumn garden, though some gardeners may not like the fact that their brittle stems are so easily broken. (It irritates me no end.) Winter hardiness depends on maintaining a small growth of basal leaves in late autumn, encouraged by ample moisture in September or October.

Despite some really wild exaggerations in nursery catalogs, agastaches have very little drought tolerance (you will always find them most spectacularly grown with constant irrigation), and some of the species should be considered only marginally hardy. They do not belong in a dry garden.

Amsonia. There are three highly desirable species in the genus, a member of the dogbane family (Apocynaceae). These are, unfortunately, rarely seen in the nursery trade. All three species are taprooted and will grow happily in the driest conditions imaginable short of asphalt.

Amsonia jonesii, found from western Colorado through eastern and southern Utah to northern Arizona, is at least occasionally available. Plants are about a foot (30cm) tall and wide, in dry years, a little taller in wetter years, with oval, acuminate green leaves two inches (5cm) long and profuse flowering bunches of half-inch-wide (1.25cm) blue stars with white centers, in May. Pipebone-shaped seedpods follow, containing seeds that some people (not including me) can germinate with ease.

The two other species can only be considered on the fringe of western horticulture, since plants are rarely offered for sale and seed is almost as scarce. *Amsonia eastwoodiana* is of variable height, from six inches (15cm) to a foot (30cm) or more tall, with narrowly oblanceolate green leaves an inch (2.5cm) long, sometimes woolly, sometimes not, with more open clusters of flowers similar to those of *A. jonesii*. Native to northern Arizona and southern Utah. *Amsonia tomentosa* is similar but with much wider, ovate, acute leaves, somewhat longer than those of *A. eastwoodiana*. *Amsonia tomentosa* is native from southern California to Arizona, southern Nevada, and southwestern Utah, but seems to be completely hardy.

Amsonia jonesii

Argemone polyanthemos

Argemone (prickly poppy). Botanists would have us believe that there are several species of prickly poppy native to the west, but for our purposes *Argemone polyanthemos* (Montana to Texas) is the one to have. This is a beautiful taprooted annual or biennial, to three feet (90cm) when very happy, with pinnately lobed prickly leaves six inches (15cm) long, or longer, with four-inch-wide (10cm) fried-egg flowers on and off all summer. Spiny seedpods follow; these are best cut off the plant rather than pulled off (one attempt at the latter will prove the wisdom of doing the former). Seed can be sown in winter; purchased plants establish quite easily.

Artemisia. *Artemisia ludoviciana* is found everywhere west of the Mississippi River, and east of the Cascades and Sierra Nevada, a distribution whose origin will become immediately apparent should you plant a single, tiny plant of this in your garden. This is not necessarily a bad thing, but *A. ludoviciana*'s furious spreading habit should be kept in mind before you thrust the trowel into the dirt. I should add that I like this plant, though I would not plant it where I didn't want it to spread everywhere, immediately.

Artemisia ludoviciana grows anywhere from one to three feet (30 to 90cm) tall (it will be at the shorter end of the spectrum in a dry garden), with white-woolly foliage and widely variable leaves. There are a number of varieties, only two of which are of real interest. *Artemisia ludoviciana* var. *ludoviciana*, the common variety on the Great Plains, and also in the Intermountain region, has more or less entire narrowly oblanceolate leaves; var. *latiloba* (eastern Washington and Oregon to Montana, south to Utah and California) has deeply divided leaves.

This is a plant that can be grown either in the driest soil or in a heavily watered garden. In dry gardens the plant is still attractive but has a looser, weedier look. The named horticultural varieties of *Artemisia ludoviciana*, possessing that extra edge of sophistication, like 'Silver Queen', 'Silver King', and 'Valerie Finnis', are better grown with plenty of irrigation, though there is certainly no law preventing anyone from growing them in a dry garden.

Bahia. A genus of a dozen or so yellow-flowered daisies, of which at least one is of interest. *Bahia nudicaulis* is native from Montana and Wyoming west and south to the Four Corners area; this is a foot-tall (30cm) taprooted plant with aromatic foliage. Oblong tapering leaves, three inches (7.5cm) long, are clustered along the stems in var. *oblongifolia* (plants from the Four Corners); leaves are more rounded in var. *nudicaulis* (Wyoming and Montana), and slightly narrower and mostly at the base in var. *desertorum* (Utah and western Colorado). The yellow daisies are two inches (5cm) wide, with relatively wide (quarter-inch, 6mm) blunt-tipped ray flowers in May and June. Even though the Rocky Mountain region is tiresomely rich in yellow daisies, *B. nudicaulis* is a good choice for a dry-as-dust garden, and it does have another trick up its sleeve: it belies the reputation of taprooted plants by producing a few runners, enabling you to have a nice colony in ten or twenty years.

Baileya (desert marigold). A couple of species native to the southwestern United States and northern Mexico are common in seed catalogs and sometimes offered as plants; these have white-woolly foliage and yellow daisies on stems a foot (30cm) or more high, blooming in spring. *Baileya multiradiata*, a perennial, has pinnately divided leaves and flowers about three inches (7.5 cm) across; *B. pleniradiata*, a winter annual, has leaves divided into lobes and flowers about an inch and a half (3.75 cm) across. Seed of both can be sown as winter wanes and, given a wet spring, you will have blooming plants in May or June; for very dry locations.

Berlandiera. Four species are native to northern Mexico, some finding their way across the border into the United States. *Berlandiera lyrata*, whose supposed common name "green eyes" has probably been universally supplanted by "chocolate flower," is a taprooted perennial to two feet (60 cm), more or less, usually flopping (or decumbent, as botanists say) with gray-green lyre-shaped leaves six inches (15 cm) long at the base, shorter, and velvety, in the inflorescence; it is smothered with two-inch-wide (5 cm) yellow daisies all summer and intensely scented of chocolate in the morning.

Berlandiera lyrata

Berlandiera lyrata must be in the top five best choices for a real dryland garden; it will tolerate any amount of heat and drought, and still go on flowering. Some of our plants spend the summer lying on concrete pavement, which is not exactly a cool surface in Denver. *Berlandiera lyrata* transplants somewhat uneasily (be careful not to disturb the taproot), but once plants are established, the seeds derived from the curious green discs left after the flowers fade can be scattered through the garden in November. Aside from northern Mexico, *B. lyrata* is found in Arizona, New Mexico, western Texas, Kansas, and Colorado.

Callirhoë. Half a dozen or so species in the mallow family, mostly found further east in prairies and woodlands of eastern North America. (I am of course just being pedantic in using the diaeresis: *Callirhoë* seems to have largely lost it, as well as its fourth syllable, in recent years.) A couple of the more upright species, like *C. digitata* and *C. papaver*, make good, if short-lived, plants in a regularly watered garden. The best-known species is *C. involucrata* (wine cups, among other common names), native from Minnesota to Wyoming south to New Mexico. This is a sprawling plant with green-gray lobed geranium-like leaves two inches (5cm) long and wide, and two-inch-wide (5cm) wine-red round flowers in June, July, and August, or sometimes off and on depending on drought. In years of good moisture the plant may spread three feet (90cm); in very dry years the green parts wither to almost nothing, but apparently the ever-widening caudex (the woody root) keeps the plant going. It needs to be regularly watered the first year. After it settles in, and after a year of good moisture, the parent plant may be surrounded by dozens of tiny wine cups.

Clarkia. A genus of about forty species of annuals, mostly confined to California, many of which are very beautiful and nicely suited to the dry garden if the plants are in the garden before hot weather comes (in Denver this would be before the first of May), or if seed is sown direct in late winter. My favorite is *Clarkia speciosa*, a sort of lolling plant to two feet (60cm) if it happens to be particularly ecstatic, with two-inch-wide (5cm) four-petaled flowers, pink shading to white at the center. Or maybe my favorite is *C. amoena* (farewell-to-spring), pink flowers with darker blotches at the center. *Clarkia bottae*, *C. dudleyana*, *C. imbricata*, and *C. rubicunda* are also good.

Not that clarkia seed is available, of course, though once in a blue moon a seed collector offers wild-collected seed (possibly some species, or seeds, may be purchased from nurseries specializing in native Californian plants). If you do find clarkia seed, and sow it, and it germinates, and you get flowering plants, save the seed for sowing next year. If you can't find clarkia seed, *Clarkia amoena* has been subject to a great deal of horticultural selection, and any of the godetias (same plant as *C. amoena*) will do. Believe it or not.

Cucurbita. The stinking cucumber or buffalo gourd, *Cucurbita foetidissima*, found from Nebraska to California south into northern Mexico, only stinks when the foliage is bruised or broken. This is, as Barr

Cucurbita foetidissima at Denver Botanic Gardens

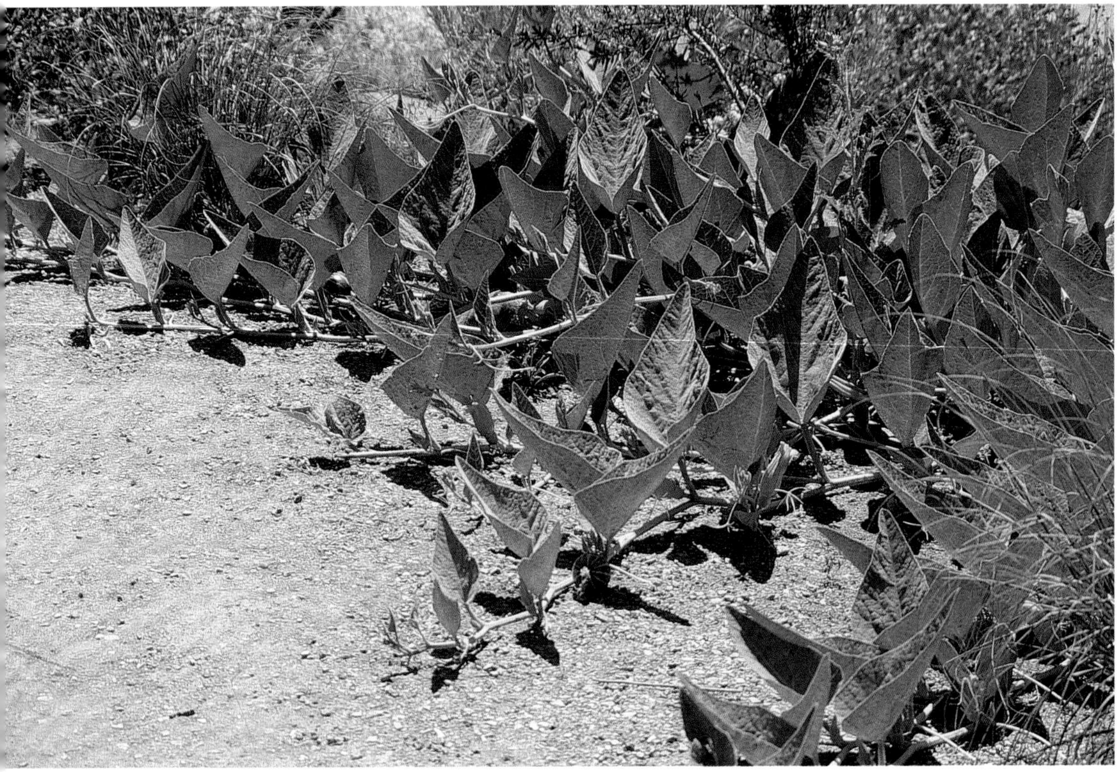

said, "a spectacular trailing vine," with sandpapery stems and gray-green rounded triangular leaves six to eight inches (15 to 20cm) long, the plant spreading to ten feet (3m) or even more. The flowers are typical yellow cucumber flowers, three to four inches (7.5 to 10cm) long, throughout the summer, followed by round inedible (at least I wouldn't eat them) cucumbers about the same length. *Cucurbita foetidissima* is fairly easily grown from seed, though I think the only way to get seed is to pick the cucumbers from plants growing by the side of the road. This would be an excellent, and different, choice for covering a large area where you can't think of anything else to grow.

Dalea purpurea

Dalea. Daleas are ornamental, temperamental clovers almost entirely residing on the extreme outer fringes of horticulture. One, *Dalea purpurea* (usually sold as *Petalostemon purpureum*), barely crosses the 100th meridian, except in var. *arenicola*, which is found in sand dunes from western Nebraska south along the Colorado-Kansas state lines into the Texas panhandle. It can be grown in clay despite its name (*arenicola* means "sand-dweller"). This has green, pinnate leaves an inch (2.5cm) or so long, growing to maybe a foot (30cm) high after wet springs, with showy purple bottlebrushes in May or June. The happiness of *D. purpurea* waxes and wanes with available moisture; the plants can be killed outright by prolonged drought.

Other daleas are only available as seed. *Dalea formosa* (southeastern Colorado south to Coahuila) is a shrublet six inches (15cm) or more high, spreading several times as wide, with bright rose-purple flowers; *D. frutescens* (Oklahoma and Texas south to Nuevo León) is another shrublet, or woody-based perennial, a foot (30 cm) tall in cold-winter gardens, with purple flowers; *D. scoparia* (broom dalea; Arizona, Sonora, New Mexico, Chihuahua, Coahuila, and western Texas) is a more or less woody shrub to three feet (90 cm) with a few leaves on the stems and a few blue flowers at the ends of the stems. Seed can be germinated by nicking it opposite the hilum and sowing it under lights, or sown direct (probably the safest method), and hoping for rain.

Datura (thorn apple, toloache). A large, poisonous perennial, or, more usually, a spindly annual, three feet (90 cm) high and as much as ten feet (3 m) wide, *Datura wrightii* (Oklahoma to California south into Mexico) has lobed, acrid-smelling green leaves six inches (15 cm) long and almost as wide, and large white trumpets eight inches (20 cm) long, heavily scented, borne all summer. Golfball-sized thorny green seedpods follow. *Datura wrightii* is common in garden centers and nurseries, though it can easily be confused with the Asian species *D. metel* (I believe all the horticultural selections are derived from the Asian datura), which is not hardy.

The taxonomy of the North American species of *Datura* is convoluted, to say the least. Some botanists segregate *D. wrightii* into various subspecies, while others seem to suggest that *D. wrightii* is synonymous with *D. inoxia*, which is also synonymous with *D. meteloides*.

Garden performance of *Datura wrightii* is equally difficult to define precisely. Some plants may fail after the first year, while others eventually grow to large plants that will tolerate considerable drought. Sometimes plants will leave dozens of seedlings that, in good years, can grow to flowering plants in the same summer. Western nurseries with a fondness for tucking away various treasures on the plant tables may have a perennial datura or two. Daturas are easy to grow from seed, if the seed is sown outdoors in winter.

Delphinium (larkspur). A handful of dryland delphiniums are occasionally available as seed from companies catering to the rock garden trade, though the plants are generally over a foot (30 cm) tall. I have had no success growing them from seed. Probably, considering the per-

Delphinium geyeri with *Gazania* Tanager™, Kelaidis garden

formance of some Central Asian delphiniums in the garden, once you get them going they will continue by seeding around the original plant. Maybe Christopher Lloyd's maxim, that some plants are simply best left to be enjoyed in the wild, applies here. If you're so inclined, some delphiniums to try are *Delphinium geyeri*, *D. nelsonii*, and *D. nuttallianum*.

Echinacea (purple coneflower). One species, *Echinacea angustifolia*, is found throughout the Great Plains until it crosses the Kansas-Colorado state line and finds the lower rainfall less to its liking. Barr called *E. angustifolia* "bold, spectacular, and beautiful," an appraisal that can only be attributed to a higher average annual rainfall than that "enjoyed" in the garden here. The plant barely survives. Original plantings gave way to seedlings that exhibited greater drought tolerance, but not by enough to make me overjoyed at the plants' performance. Here, *E. angustifolia* grows to a foot (30cm) or less, with eight-inch-long (20cm), rough linear-oblanceolate leaves, and pink-purple daisies three inches (7.5cm) wide, the ray flowers downward-pointing, as is typical with the

Echinacea angustifolia at Denver Botanic Gardens

genus. This is difficult to grow from seed, but professional growers, displaying their usual wizardry, have made plants available, which should be considered as the beginning of breeding colonies. Just don't expect too much from this plant. Unless you water it.

The other echinaceas, like *Echinacea pallida* and *E. purpurea*, with distributions much further east, are often cited as examples of plants suitable for low-water gardens. This is possibly the most bizarre situation in horticulture: not only are these species completely unacquainted with western-style drought in their native habitats, they demonstrate no drought tolerance whatsoever in the garden.

Eschscholzia (California poppy). Two California poppies are commonly available in the nursery trade as seeds or plants and probably familiar to everyone. *Eschscholzia caespitosa* 'Sundew' is the smaller of the two, with profuse pale yellow flowers in May and June; *E. califor-*

Eschscholzia californica 'Alba'

nica is, of course, orange, and the state flower of California. I like all the color forms of *E. californica* except the doubles; the cream-colored one (sold as 'Alba', among other names) is a special favorite here. *Eschscholzia caespitosa* is a native of California and Oregon; *E. californica* is found from Washington to Baja California.

Gardeners who complain that *Eschscholzia californica* takes over the garden are watering too much. In a dry garden it remains a well-behaved plant. The species can be either an annual or a taprooted perennial. Seed can be sown any time from November onward, though preferably not too late in the spring. In a good year with "normal" moisture, the plants add a special touch to the dry garden.

Gaillardia (blanket flower). Beautiful members of the daisy family with lobed ray flowers loosely spaced around the disk flower. The common gaillardia of horticulture is probably a hybrid of *Gaillardia aristata* and G. *pulchella*, sometimes called G. ×*grandiflora*; these have been bred to a richer lifestyle and wither away to nothing in the dry garden unless a very wet summer (which is possible) ensues.

Gaillardia aristata is common throughout the west (North Dakota to New Mexico, and Utah to British Columbia), a more or less (less in conditions of severe drought) two-foot (60cm), single or multi-stemmed plant, with lobed oblanceolate leaves four inches (10cm) long, vaguely resembling those of dandelions but grayer, with flowers about four inches (10cm) across, borne throughout the summer. The disk flowers are dark purple; the ray flowers are yellow.

Gaillardia pinnatifida (Colorado south to Texas and Coahuila, west to Arizona and Utah) is a more slender plant to a foot (30cm) or so, with hairy pinnatifid leaves and flowers two inches (5cm) wide in May and June. The disk flowers are wine-red, or some shade approaching that; the ray flowers are yellow.

Gaillardia pulchella has a more easterly distribution but does make its way to Texas and New Mexico. This is essentially an annual with a desire to become perennial (a desire rarely satisfied), similar in many respects to G. *aristata*, but the ray flowers are red-purple, yellow at the tips. I always considered the suitability of G. *pulchella* to dry gardens to be suspect until I observed the plants growing and seeding about over a period of years in an unirrigated lawn of buffalograss and weeds.

Gaillardias can, of course, be purchased as plants, but I think their longevity is increased by sowing seed in winter.

Helianthus (sunflower). Sunflowers are traditionally associated with moister climates than those of the west; the sunflower so often considered suitable for dry gardens, *Helianthus maximilianii*, is a plant mostly of the prairies (Manitoba to Texas). When planted in the dry garden here, several plants of this very attractive sunflower demonstrated their adaptability to drought by dying.

Ipomoea (morning-glory). *Ipomoea leptophylla* (bush morning-glory) is, to my eyes, one of the most beautiful plants in the western North American flora. Native from South Dakota to New Mexico, found growing in deep sand but not absolutely demanding it in the garden, this is a mounding plant to three feet (90cm) with six-inch-long (15cm), narrowly lanceolate green leaves, and gorgeous reddish purple morning-glory flowers, with a darker throat, about two inches (5cm) wide, opening throughout the summer. The plant makes an enormous root, for water storage; this root is sensitive to standing water in winter, so if the morning-glory is grown in clay, which is otherwise no problem, care should be taken that it's grown in a place where water does not collect in late winter. Plants are sometimes available, but *I. leptophylla* is easily grown from seed; after danger of frost is past (the foliage is frost-tender), I file a small notch in the end of the seed and soak it overnight, for planting out into the garden the next day.

Ipomoea leptophylla

Maurandya (snapdragon vine, balloonbush). Two trailing vines to ten feet (3m) or more, found growing among shrubs in the lower deserts of North America, occasionally make their way into seed catalogs. These are *Maurandya antirrhiniflora* (*Maurandella antirrhiniflora*; southern California and Sonora to Texas and Coahuila), with dark red-on-purple snapdragon-penstemon flowers, an inch (2.5cm) long and wide, on a vine with ivy-shaped leaves, two inches (5cm) long and wide, and *M. wislizeni*, essentially the same distribution except for California, with more arrow-shaped leaves and light blue or purple flowers (and, I might add, the current indignity of being forced into the genus *Epixiphium*).

These are perennials but said not to be hardy. I would agree based on my experience. They are also said to be slow to germinate from seed. I would disagree here, because nothing has ever happened when I sowed seed, and yet I have had *Maurandya antirrhiniflora* in the garden, twining and blooming over shrubs just like in the deserts. I think the secret here is either to sow seed in late winter where you want the plants, or have someone adept at germinating plants do the work for you and send you plants, though these, of course, will need more water as they establish in the first weeks of summer.

Mentzelia (blazing star). Gorgeous but difficult, taprooted plants requiring dry soil and therefore sensitive to overwatering in an attempt to get young plants established. *Mentzelia decapetala* is occasionally offered in regional nurseries and is definitely worth trying. This is a multi-stemmed biennial (or if you're lucky, a perennial) to three feet (90 cm) with serrated green leaves, six inches (15 cm) long, and six-inch-wide (15 cm) five-petaled cream-colored stars with a cluster of stamens in the center. The flowers, in good summers borne all summer, open in the afternoon and close sometime past midnight. Found throughout the Great Plains, extending into Mexico. *Mentzelia nuda* (Montana to Texas) is similar but with smaller flowers, favoring deep sand in the wild. I have never grown this one, but like many other plants growing on sand, it may adapt to clay if it is never watered.

There are other species native to the Great Plains and the Intermountain region which I have never seen offered either as seed or plants. Mentzelias can be grown from seed sown outdoors in pots in winter, or even directly into the ground, in autumn. Since most of them seem to thrive along roadsides, a little discreet seed-collecting might not be out of order. Wear gloves; the seedpods are like tubes of coarse sandpaper.

California has a number of annual species, only one of which, the yellow-flowered *Mentzelia lindleyi*, ever appears in seed catalogs. Reading Lester Rowntree's breathless prose describing these in detail makes me wish I had the opportunity to try them all.

Mirabilis (four o'clock). The wild four o'clock, *Mirabilis multiflora*, is found from Colorado to California and Baja California. Impossible to grow from seed (for me, anyway), the four o'clock has become a regular feature of nursery catalogs provided by people who can work the magic apparently needed to get seeds to germinate. This is a plant with thick, fleshy, three-inch (7.5 cm) ovate-cordate leaves on stems to two feet (60 cm) or more, but sprawling to several times that wide, so make sure you give it room. Pink-magenta flowers an inch (2.5 cm) wide are borne in profusion from July until frost, in the afternoon and evening.

Four o'clocks are slow to establish. Plants should probably not be left on their own, without watering, for at least three years.

A variety of *Mirabilis multiflora* (sometimes granted specific status, as *M. glandulosa*) with sticky flowers is found throughout the range of regular *M. multiflora*; it is said to have spring-blooming flowers that open in early morning and are "heavily rose-scented" (Weber 1987). I am unable to think of a single reason why this plant is not in our garden.

Mirabilis multiflora

Penstemon. The largest genus of flowering plants endemic to North America, and easily, aside from cacti, the richest source of plants suitable to the dry garden. Some are better than others, of course, and what follows is a personal selection based on the plants' performance during several years of severe droughts.

Garden performance—in this case meaning tolerance to heat, constant drought, wind (endless, endless wind), and hot winter sun—is best assessed over a period of about ten years during which the plants can experience most of the vagaries of the Rocky Mountain climate. Not all penstemons react to prolonged drought in the same way; even though passing knowledge of their habitat and prior experience in years of "normal" moisture might suggest otherwise, some of the dryland penstemons will collapse during a hot, dry summer following a hot, dry spring. And, of course, cold snaps in April and May can have a negative effect on the ability of some penstemons to tolerate prolonged summer drought.

All the penstemons mentioned here, except where noted, form wandlike flowering stalks that are deciduous and should be cut down before autumn, unless you're saving seed. During a hot, dry summer plants may die if allowed to form copious amounts of seed. As a rule penstemons have basal leaves that need to overwinter in order to ensure survival for the next year. Plants with these leaves may require deep irrigation from time to time in autumn if no rain falls (which is the typical scenario).

I have to admit that a lot of penstemons look much better when irrigated once a week, assuming no rain falls, but then, this is not exactly the typical situation with most penstemons, growing as they do in places where spring and summer are the rainy seasons.

Otherwise, the list is the usual suspects plus a few additions, and a few subtractions. I no longer grow *Penstemon clutei* or *P. eatonii*; both were irritatingly short-lived under extreme conditions. *Penstemon grandiflorus* is nice but acts like an annual. Many others fail to make it through a winter following a good season of bloom. I imagine that some readers will wonder why plants of the Great Plains seem better adapted to thrive under conditions of severe drought than do those of the Intermountain region and California. Penstemons in the former region are mostly smaller and more suited to rock gardens, or, if they are larger ones like *Penstemon payettensis* and *P. speciosus*, they tend to flower once and then die. This of course is no reason for you not to try them.

Hot winter sun and the resulting desiccation of overwintering basal leaves has made long-term trials of some of the Californians, like *Penstemon clevelandii* and *P. spectabilis*, problematic. The plants seem at least borderline hardy, but then things go wrong in winter, and the plants don't have enough strength to produce healthy growth in spring, or if they do, they prove the rule that plants on the cusp of hardiness do less well in drought than hardier plants.

I should add that the list of plants reflects my current opinion; I change my mind almost as often as I change my underwear. Besides, I have already made extensive lists of penstemons elsewhere and am wary of trying readers' patience to an even greater degree.

Penstemons are very easy to grow from seed, so I would advise trying any that sound nice, and making your own winter- and drought-hardiness trials. The journey alone is worth the effort.

Penstemon barbatus (southwestern Colorado, Utah, eastern Arizona, New Mexico, western Texas, Chihuahua, and Coahuila, maybe elsewhere in Mexico) is reputedly short-lived, but plants in one of the cactus gardens here have bravely come back year after year, leaving seedlings everywhere. The seedlings are hardier plants and in some years form a tiny forest of red, inch-and-a-half-long (3.75cm) sharkshead flowers on three-foot (90cm) waving stalks in June and July. The few, opposite, four-inch-long (10cm), narrowly oblanceolate leaves neither add nor detract from the display. Hummingbirds will love you for planting this one. The cultivars of *P. barbatus*, though, are best relegated to a regularly watered garden, especially 'Elfin Pink' and 'Rondo', which do not overwinter here. 'Schooley's Yellow' seems to have disappeared from horticulture altogether; my plants passed on years ago.

Penstemon barbatus

Penstemon brandegei, native to northern New Mexico and southern Colorado, is a robust creature with thick stems; slightly coarse, undulate-margined, three-inch-long (7.5cm) oblanceolate green leaves; and a massive display of inch-long (2.5cm) blue-purple flowers, white underneath, arranged along one side of the two-foot (60cm) stems, in late May and June. *Penstemon brandegei* is as drought- and heat-tolerant as the sidewalk its stems loll on, in 100F (38C) weather with five percent humidity and no rain for six straight weeks. This is often sold as *P. alpinus* in nurseries, but the real *P. alpinus* is a much smaller, more delicate-looking species found at higher elevations. *Penstemon glaber* is less robust, with flowers spaced less closely together, and nowhere to be seen in horticulture. This is a common roadside plant in its native habitat (northwestern Colorado, Wyoming, Nebraska, South Dakota), so seed is easy to collect.

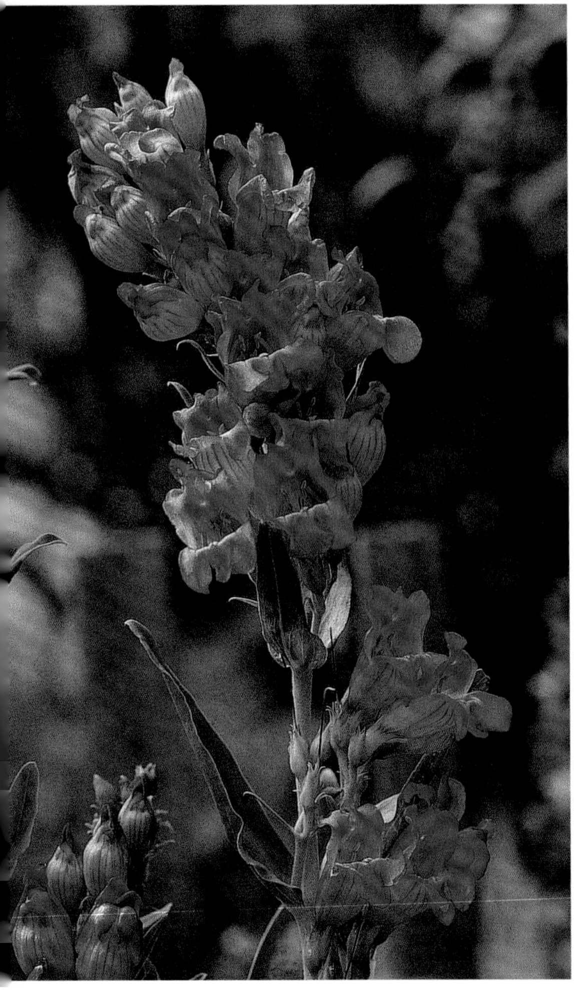

Penstemon brandegei

Penstemon cardinalis (southern New Mexico and adjacent western Texas) is a two- to three-foot (60 to 90 cm) plant with three-inch (7.5 cm) ovate green leaves and inch-long (2.5 cm) dark red tubular flowers borne from late June or early July until frost. This long-lived and dependable species will thrive when spring and summer bring an average amount of moisture, but the plants are weakened by prolonged drought and will eventually die.

Penstemon centranthifolius (scarlet bugler) has been a surprise. I had ordered seed from a population described as hardy, but this was sold out; I received instead seed from a population growing at much lower elevations, and the resulting plants have proved as hardy and reliable as almost any other penstemon. *Penstemon centranthifolius* is native to southern California and Baja California; in the garden conditions here, it is a two-foot (60 cm) plant with three-inch-long (7.5 cm) lanceolate blue-glaucous leaves clasping the stems, and inch-long (2.5 cm) bright red tubular flowers in July. Hummingbirds are of course delirious when they find this growing in the garden. *Penstemon subulatus*, a species from central and southern Arizona, which I haven't grown, is similar but with a narrower flower.

Penstemon floridus has been a disappointment here, though I ought to give it another chance. This is a three-foot (90 cm) plant with folded, toothed, blue-glaucous leaves clasping the stem, and bulging fat inch-long (2.5 cm) pink-red flowers in June. This is a penstemon of eastern California (Mono and Inyo counties) and adjacent Nevada. There is a variety, *austinii*, with shorter flowers. Plants in the garden here overwintered with difficulty, the majority of basal leaves frying to a crisp during the winter, but the plants did recover. They grew like crazy and then

Penstemon centranthifolius

fell over and bloomed lying on their sides. Applications of potash, which I failed to use, are said to help with the falling-over business. *Penstemon rubicundus*, a beautiful species from eastern California and western Nevada, with less bulging pink-red flowers, is definitely worth looking for in seed catalogs.

Penstemon grinnellii has been a favorite here for several years now. This native of mountains north of Los Angeles makes an open, somewhat sprawling plant with stems about two feet (60 cm) tall; narrowly oblanceolate, four-inch (10 cm), folded, toothed, glaucous green leaves; and fat, scented, inch-long (2.5 cm) pale pink flowers in June. After blooming, the original plants died, but left plenty of seedlings, which carry on the display. *Penstemon palmeri*, which is much more readily available, is similar, though the leaves are connate-perfoliate, and the flowers are more fragrant. This native of southern California, Arizona, and southwestern Utah is much happier in cold-winter gardens when given regular irrigation; *P. grinnellii* seems to win out when it comes to performance in the dry garden, though the display *P. palmeri* provides when watered may make the difference to some gardeners. I think it does, for me.

Penstemon incertus is one of those strange penstemons that haunt desert washes north of Los Angeles; this two-foot (60 cm) pale green plant has three-inch (7.5 cm) linear leaves on stems that grow this way and that, making the plant almost unnoticeable in the garden until its garish pink and purple flowers bloom in late June or July. *Penstemon fruticiformis* is similar, with a similar range, though it extends into Nevada,

Penstemon grinnellii with snow-in-summer

and the flowers are not slightly sticky as they are in *P. incertus*. Both of these are good in a "furnace garden" filled with cacti and soil too hot to touch in July.

Penstemon parryi has, finally, successfully survived winter temperatures of –5F (–20.5C) in the garden here and gone on to provide a reasonably exciting display of its bright pink inch-long (2.5cm) flowers. The oblong, folded blue-green leaves, four inches (10cm) long at the base, are attractive both in summer and in winter (though, as suggested, they burn to a crisp in hot winter sun). In cold-winter gardens the plants grow only two to three feet (60 to 90cm) tall. The plants flower in late May and early June and thus are dependent on ample spring moisture; if this isn't provided, the plants will be much smaller, and you will wonder what all the excitement is about. *Penstemon parryi* is native to southern Arizona and Sonora. *Penstemon superbus*, from southern New Mexico, southeastern Arizona, and Chihuahua, is similar but hardier, with a tendency to grow very tall, bloom profusely in June and July, and then fall over and die. It is a graceful exit.

Penstemon pseudospectabilis is native to Arizona, primarily, but also found in adjacent areas of California and southwestern New Mexico, and northern Sonora. Ordinarily, this is a three-foot (90cm) or taller plant, with beautiful blue-green oblanceolate leaves (even more attractive in winter, with the undersides turning deep purple) and bright rose-pink inch-and-a-half-long (3.75cm) tubular flowers in June. In prolonged severe drought, the plants may grow only eighteen inches (45cm), but still put on a show. Not many other plants can make the same claim.

[left] *Penstemon superbus*

[above] *Penstemon pseudospectabilis* with *Purshia stansburiana*

Penstemon pseudospectabilis has been in the garden here for over ten years, completely ignored, blooming every year no matter what. There are some hybrids between *P. pseudospectabilis* and *P. palmeri* floating around nurseries in the west that are extremely attractive, if short-lived, plants.

Penstemon scariosus (eastern Utah, and a few areas in western Colorado) is an attractive species along the lines of *P. strictus*, but with longer (to six inches, 15cm), more linear green basal leaves, stems to two

Penstemon strictus

feet (60 cm), and clusters of inch-long (2.5 cm) flowers arranged along one side of each stem. There are a couple of varieties: var. *garrettii* (the one grown in the garden here) with slightly smaller flowers than the typical species, and var. *albifluvis*, a rare plant with pale lavender flowers. *Penstemon scariosus* var. *garrettii*, the one most commonly available in seedlists, is easily grown from seed and long-lived in the garden.

Penstemon strictus (Wyoming, Utah, western Colorado, northern Arizona, and northern New Mexico) is easily the most commonly available penstemon in western nurseries, and its reputation as a good choice for a dry garden is well deserved, but only if spring provides its usual moisture. *Penstemon strictus* is a gorgeous, easily grown (and easily grown from seed) plant to two feet (60 cm) with four-inch-long (10 cm), narrowly oblanceolate, slightly folded green basal leaves and fat, inch-long (2.5 cm), blue-purple June-blooming flowers in a one-sided inflorescence. There is a horticultural selection, 'Bandera', which is said to be good for clay soils, as though other penstemons were not. It is otherwise indistinguishable from the species itself.

Following prolonged hot, dry springs, *Penstemon strictus* sits in the garden as a shriveled mass of leaves; a better choice might be the very similar *P. strictiformis*, native to the Four Corners area, which has proved much more tolerant of spring drought. (*Penstemon strictiformis* has less hairy anthers, and the lower lobe is more prominent; maybe this one, instead of *P. strictus*, should be called the porch penstemon.) I know that preferring a recondite species to a common species reeks of

[left] *Penstemon venustus*

[above] *Penstemon virgatus* var. *asa-grayi*

elitism; to my knowledge, *P. strictiformis* is not available in the nursery trade, except as seed, which germinates readily.

Penstemon venustus is a two-foot (60 cm) multi-stemmed penstemon with oblanceolate toothed green leaves about two inches (5 cm) long and a massive display of large, pale purple flowers an inch and a half (3.75 cm) long, in May. *Penstemon venustus* is native to eastern Washington and Oregon, and western Idaho. It is superior in every respect to the more commonly available, closely related *P. richardsonii*, which is too short-lived and too dependent on regular moisture to be a good choice for the dry garden. In fact, it is superior to most penstemons as a garden plant. *Penstemon venustus* is easy from seed, long-lived, hardy, and exhibits an amazing (and gratifying) ability to persist through year after year of drought.

Penstemon virgatus (Wyoming to New Mexico and Arizona) has a number of varieties, but the one that we want is the variety from Colorado and Wyoming, var. *asa-grayi* (some sources still wrongly insist *P. unilateralis* is a synonym). This is a multi-stemmed plant with three-inch (7.5 cm) gray-green leaves arranged along the stem, and a one-sided inflorescence of inch-long (2.5 cm) pale purple flowers with a distinctive white beard, in early June. Though *P. virgatus* var. *asa-grayi* does not live forever, it is easily one of the most cold-hardy, drought-tolerant penstemons on the planet. It is easy from seed, and sometimes available in nurseries.

Phacelia. Leafing through the various western floras reveals a staggering array of perennials and annuals in the genus *Phacelia*, a member of the waterleaf family (Hydrophyllaceae), most of which are unknown to horticulture, and definitely unknown to me. One perennial native throughout western North America (Montana to California), *P. hastata*, is a semi-moderately exciting plant to about two feet (60 cm), lower in drier areas and much taller where it receives ample moisture, with nice, silver oblanceolate leaves, and (to quote Barr, who referred to it as *P. leucophylla*, a name now subsumed under the older name *P. hastata*) "neat, uncoiling racemes of narrow-tubed florets of a hue as indefinable in its neutral lavender as the shadow of a vanished hope."

Barr's description of the flowers fits many of the species perfectly; the southern Californian annual *Phacelia tanacetifolia* (also found in southern Nevada and northwestern Arizona) has a fiddleback-shaped inflorescence too, on a two-foot (60 cm) plant with gray-green lobed leaves. The quarter-inch-wide (6 mm) light blue flowers are pleasantly fragrant, borne throughout the summer. Seed is readily available and can just be scattered on the ground and lightly covered; lucky gardeners will have a healthy colony after a few years.

Phacelia lutea (western Colorado, Wyoming, and Montana to Oregon and California) is a variable species, low, sprawling, with bright yellow

Phacelia campanularia

cup-shaped flowers. This very attractive annual would be worth growing if it were available. Sometimes confused with *P. adenophora*.

The star of the show, as far as dryland species are concerned (and as far as I know one phacelia from another), is *Phacelia campanularia*, a mounding annual from southeastern California, in dry conditions growing to about ten inches (25cm), with green, slightly fleshy or rubbery ovate leaves, and stunning bright blue, inch-wide (2.5cm) outward-facing bell-shaped flowers in June and July (or earlier, depending on the weather). This gorgeous little thing is readily available as seed, which can be sown in earliest spring, or, better, in late autumn or winter.

Psilostrophe (paperflower). The name rhymes with "apostrophe," of course. Half a dozen or so species of paperflower (so named because the ray flowers turn papery as they age, instead of falling off) are native to the southwestern United States and northern Mexico; all have woolly-hairy foliage and yellow or yellow-orange daisy flowers lobed at the tips. Seed is the most common means of obtaining plants, though nursery-raised plants are sometimes available; the latter would be my choice since my success rate germinating seed has not been very high. These attractive plants are superior choices for a hot, dry garden.

Psilostrophe bakeri, native to southern and western Colorado, is a two-foot (60 cm) plant with three-inch-long (7.5 cm) oblanceolate basal leaves and flowers an inch (2.5 cm) wide in June and July. This can be a short-lived plant but may seed itself around. *Psilostrophe tagetina* (Arizona and Utah to western Texas, south to Durango) is similar but taller and slightly less elegant, with a few lobed leaves at the base, and smaller flowers, also borne in June and July. *Psilostrophe tagetina* has persisted in the dry garden here for a number of years, mostly perpetuating itself by seed.

Psilostrophe cooperi is a shrubby species, white-woolly all over, growing to two feet (60 cm) with narrowly linear leaves, native to lower elevations from southwestern Utah through California to Baja California, Sonora, and Arizona. My impression is that this plant is winter-hardy in Denver, but it no longer grows in the garden here.

Ratibida (Mexican hat, prairie coneflower). *Ratibida columnifera* is the species we want in the garden; this is native from Michigan to Arizona (claims that the plant was introduced to the western Great Plains overlook the fact that Rydberg included this species in his *Flora of Colorado* in 1906). *Ratibida columnifera* is a very unusual daisy, blooming all summer, with columnar black disk flowers, the column about an inch (2.5 cm) long, and reflexed, oblong yellow ray flowers an inch (2.5 cm) long, on stalks two feet (60 cm), more or less, depending on available moisture, with a few pinnatifid green-gray leaves four inches (10 cm) long. Occasionally plants will have dark red ray flowers; these have sometimes been called forma *pulcherrima*. Both are irresistibly attractive plants. Their life span is shortened by prolonged drought, though they do reseed.

Rudbeckia. *Rudbeckia hirta* (black-eyed Susan) is an incomparably coarse weedy plant with six-inch (15 cm) sandpaper-rough oblanceolate green leaves and four-inch-wide (10 cm) bright yellow daises, with a black eye of course, blooming all summer but putting on the biggest

[left] *Ratibida columnifera*

[below] *Ratibida columnifera*, dark red form

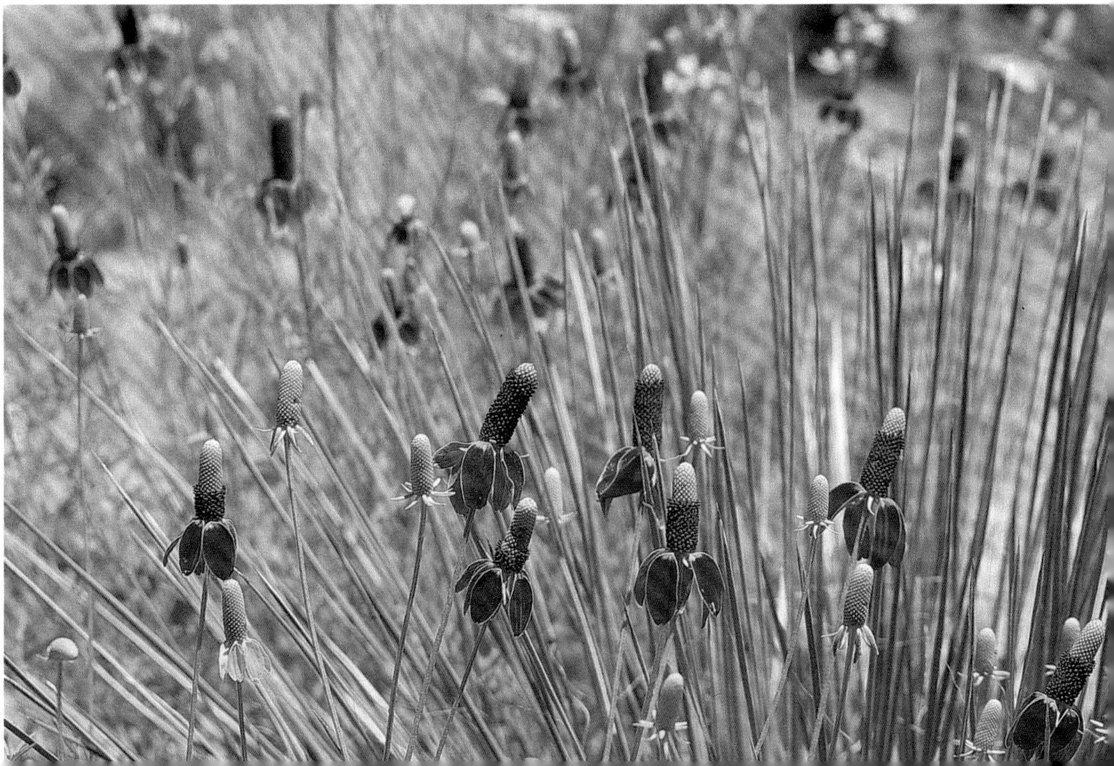

show from August onward. In some ways there is nothing like it, and a group of these can be very impressive and beautiful. *Rudbeckia hirta* is native mostly to eastern North America but is also found along the Front Range of the Rocky Mountains in Colorado. This is a biennial that can be grown from seed collected off plants growing in the wild (you're not likely to miss them even in seed), and then sown directly into the ground.

Salvia (sage). *Salvia azurea*, *S. azurea* var. *grandiflora*, and *S. pitcheri* may all be the same species, or two different species and a variety. Botanists are in disagreement, to say the least, about the name of the blue-flowered salvia native to the Great Plains, as well as the distribution of the plant, as well as its native status in some states. It is said, for instance, to have been introduced into eastern Colorado, but is mentioned by Rydberg in his 1906 *Flora of Colorado*.

Salvia azurea

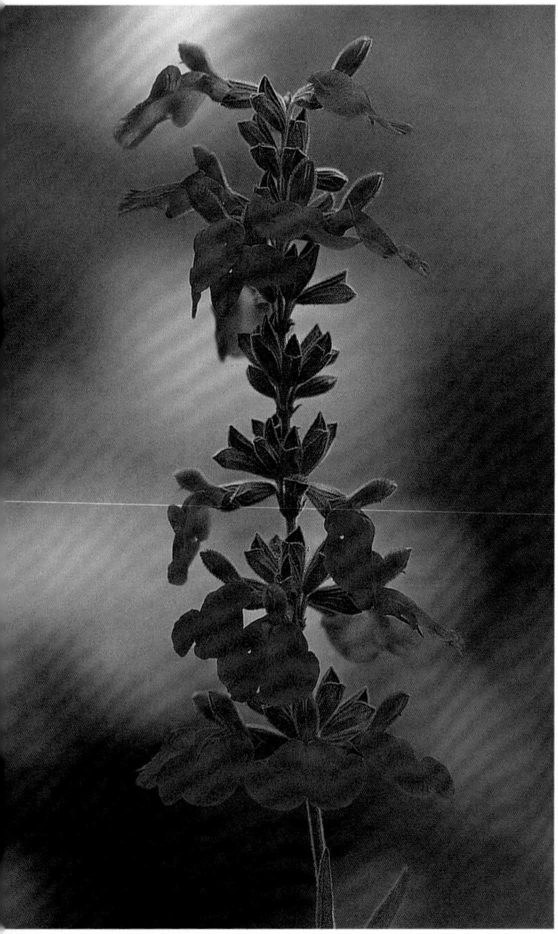

In keeping with this odd situation, only some plants of *Salvia azurea* have any drought tolerance at all; named varieties have proved impossible to keep alive in the garden here without, literally, almost daily watering in summer, though maybe these are difficult to establish when planted as large plants. Smaller plants grown from seed collected in the wild and also a variety grown from cuttings, with darker blue flowers, have proved quite drought-tolerant, flowering beautifully without any supplemental irrigation.

The basic plant throws up a few wand-like dark stems three feet (90cm) tall with folded, linear-lanceolate leaves about two inches (5cm) long, and clusters of gorgeous sky-blue, or deeper blue, typical salvia flowers an inch (2.5cm) long, starting in September (or sometimes earlier), and ending with the first hard frost. *Salvia azurea* also responds impressively to heavy watering by growing twice its normal height and producing about a hundred times more flowers. Either way, it is an indispensable addition to the garden.

Scrophularia. Penstemon relatives of the sort that would barge in unexpectedly at a family reunion and make everyone wish they were somewhere else. They are mostly leaves. *Scrophularia macrantha*, native to a few locations in southwestern New Mexico, is a three-foot (90 cm) plant (with constant moisture) with four-inch (10 cm) serrated leaves. The pea-sized, red, pregnant-guppy flowers are not much to look at. Granted, red flowers are automatically desirable if attracting hummingbirds is the aim, but gardeners can do much better than this. Established plants in the garden here have died of drought even when planted next to an irrigated lawn. *Scrophularia desertorum*, from southern California and Nevada, has still larger leaves and smaller red and cream flowers, and is even less distinguished.

Sphaeralcea (globemallow). Sphaeralceas are highly satisfactory plants for the dry garden, offering a good display of inch-wide (2.5 cm) flowers all summer, though the plants are difficult to find in any form other than seed. The seed doesn't always want to germinate in the way you think it should. (Meaning, don't plan a garden around groups of sphaeralceas before you have seedlings coming up in pots.)

The taller species are much less easy to identify than the little plants grown in rock gardens, and the flower color can vary from white to pink to grenadine-red to creamsicle-orange. I like the orange forms the best, since a good soft orange is fairly rare, but all the other colors are nice, too.

Four species are likely to be available in seedlists. *Sphaeralcea angustifolia*, native from Colorado and western Kansas to Arizona, Chihuahua, Coahuila, and western Texas, is a five-foot (1.5 m) plant with two-inch-long (5 cm) crinkled gray oblanceolate leaves, generally with no lobes (except in var. *lobata*, which has lobed leaves at the base); *S. fendleri* (roughly the same distribution except southwestern Colorado and not Kansas), a five-foot (1.5 m) plant from ponderosa pine forests with crinkled green, deeply cleft leaves covered with white hairs, and

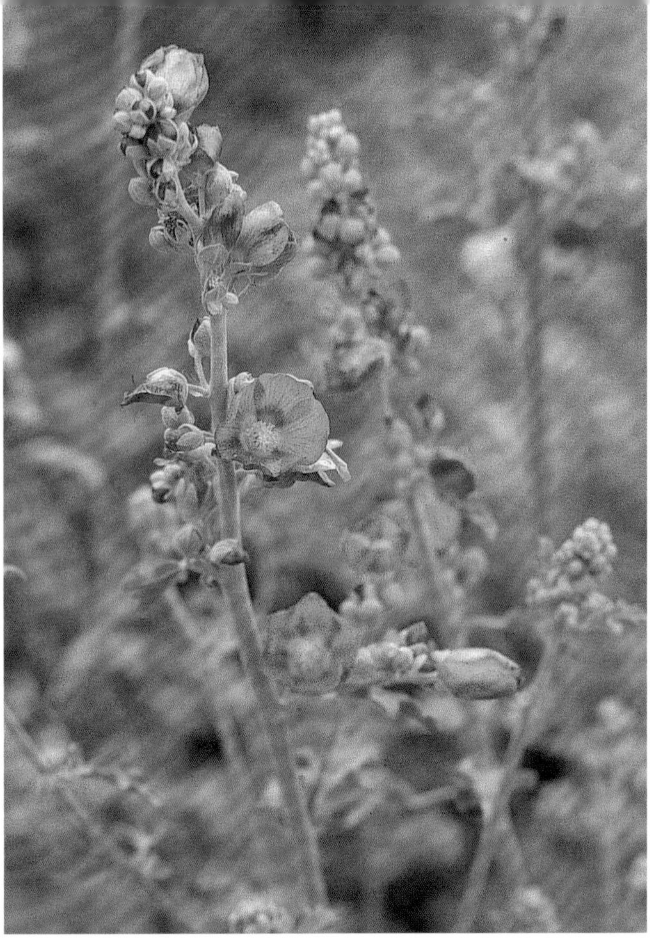

[right] *Sphaeralcea munroana*

[below] *Sphaeralcea incana*, pink form

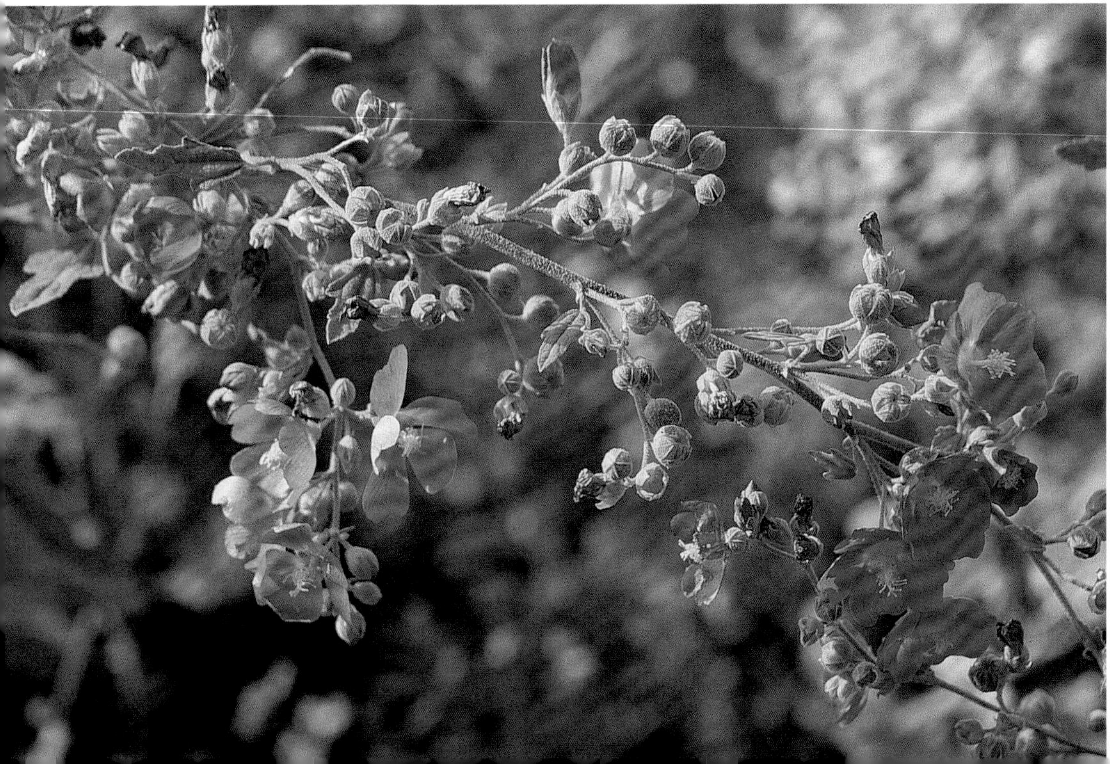

occasionally very attractive deep pink-purple flowers (the largest flowers are found on var. *venusta*, from southern Arizona and northern Chihuahua); *S. incana* (my favorite), the same size as the others (though count on only half the height in very dry years), with grayish shallowly lobed leaves covered with yellowish hairs, from Arizona, New Mexico, western Texas, and Chihuahua; and *S. munroana* (Utah to Montana, Idaho to California), a shorter plant, with green, slightly lobed leaves, though some nursery-grown forms have grayer leaves. I find this last one to be difficult to transplant, and plants grown in nursery soil have never overwintered for me.

Sphaeralceas have a running root, as they say, by which they can form a thicket, though this takes ages in a dry garden. Plants appearing where they are not wanted can simply be dug up and, occasionally, successfully moved elsewhere (usually they just die).

Stachys (hedge nettle). A few species of *Stachys* are native to North America, but none are as hardy as those from Central Asia. *Stachys coccinea*, from southern Arizona, New Mexico, western Texas, Sonora, Chihuahua, Coahuila, and maybe even further south, must be considered as barely hardy for cold-winter gardens and, even if it makes it through a winter, its struggle to regain strength makes it a profoundly thirsty plant. Even the bright red flowers do not redeem it; *S. coccinea* is not worth growing except as a heavily watered annual. The same has to be said for the even more attractive Mexican species, *S. albotomentosa*; the densely white-woolly leaves are its principal asset, but its tenderness makes it another plant needing copious amounts of irrigation.

Stanleya (prince's plume). Several species of *Stanleya* are native to western North America, but the most common, *Stanleya pinnata* (North Dakota to California and New Mexico), is the one we want. This is a three-foot (90 cm), green-leafed plant, the lower leaves elliptic in shape but pinnatifid, as though someone had taken huge chomps out of them on either side; the leaves are less gashed higher up on the stem. The inflorescence is a spectacular plume of small yellow flowers borne in late June or July.

Stanleya pinnata is a highly desirable, relatively long-lived plant in

Stanleya pinnata

the garden, eventually forming a clump of fairly woody stems. It is more or less widely available in nurseries and seeds about moderately. Plants can wilt when subjected to temperatures over 100F (38C) in the afternoon sun. Well, you would too. The plants quickly revive in the evening. *Stanleya pinnata* is considered a selenium indicator in the wild, since apparently it grows only in soils containing selenium. This seems to me to be a strange observation; in the garden it will grow perfectly happily in plain, selenium-free clay soil, so it must also do so in the wild.

Verbena. A few verbenas are of moderate value in the dry garden. *Verbena bipinnatifida* (*Glandularia bipinnatifida*) is a sprawling plant, sometimes growing as wide as two feet (60cm), with, obviously, bipinnate green leaves and heads of rose-purple flowers similar to the annual verbenas, growing to four inches (10cm). The flowers, which in a good year are produced all summer, unfortunately lack the rich fragrance of the more easterly distributed *V. canadensis* (*G. canadensis*), but at least *V. bipinnatifida* is capable of overwintering here, which *V. canadensis* has never done. *Verbena bipinnatifida* is found along roadsides, and elsewhere, from South Dakota to Texas and points south. A taller version (to eight inches, 20cm) of this, *V. wrightii* (*G. bipinnatifida* var. *ciliata*) is native from Arizona to western Texas (some botanists consider it synonymous with *V. bipinnatifida*).

The more southerly distributed *Verbena gooddingii* (*Glandularia gooddingii*) might be worth trying (though its hardiness is unproven), but most verbenas native to North America inhabit soils too moist to be considered candidates for dry gardens. The ones mentioned here are not quite elegant enough for the rock garden, and not reliable enough for me to be overly enthusiastic about them. They linger for a year or two, produce a few seedlings that may put on an unexpected display one year, and then they're gone.

Verbesina. One species, *Verbesina encelioides* (golden crownbeard, butter daisy, or, my favorite, cowpen daisy) is worth considering if you desperately need a showy yellow annual daisy somewhere in the garden. Plants grow about three feet (90 cm) tall, with toothed green leaves about three inches (7.5 cm) long, curiously winged petioles, and flowers about four inches (10 cm) across, borne from July until frost. Seed can be sown at any time, though autumn and late winter are probably best.

Viguiera multiflora

Viguiera (goldeneye). *Viguiera multiflora* (*Heliomeris multiflora*) is the only species of interest here (mostly because I don't know the other species); native from Montana to southern California and New Mexico south into Mexico, this is a three- to four-foot-tall (90 to 120 cm), or taller, branched perennial with lanceolate to linear leaves (in var. *nevadensis*) with yellow daisy flowers about three inches (7.5 cm) wide, borne from midsummer until frost. *Viguiera multiflora* is occasionally available in the trade. Seed can be sown in autumn or winter. Your neighbors may think you're growing weeds if they see this in the garden.

Wyethia (mule's ears). About a dozen species of *Wyethia* are native to western

CHAPTER THREE

Grasses

Almost all grasses with ornamental potential native to western North America, east of the Sierra Nevada, are warm-season grasses, and as a result they absolutely require the equivalent of natural rainfall (or the actual rainfall itself) in order to look like anything at all in the garden. In other words, during years of below-average rainfall, they will need to be watered if they are to flower. They are probably best planted in a garden that receives regular irrigation (twice a month at least).

Many of them are also fiendishly difficult to establish. I have planted hundreds of native grasses, never to see them again. Autumn planting is rarely recommended for any ornamental grass (there are the usual exceptional success stories that prove the rule), but even spring planting has resulted in failure of the plants to overwinter.

I suspect that one reason why many grasses fail so spectacularly is that they intensely dislike being transplanted. There appears to be some difficulty getting grasses, native and exotic, grown in nursery pots to establish in the garden; this is a story repeated with other types of plants where the roots have grown in the pot in such a way that the plant is unable to adjust to garden life by growing roots in the normal way and direction (downward). I don't have any data to back up this argument but a number of highly respected horticulturists have made the same suggestion.

Schizachyrium scoparium at Kendrick Lake

If the roots are pot-bound, they can be gently prised apart (chopsticks are a perfect tool) and the root ball allowed to soak in water for a few hours so that the soilless mix is washed away, at least a little, so the plant can be planted in garden soil.

And yet people plant ornamental grasses all the time, and the plants don't die. Thinking that the problem getting grasses established lay with me, like it usually does, I did some clandestine investigation of gardens where native grasses are successfully grown and found that, sure enough, they received regular irrigation, often on drip systems. This seems to be one key to successful establishment.

The garden performance of grasses grown from seed tells a different story. This is the way nature does it, after all, and once the plants begin to mature there is no sign of struggling with drought. If you want to bypass trying to establish potted grasses, seed should be sown directly into the soil in which it is to grow, preferably in autumn or winter, the area labeled, and seedlings thinned when they are about six inches (15cm) tall.

Of course plants are more readily available than seed. If you choose to purchase nursery-grown plants, just remember that they need constantly moist soil for at least the first two years while they are green, and to be heavily mulched with something that doesn't mat down, like pine needles, for their first winter.

During years of ample rainfall, the native grasses do add a distinctive, not-quite-green look to the garden, and if you are willing to wait out an exceptionally dry summer, you can plant most of these and expect a glorious display every few years. (Or longer.)

Only a few of these grasses can really be considered outstanding choices for a dry garden. I exclude switchgrass, *Panicum virgatum*, a common native plant with a number of very attractive cultivars, because of its insatiable thirst (its preference in the wild is for moist areas).

There are no detailed descriptions of these plants in the list that follows. They are grasses, after all, and look like grass. Most of them are bunchgrasses, growing in a bunch, but some are stoloniferous and can be encouraged to form a lawn of sorts. Of course, I've decided to display a high degree of sophistication by calling a grass stem by its proper name, culm. (Even though grasses like big bluestem are not called big blueculm . . .)

Botanists have been fooling around with the names of many of these, and sometimes you will find plants listed for sale under different names.

Andropogon (bluestem). *Andropogon gerardii* (big bluestem) is native to practically everywhere east of the Rocky Mountains and a few places in Arizona and Utah. This species is, as its common name suggests, a big grass, rarely spreading, to six feet (1.8m) in good conditions, with distinctly blue culms, especially in some of the named varieties. Big bluestem is a major component of the tall-grass prairie and really does require a considerable amount of summer moisture in order to flower well. I rate this one as extremely difficult to establish if planted after 1 June.

Aristida. *Aristida purpurea* (three-awn), found everywhere in western North America, is a moderately interesting grass growing to two feet (60cm); good in dry gardens, though the seedheads (awns) have a hard tip that may get caught in a dog's coat. Easy from seed.

Bouteloua (grama grass). The generic name is often misspelled, and *grama* is the Spanish word for "grass," so the common name is an exercise in redundancy. Two species are worth considering. *Bouteloua curtipendula* (side-oats grama), another native of everywhere (including South America), is a slightly spreading grass to eight inches (20cm) or so, though shorter in a dry garden, with a one-sided inflorescence to two feet (60cm) looking like a line of oats. Side-oats grama is easy to grow from seed sown in June or July, easy to transplant, and does well in a dry garden, though it is not spectacular.

Bouteloua gracilis (blue grama), native throughout western North America, is a major component of the short-grass prairie. Blue grama is about six inches (15cm) high, with nice light greenish blue blades appearing in June (in other words, it "greens up" in June) and feathery seedheads on culms about eight inches (20cm) tall. The seedheads remain all winter and are highly attractive in the winter garden, especially with a little snow on the ground. Blue grama makes an excellent host for paintbrushes (*Castilleja* spp.) and is worth growing for this alone. It is often recommended as an "alternative" lawn. But not by me. Alternatives to Kentucky bluegrass, the usual turfgrass in the dry, cold-winter areas of

Our blue grama front lawn, with *Penstemon pinifolius* and *Castilleja integra*

North America, should at least offer equal performance without having to make endless qualifications to our definition of what a lawn should be. Blue grama is extremely drought-tolerant but requires regular summer moisture in order to be a lawn and massive amounts of weeding with the supplemental irrigation. It is slow to recover from drought and may in fact remain dormant for the rest of its short growing season. As a lawn it is easily and inevitably invaded by weeds. It can be mowed. During the drought of 2002, our blue grama lawn turned green only in September, then went brown again in October.

Buchloë. Another native grass often recommended for lawns, usually by people who've never tried it, *Buchloë dactyloides* (*Bouteloua dactyloides*; buffalograss) is found throughout the Great Plains and is another dominant plant of the short-grass prairie, but is stoloniferous, unlike blue grama. Under dry conditions it grows about three inches (7.5cm) tall, with plumed straw-colored seedheads a little taller than this.

As a lawn, buffalograss makes a beautiful, distinctly bluish sward, starting in late May with some of the selected turf types, turning straw-colored by late September. Like blue grama it requires weekly irrigation during periods of drought in order to look respectable (in other words, to prevent it from going dormant), which raises questions about the purpose of alternative turf grasses. Even though this is a sod-forming grass it is, like blue grama, a breeding ground for weeds which, once established, are almost impossible to control since watering the lawn encourages the weeds too. Our turf-type buffalograss quickly turned into a weed-choked disaster area. I removed the lawn after about five years of pretending that it looked presentable. There may be some newer varieties with better lawn performance.

The pasture types of buffalograss are my favorite; these make a striking ground cover under shrubs, but the best application, in my view, is between flagstone pavers, where they are peerless. They can be mowed, but need heavy watering after mowing. I like them best left unmowed, for the attractive seedheads. Seed can usually be obtained from feed lots or local seed companies; some of the seed is treated for enhanced germination and has a bright blue color. Seed can be sown in June or July. (It can also be sown in winter, but you have less control over germination and the light seed is easily blown away.)

Buchloë, by the way, is a three-syllable word.

Elymus (wildrye). *Elymus cinereus* (basin wildrye) is found more or less throughout western North America (Saskatchewan to California). This is a robust, coarse grass with glaucous herbage six feet (1.8m) by three feet (1m), suitable for a place where you need a huge, slightly ordinary grass. Some species in *Elymus* (and this is one) are sometimes included in the genus *Leymus*. Rarely available in the trade.

Erioneuron. Small tufted grasses perfect for underplanting in a dry garden, or for a dryland trough (where they will need watering). *Erioneuron pilosum* (Kansas to Nevada, south to Chihuahua) is about four inches (10cm) tall under dry conditions, not spreading, with only a few roots that are easily torn up by careless weeders (I speak from experience); *E. pulchellum* (California to western Texas south to at least Chihuahua) is slightly taller, spreading, with a more serious root system.

Festuca (fescue). A trio of quite similar fescues, *Festuca arizonica*, *F. idahoensis*, and *F. ovina* are sometimes found floating around seedlists and even in a nursery or two. Though they are worth growing, none should really be considered suitable for a dry garden. *Festuca ovina* var. *brevifolia* (*F. brachyphylla*) might be an exception; this alpine grass stays about four inches (10 cm) under dry conditions, and reseeds fairly relentlessly, but only lives for two or three years. (The sheep fescue used in lawn grasses is the European variety, *F. ovina* var. *ovina*.)

Hilaria. *Hilaria jamesii* (*Pleuraphis jamesii*; galleta grass), sometimes recommended as an alternative lawn, is more often seen as a ground cover in areas for which a drought-tolerant turf-forming grass that will take traffic is required. The only problem with this idea is that you have to grow galleta grass from seed, and the tiny seeds are easily blown away by wind, or a fit of sneezing. Otherwise, this is another excellent choice for ground cover among dryland shrubs. *Hilaria jamesii* is native from Wyoming to New Mexico, west to California. It is a rapid-growing grass about six inches (15 cm) tall, with flowering culms about a foot (30 cm) tall. It can be mowed.

Koeleria (junegrass). The one species of junegrass native to North America, *Koeleria macrantha* (*K. cristata*), is found almost everywhere. I grow a nice dwarf form found in Wyoming (unfortunately this hasn't been given a name) that has tufts of green about four inches (10 cm) high and wide, with straw-colored flowers on culms twice as high, in guess what month. Junegrass takes considerable drought and is cute in a rock garden.

Muhlenbergia (muhly . . . seriously, this is the common name). The best choice for a dry garden is probably *Muhlenbergia porteri* (bush muhly, black grama, mesquite grass; Colorado to Coahuila, west to California), a nonrhizomatous, wiry, branching grass with culms to three feet (90 cm) or more, the flowers in open panicles in mid to late summer. *Muhlenbergia porteri* will take considerable drought.

Other muhlies to try are *Muhlenbergia rigens* (deergrass; Texas west to Sonora and California), a clumping grass with culms to five feet (1.5 m), though often shorter, with flowers in tight panicles in summer. Trials in the garden here did not reveal an astonishing degree of winter hardiness. *Muhlenbergia wrightii* (Oklahoma to Coahuila, west to Sonora, Arizona, and Utah) is rather similar, though only a foot (30 cm) or so tall, but it is completely hardy.

Oryzopsis (ricegrass). *Oryzopsis hymenoides* (*Achnatherum* or *Stipa hymenoides*; Indian ricegrass), found from British Columbia to Texas, is one of the best ornamental grasses for the dry garden, forming outward-splayed tufts of thick green culms a foot (30 cm) or so tall, with beautiful, open, straw-colored panicles in midsummer, or later. The cut flowers make a handsome dried arrangement. *Oryzopsis hymenoides* can be transplanted, but sowing seed in midwinter yields plenty of healthy seedlings the following spring. Unfortunately, these are relished by rabbits, who will eat the young tufts of grass (and the older ones, too) right down to the ground.

Schizachyrium. One species, *Schizachyrium scoparium* (little bluestem), is of interest, though its drought-tolerance may seem overrated until you actually get plants to make it through two or three winters, which is not the easiest thing to do. In other words, transplanted plants of little bluestem need massive amounts of water for the first two or three years, and then they can be left on their own. Little bluestem is native to North America (this is the simplest way of putting it) and is a major component of the tall-grass prairie. It is a very attractive, distinctly blue-tinted grass a foot (30 cm) tall, though two or three times taller than that with abundant moisture. There are little tufts for flowers, in mid to late summer. In autumn, little bluestem turns a ravishing russet color.

There are a couple of cultivars of little bluestem in the trade, selected for color; these, considering the years of frustration I endured trying to get regular bluestem to grow, I have ignored.

Sorghastrum. *Sorghastrum nutans* (Indian grass) is another grass native to everywhere, except the west coast, and another component of the tall-grass prairie, a big, slightly spreading, sometimes bluish grass to five feet (1.5m), with named varieties. I have tried this species half a dozen times, and each time plants, even when set out in spring, have failed to overwinter. There must be something about growing it that I don't know.

Sporobolus (dropseed). A genus of bunchgrasses similar to *Muhlenbergia* but usually having solid, pithy culms. For gardeners this means that they require a little bit more effort to cut down in late winter or spring. They show considerable resistance to drought but do require ample moisture from midsummer onward if they are to flower.

Sporobolus airoides (alkali sacaton) is widespread throughout western North America (South Dakota west to Washington, south into Mexico). When happy this is a three-foot-tall (90cm) grass with open, airy panicles in summer. *Sporobolus wrightii* (sacaton), a more southerly distributed grass, is a more robust version of this and has slightly more resistance to drought. It is sometimes considered a variety of *S. airoides*. *Sporobolus wrightii* has recently become popular as a low-water ornamental grass, a role it fulfills until it starts to sulk in August.

Sporobolus cryptandrus (sand dropseed) is native throughout western North America, except California, and ventures east to the Atlantic states. This is a three-foot (90cm) grass with less airy panicles than the other two species, the flowers tinged purple. Sand dropseed is the most drought-tolerant of the three species. All can be raised from seed sown outdoors in winter.

Stipa (needlegrass). Needlegrasses should only be planted in areas where pets will not come in contact with the seeds, which can work their way through even a heavy coat into the skin and necessitate a trip to the vet. Still, there are a couple to be considered. *Stipa comata* (*Hesperostipa comata*; needle and thread, a reference to the appearance of the seedhead) is another widespread (Ontario to the Yukon, south to California and Texas) grass, three feet (90cm) tall, give or take depending on available moisture. *Stipa speciosa* (*Achnatherum speciosum*; Colorado and

Arizona to California and Baja California) is a two-foot (60cm) grass adapted to very dry conditions but not available in the trade.

The other stipas you might want to try go under names like *Stipa columbiana* (*Achnatherum nelsonii*), *S. robusta* (*A. robustum*; sleepygrass), and *S. viridula* (*Nassella viridula*). Depending on which botanist you consult, these are the same, or different.

Stipa tenuissima (*Nassella tenuissima*), a native of Arizona, New Mexico, and northern Mexico, is a green grass, about a foot (30cm) tall with attractive straw-colored seedheads, that has become, incomprehensibly, very popular in the nursery trade. It seeds about with horrific abandon and has no place whatsoever in the garden.

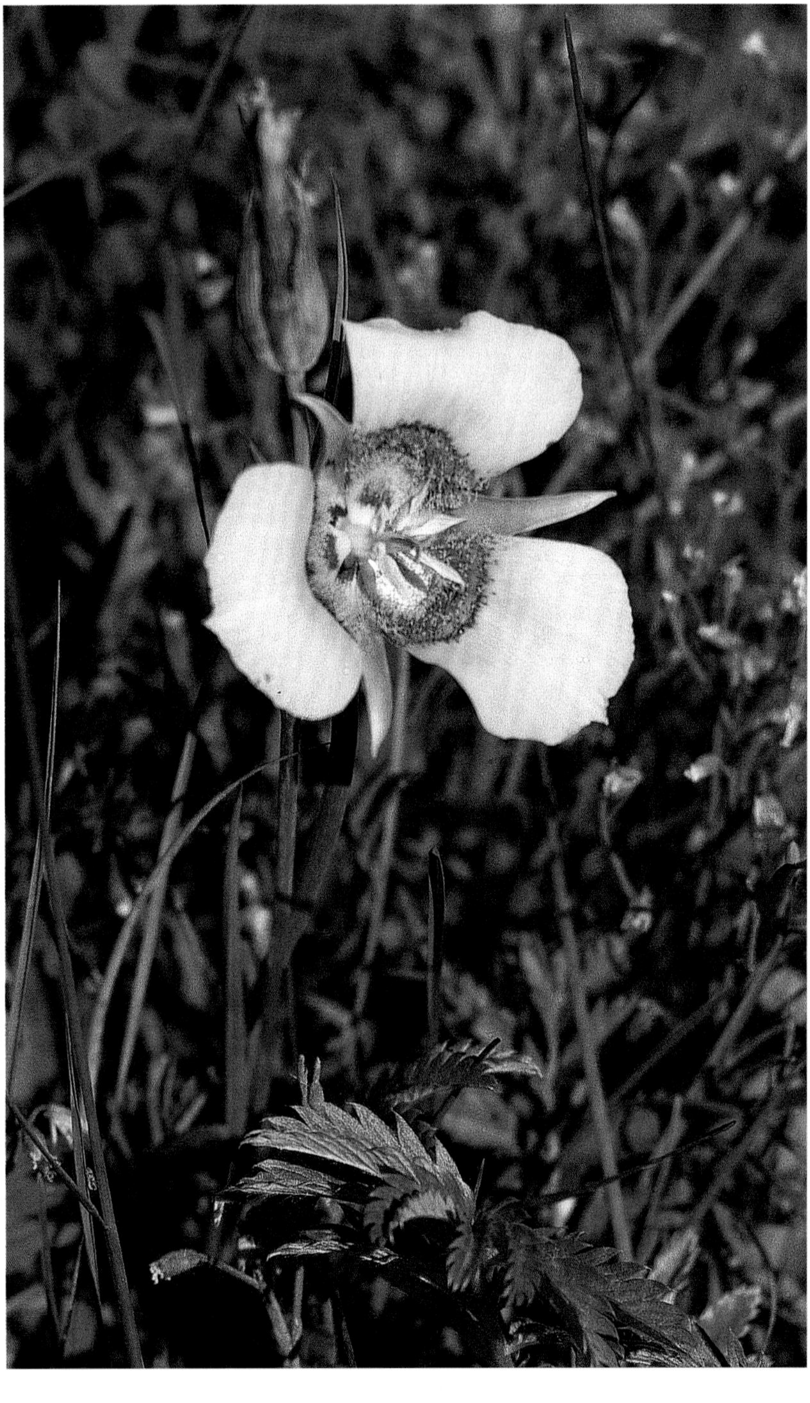

CHAPTER FOUR

Bulbs

The Rocky Mountain and Intermountain regions have a surprisingly low number of native bulbous plants suitable as ornamentals. Surprising, because more or less similar climates, like those of Turkey and Central Asia, are home to huge numbers of bulbs that are easily grown in our climate, and in fact, the high, dry, cold-winter regions of western North America offer well-nigh perfect conditions for chionodoxas (beautiful in buffalograss or blue grama lawns), colchicums, crocuses, cyclamen, eranthis, fritillaries, irises, scillas, sternbergias, tulips, and so on, if grown in clay soil. The list of suitable bulbs is practically endless.

The list of cold-hardy, drought-tolerant North American bulbs is much smaller. California has a vast number of native bulbs, but not too many of these are reliably hardy in a succession of very dry, sunny, sometimes cold winters.

The bulbs mentioned here, all of which are in the lily family, are hardy and should be treated like their Eurasian cousins: planted not too deeply in clay soil, watered once, and then left alone. The extreme planting depths suggested by some books and nursery catalogs should be dismissed as an aberration of some kind. Why the subject of bulbs and bulb planting provokes such flights of fancy (not to say sheer drivel) from horticultural professionals who ought to know better is a complete mystery to me. Bulbs are very easy to grow and need no special attention

Calochortus gunnisonii

in the high, dry regions of western North America. No bulb needs to be planted eight inches (20cm) deep, as it will spend most of its energy trying to get some sunlight in order to live, and organic matter in the soil increases the chances for rot by exponential factors. Clay, or soil resembling clay, is the soil most bulbs favor in the wild, and the natural medium for bulb growth in a climate like mine.

Probably the ideal place in which to grow most of these bulbs is a buffalograss or blue grama lawn, though keeping such a lawn weed-free is not exactly easy.

Only a few of these are commonly available in the trade. The rest have to be grown from seed, which is usually available from rock garden society seedlists.

Some bulbous species must be ruled out for inclusion here, either because they need unending amounts of moisture (*Zigadenus*), or they require regular irrigation during their summer dormant period (*Erythronium*).

Allium platycaule

Allium. The ornamental onions include quite a few virulent pests that seed all over the garden, but the North Americans seem well behaved. Possibly too well behaved—the level of excitement here is not very high. They are easy to grow from seed sown outdoors in winter or simply scattered on the ground at any time and lightly worked into the soil. Obviously, with only two species listed (North America has about seventy-five species), I don't know anything at all about this subject.

Allium acuminatum is widespread throughout western North America (British Columbia to California, Idaho and Wyoming south to Arizona); this is a June bloomer growing about eight inches (20cm) with a half-dozen or so pale pink (at least this is their color in my garden) flowers on long pedicels; the whole flower head is about two inches (5cm) across.

Allium platycaule is a Californian (also

found in western Nevada and southern Oregon) with two strap-like bluish green leaves, edged in red, about four inches (10cm) long, with a golfball-sized clustered inflorescence of pink flowers on a scape as tall as the leaves, in May.

Other alliums may be found in various private seedlists from time to time; have at them. Not all of these are dryland bulbs; ones you might try, if available, are *A. atrorubens*, *A. lemmonii*, *A. macropetalum*, *A. nevadense*, *A. passeyi*, and *A. tolmiei.*

Brodiaea. Some of the species formerly found under this name have been moved to *Dichelostemma* or *Triteleia*. Not that confusion doesn't still reign supreme with these Californians (or mostly Californians). They all look pretty much alike to me. I grow only one, *Brodiaea terrestris* (California north of the Monterrey Peninsula to southern Oregon); this is, in my garden anyway, an infinitesimal thing with purple upward-facing bell-shaped flowers the size of a thimble which sit practically on the ground, flowering for a few days in May. It grows in the most hard-packed clay soil imaginable, one of those flowers that delights, in an infinitesimal sort of way, when encountered, just because it's there, briefly. The enthusiasm for such things is often difficult to convey to other people.

Brodiaea terrestris

I once grew *Brodiaea coronaria*, about six inches (15cm) tall with blue-purple bell flowers; I suspect this native of the west coast, from British Columbia to California, needed more water, especially in autumn.

Lester Rowntree's *Hardy Californians* (1936) is a good, well-written, nontechnical account of a large number of plants including bulbs. This is well worth seeking in used bookstores (all her books are worth acquiring), especially since it gives more information than I do.

Calochortus (mariposa lily, sego lily). The sixty or so *Calochortus* species (two-thirds of which are Californian) are reputed to be as difficult to grow as bananas at the North Pole. (A few experts grow them in Britain, but that's a different story.) Not all are hardy, of course; as a generalization, there are summer growers (several of which are hardy) and winter growers (mostly Mexican and mostly not hardy).

The essential shape of the plant is a simple stem, with a few linear leaves, carrying one or more spectacular three-petaled flowers. Some flowers are nodding globes, the petal closed at the tips; some are open, upright-facing flattened bells covered with hairs (these are called cat's ears); most are open, upright-facing flattened bells with no hairs. The species listed here are all of the last kind.

Several selections of the Californian species (*Calochortus luteus*, *C. superbus*, *C. venustus*) are now available from bulb growers in the Netherlands. These seem to be perfectly hardy in my garden. Purists who bristle at the suggestion that these be considered native plants should probably consider focusing on other, more important things. I highly recommend trying some of these; bulbs are cheap, and they can be planted late in the year, if your soil is not frozen.

Seeds of several species are commonly available either in rock garden society seedlists or specialized seedlists sent out by private collectors. You can sow the seed in pots outside, or inside, but I believe the best method for dealing with calochortus seed is to sow it direct. Use a label to mark out your area; the seedlings are easily mistaken for blades of grass, and you wouldn't want to weed out your calochortus lawn by mistake.

Calochortus have two archenemies. The first one may discourage you from growing them after trying them for a couple of years. Rabbits. If your garden is open to incursion from rabbits, you might want to think twice about calochortus, for bunnies love to mow the tender leaves of calochortus right down to the ground.

The second enemy is a psychological one, resulting from an excessive amount of negative publicity originating from climates completely unsuitable to their cultivation. The cold-hardy calochortus need dry clay soil with no supplemental irrigation. They will survive perfectly well on natural precipitation.

Species worth trying, and flowering in late June a few years after seed is sown, are *Calochortus aureus* (Arizona and Utah to New Mexico), pale yellow flowers; *C. eurycarpus* (eastern Oregon, western Idaho, and Nevada), white or pale purple flowers with a red-violet blotch in the center of the petal; *C. flexuosus* (California to Arizona and western Colorado), white, tinted pale purple, with yellow and purple in the center, with stems weirdly twisting through neighboring plants; *C. gunnisonii* (South Dakota to Montana, south to New Mexico and west to Utah), white, yellow, or purple flowers (this will accept more moisture than some of the others); *C. luteus* (California), yellow flowers; *C. macrocarpus* (British Columbia to Montana and Nevada), purple flowers striped green; *C. nuttallii* (North Dakota to Arizona and Nevada; this is the "sego lily," state flower of Utah), white or sometimes pinkish purple, with a reddish purple band in the center of the flower (*C. ambiguus* and *C. bruneaunis* are similar); *C. superbus* (California), white, pale yellow, or pale purple; *C. venustus* (California), white, yellow, or purple (sometimes with strong red tints), with a dark blotch on the petals.

Dichelostemma. One species, *Dichelostemma pulchellum* (blue dicks; Oregon to northern Mexico and east to Utah and New Mexico), is a foot-tall (30 cm) plant with two or three narrowly linear leaves and a golfball-sized head of usually blue-purple flowers, each about a quarter of an inch (6 mm) in length, in June. Some botanists call this *D. capitatum*. Not incredibly exciting, but reliably hardy. *Dichelostemma ida-maia* (firecracker flower; California and southern Oregon) has red, slightly bulging flowers; this has refused to persist in the garden for more than a couple of years. Both are available as bulbs from several firms.

Fritillaria. *Fritillaria pudica* (Wyoming to British Columbia and California) is completely hardy; this variable species has yellow bells about an inch (2.5 cm) long in larger plants (to a foot, 30 cm), though the flowers, and the plants, are often much smaller. Bulbs are available in the trade. This May or June bloomer is good for the rock garden, though, frankly, I find the Turkish and Central Asian fritillaries more exciting.

There are a dozen or so Californian species of *Fritillaria* that might be worth trying in a dry garden; I've never gotten around to growing any of these.

Triteleia. The Californian (also from southern Oregon) *Triteleia laxa* (this is even available in box stores, sold as *Brodiaea laxa* 'Queen Fabiola') is a six-inch (15 cm) tall plant with umbels of good purple flowers about an inch (2.5 cm) long, in June. This has proved itself hardy in the garden here. There are other Californian species but their performance here has not been exceptional. (In other words, they all died.)

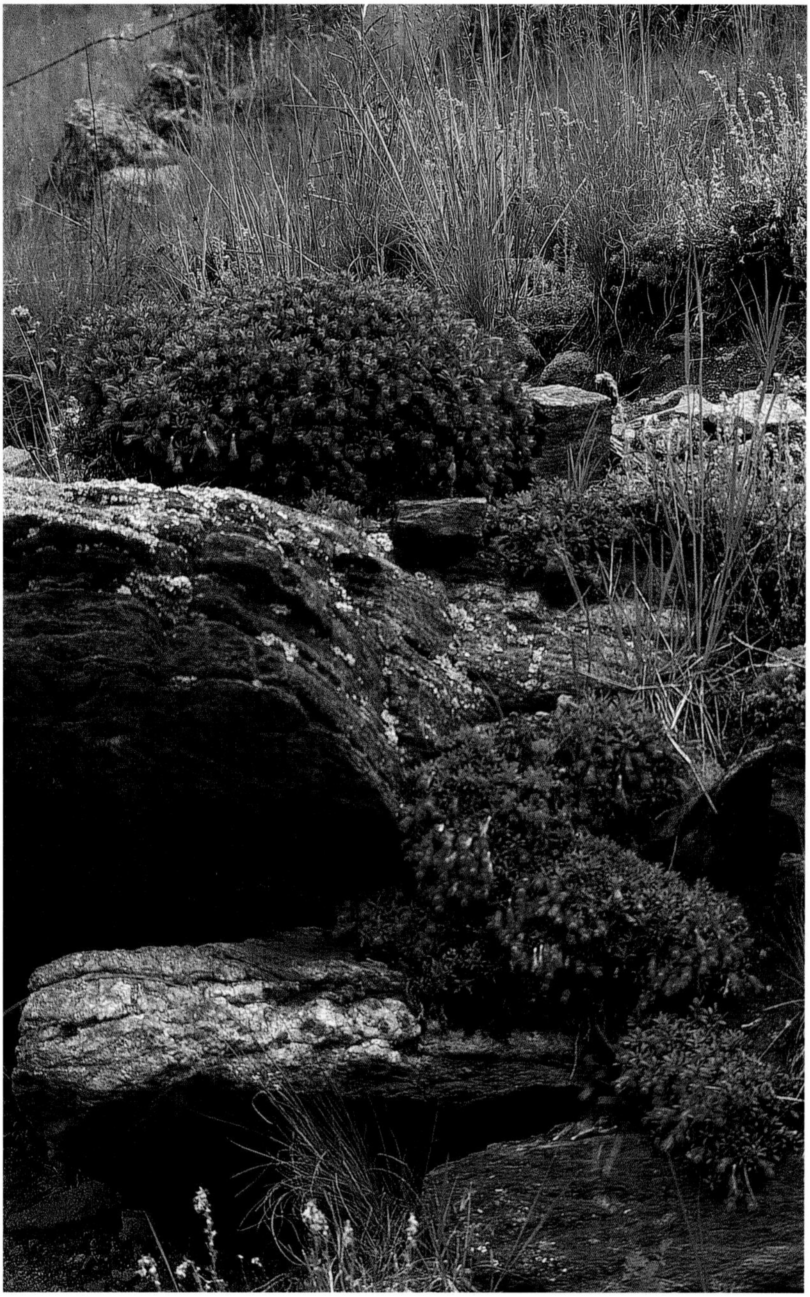

CHAPTER FIVE

Rock Garden Plants

Traditionally, rock gardening has been relegated, at least in the eyes of average gardeners, to a kind of microscopic elitist horticulture dedicated to the growing of impossibly difficult plants. Botanical names are bandied about to such a degree that it makes string theory seem comprehensible. Serious rock gardeners collect different forms of the same species and proudly display the collectors' catalog numbers on the labels, though there are some rock gardeners (myself included) that eschew labels altogether.

Rock garden plants (often called alpines outside North America, even though many are not alpine plants) are sometimes defined as plants less than a foot (30cm) tall suitable for a rock garden. I define rock garden plants as anything suitable for *my* rock garden; what follows is a personal selection.

Rock gardeners are probably the least likely to take seriously the cold hardiness and cultivation statements of gardening books; rock gardeners are constantly experimenting with plants not considered to be hardy in their climates, and you can find a wealth of first-rate cultivation information simply by joining a local chapter of the North American Rock Garden Society, not to mention joining the society itself (or the Alpine

Mounds of *Penstemon crandallii* at Guanella Pass

Garden Society, or any other society if you don't live in North America; foreign rock garden societies welcome members from all countries).

The standard rock garden texts, like Farrer's *The English Rock Garden* (1948), also offer what might be called garden travelogues, filled with information about plants growing in their native habitats. Barr's *Jewels of the Plains* (1983), a seminal work for gardeners living in the Great Plains, contains similar information, as does Lester Rowntree's *Hardy Californians* (1936), an equally valuable work for people (like me) who sometimes wish they still lived in that state. Ira Gabrielson's *Western American Alpines* (1932), a complement to Barr's book, is equally good with high-elevation (though not always drought-tolerant) miniatures from the west coast.

Likewise, the various rock garden societies offer guided tours of plant habitats timed to show the best display of flowers. Quite often the local chapters will have slide presentations given by people who have visited these locales, complete with gorgeously photographed plants that no one has ever heard of. Sometimes seed is collected from these plants and is offered for sale.

I must confess here that the enthusiasm of some rock gardeners to see plants in their native habitats is one I do not share; seeing plants in the wild is interesting, but as a gardener, I would rather visit gardens.

The selection of plants in this chapter is not intended to intimidate beginners; these plants are, for the most part, quite easily grown in our region, no matter what other rock garden literature has to say about them. Most will have to be grown from seed, though a growing number of regional nurseries offer a stunningly wide variety of native rock garden plants.

The botanical names here are dispensed with as much consideration as a drunken tank driver heading backward down a freeway at night. I apologize, sort of, but really there isn't much to be done about this, since this is what rock gardening is all about. That, and an overriding joy in the endless variety of nature.

Abronia (sand verbena). Members of the four-o'clock family that are rare inhabitants of almost any garden. Several highly desirable midsummer-flowering species, even if they choose to depart after a year or two, make as memorable an impression as any plant you may want to grow. The most impressive species, probably, is *Abronia fragrans*, an upright, or laxly upright, plant with wavy-margined leaves and snowball heads of flowers in white, or white tinged with pink. This plant, native to sandy places in the Great Plains (more or less common on roadsides in and around the Sandhills area of eastern Colorado and western Nebraska), is possibly too large for the rock garden: it can grow to two, three, or even four feet (120 cm), though rarely staying upright when it reaches that length.

More suitable for the rock garden is *Abronia elliptica*, growing to about eight inches (20 cm) with leathery elliptical leaves and, once again, white snowballs for flowers. Like *A. fragrans*, the clustered, rounded heads of flowers yield the most intense pleasant fragrance, reminiscent of nothing else in the world, yet immediately and mysteriously evocative. Some botanists consider this to be a variety of *A. fragrans*; it hardly matters.

There is a dwarf species from high altitudes in California, *Abronia alpina*, which sounds delightful. I have never seen it, let alone tried to grow it. Dwight Ripley said of this "most desirable of all sand verbenas" that it was an "inch-high mat of rounded, viscous leaves, covered at flowering time with hundreds of stemless umbels that fade insensibly from palest pink to white."

The plants are so ungrowable that they must constitute one of the gardening life's major disappointments; even germinating them from seed is difficult (Farrer's comment that "they are easily to be raised from seed" notwithstanding) and is best left to the few magicians who have mastered the arcane art of propagating these plants. Every so often it is possible to buy a few plants. They can be tried in the rock garden, even grown in clay, or in a trough filled with a very porous soilless mix. Some plants live, but most die.

Abronia villosa, an annual, is occasionally grown; one year I grew this after receiving a plant from friend. This prostrate plant has clusters of beautiful pink-violet flowers; it blooms for a long period in summer and then is gone.

Aletes humilis

Aletes. The dwarf parsleys may push the limits when it comes to plants with immediate appeal, but some rock gardeners, myself included, still find room for a few of these. Both species probably prefer more moisture but bravely endure drought by disappearing at inconvenient times and reappearing when more moisture is available. *Aletes acaulis*, a fairly common plant along the foothills of the Front Range in Colorado, is a miniature parsley (Italian, not curly-leafed) about four inches (10 cm) across with deep green leaves and upright stems carrying umbels of tiny yellow flowers in May or June. *Aletes humilis* (Larimer parsley), a rare inhabitant of northern Colorado and southern Wyoming, is smaller, with the stems splayed out from the center of the plant. The effect is charmingly insignificant.

Antennaria (pussytoes, cat's ears). A genus of about three dozen species, some of which are undistinguished ("coarse and really ugly weeds"—Clay), but a number of which are highly desirable in the rock garden, either as individual mats or as ground covers, flowering in midsummer. Most of these will tolerate considerable, but not total, summer drought; some may appear to be lost after a hot, dry summer and then come to life again in autumn, or any time after a good, soaking rain. Sometimes their reincarnation is only partial, and large patches of the plant will have died. All can be grown in plain clay soil. Reseeding, sometimes excessively prolifically, is the rule.

The European *Antennaria dioica*, in its 'Nyewood's Variety' (red-pink flowers), may be hard to beat, but western North America excels in a number of worthy gray- or silver-leafed mats that are perfect for any rock garden.

Antennaria sp.

There seems to be some disagreement among botanists where names are concerned. In fact, the taxonomy of *Antennaria* appears to be hopeless at best, so probably the best thing to do is to read carefully the descriptions in seed catalogs (pussytoes are an exception to the rule that plants that reseed freely in the garden are not easy to grow from purchased seed), or just take a chance. Nurseries specializing in rock garden plants and seed collectors only sell the most desirable kinds of pussytoes.

My current favorite is *Antennaria aromatica*, a tundra plant from Colorado and Wyoming, an easily pleased mat of nice silver leaves with attractive (to me) flowers of black and gold. The specific epithet refers to

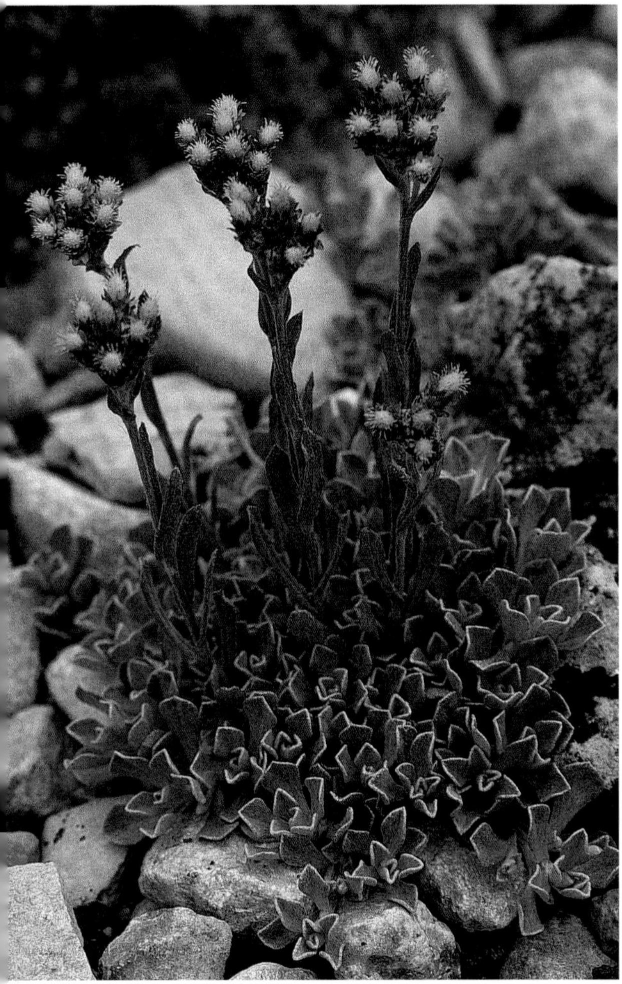

Antennaria aromatica

the scent of citronella that the plant has when crushed. This one is beyond easy to grow from seed; beware planting it in a trough.

Antennaria umbrinella is similar but scentless and not glandular; definitely worth growing. *Antennaria microphylla* is, as the name suggests, a tiny-leafed silvery mat. *Antennaria rosea* is what you might call garden-variety pussytoes; easy, accommodating, and resistant to drought. The flowers on this one are usually pink, though not excitingly so.

Another pink-flowered pussytoes is *Antennaria parvifolia*, common in Colorado and Wyoming; this one has somewhat larger leaves than its name suggests. (*Antennaria parvifolia* has swallowed up Barr's *A. aprica*; see Barkley 1986) This is a first-rate ground cover; both it and *A. rosea* are stunning when allowed to flow into and along the spaces in red or pink flagstone paving.

Antennaria parvifolia gives it name to a flowerless variety, 'McClintock'. One usually relies on minute details of the phyllaries (bracts in the flower head) to determine which species is which; it must have been a leap of faith that assigned a specific name where no flowers exist. Another nonflowering variety is 'Adams Dwarf', which is probably not *parvifolia*; this one is 'McClintock' but with leaves about half the size.

Siskiyou Rare Plant Nursery sold a species which they identified only as being from Devil's Tower in Wyoming. This is less silver than the rest but is again a reliable ground cover. One year I raised a number of antennarias from seed and found one that exactly matches Devil's Tower, but forgot to note which species it was. Such is life.

Barr lists at least another half-dozen. The species hybridize in the wild, and trying to identify plants out of flower suggests that his was a more hopeful outlook.

Aquilegia (columbine). Only a couple of columbines fit the dryland plant bill; one is *Aquilegia barnebyi* (oil-shale columbine), with pink-and-yellow flowers in June and July, often continuing to flower into August. This one can bake for years in the hot sun on a clay slope; eventually the plants will die but will leave plenty of children to carry on. Not the most exciting columbine in flower, but the gorgeous clumps of blue-silver leaves are an asset through the summer, and the flowers are favored by hawkmoths in spring.

The other columbine is, to most rock gardeners, the ultimate columbine, *Aquilegia jonesii*. Possibly not fitting the definition of a dryland

Aquilegia barnebyi

Aquilegia jonesii

plant, being native to limestone mountains from northern Wyoming into Alberta, but certainly more successful when treated like one, this is a low, blue-leafed cushion two inches (5 cm) high by, when happy, eight inches (20 cm) wide, with large blue-purple spurless flowers almost smothering the plant. The garden climates in the Rocky Mountain region offer perfect conditions for easy flowering of *A. jonesii*; do not be afraid to put this one in the hottest, driest spot in the rock garden. Applications of blossom booster in February may improve flowering, which in our garden is mid-March . . . just in time to be flattened by heavy, wet spring snow.

In winter, columbines withdraw to a tiny cluster of leaves almost at ground level. *Aquilegia jonesii*'s leaves sometimes become almost invisible, but by February you should begin to notice some of the tiny leaves starting to unfurl.

In troughs, I give *Aquilegia jonesii* an extra helping of horticultural lime when planting (this might be the one time that the otherwise inviolable rule of not adding limestone is broken); other than that, cultivation is pretty straightforward. The plants do not live for ever.

Arctomecon (bearpoppy). Legendary, gorgeous cold-desert plants. These are fuzzy-rosetted, taprooted poppy-flowered natives of the Mojave Desert, found around Las Vegas westward to California, also in extreme southwestern Utah, growing in gypsum- or lime-rich soils. Their hardiness to cold is unproven; their seed is often contraband.

There are three species. *Arctomecon humilis* is the smallest, to about eight inches (20 cm), with slightly hairy leaves and four-petaled white flowers. *Arctomecon merriamii* has hairy leaves, six-petaled white flowers, few to a stem, and is about eighteen inches (45 cm) tall. Both are listed as endangered species. *Arctomecon californica*, whose "bluish leaves, clothed in long pale hairs, sit comfortably on beds of alkaline clay as white and stodgy as nougat" (Ripley), is about two feet (60 cm) tall and graced with plentiful eggyolk-yellow flowers.

Apparently these are plants that suffer the attentions of people who like to try to dig up plants in the wild and bring them home to their gardens. The phrase "torn up by the roots" is a good operative one here; dead plants transplant badly. The principal threats to these plants seem to be the usual ones of development and "recreational" use of off-road vehicles.

Visitors to our garden who expect to find wide drifts of bearpoppies will be disappointed.

Arenaria (sandwort). Few plants have a more appropriate common name: on a windswept plateau in northern Colorado, near the Wyoming border, and in spectacular view of the Pawnee Buttes, large, ancient green cushions of *Arenaria hookeri* collect windblown sand and loess. The plants are half mineral and half vegetable—not necessarily a desirable, or easily duplicated, feature in the rock garden, but an amazing sight nonetheless. In the garden, *A. hookeri* forms tight green domes covered with white flowers in spring.

Arenarias are not in the absolutely first rank of rock garden plants, but they fulfill a need for greenery in the predominantly gray, silver, and blue foliage of the dry rock garden. They flower in May. *Arenaria obtusiloba*, a low, tight-leafed mat plant from high alpine regions in the Rockies, will also take quite dry conditions. *Arenaria franklinii* ("particularly glaucous, harsh, and prickly-leaved, with very close flat-topped bunches of flower on the two- or three-inch leafy stems," according to Clay, though he was mistaken in saying that *A. hookeri* was similar) and *A. kingii* are more open-structured but equally desirable sandworts from sagebrush regions in the Great Basin and points west.

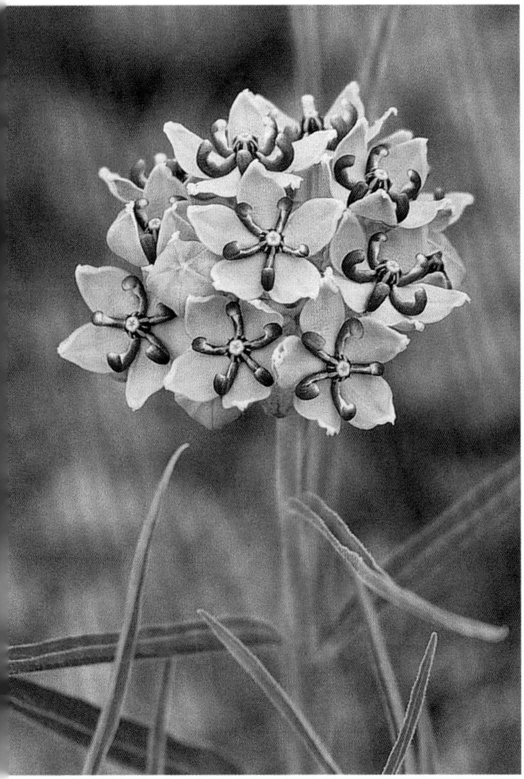

Asclepias asperula

Asclepias (milkweed). Gardeners who are not avid rock gardeners may be surprised to learn that there are dwarf milkweeds that positively ache for an open, sunny, bone-dry site on clay soil in which to grow. Avid rock gardeners may know this quite well, and prefer to change the subject. I have no choice but to go on.

Asclepias pumila and *A. uncialis*, both species of the Great Plains, have a vague something that admirers of wildflowers might call charming, while rock gardeners who pride themselves on their sophisticated taste will dismiss them as boring. Barr, who was both a lover of wildflowers and a sophisticated rock gardener, admired *A. pumila*: "Everywhere it flowers freely and with its close-colony habit produces masses of attractive, honey-scented blooms." I have yet to acquire this plant. *Asclepias uncialis* is very dwarf, with pink or greenish flowers.

Asclepias asperula (antelope-horn) is another plant of the Great Plains, growing about eight inches (20 cm) high with long, almost linear, raspy green leaves and oddly beautiful greenish brown flowers. Wonderful in the rock garden but likely to be passed by unless you look at every plant in your garden every day.

Asclepias ruthiae is another dwarf, from central Utah, whose "furry oval leaves are sharply pointed at the tips, suffused with lavender on both surfaces, and hemmed around with a thin margin of white" (Ripley), though the purple flowers are possibly smaller than any but the most avid asclepiaphile would accept. Still, purple flowers and purple leaves—not the worst way to dress in the desert.

Farrer passed *Asclepias* by without the slightest murmur, which is a pity for I lack his ability to bemoan endless failure in a long series of sobbing laments. And yet, hear my sad tale, for I speak now of the most desirable of all milkweeds, the unutterably glorious *Asclepias cryptoceras*, "one of the crown jewels of our [Colorado] flora," according to

Weber (1987). For years I longed to grow this oval-leafed, cream-and-purple-flowered gem in the rock garden or in troughs. I obtained seed, both of the type species and of var. *davisiana*, which has larger flowers, germinated it, planted the little parsnip-like roots into a suitable clayey or rocky-sandy soil, and never saw the plants again. Meanwhile, a non-gardening friend who has an interest in milkweeds and a determination to ignore my supposedly expert advice, successfully germinated seeds and grew the plant well, frequently calling me to report on its progress. After that, I gave up trying to grow the thing.

Aster. In autumn, as the large and beautiful cultivars of *Aster novae-angliae* (*Symphyotrichum novae-angliae*) are blooming in the garden here, the unimproved wild species is blooming along roadsides all over eastern Colorado, and elsewhere. Barr's description of this species as "beautiful and stately" makes me curious to see the plants he had in mind; as I know it, it is a pathetic and worthless purple-flowered weed with no place in the garden (or in the wild, for that matter).

I also do not know the form of *Aster ericoides* (*Symphyotrichum ericoides*) he called *A. batesii*, though the photograph in *Jewels of the Plains* looks enticing. *Aster ericoides* itself is as valuable as *A. novae-angliae*, except that it is white-flowered.

Aster fendleri (*Symphyotrichum fendleri*), in its form 'My Antonia', is a fairly nice, low (eight inches, 20 cm) plant with sprawling stems and white flowers in mid to late August. I would not go so far as Barr did in calling it "the prime rock aster of the Plains," but it does not revolt me.

A friend is enthusiastic about *Aster porteri* (*Symphyotrichum porteri*); this is an eight- to sixteen-inch (20 to 40 cm) plant with green leaves and white flowers. I have not grown this, being, as is possibly evident, dubious about the garden value of many of the western asters. I will take her word for it.

Barr made quite a few selections of Great Plains plants; most of these are out of commerce now, which is a pity, since all the ones I have been able to acquire were outstanding. 'Dream of Beauty', his pink-flowered selection of *Aster oblongifolius* (*Symphyotrichum oblongifolium*), or *A. kumleinii*, as he called it, took me years to find; it is easily the best aster I have ever grown in my dry garden. This one is rhizomatous and would

Aster oblongifolius 'Dream of Beauty'

probably be a pest with more moisture. Here, it forms large clumps one year, then the next year moves to a different spot, or doubles in size, or shrinks. Barr wrote that the plant is eight to fifteen inches (20 to 38cm) tall "and compact when not influenced by much moisture"—makes me wonder about the difference in moisture regimes between our garden and his. In our garden, the plant never gets taller than ten inches (25cm), even in a wet year.

Astragalus (milkvetch, locoweed). Said to be the largest genus of flowering plants (but who's counting?), *Astragalus* has more than its share of fine rock garden plants native to western North America. There are three types of interest to rock gardeners, mat-forming, cushion, and more upright branching plants, flowering in May, sometimes, with luck, continuing into June. These, with one glaring exception, have white, pink, or purplish pea flowers; as a lagniappe, some have improbably inflated balloon-like seedpods, equally improbably colored on the outside. And few plants create such a satisfying impression in a typically open winter as do the mat-formers, silver-leaves shining in the sun, waiting for spring.

Astragalus are mostly easy from seed. They can be sown in the usual manner outdoors in pots, though nicking the seed opposite the hilum (the part attached to the seed capsule) helps moisture enter the sometimes hard seed coat. There is supposedly a problem with alellopathy in germinating astragalus seed; some growers recommend planting a single seed to a pot to prevent the alellopathic hormone from killing successive seedlings once one seedling has started growing in the pot. I've tried this and not noticed much difference.

Once germinated, seedlings try to leap out of the pot; the root grows faster than the stems, so it's a good idea to plant the seed more deeply than usual.

The taprooted species, especially, are exceedingly difficult to transplant from seedpot into the garden. If the fine root hairs are disturbed, or if the root is damaged in any way, the plants linger for a few hours and then die. Patience and skill, of brain-surgeon caliber, is required to keep the plants alive during this process.

Sowing in situ is a way to avoid these difficulties and can be successful, but only if you remember to water the area where you sowed the seed, unless of course it rains or snows.

Desirable astragalus are found in dry, rocky, sandy, or clay soils throughout our region. All do well in sunny sites completely exposed to sun and wind, and, with one exception, all will endure the most intensely mind-numbing cold imaginable. I find them less easy to grow, though, than their Turkish counterparts like *Astragalus creticus*.

What follows is anything but a comprehensive list of astragali you might want to seek out.

Astragalus amphioxys is a short-lived perennial, distributed from south-central Utah south into New Mexico and west Texas. This is a variable species, about four inches (10cm) tall, with silvery pinnate foliage and, in var. *amphioxys* at least, relatively enormous purplish pink flowers the size of a lima bean. It's fun while it lasts.

The odd-astragalus-out in the group, surely, is *Astragalus asclepiadoides*, which has, as the name suggests, milkweed leaves, round and slightly heart-shaped, with large or small purple flowers. Found in Utah and western Colorado (forms from the latter area are said to have larger flowers). This is an upright plant to about a foot (30cm) tall, branching, with fat purple-mottled seedpods. You could grow this as a conversation piece if for no other reason, though the common name, milkweed milkvetch, has its own dairy-like euphony.

Barr's milkvetch, *Astragalus barrii*, is a cushion plant, at least as I know it, an inch (2.5cm) tall, with large pink or reddish pink flowers held a little above the silvery, palmately trifoliate leaves. Barr says it can spread to twenty inches (50cm), but with me it grew only to about four inches (10cm) before being carried away in the drought of 2002. This rare inhabitant of slopes and hills in western South Dakota, northern Wyoming, and adjacent Montana is in cultivation possibly the most amenable of all American astragali, and a prize plant for a trough. At least a couple of Colorado nurseries propagate and sell this plant (as well as a number of other first-rate astragali).

Astragalus ceramicus, a species of the Great Plains (especially in the Nebraska Sandhills, var. *filifolius*) and southern Idaho (var. *ceramicus*), is the least impressive of astragali, except when it sets seed. Imagine a bunch of gray sticks, either upright or trying to be upright, four inches (10cm) to a foot (30cm) tall, with few, single leaves and tiny off-white or purplish white flowers. The sort of thing you would pull up if you found it in your garden without knowing what it was. But then, say in July, the seedpods form, swelling up to as much as two inches (5cm) long and half an inch (1.25cm) wide, cream-colored, with purple or red mottling: a rock garden Christmas tree in summer. During a day open to garden visitors, the pods will disappear one by one; even the most trustworthy people seem to lose control in the presence of the pods.

Astragalus chloödes (grass milkvetch), from the Uinta Basin in eastern Utah, is another oddity, looking, as the specific epithet suggests (*chloödes* means "grass-like" and is a three-syllable word, hence the diaeresis), like a tuft of gray-leafed grass about six inches (15cm) tall. The small pinkish purple flowers create almost no impression except the intended one of surprise, when serious rock gardeners look closely at the plant.

Astragalus barrii

Astragalus coccineus, "by far the most sensational of its genus" (Ripley), is native from around Las Vegas, Nevada, southward through southern California, western Arizona, and northern Baja California. I would not swear that this one is completely hardy, though it has overwintered in our garden and bloomed more than once. It makes a white-woolly dome about four inches (10 cm) high and wide, and is fairly unbelievable when it actually opens a few flowers. This is an astragalus pollinated by . . . hummingbirds. "The leaves are clothed [Ripley again] in dense white silk (as are also the seedpods), and from their snowy mats rise up in early spring, on short stems, the heads of comparatively few pea-flowers, nearly two inches [5 cm] long, of intense scarlet."

Astragalus detritalis is a dwarf, with silvery, more or less palmately trifoliate leaves on ascending stems and bright pink-purple flowers held above the foliage, making the plant a towering four inches (10 cm) tall.

Astragalus detritalis, Kelaidis garden

Perfect for a trough. *Astragalus detritalis* is a plant of barren soils in the Uinta Basin and adjacent western Colorado.

Astragalus gilviflorus is another tripartite-leafed cushion plant, growing an inch (2.5cm) or so high and maybe six inches (15cm) wide, with handsome blue-silver foliage, this time with long white flowers. *Astragalus gilviflorus* is common on the Great Plains, also entering Utah and Idaho, growing in clay, limestone, and other soils (or "soils," meaning just plain dirt).

Astragalus kentrophyta, rare on the Great Plains, a frequent inhabitant of sagebrush areas in the Rockies, and much more common in the Intermountain West, is a variable species with pinnate gray foliage, the leaves often sharp-tipped, with white flowers tipped with purple, or purple flowers tipped with white. This is mostly a mat about half an inch (1.25cm) high and several times as wide, if you're lucky. This one I find appallingly difficult to transplant; my success with *A. kentrophyta* does not represent the finest moment in my gardening career.

Astragalus loanus is a miniature, two inches (5cm) high by four inches (10cm) wide, for troughs, found only in central Utah, with silvery clover leaves on ascending (but not very) stems and white flowers tipped with light purple. The hairy, but not mottled, seedpods are absurdly outsize on this tiny plant.

Astragalus musiniensis, from eastern Utah and western Colorado, has greenish white-hairy foliage, ascending stems with generally three leaflets at the tip, and the usual pink-purple flowers. In some forms the flowers have a redder tint, which might provide some relief in an all-astragalus garden. *Astragalus musiniensis* is, say, four inches (10cm) high by six inches (15cm) wide. Native to central Utah and western Colorado.

Astragalus purshii is another widespread, variable species, found throughout the Great Plains and the Intermountain West. This one has white-woolly pinnate foliage and grows to about four inches (10cm) tall, forming a loose mat with slightly floppy stems. Flower color is anything from white to purple, possibly the best coloration is in var. *tinctus*.

Astragalus sericoleucus is a mat-former, sending out branches to form a very low carpet to a yard (90cm) wide or more (don't depend on it), with beautiful silvery white hairy (*sericoleucus* means "silky white") palmately trifoliate leaves about half an inch (1.25cm) long. The smallish but plentiful flowers are purplish pink, though white forms have been reported. Native to rocky slopes and hills in western Kansas, Nebraska, northeastern Colorado, and southeastern Wyoming, plants and seeds are rarely offered for sale. A condensed form of *A. sericoleucus* growing, mostly, in central and southwestern Wyoming, is sometimes called *A. aretioides*. This is even more desirable. *Astragalus tridactylicus* is similar to *A. sericoleucus*, but with larger flowers; this is common in Wyoming and also found on shale outcrops next to the eastern foothills of the Rockies in Colorado.

Astragalus spatulatus is another great plant (in Barr's words, "It would be difficult to blueprint a more perfect plant for the sunny, dry rock garden"). This is another cushion plant, half an inch (1.25cm) tall to about six inches (15cm) wide, with spatulate silvery hairy leaves, the flowers purplish pink with white tips held slightly above the foliage. Common on the Great Plains from Kansas and Colorado north into Alberta and Saskatchewan. *Astragalus simplicifolius*, a native of Wyo-

Astragalus utahensis, Kelaidis garden

ming, is somewhat similar but with flowers twice the size of those of *A. spatulatus*, so it must be considered twice as good, and therefore twice as perfect.

Astragalus utahensis is a fabulously showy plant, abundant in the Wasatch Mountains of Utah but found elsewhere (southwestern Wyoming, southern Idaho, eastern Nevada), and a constant source of embarrassment to yours truly. (Everyone else can grow it.) A six- by six-inch (15 by 15 cm) plant, with "clumps of fat little leaves clothed in dense white wool and flowers of brilliant purple" (Ripley)—for some people, at least. It's relatively easy from seed, and plants can be had, at times, from various nurseries.

Astragalus whitneyi, native to the eastern slopes of the Cascades and Sierra Nevada, and as far east as Idaho, is a yawn until it goes to seed. It has green or silvery pinnate flowers, tiny white pea flowers, and, after all that is finally over, enormous balloon seedpods mottled red.

Astragalus whitneyi

Bolophyta. These little plants, sometimes placed in *Parthenium*, are admittedly an acquired taste: gray-green-silver-leafed dwarf feverfews, an inch or two (2.5 to 5 cm) tall, with mutant, almost-rayless daisy flowers hidden in the foliage. There are three quite similar species, distinguished by the presence of hairs and wings on the achenes, microscopic differences of little interest to anyone but botanists.

The nonalpine *Bolophyta alpina* (Wyoming feverfew) grows in barren shale in desolate windswept grasslands in south-central Wyoming and northern Colorado, forming small cushions with the tiny, extraterrestrial flowers nestled in the white, marcescent leaves (last year's dried leaves), looking like nothing so much as dried grass. Apparently this species was thought to be quite rare, but new populations have been found recently, a remarkable testament to botanists' eyesight.

Bolophyta ligulata, more or less common on barren clay and limestone in the Uinta Basin in Utah, with scattered populations in adjacent areas in Colorado, where it sometimes grows on oil shale, has somewhat more oval leaves and appears to be the tidiest of the three species.

Bolophyta tetraneuris (Arkansas River feverfew) is found on white limestone in a few places in central and southern Colorado. I have this one growing in a white shale trough where it looks pretty good, shale troughs being just about the epitome of the possibilities in the sunny west (I still plan to make an oil shale trough one day), though the plants are passed by without comment when the garden is open to visitors.

Calylophus. Yellow-flowered evening primroses, segregated out of *Oenothera* because of their stigmas, which are entire instead of lobed, and their lack of basal leaves (all the leaves are on the stems), but in some ways quite similar (the four-petaled flowers bear a strong family resemblance to those of oenotheras). Calylophi (calylophi?) begin flowering in the evening, as you might guess, and by the next day their withered flowers have turned to orange and pink. On rare overcast mornings the flowers will continue to bloom. Members of this genus lack the refinement of some oenotheras, and most of them may actually be too tall for inclusion in smaller rock gardens. All are easy—and then some—to grow from seed.

Calylophus berlandieri is a species more of the eastern part of the Great Plains (the southwestern part, actually; southwestern Kansas south through eastern New Mexico, the Texas panhandle, and down into Mexico) with more or less upright stems to two feet (60 cm). The stem leaves are linear to oblanceolate, slightly toothed (sometimes almost microscopically so), with crinkly-petaled flowers about two inches (5 cm) wide.

Calylophus drummondianus is a mouthful of a synonym for *C. berlandieri*. Some botanical treatments consider *C. berlandieri* subsp. *berlandieri* to be *C. drummondianus* subsp. *berlandieri*, and *C. berlandieri* subsp. *pinifolius* (a form found further east) to be *C. drummondianus* subsp. *drummondianus*. When called *Oenothera berlandieri*, as it sometimes is, it's frequently confused in horticulture with *O. speciosa*. The two are not the same plant.

Calylophus hartwegii, another species from the southwestern part of the Great Plains and south to Mexico, has weakly ascending to upright stems to two feet (60 cm) with mini-milkweed leaves, though sometimes these are toothed, with fine large crinkly-petaled flowers. *Calylophus fendleri* is considered by some to be a subspecies.

Calylophus lavandulifolius, the best species, is a smaller plant with lavender-like leaves and four-parted flowers. Found throughout the Great Plains and in parts of southwestern Wyoming and adjacent Utah. In our garden this made a plant about six inches (15 cm) by ten inches (25 cm).

Calylophus serrulatus has upright stems with oblanceolate or linear slightly toothed leaves, and small flowers less than an inch wide. This would-be shrub is found throughout the Great Plains. Barr praised this plant (as *Oenothera serrulata*), calling it "well behaved in the garden," which is the last thing in the world I would say about this plant. In our garden it seeded about so viciously that when the last plant was ripped out I uttered a cry of triumph heard throughout the state. Barr's mention of a form with flowers two inches (5 cm) across is interesting. I wouldn't want it.

Castilleja (paintbrush). A genus of some two hundred hemiparasitic relatives of penstemons and snapdragons admired, in some species, for their brightly colored bracts. (The bracts surround the flowers, which are usually inconspicuous.)

I've never quite been sure what makes a plant *hemi*parasitic instead of just plain parasitic, though the botanical descriptions never mention the presence of haustoria, which characterize a true parasite. Maybe I should read more. Anyway, the plants do seem to require the presence of a "host" in the wild; they never grow by themselves in the wild as far as I know. The term "facultative parasite" is used to describe plants that can grow with or without a host, but the host (almost always sagebrush) is thought to allow paintbrushes greater resistance to drought than they might have growing on their own.

Because of this, paintbrushes have acquired a reputation of being difficult to grow. Farrer's mournful sighs notwithstanding, paintbrushes are fairly easy to grow, if you give them the conditions they seem to require. Most of the species are found in western North America in a wide variety of habitats (we're only interested in the dryland species here), and the ones I mention may seem too large for the average rock garden, but they're exactly the sort of plants that benefit from the finicky, dedicated precision most rock gardeners apply in growing their plants.

Paintbrushes are grown from seed, though a few nurseries in Colorado, at least, do offer plants propagated by local growers. (I hear that one nurseryman is even hybridizing plants and selecting for color.) Paintbrush seed is covered with a soft, dry, spongy, reticulated coating, or testum, that you remove by putting the seed in the palm of one hand and lightly rubbing the coating off. At this point you will want to resist the temptation to blow the chaff away; sow both in seed pots and set them outdoors in January as you would other seed. (It isn't necessary to provide a host yet.) When the seedlings are of adequate size, usually by August of the next year, they can be planted within a few inches of a suitable host. *Artemisia frigida*, being a low plant, and blue grama (especially as a lawn) are excellent choices for hosts, though in the wild the larger artemisias are usually the hosts. The red-flowered species will, of course, attract their principal pollinator, hummingbirds.

Paintbrushes suffer from few pests, though the flea beetle that attacks penstemons will try to devour paintbrushes, too. The plants are exceptionally resilient to drought, disappearing completely during prolonged drought, and then reappearing with renewed strength during wetter years. I'm not certain that the alpine species have a built-in resistance to drought like some of the alpine species in *Penstemon* do, but there is no reason why these couldn't be tried as well.

The species in *Castilleja* are difficult to key out, and often the major differences are in the way the bracts are cleft, and even this is not always a reliable method of identification. Buying seed from collectors like Northwest Native Seed is probably the best way of getting the plants you want.

Here are a few species that are worth trying. With any luck, success with these will encourage you to try more.

Castilleja angustifolia, in one of the most beautiful forms with violet or pink-purple bracts (the color range is pink to purple to orange to yellow), has rough-hairy linear leaves and grows to about two feet (60 cm) tall. Grows with *Artemisia tridentata*, western Wyoming and Montana east through southern Idaho, northern Utah, Nevada, and Oregon.

Castilleja integra

Castilleja applegatei is found in sagebrush areas, and also at higher elevations, east of the Cascades and Sierra Nevada, to central Idaho. This has sticky-hairy wavy-margined leaves and stems to two feet (60 cm), with red, or sometimes orange or yellow, bracts.

Castilleja chromosa is very similar to *C. angustifolia* and might even be considered a variety of this, though apparently it never has the beautiful purple coloration to its bracts. *Castilleja chromosa* is common throughout the Intermountain West, venturing even as far south as northwestern New Mexico and northern Arizona.

Castilleja integra is a species of the southern Great Plains, from southeastern Colorado into New Mexico and northern Mexico, also in west Texas and Arizona, with lightly woolly linear leaves to about one foot (30 cm), sometimes taller, and bright orange bracts. Plants in the garden here, grown in a blue grama lawn for about ten years, have even produced seedlings.

Castilleja linariifolia is a beauty, with smooth or lightly hairy narrowly linear leaves and red, or sometimes orange-red, bracts, growing from one to three feet (30 to 90 cm) tall. New Mexico to Wyoming (where it is the state flower) west to Oregon and California. Yellow forms also exist.

Castilleja scabrida is a gorgeous dwarf (to six inches, 15 cm), found from eastern Nevada to western Colorado, with rough-hairy stems, linear leaves, and bright red bracts.

Castilleja sessiliflora is one of the boring ones. I only mention it because I've grown several forms, and none has been spectacular. This is a common species found throughout the Great Plains and further, from northern Mexico all the way up into Saskatchewan and Manitoba. My plants are about six inches (15cm) tall, with downy linear leaves, greenish bracts, and wan yellow flowers.

Chamaechaenactis. A genus of one species, *Chamaechaenactis scaposa*, a low, choice cushion plant found in clay and sandy soil in sagebrush, from western Wyoming and Colorado south through Utah to northern Arizona. A multi-stemmed plant, with little ovate leaves, and small half-open daisy flowers, white aging to pink. Three inches (7.5cm) by five inches (12.5cm), maybe. Easy from seed, but taprooted, so it transplants unwillingly if allowed to get too big for its pot.

Cheilanthes (lipfern). It seems absurd that there might be ferns suitable for our dry rock garden, but here they are. (We will meet them again when we come to *Notholaena* and *Pellaea*.) *Cheilanthes*, a genus found throughout the world, has a number of xerophytic species native to western North America, growing mostly in rock crevices or among boulders, that have to count among the most highly desirable yet frustratingly unavailable plants in the whole of this book. Frustrating that they're unobtainable, yes, but it's also understandable, since propagating ferns for dry climates would be outside the purview of about one hundred percent of nurseries specializing in ferns.

Cheilanthes are not entirely unavailable, though; some nurseries catering to the rock garden trade do occasionally offer one or two species. I've been able to acquire a number of species from time to time. Culture is the same for all species, the preferred site being in, at the most, light or dappled shade, or on the north side of a rock garden, wedged between rocks with at least some soil so that the roots can find a cool rooting medium in their search for moisture. For the first year they should be treated like any other ferns and given water at almost every possible opportunity. Prolonged drought may cause the fronds to curl right down to the crown of the plant, a condition remedied by rain or a brief session with the hose.

Pteridophiles have a number of recipes, all vaguely similar, that are said to produce ferns by sowing spores. I've tried it; my wife eventually forced me to throw away the boxes of resulting fungus.

Cheilanthes eatonii, one of the largest at a foot (30 cm) tall, with gray-green hairy pinnae, scaly on the underside, is found from roughly the Oklahoma Panhandle south into New Mexico, Arizona, into Mexico, and also west to Utah.

Cheilanthes feei, found throughout the Great Plains, in fact almost everywhere in North America, is shorter, to about eight inches (20 cm), without scales on the pinnae, generally giving the effect of a slightly smaller *C. eatonii*, and gorgeous when allowed to weave its way through rock crevices. I know of a spectacular example of this, with the ferns grown in the full, blazing Denver sun.

Cheilanthes fendleri, also growing to about eight inches (20 cm), has glabrous pinnae, found from Colorado to Arizona through New Mexico to west Texas.

Other species to look for are *Cheilanthes wootonii*, and, if they're hardy (this would be a double test, to see if you can find the plants and then see if they make it through a cold winter), *C. covillei*, *C. lindheimeri*, *C. pringlei*, *C. parryi*, and *C. wrightii*.

Chrysopsis will be found, unfortunately, under *Heterotheca*.

Clematis. Of the half-dozen or so species native to North America, three are of interest to us here. Fortunately, the vining and trailing types are less tolerant of drought; otherwise, I would have to try to sort out the incomprehensibly convoluted mess of names attached to them (Barr's *Clematis occidentalis*, which might do well in climates with slightly more rain than mine, is *C. columbiana* is *C. columbiana* var. *tenuiloba* is *C. tenuiloba*).

Clematis fremontii, from Kansas and Nebraska, mainly, would be identified as anything but a clematis out of flower; it has widely ovate, veined, leathery green herbaceous leaves about four inches (10 cm) long and two or three inches (5 to 7.5 cm) wide. The flowers, produced in late April to May, are of the viorna type, an upside-down urn with the sepals curved upward, purple with whitish margins, making them look faintly striped.

This is a perfect plant for plain clay soil, but care must be taken to ensure that melting snow in spring does not collect around the woody

[right] *Clematis fremontii*

[below] *Clematis hirsutissima* at Denver Botanic Gardens

crown. Siting the plant on a slope, in full sun, would be best. (This advice is from bitter experience.)

As with most members of the buttercup family, sowing fresh seed is the second best idea, since older seed can take years to germinate. The best idea is to buy plants from nurseries skilled in clematis propagation.

Clematis hirsutissima (sugarbowls) grows to about eighteen inches (45cm) with divided linear leaves on erect stems and purple viorna flowers, the sepals upturned at the edges. The plant is hairy throughout. Native to moist meadows and dry sagebrush throughout the northern Great Plains (northern Colorado, Wyoming, Montana, Idaho, and so forth). In dry gardens the plants grow achingly slowly, but they still grow, a little better with dappled shade. Some selected forms exist on the outermost fringes of horticulture.

For some reason, *Clematis hirsutissima* has always been identified, particularly across the Atlantic, as *C. douglasii.*

Clematis scottii (*C. hirsutissima* var. *scottii*) is a sprawling plant with stems about eighteen inches (45cm) long, the leaves glaucous and elliptical, with flowers of the viorna type minus the upturned sepals. Native to southern Colorado and northern New Mexico, maybe further south. This one would, again, appreciate some light shade if it's going to be grown dry.

The plant pictured in Graham Stuart Thomas's lovely book *Treasured Perennials* as *Clematis hirsutissima scottiae* is *C. scottii.*

Cryptantha. A genus of mostly weedy borages from dry places throughout the west (and also in South America), full of the bristling hairs and sandpaper leaves associated with this family. The flowers, borne through the summer, are forget-me-nots; the prevailing color is white with a yellow eye, which could be why some cryptanthas travel under the common name of popcorn flower.

The growing of cryptanthas, I should warn you, is one of the more arcane areas of horticulture, even of dryland horticulture. Finding plants for sale at a nursery would be a rare phenomenon, but they can be grown from seed using the usual outdoor treatment.

Passing by in disdain the mostly annual weeds, we concentrate on species placed in the section Oreocarya (some botanists use this name as the generic name instead). There are a couple of biennials that may be of interest. *Cryptantha celosioides* (Barr's *C. bradburiana*), the butte candle, found throughout the Great Plains, has a first-year rosette of gray-woolly spoon-shaped leaves, then the next year it sends up several foot-tall (30cm), or taller, stems with smaller, less woolly leaves, and clusters of white flowers in the leaf axils. *Cryptantha virgata* is similar but with linear basal and stem leaves; this is found along the eastern foothills of the Rockies in Wyoming and Colorado.

Then there are the upright-stemmed perennials of the Intermountain West, some of which are attractive enough in the rock garden, though rarely available even from seed collectors. *Cryptantha confertiflora* and *C. flava* are popcorn flowers with extra butter; both have yellow flowers, in the case of *C. confertiflora*, sometimes even with a tint of orange. Both have gray-green, upright, linear-oblanceolate, rough hairy basal leaves and flowering stems from six inches (15cm) to a foot (30cm) tall, give or take, with clusters of flowers in the axils of the stem leaves. *Cryptantha johnstonii*, from the San Rafael Swell in central Utah, is a smaller plant, four inches (10cm) to ten inches (25cm) tall, with gray-green oblanceolate leaves and white flowers, larger than most other cryptanthas.

Lastly, there are the *other* cryptanthas, the cushion plants, a group of highly desirable, terrifyingly recalcitrant plants, as aristocratic in their own way as their cousin, *Eritrichium nanum*, but even more difficult to grow. Some of these rot away to nothing at the slightest hint of summer humidity (about thirty percent humidity kills them), others rot away if you look at them. Fortunately, seed collectors know their cryptanthas, and a number of these plants are offered on a regular basis.

Cryptantha caespitosa, growing in dry clay or sandy soils from southwestern Wyoming east into Idaho, is a somewhat spreading plant, with gray, downy oblanceolate leaves and smallish flowers on weakly ascending (to about two inches, 5cm) stems. This is one for a dry trough.

I admit I don't know everything, but *Cryptantha cana*, from western Nebraska and nearby areas in South Dakota, Wyoming, and Colorado, is the best in the genus and certainly the best cryptantha ever to have been grown in the garden here. This is a fat, silky cushion to about six inches (15cm) and at least twice as wide. The gray-silver leaves are oblanceolate; the flowering stems are not much taller than the leaves.

Cryptantha caespitosa

Barr's statement that the cultivation of this plant (native to areas practically at his doorstep) is "a challenge still to be met" is a precise one, though plants lived in the garden here for a few years, and then gave up the ghost for no apparent reason.

Cryptantha compacta, from western Utah, is a gem. This has downy, silvery gray leaves, slightly spoon-shaped, huddling together in a tiny cluster about an inch (2.5cm) high, with flowering stems only slightly higher. Like other cryptanthas, this has a taproot, but seedlings transplant with surprising ease. *Cryptantha compacta* belongs in a trough, watered sparingly during prolonged drought and covered (a clear plastic seed tray cover will do) during damp periods in summer. *Cryptantha humilis*, despite its name, is a taller, upright version of *C. compacta*.

Cryptantha jonesiana, from the San Rafael Swell in central Utah, is an upright plant, with greenish spatulate leaves, to six inches (15 cm) tall, with a few flowers in the leaf axils and clusters of white flowers at the tip of the stalk. This is a rare beauty for a trough, less annoyingly sensitive to excessive humidity.

Cryptantha paradoxa is another upright plant, to four inches (10 cm), with downy silvery oblanceolate leaves and, again, white flowers clustered at the top of the stem. This one is native to central and eastern Utah, western Colorado, and northwestern New Mexico, and once again a prime candidate for a sunny, dry trough.

Douglasia. A genus of cushion plants properly belonging to the watered alpine garden, and yet . . . Some years ago I noticed a small plant, that had been growing there for a few years, blooming in one of our unwatered gardens, next to some agaves. I bent over to look at it (carefully); it was a douglasia, though it didn't quite look like any douglasia I knew from what was growing in the troughs. I must have thrown out the con-

Douglasia nivalis

tents of an old seed pot there after waiting the requisite five years for something to happen. A piece was sent off to an expert in *Douglasia*, who identified it as a form of *D. nivalis*.

Thinking that having a douglasia growing in dry clay soil was somehow contrary to the universal laws of rock gardening, I transplanted the plant into the trough where the other, more common forms of *Douglasia nivalis* were growing. The poor plant died the next day. No doubt there is a moral to this little story.

Anyway, *Douglasia nivalis* is native to the eastern slopes of the Cascades in Washington, and also in areas of British Columbia and Alberta. It has grayish, tiny oblanceolate leaves, forming a loose or tight cushion, about one inch (2.5cm) high, and, as I know it in the garden, about six inches (15cm) wide, with clusters of red or wine-red flowers, blooming any time from mid-January to mid-March in the garden here. If seedlings should appear in places where they don't belong, leave them alone.

Dudleya cymosa subsp. *pumila*, garden of Ann and Dick Bartlett

Dudleya. Hen-and-chickens lookalikes, but with gray, silver, or glaucous green fleshy leaves, from California, Arizona, and Mexico. Most are hopelessly tender. One species, *Dudleya cymosa*, has proven itself hardy in Denver-area gardens. Usually subsp. *pumila* is the one grown, though subsp. *cymosa* should also be tried. Plants are now routinely offered at rock garden plant sales in the Rocky Mountain area; I believe the form grown is from high elevations in the San Gabriel Mountains of southern California. The plant forms a golfball-sized rosette of gray, more or less oblanceolate leaves with a sharply acute tip, and clusters of beautiful red and yellow flowers held on a short stalk. In winter the plant pulls itself together tightly and huddles against the soil for warmth.

Dudleyas are easily grown from seed sown under lights; the fine seed should be barely covered with fine sand to keep it moist. The plants transplant like a charm.

Enceliopsis. A small group of daisies with gray or green basal leaves from which rise stalks carrying large yellow flowers. *Enceliopsis nudicaulis*, a species found growing in dry areas throughout the Intermountain West, has widely obovate, mucronate leaves arising from woody stems about eight inches (20 cm) tall, with flowers an inch and a half (3.75 cm) wide. This taprooted plant does quite well on the hot slopes of a southwest-facing raised bed, though it tends to wear out its welcome as it looks progressively trashier after a few years. *Enceliopsis nudicaulis* is easily raised from seed.

Eriastrum. Phlox relatives, mostly annuals, from California, with at least one nominal perennial that might pique our interest for the few years that it lives in the rock garden. This is *Eriastrum densifolium* subsp. *austromontanum*, a six-inch-high (15 cm) plant with tiny, pinnately lobed leaves, and heads of long-tubed, light blue typical phlox flowers. Easily grown from seed.

Erigeron. An absolutely dizzying array of very attractive daisies, large and small, usually with plentiful ray flowers arrayed in several rows (in this they are different from asters, which have the ray flowers arranged in a single row), and blooming mostly from May to July. Erigerons are something of a western specialty. The small ones, which concern us here, range from abominable weeds to congenial members of the rock garden to frightfully choice and difficult miniatures. Some of these last are alpine plants too aristocratic to deserve rough treatment; we allocate these to the watered rock garden and trough.

The differences between species can sometimes be excessively technical. Good erigerons are mostly obtainable from seed collectors and nurseries specializing in rock garden plants. Seed is easily germinated using the outdoor treatment; some plants will reseed at will once they are established. The plants are mostly taprooted, so plant them where you're sure you want them.

Erigeron bloomeri, a plant of eastern Washington and Oregon, Idaho, northern California, and Nevada, growing in sagebrush, with finely white-hairy upright-growing linear leaves to about two inches (5 cm), with rayless, solitary yellow flowers on stalks about three times as high as the leaves. A curiosity, maybe, but still a nice plant.

Erigeron chrysopsidis, another sagebrush plant of eastern Washington and Oregon, Nevada, and Idaho, forms a kind of cushion of linear-oblanceolate hairy green leaves about two inches (5 cm) long, with golden yellow flowers held singly on stalks anywhere from an inch (2.5 cm) to six inches (15 cm) tall. In varieties in the southern part of the range, the ray flowers are quite short; the northern form has longer ray flowers and makes a more attractive plant. A beautiful selection of *E. chrysopsidis*, named after Grand Ridge Nursery in Issaquah, Washington, has flowers

Trough with erigerons and cacti, Kelaidis garden

that bloom all summer, but I have never tried growing this one in the dry garden.

Erigeron compactus, found here and there from southwestern Wyoming and western Colorado to California, is a cushion erigeron of the utmost refinement, as good as any of the high alpine species. The tiny linear gray leaves are rather untidily arranged in the cushion; the flowers, white or pale pink, are borne singly on stems three inches (7.5cm) high. Look for var. *consimilis*, with larger flowers about an inch (2.5cm) wide. This one is easy to grow from seed but not so easy to keep alive, especially during wet summers.

Erigeron compositus is a widespread erigeron (native even to Greenland) growing mostly at high elevations in the Intermountain West, but at lower, drier elevations in the Great Plains. Despite its preference for higher elevations in the drier west, this species is without a doubt utterly drought-tolerant. The plant has loose tufts of gray, thrice-divided leaves, sticky or not, with flower heads of white, pink, blue, or lavender on stems about four inches (10cm) tall, though it can be taller in some forms. (Get the small ones.) Other forms have rayless flowers, which is undesirable in this species. 'Goat Rocks', a hybrid with *E. aureus* (an alpine species of the Cascades), has beautiful pale lemon-yellow flowers all season; I have not tested this one for drought resistance.

Erigeron elegantulus is a little beauty from eastern Oregon and northeastern California, with quite narrow, upright linear leaves and white or bluish flowers on six-inch (15cm) stems. *Erigeron linearis* is similar, but taller (in some forms), with yellow flowers. *Erigeron filifolius* is close to both of these but has blue, white,

Erigeron compactus var. *consimilis*

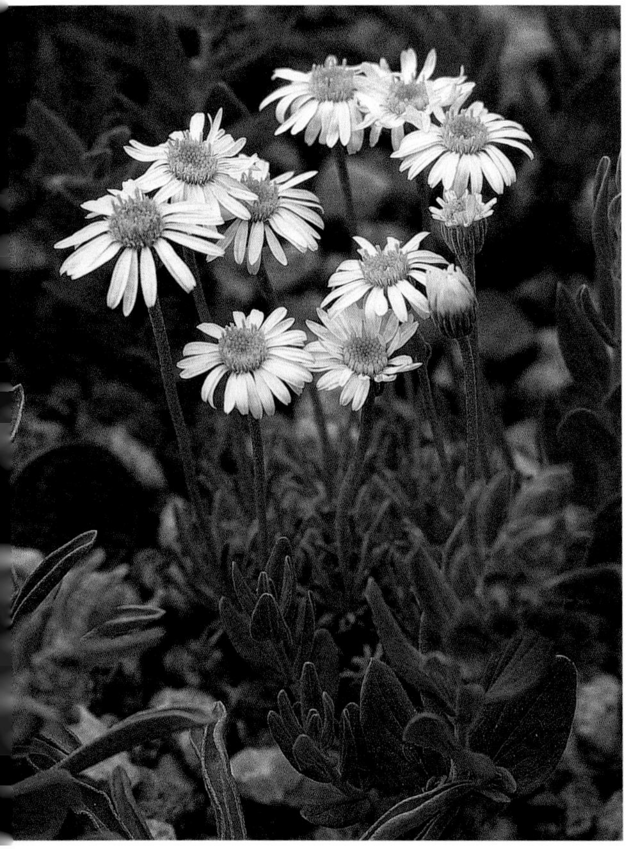

or pink flowers, branched on the stem, and an apparent, but unfulfilled, desire to become a shrub. A larger form is found in Washington and Oregon.

Erigeron flagellaris (whiplash daisy) is a short-lived perennial; it's a pity that it lives at all. This has small obovate-spatulate green leaves and attractive white daisies. It sends out stolons (the whiplash) that root at the stems, and it produces seeds. All the seeds germinate. The next year there is a hideous tangle of whips, living and dead, everywhere; these are difficult to remove and even if all are pulled out, plants still appear. This species is native throughout the Great Plains, and in many parts of the Intermountain West. Beware.

Erigeron poliospermus, from eastern Oregon, Washington, and British Columbia, has linear-oblanceolate, upright, hairy green leaves, and flowers of pink or purple on stems four inches (10 cm) tall. My plants had purple flowers; a deep blue form is also known, which I fairly desperately yearn for. Originally described as a variety of *E. poliospermus*, *E. latus* is an equally fine species from a small area in northern Nevada and adjacent Idaho, with almost spoon-shaped sticky, hairy leaves, and inch-wide (2.5 cm) purple flowers, though white or pink forms are also known. The stems are four inches (10 cm) tall.

Erigeron nanus, from Wyoming, Idaho, and Utah, is rather similar to *E. latus*, though the hairy basal leaves are more linear. This also is about four inches (10 cm) tall with blue or purple flowers, though white forms are known, too. *Erigeron rydbergii* is a slightly smaller plant, with purple or white flowers and less hairy leaves, found in Wyoming, Montana, and Idaho. *Erigeron untermannii* is again similar but with shorter hairs (one of the—literally—microscopic differences), and usually white flowers. Found in eastern Utah. All of these are of equal effect in the garden.

Erigeron ochroleucus is a plant of the northern Great Plains, Alberta and Saskatchewan to Wyoming and Nebraska, with, again, linear to lanceolate basal leaves and white, purple, or blue flowers. In var. *scribneri*, which is the variety of interest to rock gardeners ("of the Great Plains daisies," Barr wrote, "the crown jewel"), the flowering stems are no more than two inches (5 cm) high.

Erigeron pulcherrimus, from western Wyoming and Colorado, eastern Utah, and northwestern New Mexico, has the linear to somewhat

Erigeron ochroleucus var. *scribneri*

lanceolate leaves we have now come to expect, though this time they are grayish, and this is a taller plant, anywhere from four inches (10 cm) to a foot (30 cm) tall, with fine, inch-wide (2.5 cm) white or light purple flowers.

Erigeron pumilus, a highly variable species found throughout the Intermountain West and also on the Great Plains, has mostly narrowly oblanceolate leaves, though in some varieties these can be more linear, and white, pink, or blue flowers of varying sizes. The stems can be anywhere from four inches (10 cm) tall to almost two feet (60 cm) tall in var. *euintermedius*, from the dry parts of the Pacific Northwest and California east of the Sierra Nevada (this one may be too tall for some rock gardens).

To answer the inevitable question, "Aren't there any desirable erigerons that don't have narrow leaves?" I would draw your attention to the amazing little mat plant from northern Arizona, *Erigeron scopulinus*. This has tiny, quarter-inch-long (6 mm), spoon-shaped leaves, forming an ever-widening mat with tiny white flowers held barely above the green leaves. I find *E. scopulinus* best served by being grown on the north side of the dry rock garden, on a raised bed, where it can receive a little shade; it can be severely damaged by prolonged drought.

There are, of course, other erigerons besides these.

Eriogonum (wild buckwheat). These members of the buckwheat family include some of the most desirable, not to say legendary, plants suitable for the sunniest parts of the dry rock garden. Generally the effect is of a mat- or cushion-forming plant, or a shrub, with small leaves and

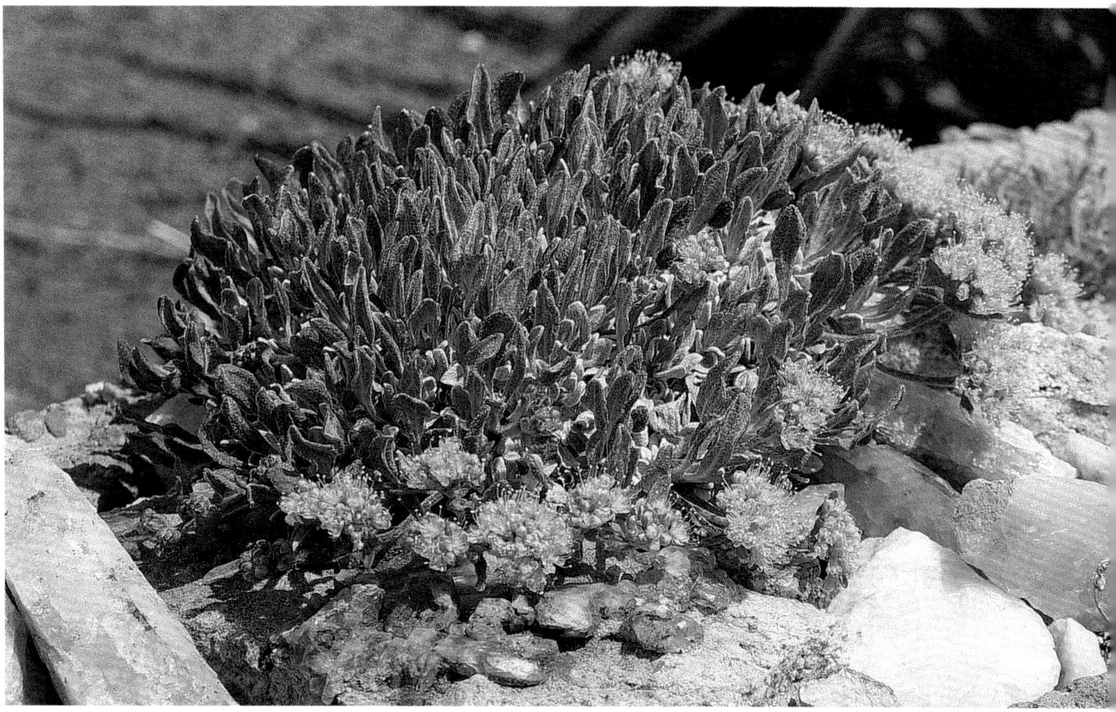

Eriogonum arcuatum var. *arcuatum*, Kelaidis garden

clusters of flowers in cymes or umbels. Some species are dioecious with staminate (male) and pistillate (female) flowers; the pistillate flowers are usually larger. The flowers quite often age to a pinkish or rust color, forming a beautiful combination with the newer flowers, which are produced in succession all summer.

There are also a number of annual and biennial weedy-looking things, but fortunately seed collectors and nurseries take no account of these.

Here, especially, ignoring conventional cultural advice from climates possibly unsuited to the culture of dryland plants is the best recipe for success. Eriogonums are easy to grow in dry clay soil mulched with gravel. Still, prolonged humidity in excess of thirty percent (it does happen now and then) in summer can be a problem for some of the woolly-leafed species; a black fungus appears on the leaves and is difficult to control after that, until the plant dies, and then there are no more worries. Naturally, the rarer the species, the more vulnerable it is.

There is a serious pest of eriogonums whose identity remains a mystery, at least to me. The first sign of trouble is what looks like cobwebs on the leaves, then the whole plant is covered, and then soon after that the plant is dead, eaten right down to the ground. If you touch the cobwebs, a tiny creature can be seen to disappear into the depths of the plant. All species can be afflicted. Pyrethrin is an effective control.

Few of these plants are readily obtainable in the trade, and even though nurseries in the Rocky Mountain and Intermountain regions may surprise you with their selections, don't expect too much. This is what the seedlists are for. At least a couple of the better known lists routinely offer a good selection of eriogonums. Seed germinates readily in earliest spring, using the outdoor method; the plants transplant with ease. (To avoid the wrath of Nemesis, and maybe a dash of guilt, I'll pass by some of the rarer eriogonums considered to be threatened in their native habitat, like *Eriogonum butterworthianum*, *E. chrysops*, and *E. twisselmannii*, though, thanks to the occasional tiny packet of seed slipped into my hands, these have also been successfully grown in the garden here.) And I must acknowledge the bitter truth that many of these plants, rare or not so rare, passed into the Great Beyond after the droughts of 2001–03.

Telling one eriogonum from another is sometimes a job for specialists. Some of the cushion species differentiate themselves with qualities so subtle that one may be easily mistaken for another. The treatment of *Eriogonum* in *Flora of North America* is an excellent technical reference.

Eriogonum acaule, one of the most desirable of all rock garden plants, is from central and southern Wyoming (also in northwestern Colorado, where it is extremely rare) and forms mats or cushions of tiny upright linear to oblanceolate silvery leaves that might possibly reach half an inch (1.25cm) into the air in an unusually wet summer. The yellow flattened pom-pom flowers lie almost stemless on the cushion, which at its utmost may be eight inches (20cm) wide. One year I decided to move my plant to a "better" location, and that was the end of that. Seed of *E. acaule* is difficult to collect, thus rarely available, and when it is, is priced accordingly.

Eriogonum androsaceum is a condensed mat-former, an inch (2.5cm) or so high by a foot (30 cm) or so wide, closely related to *E. flavum*, with light yellow flowers. The leaves are all basal, elliptic, narrow, green with white-woolly tips. This is a moderately high elevation species from northwestern Montana and southern Alberta but quite growable in a sunny dry location. Seed and plants are rarely offered.

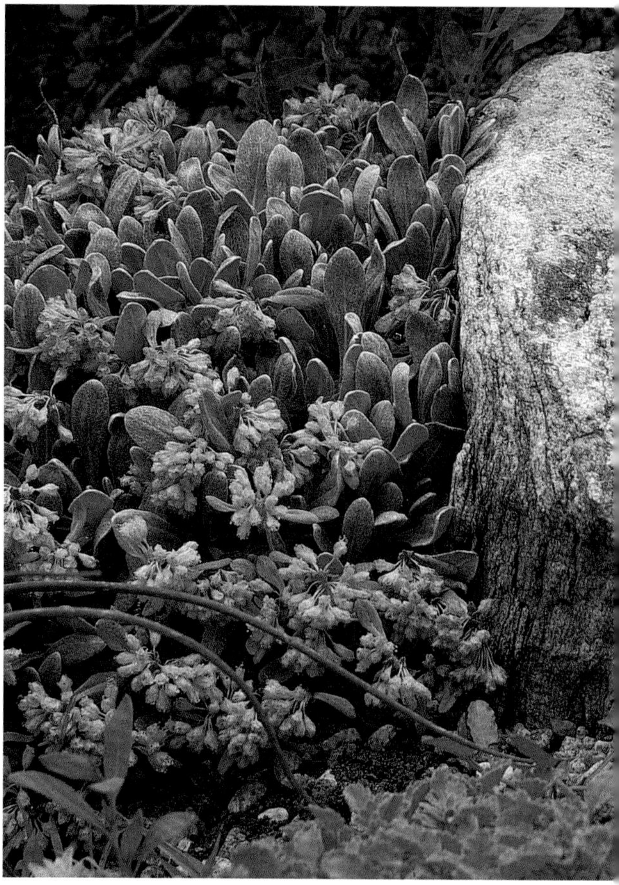

Eriogonum arcuatum var. *xanthum*

Eriogonum arcuatum is the preferred name for the plant we knew as *E. jamesii* (in its varieties *flavescens* and *xanthum*). The differences between the two species strike me as arcane, except that *E. jamesii* tends to be shrubbier and has white or cream-colored flowers. So now, of course, we have two eriogonums to buy instead of one, and this is good.

Eriogonum arcuatum and *E. jamesii* are both plants of the Great Plains, though *E. arcuatum* winds up in eastern Utah and northern Arizona, while *E. jamesii* is also found in New Mexico, Arizona, Texas, and northern Mexico. *Eriogonum arcuatum*, in the varieties *arcuatum* and *xanthum*, are excellent, beautiful cushion plants three inches (7.5 cm) by eight inches (20 cm) with green-woolly narrow or oblanceolate leaves and clusters of yellow flowers. Despite var. *xanthum*'s provenance (it comes from higher elevations in the Rockies), it is an easy one for the dry rock garden.

I almost hesitate to include *Eriogonum aretioides*, an endemic of Garfield County in southern Utah with tiny, white-woolly, oblanceolate wavy leaves and yellow flowers sitting right on the cushion. This fearfully choice eriogonum forms mounds a couple of inches (5 cm) high by maybe a foot (30 cm) wide and grows at higher elevations than one would ordinarily associate with dryland plants, so in theory would require more moisture, but *E. aretioides* does fine in a dry rock garden, particularly on a north-facing exposure. It is probably better suited to a trough. Seed is offered once in a blue moon. *Eriogonum tumulosum* is similar but with white flowers; this one is from eastern Utah (the Uinta Basin) and a few areas in northwestern Colorado. I grew this for a while and then, in a mindless moment, decided to transplant it . . .

Eriogonum bicolor is an attractive mounding shrublet from southeastern Utah, maybe two inches (5cm) high by six inches (15cm) wide, with tiny fuzzy club-shaped leaves and clusters of white or pink flowers veined with purple. *Eriogonum bicolor* is suitable for the driest, most exposed sites imaginable. This one is quite easy from seed, if you can find it.

Eriogonum caespitosum

Eriogonum caespitosum is widespread in dry areas from Wyoming westward. This is very occasionally available from mail-order nurseries, but seed is more or less regularly listed. *Eriogonum caespitosum* is a mat, with green-gray leaves, never more than an inch (2.5cm) tall as I know it, and slowly expanding to an as-yet-unknown width. A mat one to two feet (30 to 60cm) wide does not seem unreasonable. The flowers are yellow, sometimes with a reddish tint, and are on stems barely taller than the plant. This one has to rank among the most accommodating and easily grown of the mat-forming eriogonums; practically perfect in every way, and not so difficult to find as some of the others.

Eriogonum compositum is a beauty from east of the Cascades in Washington and Oregon; this has olive-green lanceolate woolly-tipped leaves on fairly long petioles and forms mounds about six inches (15cm) wide. The fat flowering stems, six inches (15cm) tall, look like healthy dandelions carrying golf-ball-sized clusters of cream-colored flowers (as I know it), though the flowers can be light or bright yellow as well. *Eriogonum compositum* is long-lived and has superior drought resistance; the two varieties in the garden here, var. *compositum* and var. *leianthum*, are similar in appearance (though var. *leianthum* is smaller) and disposition.

Eriogonum corymbosum is a small hemispherical shrub, about two feet (60cm) by three feet (90cm), though it can be smaller, or much larger. This has gray-silver-woolly leaves (less or more so depending on the variety) arranged along the stems, and white or pink flowers (yellow in var. *aureum* and var. *glutinosum*) in cymes, the flowers aging to pink and rust as they age. Resembling nothing so much as a tiny-leafed baby's breath in flower, *E. corymbosum* is native throughout the Intermountain West. In autumn after the flowers have fallen, the chicken-wire appearance formed by the remnants of the flowering stems is most attractive. Plants grow slowly. This is easily one of the all-time great plants of the Intermountain West, but do take into account its eventual size when setting out plants.

Eriogonum douglasii is vaguely similar to *E. caespitosum* but seems to me to be a slightly larger plant, or taller, anyway; my plants are any-

Eriogonum douglasii

where from an inch (2.5 cm) to three inches (7.5 cm) tall, slowly spreading to a foot (30 cm) or more wide. The leaves on one plant are oblanceolate, greenish-woolly, and on the other are more silvery. One plant has clusters of yellow flowers held slightly above the leaves, the other has pinkish red flowers on stems about an inch and a half (3.75 cm) tall. *Eriogonum douglasii*, native to dry parts of the Pacific Northwest (including northern Nevada and California), is another great one for the rock garden and easily grown from seed.

Eriogonum effusum, from the Great Plains, is another small shrub, with gray-woolly oblanceolate to obovate leaves along the stems, though there is great variety in its appearance. The plants are about a foot (30 cm) high; in the garden here the stems tend to something less than upright, with sprays of yellowish flowers. This is another very accommodating eriogonum; I grew my plants from ten-year-old seed collected near the Pawnee Buttes in northern Colorado.

Eriogonum fasciculatum (California buckwheat) did not live long in the garden. This one is possibly only borderline hardy, or this is just a case of brown fingers. *Eriogonum fasciculatum* is a highly variable species with clusters of small, thick, linear to oblanceolate green or grayish leaves along the stems, with white or pink flowers in multiple heads. It can be a huge plant the size of a Volkswagen, or it can be much smaller. This is essentially a warm-desert (Mojave Desert) plant, native to California, Nevada, southwestern Utah, Arizona, and Mexico, but sometimes these warm-desert plants surprise you with their hardiness. I tried var. *polifolium*, hoping it would be smaller, and it turned out to be even smaller than I had imagined. Although come to think of it a few very large specimens would solve any problems you might have trying to figure out what to plant in a rock garden. "It is not," Lester Rowntree wrote, "a striking plant in the garden, where it responds eagerly to a little kindness, although it has its uses in the wild garden. But it is so much a part of chaparral and mesa that it must have found a place in the affections of others besides myself."

Eriogonum flavum is primarily a plant of the Great Plains, but it also ventures into eastern Washington and Oregon, southern British Columbia and Alberta, even Alaska and the Yukon; this has variably oblanceolate leaves, green above, white-woolly beneath, often in rosettes, an inch

(2.5cm) or so high, and eight inches (20cm) or more across. The stems, smothered with yellow flowers in clusters, may be six inches (15cm) tall. Plants or seeds from the Great Plains will be var. *flavum*, plants from Washington and Oregon will probably be var. *piperi*. The differences are minimal enough that any variety will have the same garden effect.

Eriogonum gracilipes, from the White Mountains in California, is another choice dwarf plant, about four inches (10cm) by six inches (15cm), with silvery white-woolly elliptic leaves and white or rose-pink flowers. The rose-colored forms are especially beautiful, and this is what you would expect to find in the trade. Even though this is a high-elevation eriogonum, the White Mountains are not exactly rain-drenched, and this species will perform quite well in a dry site in clay.

Eriogonum heermannii, like *E. fasciculatum*, is a variable species of southern California, Nevada, and Arizona, of potentially the same size as *E. fasciculatum*, and the same hardiness. It probably would do best in a protected location (a location where a shrub the size of a small car would fit in nicely). The linear to spatulate woolly green leaves are again clustered along the stems; the flowers are in single heads of white, yellow, or rose. Variety *humilius*, from the White Mountains, should be tried, as well as var. *argense* from higher elevations in the Mojave Desert. Once the cultivation of this and *E. fasciculatum* have been mastered in cold gardens, then possibly *E. giganteum*, which is, obviously, even bigger, could be tried.

Eriogonum heracleoides is found more or less throughout the Intermountain West; this is a mat-former with more or less oblanceolate gray-green leaves, generally woolly beneath, and flowering stems to six inches (15cm), bearing white, or sometimes yellow flowers. These stems have a funny little whorl of bracts, which helps to distinguish this species, though distinctions like this may cause most gardeners' eyes to glaze over. A dwarf form, *E. heracleoides* var. *minus*, hails from eastern Washington, and makes a small rosette of grayish leaves with stems about three inches (7.5cm) high; this is the variety of choice for a rock garden filled with small treasures, or for a trough.

Eriogonum incanum, from high elevations in the Sierra Nevada, and adjacent Oregon, is a white-woolly thing of the kind whose existence is noted wistfully or even tearfully by alpine garden writers staring out the window at the winter rain. Clay mentioned it; Lester Rowntree, in her delightful book *Hardy Californians*, did not, but by her own admittance her cool, foggy garden on the California coast was not an ideal place for a lot of woolly-leafed plants. As I write this, in mid-December, the idea of rain sounds so pleasant and so impossible that it's difficult to persuade me that a sunny, dry, windy, and often revoltingly cold winter is a justifiable exchange for being able to grow things like *E. incanum* without too much trouble. Whatever. *Eriogonum incanum* is a mat, to eight inches (20cm) tall, and twice as wide, with woolly white, or sometimes yellowish, elliptic leaves, with yellow or red flowers. I like the red best.

Eriogonum jamesii (antelope sage), as we now know, if we were reading alphabetically, has been stripped of the yellow-flowered varieties we knew as *E. jamesii* var. *flavescens*, and is now the white-flowered eriogonum of the Great Plains with a distinct tendency to shrubbiness. (Well, it was always the white-flowered eriogonum; the relationship of names to plants has been clarified.) This is a larger plant than *E. arcuatum*, two to eight inches (5 to 20cm) tall to a yard (90cm) or more wide—possibly too large for an average-sized rock garden unless you have already found and planted everything you want and still have empty space to fill.

Eriogonum kennedyi is one of those plants that takes a rock gardener's breath away. This mid- to high-altitude Californian (though it also appears in western Nevada) has densely clustered, tiny, more or less elliptic gray-woolly leaves, no more than half an inch (1.25cm) long in the largest-leafed varieties, and heads of white or rose-colored flowers. A couple of varieties have appeared in the seedlists (notably Northwest Native Seed); these are easily grown from seed and easy to grow, especially in troughs. *Eriogonum kennedyi* var. *alpigenum*, the most condensed of all, is found at the highest elevations, though var. *kennedyi* is not much larger. *Eriogonum kennedyi* var. *austromontanum* is slightly larger and grows at lower, drier elevations; it too is quite amenable to cultivation. Variety *purpusii*, from middle elevations mostly in Inyo County, California, and adjacent Nevada, has white-woolly leaves; this one I would like to try.

Eriogonum lobbii has basal rosettes of round, woolly leaves forming a mound six inches (15cm) tall and twice as wide, though sometimes much smaller, with stems about six inches (15cm) long, usually prostrate (flopping in a circle around the basal leaves), and more or less round clusters of white flowers, aging to rose. An ultra-large rosetted form from western Nevada, *E. lobbii* var. *robustum* (*E. robustum*), has white-woolly leaves and pale yellow flowers.

Eriogonum mancum is another classic rock garden plant, a beautiful thing with silver-woolly obovate basal leaves forming a mound, or mat, about two inches (5 cm) tall, and four to six inches (10 to 15 cm) wide, with flowering stems about four inches (10 cm) tall. The flowers are in clusters of rounded heads, cream-colored aging to raspberry, a spectacular effect in such a miniature. The leaves are, unfortunately, especially susceptible to excessive summer humidity. *Eriogonum mancum* is native to middle altitudes in western Montana, and adjacent areas of Idaho and Wyoming.

Eriogonum niveum, a plant of the dry areas of the Pacific Northwest, is one of the best of the larger eriogonums, silvery whitish gray-woolly, with usually erect stems to eight inches (20 cm), maybe more, and growing about twice as wide. Though *E. niveum* can have basal leaves, usually these are arranged along the stem, and are more or less lanceolate; the stems have leafy bracts at the nodes. The inflorescence is a series of

Eriogonum mancum

cymes arranged along the nodes, with white, sometimes tinged with red, flowers. The flowers hardly matter. The whole plant is so perfectly silver and woolly, it makes a beautiful contrast with blue acantholimons and dwarf forms of ponderosa pine, among other things.

Though Ira Gabrielson rated *Eriogonum nudum* as the "outstanding success" in his garden, I find this one unattractive. The long-petioled, ugly (in an indefinable way) leaves are obovate, or elliptic, greenish, woolly beneath, in rosettes or arranged on the stems for a short distance. The flowering stems are bare (hence the *nudum*), with tiny clusters of white, yellow, or red flowers. Common in California, also found in Oregon and Washington. There are about a dozen varieties, and it's possible I acquired the hideous one. (I picked up the plant despite the reaction of another gardening friend, who put the plant down as quickly as he picked it up.) Gabrielson said it was biennial or short-lived; mine died after a few years of trying to get rid of it through buyer's remorse.

Eriogonum ovalifolium is a variable species, found throughout western North America in dry areas, including higher elevations. This has, unbelievable as it may seem, oval leaves (though their shape can vary), generally woolly, velvety, and silver or gray, sometimes with brownish margins that give the plants a beautiful silver and olive-brown effect, which is most strongly pronounced in winter. *Eriogonum ovalifolium* is a cushion or mat plant, rarely taller than an inch (2.5 cm) high, sometimes forming mats a foot and a half (45 cm) wide, though in the garden these are usually smaller. The pom-pom flowers may be white, yellow, pink, rose, or even (gasp) purple.

There are about a dozen varieties of *Eriogonum ovalifolium*. All are worth acquiring: this, in case the preceding half-hearted attempts at describing one of the most beautiful species of *Eriogonum* didn't make it clear, is one of North America's finest rock garden plants. Two varieties in particular deserve attention; both are available from seed collectors. *Eriogonum ovalifolium* var. *depressum*, from Alberta through eastern Oregon, is a more greenish-leafed, somewhat less woolly, congested mat; *E. ovalifolium* var. *nivale*, from the Sierras and mountains in Nevada, is even more condensed, with silver leaves, oval and slightly wavy, sitting right on the ground. Both are quite growable in the rock garden, or troughs, and are as good as it gets.

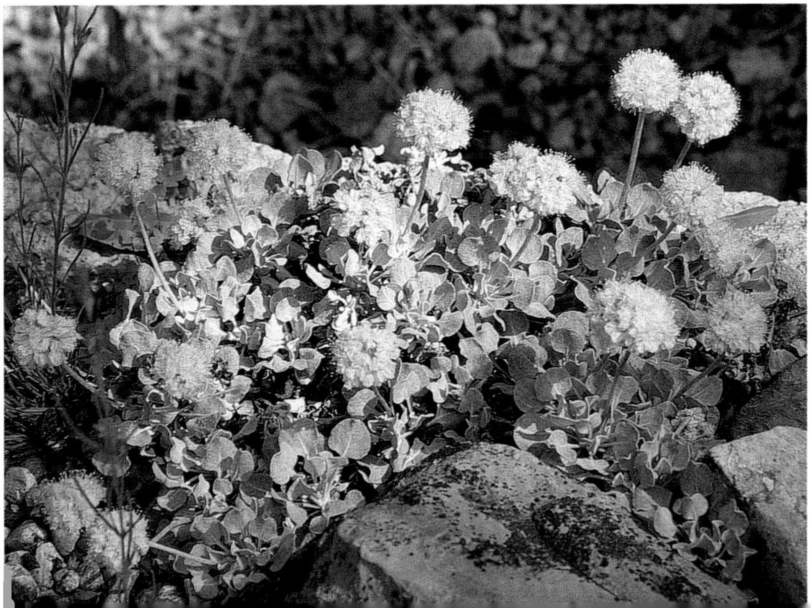

[above left] *Eriogonum ovalifolium*

[above] *Eriogonum ovalifolium* var. *depressum*

[left] Hybrid between *Eriogonum ovalifolium* var. *nivale* and *E. o.* var. *depressum*

Eriogonum panguicense, from Utah, is probably only of interest to gardeners wanting new plants for their troughs. This is a tiny one, at least in the variety I know, var. *alpestre*, and even though this is a higher-elevation plant it does quite well at the top of our dry rock garden, where it's barely noticeable. *Eriogonum panguicense* has tiny, green, linear leaves (the species has a rather wide spectrum of leaf shape in the wild), basally and along the stem, with small puffs of flowers, white with red anthers.

Eriogonum pauciflorum (*E. multiceps*) is a common mat-forming plant, found throughout the Great Plains, including Saskatchewan and Manitoba. A variable species, the plants you are likely to get from nurseries or seedlists will be a mat about an inch (2.5cm) tall with gray, linear to spatulate or oblanceolate leaves eventually widening, if the plant doesn't die, to almost a foot (30cm) across. The flowering stems are about four inches (10cm) tall with heads of white, yellow, or pink flowers. "It has a cleanness of foliage," wrote Barr, referring to what he called *E. depauperatum*, "and a certain squat charm in keeping with its favorite badland habitat—hardpan littered with gravel and shared with a few prickly pears." Variety *gnaphalodes* is especially woolly and more densely compressed; this is one to look for.

A natural hybrid between *Eriogonum pauciflorum* and *E. effusum*, *E.* ×*nebraskense*, is found in western Nebraska, southern Wyoming, and northern Colorado; this has white flowers on branching stems. (The plant once known as *E. multiceps* is sometimes referred to as *E. pauciflorum* var. *nebraskense*, but this latter combination is actually our hybrid.)

Eriogonum saxatile, from California and parts of Nevada, is a superb foliage plant with large basal rosettes of long-petioled, large (an inch, 2.5cm, wide), round to elliptic, silver-white-woolly leaves four inches (10cm) high (the floras suggest that this plant can get much larger, but mine never did) and as wide (it can get much wider in real life). The white or yellow flowers are borne on stems a foot (30cm) tall, though you grow this for the leaves. My plants did not live very long, possibly because of my insufficiently Californian climate, but *E. saxatile* is so easy from seed it can be grown as an annual.

Eriogonum shockleyi is yet another choice cushion plant, found throughout the Intermountain region, a tightly congested bunch of gray or slightly green oblanceolate to elliptic woolly leaves, maybe an inch (2.5 cm) tall, growing to a foot (30 cm) or so wide under perfect conditions, but more often getting smaller and smaller until it disappears, suffering death from excessive summer humidity, even in Denver. *Eriogonum shockleyi* is not terribly difficult to grow from seed and is perhaps best suited to a dry trough, and summers with high temperatures and little rainfall. Sprinkling a little Bordeaux mixture on the leaves seems to help combat the fungus that attacks the leaves.

Eriogonum siskiyouense is a mat-former, with greenish yellow, more or less round leaves, woolly beneath, an inch (2.5 cm) high by half a yard (45 cm) wide, according to descriptions of the plant in the various floras. In my troughs, after seven years, the plants can be completely covered by the palm of my hand. The flowers are the usual yellow in solitary round heads, but I've never seen them. *Eriogonum siskiyouense* is native to a small area of northern California, growing at moderately high elevations in serpentine. It could very well be that the soil mix in my trough lacks the necessary magnesium provided by serpentine. I should pour some milk of magnesia over the plants. Easy from seed, but after that, slow as molasses in January.

Eriogonum soredium is *the* eriogonum to serious rock gardeners, though forms of *E. kennedyi* rival it in compactness. Native to a small area in Beaver County, Utah, at moderate elevations, *E. soredium* is a tightly congested cushion of white-woolly narrow, elliptic leaves so small that the plant, when young, looks like a silver rock. The cushion may be as tall as an eighth of an inch (3 mm), spreading to almost a foot (30 cm). The white flowers sit on the cushion. This is a rare plant in the wild, but even rarer in cultivation, possibly because it seems to resent violently any summer humidity; I lost my plants during a horrible bout of thirty percent humidity one summer, though, in truth, you almost needed a microscope to see them when they were alive. Probably for hopelessly fanatical rock gardeners only, and almost definitely only for those living in dry climates.

Eriogonum sphaerocephalum is a small shrub native to much of the Intermountain region, growing in sagebrush. It can supposedly be over a foot (30 cm) tall by two feet (60 cm) wide; I've never seen it in the wild.

If these measurements are correct, the plants must be thousands of years old. My plant, which is about fifteen years old, is a neat shrub six inches (15cm) high by eight inches (20cm) wide. It looks dead for most of the year. Then in late spring the narrow, oblanceolate green leaves appear on the stems, and later, clusters of yellow or light yellow flowers appear from short stems arising at the nodes of this year's branches. A first-rate little plant for very dry situations.

Eriogonum strictum is a mat-former with round green leaves, about an inch (2.5cm) tall and eight inches (20cm) wide (in the garden, anyway). The flowering stems are four to five inches (10 to 12.5cm) tall with yellow, white, rose, or purple flowers in cymes. Native to northern California and eastern Oregon and Washington to Montana. Two varieties in particular should attract our attention: var. *proliferum*, with elliptic leaves and flowers of yellow, white, rose, or purple, and var. *greenei*, with densely white-woolly leaves and white flowers. Variety *greenei* is quite close to *E. ovalifolium*, and equally desirable. Both varieties are offered as seed from time to time.

Eriogonum thymoides, native to a few scattered areas in the dry parts of the Pacific Northwest, is a beautiful little shrub, maybe six inches (15cm) tall by a foot (30cm) wide, with linear gray leaves, tiny and thyme-like (hence the specific epithet), clustered on the stems, and white or yellow flowers aging to rose-pink on short stems. *Eriogonum thymoides* is fairly easy from seed, though the plants grow infinitesimally slowly in cultivation.

Eriogonum umbellatum (sulfur flower) is probably the most familiar of eriogonums, found throughout the west. Generally this species has green elliptic or oblanceolate leaves on short spreading stems, with umbels of yellow flowers on stems, without leaf-like bracts, six inches (15cm) tall. There are over forty varieties; all are worth growing. The most common is var. *umbellatum*, with the characteristics just described. Variety *bahiiforme* (sometimes spelled "bahiaeforme"), from the coastal ranges of California, has densely woolly leaves with yellow flowers aging to orange; var. *hausknechtii* (middle elevations in the Cascades, Oregon and Washington) has olive-green elliptic leaves clustered in tight rosettes and yellow flowers; var. *humistratum* (northern California, on serpentine) has elliptic leaves covered with white wool; and var. *speciosum* is

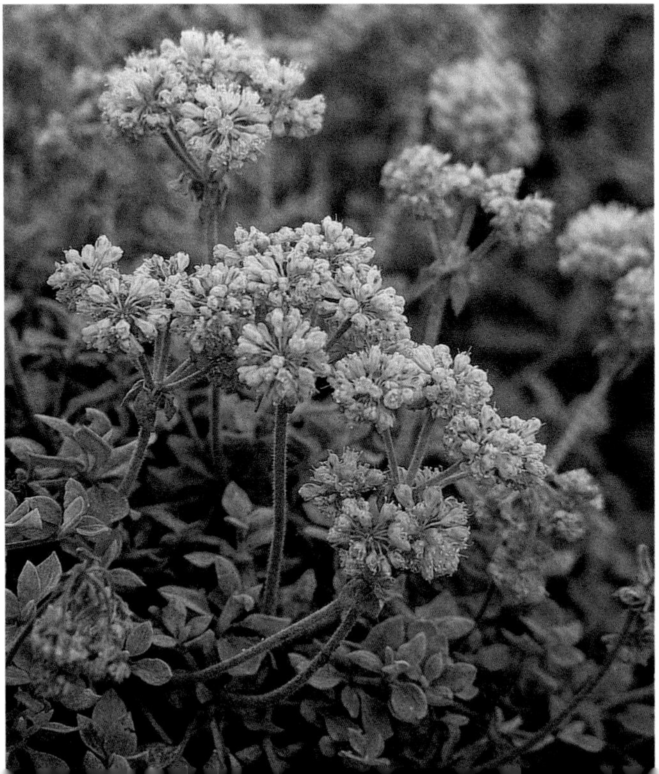

[above] *Eriogonum sphaerocephalum*

[left] *Eriogonum strictum* var. *proliferum*

a shrub with gray-green-woolly leaves growing two feet (60cm) or more high by as much or more wide. *Eriogonum umbellatum* var. *speciosum* is another serpentine plant from fairly low elevations in California, but has proved hardy in my garden—so far.

Eriogonum wrightii (bastard-sage) is widely distributed from Texas and Mexico west to California and Nevada. Plants in my garden resemble a looser form of *E. kennedyi* while still in the rosette stage, a cluster of small silver-gray-woolly leaves, but when they bloom the white flowers, aging to pink, are in sprays on foot-long (30cm) stems. This could be var. *subscaposum* (I lost the label). It behaves like a biennial in the garden, flowering and then leaving hundreds of seedlings everywhere, which can be either desirable or undesirable, depending on your point of view. Definitely an easy one to grow from seed.

Eriophyllum. A genus of woolly-leafed (the generic name means exactly that) daisies, most of which are Californian annuals.

Eriophyllum lanatum (Oregon sunshine) is an extra-woolly, variable species with handsome, usually green pinnatifid leaves and profuse woolly yellow daisies borne most of the summer on stems about eight inches (20cm) tall (it might get much larger in an irrigated garden). I found this difficult to get started the first time; the second time, after ample watering to get it going for the first few months, it took off and never looked back, until carried off by the drought of 2002. The several varieties have essentially the same effect in the garden.

Eritrichium. A genus in the borage family with a few weedy annuals and a half-dozen or so (depending on which authority you consult) woolly-haired (a translation of the generic name) cushion plants with sky-blue flowers whose existence causes a noticeable increase in the pulse of most rock gardeners. Just mentioning the name will cause some rock gardeners to faint dead away. Farrer devotes several eloquent, worshipful, and ultimately elegiac pages to *Eritrichium nanum*, the "King of the Alps" (even though the generic name is in the neuter gender); apparently the cultivation of these little cushions causes problems in climates where it rains in winter, or where summer humidity is too high. The North American version of this, *E. aretioides* (*E. nanum* var. *aretioides*,

[above] *Eriogonum umbellatum*

[left] *Eriogonum umbellatum* var. *humistratum*

Eritrichium howardii

E. elongatum) is said to be easier in cultivation, yet still hopeless. Rock gardeners have to resort to all sorts of machinations in order to get the things to grow, let alone flower, and even then, the wailing can be heard halfway across the planet.

And yet . . . these plants are not particularly difficult to grow here. But they do require plenty of summer irrigation, and so remain outside the scope of this book. One species, native to dry limestone hills in northwestern Wyoming and Montana, is *Eritrichium howardii* (which Farrer confused with *E. aretioides*). This is a tiny (less than an inch, 2.5cm, high) cushion with silvery woolly oblanceolate leaves, and clusters of sky-blue flowers, emerging from red buds, in June. The plant is so small it probably should be grown in a trough (which is where it is in the garden here) rather than in the rock garden. *Eritrichium howardii* does quite well in full sun, with limited water; excessive humidity (over thirty percent) in summer may cause fungus to develop on the leaves, and then, even here, the wailing will begin.

Gilia. Members of the phlox family mostly native to western North America, and mostly annuals. Because of my arbitrary nature, you'll have to look in the section on annuals for the annual gilias, but the larger gilias are discussed here, even though they also look good in a garden of plants generally too tall for the rock garden.

Some of the species here with salverform, uniformly colored flowers have been placed in the genus *Ipomopsis*, but, remembering what was said about plant names earlier, not all botanists accept this, so with any luck you won't be pummeled by those who insist that proposed name changes are the accepted ones. Beside, typing *Ipomopsis* over and over again is too much work.

The plants are grown from seed, sown under lights (I buy seed, give it to a skilled professional propagator, and take my cut from a selection of healthy plants in spring), though plants of *Gilia aggregata* are sometimes available in nurseries. Seed can be saved as soon as the flowering stems dry; I collect the stems and jam them, seedheads down, into a paper bag, crush the bag lightly (this is instead of crushing each of the hundreds of dried seedpods, each in turn), shake it, and the seed falls to the bottom, along with some chaff, which is inconsequential. Then I scatter some of the seed where I want plants, and save some for sowing in pots.

Gilias will take considerable drought but, because they tend to bloom after midsummer, are even happier with ample moisture. *Gilia rubra* (standing cypress), a gorgeous red-flowered biennial from further east than our region (Oklahoma and Texas and throughout the southeast), will reseed happily in a dry garden but really requires ample summer rainfall to avoid a drought-induced fungus and stunted growth. Monsoonal moisture in August may ameliorate this condition somewhat and help the plants to bloom, but regular summer rainfall or irrigation makes for happier plants.

Gilia aggregata (skyrocket), common throughout the west from Mexico to British Columbia and a favorite with hummingbirds, is a tallish plant, to two feet (60cm) or more during wet years; it forms rosettes of semi-fernlike pinnatifid green leaves the first year, then sends up one or several stems with bunches of long-tubed, funnel-shaped flowers with flaring stars on the ends (hence the common name). White forms are also known; these are just as beautiful. A form with larger, pink flowers is sometimes called var. *macrosiphon*, sometimes a species in its own right, *Gilia tenuituba* (and some botanists think these aren't the same).

Gilia aggregata, like some of the others, can be a biennial or short-lived perennial; the rule seems to be (not that nature has rules, which is why I say "seems to be") that during exceptionally wet years plants in flower are able to produce enough energy to flower again the next year; otherwise, the plants die after flowering (this is better than dying before flowering, anyway). Save the seed.

As is the case with so many other genera, *Gilia* has a number of dwarf species suitable for the rock garden, and in *G. caespitosa* we have another superior, aristocratic rock garden plant. *Gilia caespitosa* is found in just two areas in south-central Utah. This taprooted plant has ultra-sticky oblanceolate leaves clustered together in a tight cushion about half an inch (1.25cm) high and a couple of inches (5cm) wide, with pinkish red

Gilia caespitosa

tubular flowers on stems about four inches (10 cm) tall. Seed is rarely available, and germinates reluctantly. (I used the outdoor method.)

Gilia congesta, found from Nebraska to central Oregon, is a widely variable species but identifiable by the capitate (ball-shaped) cluster of flowers at the end of the stems. Though the other varieties are okay, the one we want is var. *montana*, from areas east of the Cascades in Oregon and east of the Sierra Nevada in California. This is an alpine or subalpine plant but is amenable to cultivation on the north side of a dry rock garden; it has three-pointed lobed leaves forming a lax mat, with white flowers on stems about three inches (7.5 cm) tall (it might get taller in a watered rock garden). I wouldn't go so far as to recommend *Ipomopsis* (I've never seen it called *Gilia*) *globularis*, a rare native of alpine tundra in Colorado with linear leaves and heads of heavily scented, woolly pale blue flowers, for the dry garden, though it might work; it is perfectly growable in a watered trough.

Gilia macombii, from northern Mexico and southern Arizona, is somewhat similar in appearance to *G. aggregata*, though its multiple stems are shorter (to one foot, 30 cm), on a wider plant, sometimes spreading to a foot and a half (45 cm). *Gilia macombii* forms first-year rosettes, larger and more sprawling than those of *G. aggregata*, of pinnatifid blue-green leaves, slightly woolly, and ravishingly beautiful during winter. The next summer, the plant bears clusters of light blue, inch-long (2.5 cm) flowers, and then it gives up. *Gilia macombii* is easy from seed, so be sure to save it.

Gilia rigidula (blue bowls), of dry areas from southwestern Kansas, south into west Texas and Mexico, is a smallish (maybe eight by eight inches, 20 by 20 cm), branching, almost shrubby plant with narrow pine-needle leaves and beautiful, bright blue or purple-blue flowers. This is one species that remains a gilia when the genus is split up, though the rotate (meaning the petals appeared united in the shape of a flat wheel) flower prompts some to call it *Giliastrum*; some botanists also divide the species into two varieties, one of which, var. *acerosa*, is more compact and perfect for the rock garden. It is not incredibly easy from seed.

Gilia spicata is a plant of the Great Plains, its range reaching west into Idaho; as the specific name suggests, this is a spiky thing to a little more than a foot (30 cm) tall with long, gangly linear leaves, sometimes with two or three pointed at the ends, and white or cream-colored flowers clustered around the top of the stem. Not in the top flight of gilias but still worth growing; var. *orchidacea*, really more of an alpine or subalpine plant with slightly larger flowers in a more rounded head, is the form usually offered as seed.

A dwarf relative of *Gilia spicata* from Utah is *G. tridactyla*; this is vaguely similar in appearance to *G. congesta* var. *montana*, with pretty much the same garden effect.

Gilia stenothyrsa is a biennial from the Uinta Basin in Utah, with sticky pinnatifid leaves on a single stem to two feet (60cm). The half-inch-long (1.25cm) white flowers are arranged along the stem in a virgate (wand-like) inflorescence. This is one that looks better in groups than singly; probably better in a wild garden than a rock garden.

Gilia subnuda, despite a weedy-looking rosette—a rosette that has been ripped triumphantly out of the garden more than once during weeding sprees—of oblanceolate, lightly toothed green leaves, is one of the best. This is, in its second year, a single or sometimes multi-stemmed plant to two feet (60cm), branching halfway and exploding into a profusion of red (or some shade of it) tubular, salverform flowers about a half-inch (1.25cm) long and wide. Native to Utah, the Four Corners area, and other parts of northern Arizona. This one is obviously a hummingbird magnet and because of its garish showiness is more often offered as seed than some of the others. I find seed slightly recalcitrant when it comes to germination, but it could just be me.

Gilia thurberi, from northern Mexico and southern Arizona and New Mexico, has the same ferny filigree foliage on multi-stemmed plants about a foot (30cm) tall, at least as I know it in the garden, but with large, fat flowers of the most gorgeous wine-purple imaginable. I'm not sure this one is perennial, since it seems to play the die-right-after-it flowers game like many of the others, but this is easily one of my favorite plants. This is the latest blooming of all, sometimes not even starting until September, and really glorious after a wet summer. Easy from seed.

Gutierrezia (snakeweed). Members of the daisy family found throughout the Great Plains and Intermountain region. The most common species offered is *Gutierrezia sarothrae*, a more or less shrubby plant with stems carrying linear green leaves and heads of tiny yellow flowers, spread by overgrazing in the wild. A plant utterly devoid of charm and garden value, as much of a weed in the garden as it is in the wild. The Utah endemic, *G. petradoria*, with much larger flowers, looks at least slightly promising. There are other species, but I don't care.

Haplopappus. "There are no species of *Haplopappus*," a botanist recently told me rather sternly, "native to North America." Except in this book. Even though I may already have provoked the wrath of taxonomists in brushing aside *Ipomopsis* so lightly, the segregation of species formerly described as *Haplopappus* puts a few yellow-flowered species into *Machaeranthera*, a genus of daisies with mostly white-flowered plants; the inclusion of, say, *Haplopappus spinulosus* into *Machaeranthera* is almost always accompanied by a note suggesting that this species really belongs somewhere else, as though *Machaeranthera* were a sort of halfway house for species waiting for a suitable genus. Some of the herbaceous species are now described (by some) as *Stenotus* (Nuttall's name, but not the first he used for these plants), others as *Tonestus* (an anagram of *Stenotus* . . .), some as *Macronema*, some as *Chrysothamnus*. It's enough to make anyone give up completely.

Back to rock gardening. A number of these yellow-flowered daisies are well suited to the dry rock garden (I am omitting the otherwise desirable *Haplopappus apargioides* and *H. lyallii*; these are alpine or subalpine plants that I've never tried in the dry garden). The plants are easy to grow from seed, and easy to grow in the garden, generally blooming from mid-May to mid-July.

Haplopappus acaulis (*Stenotus acaulis*) is found throughout the Intermountain area and on the Great Plains from Colorado to Saskatchewan. This is a cushion plant with upright, oblanceolate, sandpaper-rough inch-long (2.5cm) leaves clustered at the woody base, with flowering stems to almost six inches (15cm). This is one of the best.

Haplopappus armerioides (*Stenotus armerioides*) is a mat-forming plant of the Great Plains, also found in Utah and Arizona, with narrowly oblanceolate upright leaves, three inches (7.5cm) long, with stems to six inches (15cm). A form found in eastern Utah, with very narrowly linear leaves, is var. *gramineus*; both of these are desirable.

Haplopappus lanuginosus (*Stenotus lanuginosus*) has more or less woolly, upright, narrowly oblanceolate leaves about four inches (10 cm) long, with flowering stems to eight inches (20 cm), though usually shorter when grown dry. Native to dry areas from northern California to eastern Washington, and western Montana.

Haplopappus spinulosus (*Machaeranthera pinnatifida*) is a larger plant, widespread throughout the west (Alberta and Saskatchewan to northern Mexico); this has tiny bristly green leaves on multiple stems (very different from the other species listed here) a foot (30 cm) tall, on a plant about as wide, the stems carrying a massive profusion of golden daisies in late summer. The combination of bristles, wiry stems, and seedheads makes this an incredibly dusty, prickly thing to deadhead in late winter; I use gloves and hold my breath.

Haplopappus stenophyllus (*Stenotus stenophyllus*), from northern Nevada and California to Idaho and Washington, has linear, sticky, sandpaper-rough green leaves, half an inch (1.25 cm) long, clustered around the bases of the flowering stems for an inch (2.5 cm) or so. The flowering stems themselves are four inches (10 cm) tall.

Hedeoma (pennyroyal). The hedeomas are tiny-flowered plants with aromatic leaves, mostly native to the southwestern United States and Mexico, not exactly in the first rank of rock garden plants but still worth growing. *Hedeoma drummondii*, native throughout the Great Plains and Intermountain West, is sometimes offered in the trade; it is more or less perennial, with lavender or pink flowers, growing to eight inches (20 cm) high and wide. This is one to tuck away here and there in the rock garden just so you can brush against its leaves.

Heterotheca. A genus of yellow daisies formerly known as *Chrysopsis*. *Heterotheca jonesii* (from southwestern Utah), which has only recently gained a place in rock gardening, is a compact mound with tiny, silver, quarter-inch-long (6 mm) oblanceolate leaves, slowly but surely widening to at least a foot (30 cm) or more. Tiny yellow daises sit almost on top of the plant, rarely producing viable seed, but their tiny dried seedheads are attractive enough. Some nurseries carry this plant; how they get seed to germinate is beyond me.

Heterotheca villosa is a ubiquitous weedy-looking autumn-flowering plant of the Great Plains, highly variable in appearance (hence the ridiculous profusion of synonyms by Green and Rydberg), which can safely be dismissed as a plant not to be brought into the garden. Variety *hispida* (var. *minor*), sometimes referred to as a species in its own right, is somewhat more elegant, with stiffer, hairy stems and showier flowers; this is a plant of the Intermountain region as well as northern parts of the Great Plains.

Heuchera (alum root, coralbells). I wonder if I should include these, members of the saxifrage family with a penchant for growing on damp cliffs or other places where moisture is not too far away. But so many of our plants rely on moisture found deep beneath otherwise bone-dry soil. There are a few species that, while they have an obvious preference for wetter conditions, will not actually die during periods of prolonged drought. The common hybrids involving the Mexican monsoonal species *Heuchera sanguinea*, require, as might be expected, more summer moisture.

These heucheras are also a far, far cry away from the cultivars popular today, with leaves of every possible color. All are easy from seed, sown outdoors in winter.

Heuchera pulchella is a tiny thing, to about four inches (10cm) in flower, with rose-pink flowers in a one-sided (secund) inflorescence. Native to the Sandia Mountains in New Mexico. *Heuchera pulchella* has formed an ever-widening mat in the garden here, the little, half-inch-wide (1.25cm) scalloped leaves staying green, or almost so, on a bed of last year's brown leaves. This has survived despite considerable neglect by the gardener.

Heuchera rubescens is found throughout the Intermountain West, California, Texas, and northern Mexico. This is a highly variable species, in its dwarf forms not much different, visually, from *H. pulchella*; my impression is that the leaves on *H. rubescens* are more finely serrated than those of *H. pulchella*. 'Troy Boy', a dwarf selection made by Roy Davidson, is a lovely thing.

Horkelia. A moderately exciting genus in the rose family, with sticky, resin-scented foliage, mostly native to California. Worth trying is *Horkelia hispidula* from the White Mountains on the California-Nevada border. This has tiny, gray cylindrical leaves with clusters of white strawberry flowers on eight-inch (20 cm) stems. Other species are worth trying, but neither plants nor seed is commonly available.

Hymenoxys. The plants we used to know as species of *Hymenoxys* (e.g., *H. grandiflora*, old man of the mountain, which prefers alpine treatment in a trough) or *Actinella* are now in *Picradenia*, *Rydbergia*, and *Tetraneuris*. So, naturally, I'll call them *Hymenoxys*. Even though Farrer dismissed them ("a little race of not very interesting American Composites with golden flowers"), some are well worth growing.

Hymenoxys acaulis (*Tetraneuris acaulis*) is found scattered throughout the Great Plains and Intermountain region. Clusters of erect, narrowly linear to narrowly oblanceolate green, sometimes silky gray-green, leaves arise from a woody base wrapped in wool. The leaves are upright, anywhere from an inch (2.5 cm) to four inches (10 cm) long, depending on the variety, of which there are several. Most common in the trade is var. *acaulis*; I have had this one growing happily in dry clay soil for almost twenty years. Variety *caespitosa* is hairier; this one, with its yellow flowers, has been brightening a trough here for almost the same amount of time. Variety *arizonica* is larger, var. *epunctata* is less spotted (admittedly a rather trivial feature to anyone but a collector). Another variety, var. *nana*, from the San Rafael Swell in east-central Utah, has almost stemless flowers on a tiny cushion; this sounds wonderful, but I haven't grown it. *Hymenoxys torreyana* is similar to *H. acaulis* var. *acaulis*, but somewhat less refined.

Hymenoxys argentea (*Tetraneuris argentea*), found from New Mexico and Colorado west to Utah and Arizona, is a taller plant, with foot-tall (30 cm) stems. This has the same woolly base as *H. acaulis*—upright, narrowly oblanceolate, silvery silky-hairy leaves—and some stems on the leaves. *Hymenoxys argentea* is probably better in a perennial border with other dryland plants.

Hymenoxys richardsonii (*Picradenia richardsonii*), widespread throughout the Great Plains, also in Arizona and Utah, is another species with a white-woolly base, with spare clusters of linear leaves at the base, and along the stems, to a foot (30 cm) tall. This belongs, I think, in a wild garden. *Hymenoxys richardsonii* (Colorado rubber plant) was the

Hymenoxys acaulis var. *acaulis*

subject of some interest at the turn of the last century for the potential of extracting the latex in the roots, hence the common name.

Hymenoxys scaposa (*Tetraneuris scaposa*), a plant of the Great Plains, has green narrowly linear, usually woolly leaves clustered at the base of the stems. The flowering stems are six inches (15cm) tall, maybe much taller in wetter years or in an irrigated garden. For Barr, *H. scaposa* was "a valued garden plant"; for me, its tendency to seed everywhere makes it much less attractive than some other plants.

Hymenoxys subintegra (*Picradenia helenioides*) is a biennial from northern Arizona grown in the rock garden for its first-year rosette of silvery, narrow leaves, the whole thing about three inches (7.5cm) tall and twice as wide. It should be ripped out at the end of the first year. The next year, the flowering stem starts to elongate into a hideous monstros-

Hymenoxys scaposa

ity that turns yellowish and falls over when it reaches a foot (30 cm), the clusters of yellow daisies this time just adding to the offense committed in the garden.

Iris. The majority of irises native to North America taunt us from beyond the Sierra Nevada and the Cascades; these are the Pacific Coast irises, of course, in section Californicae. A few of these, including *Iris douglasiana*, *I. innominata*, *I. tenax*, are amenable to cultivation here but are definitely not evergreen in winter and not tolerant of summer drought; they're grown like Siberian irises, with summer watering.

More suitable to cultivation in the dry garden are the Middle Eastern irises in section Oncocyclus, but these are practically impossible to find as the iris market is not exactly geared toward gardeners living in climates where rain is relatively rare. (Some people like the arilbreds, hybrids between oncocyclus and other bearded irises.)

Back to earth now, the most widely distributed iris in North America is *Iris missouriensis*, an incredibly elegant plant with gray-green narrow leaves and classic iris flowers in pale lavender, light blue, or sometimes white. The plants, as I know them, grow about ten inches (25cm) tall.

Iris missouriensis commonly grows in seasonally wet areas; the fens in South Park in Colorado are filled with irises in July. I collected seed some years ago (this one, unlike some others, is easy from seed) and also dug up a plant from the middle of a dirt road. (I don't dig up plants in the wild, but I felt sorry for this one and made an exception.) Today the plants are thriving with minimal care. Barr said some of his irises seeded into his unwatered gumbo clay, so I feel safe in recommending *I. missouriensis* for the dry garden, though it may be happier with more moisture.

Lepidium (peppergrass). A genus of annuals and perennials in the mustard family of no interest to the rock gardeners (or anyone else), but with one species showing the characteristic expression of adaptation to severe climates and habitats. *Lepidium nanum* is a tightly congested cushion of green, or gray-green, leaves with tiny yellow flowers held a half-inch (1.25cm) or so above the surface of what really looks like an inch-tall (2.5cm) green rock. The cushion slowly expands to four inches (10cm) or so. Native to mountains of central Nevada, and, some say, western Utah; North America's answer to *Draba rigida* and *Arenaria tetraquetra* var. *granatensis*. Semi-easy from seed.

Leptodactylon (prickly phlox). Phlox relatives with a dinosaur name meaning "narrow finger," a reference to the clusters of needle-like leaves arranged on the stem. The five-petaled flowers, usually white or cream-colored, have caused even botanists to confuse these with phloxes. Flowering time is early spring, for the hardy ones.

Leptodactylon caespitosum (*Linanthus caespitosus*) is a cushion plant, maybe an inch (2.5cm) tall by a foot or two (30 to 60cm) wide, native to clay or shale in Utah, Wyoming, and Nebraska. I seem to recall Barr making a disparaging comment about this plant somewhere. This is a plant reeking of promise to the rock gardener, until it opens its almost infinitesimally small flowers. Nature does occasionally disappoint.

Leptodactylon californicum is the ultimate prickly phlox, growing to three feet (90 cm), with pink flowers, but unfortunately it insists on growing in the coastal counties of California from about Santa Barbara southward (as well as Baja California unless you want to call this one *L. veatchii*). It could be that this plant only pretends not to be hardy to Arctic temperatures by growing where it does, but I wouldn't count on it. Seed is occasionally offered for those willing to experiment, as well as for real Californians, of course.

Leptodactylon pungens (*Linanthus pungens*) is a subshrub or shrub found throughout the west, the foliage often pleasantly scented, growing to two feet (60 cm) or more. The fragrant flowers are variably colored, white to pale violet or pinkish, though they seem to have a difficult time trying to open. *Leptodactylon pungens* is probably best suited to a wild garden, or grown amongst low grasses (blue grama would be good).

Leptodactylon watsonii (*Linanthus watsonii*) is probably the best of the definitely hardy ones, from Utah, western Colorado and Wyoming, and southern Idaho, growing to eight inches (20 cm) or so, with the usual off-white flowers. Easily grown from seed. The stems do tend to sprawl, which may offend tidy gardeners, unless grown in full sun in a very dry position.

Lesquerella (bladder pod). Dwarf mustards from the Great Plains and Intermountain region of varying degrees of desirability. The common name, which refers to the inflated silicles (short siliques, seed capsules common to the mustard family), is rarely used in polite conversation. Rock gardeners call them lesquerellas.

Differences between some of the species are more noticeable to botanists and other lesquerellas than to gardeners, especially to this gardener. The basic form, of the desirable ones anyway, is that of a rosette of silver-gray leaves with stems erect or splaying outward and clusters of four-petaled yellow mustard flowers on the ends of the stems, though in some species the stems are much shorter, as though the plant has withdrawn into itself, perhaps out of fear of the habitats and climate they choose to live in.

Lesquerella alpina, despite its name, is found in dry areas of the northern Great Plains (Nebraska, Colorado, and Wyoming north to southern Saskatchewan and Alberta) and also in Idaho and Utah, often growing on rocks. This is a cushion plant, maybe four inches (10cm) high and wide, with gray-hairy linear-oblanceolate leaves; the flowering stems are both erect and sprawling, so the plant is covered with flowers in early spring. "In full flower," Barr wrote, "it is a startling gold tuft or bun, dropped by chance on solid, gray or brown rock." Barr went on to tell a sad tale of the survival of plants in his garden; though it can be grown fairly easily even in bone-dry clay, my plants are dead too. A compact version, var. *condensata* from southwestern Wyoming, is the one to be sought.

Lesquerella arizonica is the best of the legal lesquerellas, and quite amenable to cultivation. A cushion plant native to northern Arizona and parts of southern Utah, this has tiny half-inch-long (1.25cm) oblanceolate silver-gray leaves with flowers on short stems covering the cushion in good years. *Lesquerella arizonica* is less than an inch (2.5cm) tall; the plant in my trough is six inches (15cm) wide after about ten years.

Lesquerella arizonica, Kelaidis garden

Lesquerella congesta is a golfball-sized golfball of, naturally, congested leaves, smothered with flowers in early spring. *Lesquerella congesta* is native to a tiny area of western Colorado, growing on oil shale. Because of its rarity it is listed as threatened under the Endangered Species Act, though possibly, before the reported new interest in oil shale production becomes an expensive reality, some seed will drift into the hands of people interested in preserving this delightful little species.

Lesquerella fendleri, common throughout the Great Plains south into New Mexico and northern Mexico, has silvery elliptical basal leaves and mostly erect stems to ten inches (25cm), sometimes shorter, sometimes taller. It is only moderately exciting, but it would fill spaces where silvery-rosetted yellow-mustard-flowered plants are desperately needed (though I would opt for physarias in this case). Other species in this vein are *L. kingii*, *L. ludoviciana*, *L. montana*, *L. occidentalis*, and *L. wardii*. They mostly look alike to me and have essentially the same garden effect.

Lesquerella hemiphysaria, native to central Utah, is, as I know it, a tiny smidgen of a thing with a rosette of silvery gray-green obovate basal leaves and clusters of yellow flowers on almost completely prostrate stems. A mouse falling asleep on the plant might smother it. A cute thing for a trough, but not very long-lived. *Lesquerella multiceps* and *L. paysonii* are two other species good for rock gardens or, especially, troughs.

Lesquerella tumulosa is another exception to the rule that says that endangered members of a genus are the least attractive, for this is the most desirable of all lesquerellas. As the name suggests, this is a mound-forming plant native to a small area of white shale hills in southern Utah; the plant has tiny, silvery gray-green half-inch (1.25cm) narrowly spoon-shaped leaves tightly clustered together, with tiny yellow flowers on short stems. *Lesquerella tumulosa* has been listed as endangered under the provisions of the Endangered Species Act.

Leucocrinum (star lily). The one species, *Leucocrinum montanum*, is a nonbulbous member of the lily family, native from New Mexico northward to South Dakota and Montana, and west to California and Oregon. This forms a tuft of linear green leaves about six inches (15cm)

Leucocrinum montanum

long, with white flowers an inch (2.5cm) or so across borne in May, on stems emerging from underground. Seeds are formed underground, as with some crocuses. The plant disappears in summer.

Leucocrinum montanum grows almost within walking distance of our home, in the foothills of the Rockies, in heavy, red clay soil. The plants, which are occasionally available from mail-order nurseries catering to rock gardeners, do equally well in the garden in similar soil, but their place needs to be marked, since they dislike being smothered by larger plants.

Lewisia. A succulent-leafed genus in the purslane family favored by rock gardeners, though not many are available for sale as plants. All the cultivation information written about lewisias comes from rainy climates; we can safely ignore all of it and simply plant lewisias in ordinary clay soil with a mulch of pea gravel around the plants' crowns. I've never met a lewisia I didn't like, but most of the species require summer irrigation in order to survive here, and so my selection will be a little limited. The popular *Lewisia cotyledon*, the one most readily available, is one that needs regular summer watering in dry climates. Some of the subspecies of *L. columbiana* (subsp. *columbiana* and subsp. *wallowensis*) grow on the drier, eastern side of the Cascades and might tolerate extended periods of drought, but I water mine just in case. Lewisias are easily grown from seed sown outdoors in January.

Lewisia brachycalyx, a native of mountains in central Arizona and southern California, depends on snowmelt, or at least adequate moisture in late winter and early spring, in order to produce its inch-wide (2.5 cm) flowers, usually white, but sometimes pink, on plants barely that tall in spring, and then it disappears for the summer. New growth begins, in my garden anyway, sometime in mid-January. You need to make a place for them that doesn't get overcrowded by other plants; a crevice, or narrow planting area between two upright rocks, filled with clay soil, then a layer of sand (about two inches, 5 cm, is perfect) then a mulch of fine pea gravel should allow you to grow these plants quite easily.

Lewisia rediviva (bitterroot), the state flower of Montana, is found from northern Arizona north into British Columbia, and northwestern Colorado into Wyoming and of course Montana, growing in a wide variety of soils including heavy clay. Boldly taking a cue from nature for once, bitterroots in the garden here thrive in raised beds of unamended alkaline clay soil. Like *L. brachycalyx*, bitterroot vanishes in the hot summer months, only to re-emerge in winter, its tiny green succulent leaves barely noticeable above the soil.

The flowers of bitterroot are as ravishingly beautiful as any in the North American flora (but wait until you get to *Lewisia tweedyi*), usually huge cottoncandy-colored waterlilies two inches (5 cm) across, though equally gorgeous white forms are known. The flowers bloom along with the leaves, which apparently is a phenomenon more commonly encountered in cultivation; in nature the leaves usually wither before the flowers open. Bitterroot seed is readily available; seed often germinates at subfreezing temperatures when sown outdoors, and if it does, just leave it alone. No harm will be done bringing the pots indoors, but the plants have adapted to germinating under adverse conditions, so they just keep growing.

A smaller relative of *Lewisia rediviva*, *L. maguirei*, comes from mountains in central Nevada, but this is really more of a collector's variety.

[above] *Lewisia brachycalyx*

[left] *Lewisia rediviva*

Lewisia tweedyi

Lewisia tweedyi (*Cistanthe tweedyi*) is a native of the eastern slopes of the Cascades in Washington and British Columbia, growing mostly on unstable rocky slopes. This is a larger lewisia, growing six inches (15cm) tall and maybe, if you're lucky, ten inches (25cm) wide, smothered in late May with pale peach-pink flowers about two inches (5cm) wide. This is best grown on a north-facing slope, on a base of clay with a heavy mulch of gravel.

It would be difficult to judge a beauty contest between *Lewisia tweedyi* and *L. rediviva*. The rare white forms of *L. tweedyi* are especially gorgeous, but the easy way out of this dilemma is to grow both species. Seed of *L. tweedyi* is available from rock garden society seedlists, though some mail-order nurseries sell plants.

There are two things you need to know about *Lewisia tweedyi*. Firstly, flower buds are extremely susceptible to hard frost in late spring, so protect your plants if the weather forecast calls for frost, if you want flowers. Secondly, it is often claimed that *L. tweedyi* can't be watered in summer. Ignore this. *Lewisia tweedyi* will sail through a typical intermittently rainy summer, but, during a prolonged drought, it will die if not watered at least once a month in June, July, August, and September.

Linanthastrum. A phlox relative found throughout the Intermountain region, and south into New Mexico and Mexico, with aromatic foliage and needle-like leaves arranged in clusters like those of *Leptodactylon*, but not as prickly. There is one species, *Linanthastrum nuttal-*

lii (*Leptosiphon nuttallii*), a multi-stemmed plant growing upright to a foot (30cm) tall, though usually shorter, with clusters of whitish phlox flowers at the ends of the stems. A nice plant; this used to be offered by one alpine plant nursery, now defunct; I don't recall seeing the plant, or seed, for sale by anyone in the last few years.

Linum (flax). Only a couple of species of flax tempt the rock gardener, though the yellow-flowered annuals (*Linum aristatum*, *L. australe*, *L. puberulum*) might go well in a wild garden. The plants bloom all summer, the petals falling by noon, or thereabouts, but the flower production is constant.

Linum kingii is an odd sort, sometimes put into the Eurasian genus *Cathartolinum*, with glaucous linear leaves crowded on stems to a foot (30cm) high, with yellow five-petaled flowers shaped like an air-conditioning fan. The variety usually offered is var. *sedoides* ("like a sedum", describing the unusual leaves). Native to Nevada, Utah, Colorado, Idaho, and Wyoming, usually at higher elevations, but also found at lower elevations in drier situations.

Linum lewisii is a common plant, found throughout the west (Alaska to Mexico), in various habitats. There is some disagreement among botanists whether or not this is the same plant, or a variety of, the European flax *L. perenne*. Linear green leaves on stiff wiry stems to a foot (30cm) or so (somewhat shorter in unirrigated gardens) carry a profusion of clustered blue flowers. Probably best for the wild garden: *L. lewisii* does seed about furiously. The seedlings are difficult to pull up with your hand and even turn aside a fish-tailed weeder. A dwarf form, four inches (10cm) tall, should be sought out for the rock garden.

Lomatium (desert parsley, biscuit root—the roots of *some* species are edible). Desert parsleys are rumored to be choice and desirable plants but ones that would probably be passed by at a plant sale or nursery, only to be grabbed by a fanatical rock gardener.

Well, such is the lot of those who write about plants; introducing a perhaps unfamiliar genus, we resort to humor like this. In truth, lomatiums are attractive plants, some of which are much too big for our subject in this chapter, properly belonging in a border of dryland perennials or a wild garden. *Lomatium dissectum*, for instance, is a large plant, to four feet (120cm), found throughout the west in meadows and on slopes, with large ferny leaves and umbels of yellow or (if you're lucky) purple, ball-shaped flowers.

Lomatium nudicaule is another large one, though in its smaller forms, it is a good rock garden parsley, to two feet (60cm) or more, with large leaves composed of oval, green leaflets and open umbels of yellow flowers. *Lomatium nudicaule* is found throughout the Intermountain West, growing with sagebrush. *Lomatium cous* (eastern Washington and Oregon to Wyoming and south to Nevada and Utah) is slightly smaller, though this time with the ferny leaves typical of plants in the carrot family.

A number of smaller lomatiums are sure to tempt the rock gardener, or maybe even the curious who want to grow something different.

Lomatium foeniculaceum is a widespread species, found on both sides of the Continental Divide, mostly single stalked with yellow flowers, but with two good dwarf varieties worth seeking out, var. *inyoense* (from Inyo County, California) and var. *macdougalii* (pretty much throughout the Intermountain region). *Lomatium gormanii*, from northeastern California, eastern Oregon and Washington, and Idaho, is a sparse-leafed

Lomatium nudicaule

plant, to about six inches (15 cm), with purple-anthered white flowers (giving the plant its common name, pepper and salt, though sometimes the flowers are completely purple) and a delight. *Lomatium grayi*, another species widespread through the Intermountain area, is a nice, if smelly, delicately fern-leafed species to a foot (30 cm), more or less, with open umbels of yellow ball flowers; *L. minimum* is a tiny one (four inches, 10 cm) from around Bryce Canyon in southern Utah, best in a trough.

There are others. Lomatiamania does require some time dedicated to seed raising, since lomatiums are not exactly on every nursery list on the continent, but seed is easily germinated using the outdoor method.

These all do well in clay soil, even hard-packed clay.

Lupinus. Well over a hundred species of lupines are native to North and South America, the best known of which are the border lupines derived from *Lupinus polyphyllus*, a plant of the wet areas in California and the Pacific Northwest, and the annual *L. texensis* (Texas bluebonnet). *Lupinus arboreus* (tree lupine) seems to be a favorite in Britain, though its propensity to seed about in its native California has caused it to be the object of some genuinely bizarre "nativist" activity, exterminating plants because they grow in the "wrong" county—as though nonnative plants were the only ones whose purpose in life was to expand their territory wherever possible.

Botanically, the genus is a taxonomic nightmare (though nothing compared to cactus). A few years ago I had occasion to correspond with a botanist about nomenclatural confusion in another genus, and his response was, "You think that's bad, you should try *Lupinus*." No thank you. I'm relying on the treatment in *Intermountain Flora* (Cronquist et al. 1972–97) written by Rupert Barneby, the twentieth century's foremost authority on the Fabaceae, for the names used here ("the taxonomy of the small-flowered perennial lupines is notoriously difficult, is likely always to be so, and is clouded by a diffuse and contrary literature").

A few of the perennial species are of interest to the dryland gardener. There would probably be more mentioned, if only the things were not so infernally difficult to grow. As it is, the ones I list have had but brief careers as living plants in the garden here.

To get them going, generally, the seed is nicked opposite the hilum and sown in a soilless mix, or sown in situ, with or without the nicking. The latter method is probably the best. Lupine roots are as delicate and finicky as astragalus roots when it comes to transplanting, and a less than surgically precise removal from the seedpot, and equally precise planting, is the cause of many a failure. The plan is that once the lupines are established, they may seed around; self-sown lupines are much tougher plants than ones set out in the garden from pots.

Lupinus argenteus at Denver Botanic Gardens

Lupinus argenteus is widespread throughout the west, with a dozen or so varieties. As I know it, this is a plant with silvery leaves, multiple stems about a foot (30cm) tall, and smallish blue or light blue flowers arranged on the stalk in typical lupine fashion, blooming in May and June. I suspect that my plants were var. *argophyllus*, mentioned by Ripley but no one else.

You can almost hear the plants scream when you set them out into the garden. I went through an embarrassingly large number of plants, purchased from nurseries, before I finally got one to settle in. After that, I began to see tiny plants of *Lupinus argenteus* here and there in the garden, and knew I had arrived as I grower of dryland lupines. And, several years later, I suddenly realized that there were no more left.

Lupinus lepidus is the ultimate rock garden lupine by almost anyone's standards, especially in the subalpine or alpine var. *lobbii* from mountain ranges in California, Oregon, British Columbia, and Idaho, but this needs special treatment (ultra careful planting, incantations, long vigils, watering, and so forth). Another variety, essentially a larger form of var. *lobbii*, native to eastern Washington and Oregon, Nevada, and Utah, is *L. lepidus* var. *aridus*. This makes a mound of silvery silky-hairy leaves with flowering stems to eight inches (20 cm), in exceptional forms, with miniature spires of blue flowers (var. *lobbii* has a more capitate inflorescence and is half the size).

Of course (sigh), with *Lupinus lepidus* var. *aridus*, you do not exactly go out to a nursery, make a purchase, plant, and suddenly have drifts of flowering dwarf lupines in the rock garden. You buy seeds, in the rare years that they are available. After the seeds are nicked, they should be planted where they are to grow, about half an inch (1.25 cm) below the soil surface.

Lupinus polyphyllus, ordinarily, as I said earlier, a plant favoring wet locations, has a couple of xerophytic incarnations worth pursuing. *Lupinus polyphyllus* var. *ammophilus*, found on both sides of the Utah-Colorado border south to northwestern New Mexico, has, unusually, flowering stems rising from a buried woody trunk, or caudex. Even though the specific epithet means "sand lover," this is, like the others, a plant for dry clay gardens. This can be almost two feet (60 cm) tall, under the happiest of situations. *Lupinus polyphyllus* var. *saxosus* is a little shorter, with hairy green leaves; this is found more or less throughout the Great Basin.

Melampodium (blackfoot daisy). *Melampodium leucanthum* (sometimes confused with *M. cinereum*) is a low, almost shrubby plant, to ten inches (25 cm), and as wide, with narrowly oblong hairy green leaves and white daisies with yellow centers. Possibly a little too unrefined for a small rock garden, but good in a larger rock garden, a perennial border of dryland plants, or a wild garden. *Melampodium leucanthum* prefers dry alkaline clay soil. Native from southern Colorado south into Texas and northern Mexico; not so easy from seed but readily available from nurseries in New Mexico and Colorado.

Mertensia (bluebells). The pattern of the familiar Virginia bluebells (*Mertensia virginica*) is repeated throughout the wide variety of western species of *Mertensia*, with the exception of the high-elevation *M. alpina*, from mountains in Idaho, Montana, Wyoming, and Colorado (only on Pikes Peak), a cushion plant with flat-faced flowers, more like miniature gongs than bluebells.

A few species are adapted to drier situations and can be grown in the rock garden without irrigation, though like most dryland plants they are heavily dependent on moisture at just the right time, which in this case would be late winter and very early spring. I find them difficult to get going. Though they're easy from seed, I have had no luck at all establishing *Mertensia longiflora* or *M. oblongifolia* in the garden. The former is a dryland plant from southern British Columbia to Oregon east of the Cascades, to parts of Montana west of the Rockies, a plant growing to ten inches (25cm) with elliptic leaves; the latter is a taller plant, from roughly the same range as *M. longiflora*, though it also occurs in Nevada and Wyoming, with oblanceolate leaves and shorter flowers (those botanical names do occasionally mean something).

Mertensia lanceolata

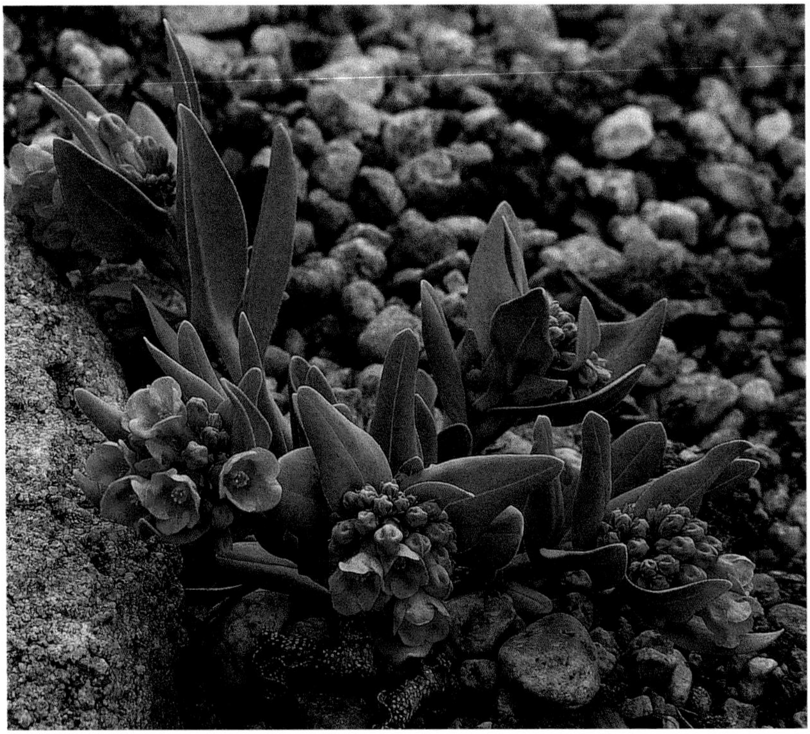

For years I tried to get *Mertensia lanceolata*, a ravishingly beautiful plant native to the foothills of the eastern slopes of the Rocky Mountains (as well as Wyoming and Montana), almost within walking distance of our house, established in the garden, but either the seeds failed to germinate, or the plants I purchased died within weeks. Then one year some plants I set out decided to live, and for some years now we have had an ever-expanding colony of these plants. *Mertensia lanceolata* is a variable species about six inches (15 cm) tall, with glaucous green oblanceolate or lanceolate leaves, and large drooping clusters of sky-blue flowers emerging from reddish buds. A few plants in the garden here have borne white flowers. To me, nothing means the end of spring (and the end of snow) more than May, and the opening of the first flowers of *M. lanceolata*. Plants bloom for a couple of weeks, set seed, and then disappear completely for the summer, only to emerge again the next spring.

Mimulus (monkey flower). A genus of plants related to snapdragons and penstemons, the majority of which are native to California, though some are found in other parts of the world. Monkey flowers can be annuals, perennials, or shrubs (though these Californians are sometimes placed in their own genus, *Diplacus*) and are almost always recommended for constantly moist garden conditions, at least during the growing season.

It may come as a surprise to learn that there are monkey flowers, annual ones, suitable for the dry rock garden. These little plants, in section Eunanus, are distributed east of the Cascades and Sierra Nevada, some entering Idaho, others venturing further south into Arizona and Baja California. These are gorgeous little plants rarely offered as seed; my recommendation is to sow the seed of the hardy species directly into the garden any time from September to January, and hope for plenty of snow in March and April to get the little plants going. I've had them appear spontaneously in seed pots where I thought I had sowed seed of other plants.

Mimulus cusickii (Oregon to northeastern California to Idaho) is eight inches (20 cm) tall, with sticky-hairy, smelly ovate leaves, and violet flowers with two yellow spots on the palate (the lower part of the opening of the flower's throat, where the beards are), and darker violet inside.

Mimulus nanus has a range similar to that of *M. cusickii*, but extends to Montana and Wyoming, and also further north into Washington, often growing around anthills (not that growing it would attract ants, but . . .). *Mimulus nanus* is much smaller than *M. cusickii* (to three or four inches, 7.5 to 10 cm), more branched, with less-smelly foliage. The flowers are pink or violet or yellow, with two yellow spots on the palate (when the flowers aren't yellow, that is).

There are other species worth trying, too.

Monardella. Mostly Californian mints, with at least one species, *Monardella odoratissima*, found throughout the west. Not really one for the rock garden, this has green or gray foliage, stems to one foot (30 cm) with variously oblanceolate to obovate leaves, and clusters of purple to white flowers in small heads. This aromatic, minty-smelling plant is good for places where you might brush against it, or grown below old roses.

Dwarf, or at least smaller, forms of *Monardella villosa* (coyote mint) have so far failed to overwinter for me, and the alpine *M. cinerea* seems to need protection from the hot winter sun here (meaning, it died).

A third failure (now I'm wondering why I bothered with this entry) which apparently is successfully grown elsewhere, since it's occasionally offered for sale in Denver, is *Monardella macrantha*, a low creeping thing with leathery bright green triangular leaves, and, at the upturned ends of the stems, "large fat and rather heavy bunches of narrow calyces, held together in a double frill of flat green bracts, from which project long tubular flowers, which may be coral red, orange-red, yellow-scarlet, orange-yellow, salmon, light yellow, or sometimes light pink" (Rowntree 1936). Oh well.

Nama. A genus of mostly annuals in the waterleaf family. Two perennials are of interest. *Nama lobbii*, from southern Oregon, northeastern California, and northwestern Nevada, is a mat-former with woolly oblanceolate leaves and stems to a foot (30 cm) or more, the planting spreading to at least twice that much, with clusters of purple or pink bell-shaped flowers in the leaf axils and at the ends of the stems. Maybe a little big for a smaller rock garden.

Nama rothrockii has erect stems to a foot (30 cm), with serrated leaves and clusters of light blue or pink funnel-shaped flowers. This spreads by rhizomes, so care should be taken before planting. Native to Nevada, southern California, and northwestern Arizona.

Notholaena (cloak fern). Mostly xerophytic rock ferns halfway between *Cheilanthes* and *Pellaea* in morphology, these are rare as hen's teeth in the rock garden trade (and even rarer in the fern trade).

At least three species are worth trying, though it's unlikely that anything other than spores would be available, and these only from specialized seedlists or rock garden society seedlists. *Notholaena fendleri* (*Argyrochosma fendleri*) is a small fern with triangular green blades (fern-speak for leaves) with white wax below, to eight inches (20 cm), from New Mexico to Wyoming; *N. sinuata* (*Astrolepis integerrima*), a larger one with linear, scale-covered blades to one foot (30 cm), Oklahoma, Texas, and New Mexico west to California and south to Mexico; and *N. standleyi*, the same height (sometimes smaller), with pentagonal blades, yellow wax below, southeastern Colorado to Mexico, west to Nevada. The ferns' habitats—exposed, sunny, hot south-facing rocks—should suggest their suitability for dry rock gardens, as well as the reason why they are utterly absent from the trade.

Oenothera (evening primrose, sundrops). A large genus related to fuchsias but looking nothing like them, mostly native to western North America, *Oenothera* has a number of gorgeous plants suitable for the rock garden or wild garden. All do well in heavy clay soil. A number of species increase themselves by freely running roots and will spoil a large area in a single year; *O. pallida*, a white-flowered species with branched stems native to the Great Plains and much of the Intermountain region, is one of the worst, and should be avoided like the plague.

There are a number of upright-growing yellow-flowered species, mostly biennials, that need regular irrigation in our area. I don't grow any of them.

Oenothera caespitosa is, I think, the most widespread species (Alberta and Saskatchewan to west Texas and Mexico, eastern Washington to southeastern California), and in my eyes the most beautiful. The basic plant is a tuft of long-petioled green or gray-green, usually softly hairy leaves on a plant maybe a foot (30cm) across after a few years; the sizable (sometimes to four inches, 10cm, across) white flowers open at sunset, their lemon scent pervading the night garden in May and June. By dawn, the flowers have faded to pink or purple, crumpled like discarded tissue paper, unless the morning is overcast, when they remain open almost until noon.

There are six subspecies; all are worth growing, even though the differences in the garden might not be as substantial as they are to botanists, or to the hawkmoths that pollinate them. The typical subspecies, *Oenothera caespitosa* subsp. *caespitosa*, is the most northerly distributed (central Nevada to Colorado, and northward) and is either a glabrous or pubescent plant; the faded flowers are rose-purple. The rest of the subspecies have flowers that fade to pink, with no purple tints; this can be considered diagnostic if no other differences are apparent. Subspecies *macroglottis*, though, has flowers with, as the name suggests, large throats at least half an inch (1.25cm) wide, with curved seed capsules tapering to the tip, found from southern Wyoming south to northern New Mexico. Subspecies *marginata* has a less conspicuously gaping throat, with straight seed capsules; this is found from western Texas

Oenothera caespitosa subsp. *caespitosa*

to California and Washington. Subspecies *navajoensis* is found in the Four Corners area, and north through Utah and western Colorado to the Wyoming state line; this has woolly leaves and stems. Of course the subspecies intergrade where they come in contact with each other, but genuine examples of all the subspecies can be obtained from seedlists, and all are worth having in the garden.

One subspecies is rather different from the rest in its size. *Oenothera caespitosa* subsp. *crinita* is a tiny plant, an inch (2.5cm) tall and two inches (5cm) across, with flowers about an inch (2.5cm) wide, perfect for the smaller rock garden. Native mostly to Nevada, but also found in northwestern Arizona, western Utah, and extreme eastern California.

One of the more unusual habitats of some of the subspecies of *Oenothera caespitosa* is at the margins of harvester ant hills, the plants forming a ring around the central anthill. This would be a good way to collect some seed, since this is a pretty obvious arrangement. Say your car broke down on a lonely road somewhere in the west; you could spend time looking for anthills and oenothera seedpods (wrinkled brown, dried-up okra pods near the base of the plant), while someone else walked to the next county looking for a telephone.

Plants are readily available at nurseries in the Rocky Mountain region; *Oenothera caespitosa* is also easy to grow from seed, either sown in winter in pots, or just scattered on the ground. Barr's statement that *O. caespitosa* "has no facility for colonizing except by seed" is not entirely accurate; some plants do colonize by means of short spreading roots, but nowhere near the extent of the really wicked species.

Oenothera flava, native throughout the Great Plains, northern Mexico, much of the Intermountain area, and California, is a smaller oenothera, looking like a dandelion with twenty times more leaves, forming rosettes about six inches (15cm) across and three inches (7.5cm) high, with yellow flowers about two inches (5cm) across. *Oenothera flava* is not incredibly exciting but still worth growing; it flowers in early summer. Rather subject to attack by flea beetles, but it quickly recovers. *Oenothera xylocarpa*, from the east slopes of the Sierra Nevada, with lyre-shaped leaves and much larger yellow flowers, would probably be a better choice.

Oenothera howardii, until recently considered the same as *O. brachy-*

carpa, a species of west Texas, southern New Mexico and Arizona, and northern Mexico, is a plant of heavy clay soils in western Kansas, Colorado, Wyoming, Utah, and Nevada. This forms a tuft of oblanceolate, slightly wavy-edged green leaves about six inches (15cm) long, the leaves appearing glabrous but really covered with microscopic hairs. The flowers are enormous, four to five inches (10 to 12.5cm) wide, lemon-yellow, held on stems about four inches (10cm) tall, opening at sunset, in early summer, and fading to orange, pink, bronze, or red by morning, though, as usual, staying open if the next morning is overcast.

Oenothera howardii

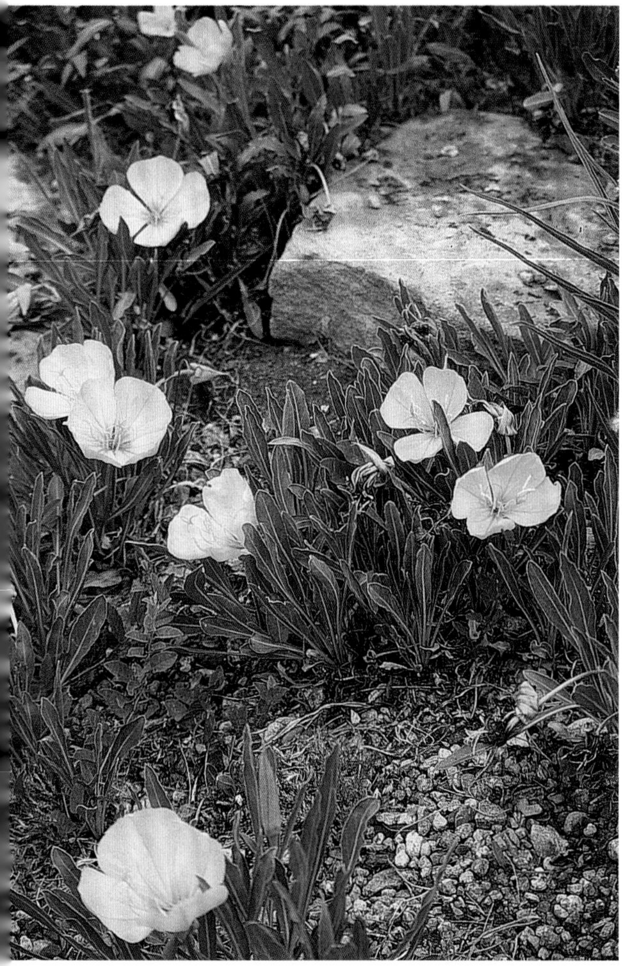

Oenothera howardii is a spreader but not a hyper-aggressive one. It's such a beautiful plant that I can forgive it this tendency, though you might not want to. Easily raised from seed. Less subject to attack by flea beetles than some.

Oenothera macrocarpa is the accepted name (Nuttall's original name) for *O. missouriensis*, possibly the best-known oenothera, but really outside of our area, being a plant of, surprise, Missouri and surrounding states. It does reveal its native habitat by showing poor drought tolerance in the garden here (Barr's experience, too) but is a beautiful plant for an irrigated garden.

A couple of subspecies of *Oenothera macrocarpa* are of interest here, though the family resemblance is difficult to see in *O. macrocarpa* subsp. *fremontii* (*O. fremontii*), a plant growing on chalky soil in southern Nebraska and northwestern Kansas. This has, as I know it, fairly linear green leaves, four inches (10cm) or so in length, on a mounding plant about a foot (30cm) tall by as wide, or perhaps wider, with "relatively enormous" (Barr) yellow flowers (they're about four inches, 10 cm, wide). This plant has shown good resistance to drought in the garden here and established easily from a plant purchased at a local nursery.

Oenothera macrocarpa subsp. *incana* strongly resembles the Missouri evening primrose but has beautiful silver leaves ("the to-be-expected different aspect of an adapted High Plains plant"—Barr), this on a plant about eight inches (20 cm) tall by a foot (30 cm) wide, with flowers the size of subsp. *fremontii*. Subspecies *incana* is native to the area around the Texas and Oklahoma panhandles. Barr reported great success with this plant, in a climate somewhat rainier than mine. I have had no success, in several attempts, in getting subsp. *incana* to be anything more than a straggling plant with a few leaves, but this one is definitely worth at least one more try.

Oenothera neomexicana is one of the spreaders; it will take over an area the size of your garage in a single season. It usually waits a year or so and then it takes off, racing to the horizon. *Oenothera neomexicana*, native to guess where, has attractive small serrated gray-green leaves on a plant about a foot (30 cm) tall and a little wider, depending on how crowded it gets, with plentiful gorgeous white flowers about three inches (7.5 cm) across, opening at sunset and withering to pink the next day. This is such a beautiful plant that it's a pity it has no self-control; it reminds me of some people I know. Not for the rock garden, but I have it in the front yard, where it can go crazy if it wants. *Oenothera neomexicana* is easy from seed. *Oenothera organensis*, from the Organ Mountains in southern New Mexico, looks like a yellow-flowered version of this.

As an aside, *Oenothera speciosa*, another spreader, is an upright plant to two feet (60 cm) or more, with oblanceolate to ovate leaves, lobed on the edges and ending in a larger lobe. Flowers are white, about three inches (7.5 cm) wide, opening in the evening. Pink-flowered tetraploid forms are found in the wild; these open in the morning. Native to eastern Nebraska and Kansas, south through Missouri into Texas and Louisiana. In the dry garden it lives for a year or two, hardly spreading at all unless the summer is a wet one. Eventually it disappears. *Oenothera rosea* (Texas and Mexico), often confused with *O. speciosa*, has rose or rose-purplish flowers about an inch wide; this is not much of a spreader and has the same moribund tendencies.

Oxytropis (locoweed). Dwarf members of the pea family, quite similar in appearance and garden value to *Astragalus*, except that in *Oxytropis* the keel (the structure formed by the two lower petals) has a beak at the tip. The species are mostly differentiated by features of sometimes doubtful importance to gardeners (length of the seedpod, etc.), but it may be that out of two species very similar in appearance one will like your garden better than the other, so both should be tried.

Some species, like *Oxytropis campestris* and *O. parryi*, inhabit more subalpine regions, or in the case of *O. splendens*, soil with more moisture in them, so I haven't tried growing these in the dry garden; remembering the rule that habitat does not necessarily mean preference, these could be tried as well.

Oxytropis are more or less easy from seed; the seed can either be nicked opposite the hilum and planted directly out into the garden sometime after mid-March, or it can be sown outdoors in pots in January. Direct sowing avoids the perils of transplanting (the roots are as finicky about being touched as those of astragalus), but germination is dependent on regular moisture. A few specialist nurseries offer plants grown in small pots; these require extreme care in transplanting out into the garden.

Oxytropis besseyi, native from Montana, Wyoming, and Colorado west to Idaho and Nevada, has silvery silky-hairy leaves and bright purplish pink, inch-long (2.5 cm) flowers. One variety has leaves and stems almost eight inches (20 cm) long (the flowering stems shorter than the leaves), but the ones to get are var. *argophylla* and var. *ventosa*, much smaller plants forming tufts about an inch (2.5 cm) high with flowering stems about twice that height. Variety *argophylla* has tiny congested leaflets; var. *ventosa* has larger (but still small) leaflets in fives.

Oxytropis lagopus is another silky silver-leafed tuft, to about three inches (7.5 cm) high, and not much wider, with bright red-purple flowers, at least in var. *atropurpurea*, on stems about four inches (10 cm) tall. Called the hare's-foot locoweed for reasons unknown to me (not that I am the most observant of people), except possibly because of the mixture of short black and long white hairs on the calyx. Native to Wyoming, southern Montana, and Idaho.

Oxytropis lambertii, widespread throughout the Great Plains, and in the Intermountain region in Utah and Arizona, is a variable species, with green or grayish pinnate leaves from two to eight inches (5 to 20 cm), with flowering stems from about four to ten inches (10 to 25 cm) tall, with clusters of purplish pink, pink, pale purple, blue-purple, or white flowers. This notorious poisoner of livestock is the most commonly available locoweed in the trade, readily available as plants.

Oxytropis multiceps is a delight. This diminutive native of Colorado, Nebraska, and Wyoming (with a larger-flowered disjunct population in northeastern Utah) is a perfect choice for the dry rock garden. This has, again, silvery silky-hairy pinnate leaves about an inch (2.5 cm) tall, forming a cushion about four times as wide, with good-sized pink-purple flowers on stems barely taller than the leaves. In Barr's words, expect "one, two, or four blossoms to the scape, which may fail to lift them upright; they loll in the sun for a few days or a week, content upon their silken cushion." I have lost more than my share of these plants, mostly, I suspect, to brown fingers, though the standard excuse is prolonged

Oxytropis multiceps

drought. *Oxytropis multiceps* is a great choice either for a sunny, totally exposed clay slope (mulched with rock, of course) or a trough. Offered by a handful of mail-order nurseries catering to rock gardeners.

Oxytropis nana is slightly larger in its parts than *O. multiceps* (to about four inches, 10 cm) with the usual silvery silky leaves, but with a leathery calyx as opposed to the papery one in *O. multiceps* (like this makes a difference in the garden), with purple or pink-purple flowers. Native to central Wyoming, blooming in May or early June in the garden. A few nurseries occasionally carry plants, but as far as I'm concerned this highly desirable plant is a difficult one to keep going.

Oxytropis oreophila is a plant of south-central Utah, northwestern Arizona, southern Nevada, and southern California, where it even finds it way to the San Bernardino Mountains. This is a little one like *O. besseyi* and *O. nana*, with the usual pink-purple flowers in May or June, definitely worth growing in var. *oreophila*, which is the largest (six by six inches, 15 by 15 cm) of the varieties, found at higher elevations (*oreophila* means "mountain lover"). The really desirable ones are var. *jonesii* and var. *juniperina*, found at lower, drier elevations. Variety *jonesii* has tinier leaves and larger flowers (the rock gardener's delight!) than var. *juniperina*, but here "larger" only means by a millimeter or two.

If you were lucky, and you were able to give *Oxytropis oreophila* var. *jonesii* (or var. *juniperina*) exactly what it needed over a period of years, which *might* be low rainfall twelve months of the year, the rainfall coming at just the right time for the plants (maybe mostly in February and March, but in the form of snow), and dry, alkaline soil, with little cloud cover, plenty of wind, and a wide range of what they call "weather events," then maybe, just maybe, you would wind up with a mound ten inches (25 cm) high and wide, possibly even larger, of white-woolly tightly congested pinnate pea leaves. If you aren't lucky, then you can just dream about such things, like I do.

Oxytropis sericea is a larger plant, found throughout the Great Plains and also common in the Intermountain region, often growing on road cuts, blooming in late May or early June, with silky green or gray (*sericea* means "silky") leaves about six inches (15 cm) long, with flowering stems to a foot (30 cm), with clusters of good-sized white flowers. Smaller forms exist, too. *Oxytropis sericea* is less of an aristocrat than some of

Oxytropis nana

Oxytropis oreophila var. *jonesii*

the other locoweeds, possibly better grown in a wild garden, but it's also much easier to grow.

Paronychia (whitlow-wort). Mostly mat-forming plants related to pinks. The almost infinitesimal flowers prompted Barr to write, "One questions their purpose in the floral scheme," but some people like them. *Paronychia depressa* is a mat-former with flowers in clusters, sometimes growing to four inches (10 cm) tall and two or three times as wide, found in eastern Wyoming and adjacent South Dakota, Nebraska, Colorado, and Kansas; *P. sessiliflora* is similar but with solitary flowers, found throughout the Great Plains. *Paronychia jamesii* is a little shrub about ten inches (25 cm) tall, widespread in the Great Plains from Nebraska southward, and into Arizona and Mexico. The European species are better. "Hardly," to give Barr the last word, "worth space in the garden, except as a novelty."

Pellaea (cliff-brake). Alphabetically, the third in the trio of xerophytic ferns (*Cheilanthes*, *Notholaena*, *Pellaea*), and, with one exception, just as unavailable in the trade. Basically these are small ferns (less than a foot, 30 cm, tall) with dark, wiry petioles (leaf stems) and leathery green pinnate blades, good for tucking away between rocks in a north-facing, dry rock garden. *Pellaea atropurpurea*, common from New England to Mexico, finds it way into the Great Plains in rocky places from the Black Hills to southeastern Colorado. This one, with tiny hairs on the petioles, is fairly common in the trade and is the easiest to grow of all the rock ferns. One has actually lived in the garden here for many years, but my photographer remains unimpressed.

Other cliff-brakes worth trying (meaning, worth trying to find and then trying to grow from spores) are *Pellaea breweri*, a fern of the Intermountain region with clusters of old petioles at its base and few hairs on the petioles. *Pellaea glabella*, found in the extreme eastern edge of the Great Plains east to New England but also in the Intermountain region from British Columbia to Arizona, is like *P. atropurpurea* but without the hairs on the petioles, and without the stumps of old petioles at its base. *Pellaea mucronata* is more westerly distributed, southern Nevada through southern California to Baja California, with mucronate blade-tips. I had a tiny version in the rock garden for a few years, and then, when I looked for it one day, it was gone.

Penstemon. The largest genus of flowering plants endemic to North America, these snapdragon relatives also offer more for the dry rock garden than any other group of plants, and by a considerable margin, too. There are upright plants, sprawling plants, mat-formers, buns, small shrubs—practically everything a rock gardener could desire. Flower colors range from bright red, orange, yellow, and white, to various shades of purple, brilliant sky-blue, and intense deep blue.

Penstemons are easily grown from seed sown outdoors in January. Seed can also be simply scattered on the ground, though maybe this isn't the brightest idea with seed of some of the rarer species. Seedlists, from collectors and those from rock garden societies, offer a huge variety of species. Nurseries catering to the rock garden trade also offer a wide variety of choices.

It's worth remembering that flower color is not precisely fixed in the majority of species; those with blue flowers can also have blue-purple, pink-purple, or white flowers. Red- or orange-flowered species can also have yellow-flowered forms, and so on.

The smaller penstemons mentioned here have varying degrees of longevity in the garden. (The taller species are relegated to the section on perennials.) Deadheading prolongs life by preventing plants from spending too much energy ripening seed instead of growing new leaves to carry the plant through the winter. One way to perpetuate the shorter-lived penstemons is to encourage a few plants to set seed, or to save a few flowering stems from the secateurs while deadheading. Once the seed capsules have dried, the stems can be cut and laid in the garden, or the capsules split and the seed sown right on the ground.

All penstemons, regardless of native habitat, have a considerable amount of drought-tolerance, and all do quite well grown in plain clay soil; the ones that follow are some of the best.

Penstemon acaulis, native to a tiny area in Wyoming and Utah west of Flaming Gorge Reservoir, is perfectly fitted to its tiny habitat. This most unusual penstemon is an inch (2.5cm) tall by a foot (30cm) wide, with tiny linear green leaves and, in late May, fat, sky-blue, half-inch-long (1.25cm) flowers peeking up through the leaves. *Penstemon acaulis* is occasionally available from mail-order nurseries; the plants are so small they need extra care (careful attention to watering, for instance) for the first few years. *Penstemon yampaënsis*, native to northwestern Colorado (incidentally, one of the coldest places in North America: the town of Maybell has recorded an unofficial low of −61F, −52C), has foliage about twice the size of that of *P. acaulis*. This one, as seed or plants, is rarely seen in the trade.

Penstemon albidus is common throughout the Great Plains from Saskatchewan to New Mexico; for some reason this species has been maligned by rock gardeners. There seems to be some color variation in the white flowers, though the plant as I know it has good-sized white flowers with an occasional purplish tinge, on a multi-stemmed plant ten inches (25cm) high and wide. *Penstemon albidus* flowers in late May or early June. In the wild, especially in years of good moisture, it can be twice the height of plants grown in dry gardens. Will tolerate long periods of drought if grown in heavy clay.

Penstemon ambiguus, native from Utah south to Arizona, and northeastern Colorado south into Texas and northern Mexico (Chihuahua), is another unusual species, a shrub with tiny green thread-like leaves and white phlox-like half-inch-wide (1.25cm) flowers with a pink throat, stuck on the end of a tiny pink tube. Plants in northeastern Colorado grow in deep sand, forming large colonies; there the plants are about ten inches (25cm) tall, and of great age, as evidenced by the thick woody trunks at their base. In the garden, *P. ambiguus* does perfectly well in clay soil; it does not require sand, or "drainage." *Penstemon thurberi*, from southern New Mexico and Arizona to southern California and Baja California, is quite similar but with funnel-shaped violet-blue flowers; it seems to be just as hardy and accepts the same conditions in the garden.

Over the last several years, *Penstemon amphorellae* has proven itself to be one of the most drought-resistant of plants, sailing through the drought of 2002 and still blooming at its usual time, late July or August well into October. *Penstemon amphorellae* is a multi-stemmed plant about ten inches (25cm) tall, with linear green leaves a little over an inch (2.5cm) long with fat, jug-shaped purple flowers (the specific epithet means "little jars," a reference also to the Mexican common name for penstemons, *jarritos*, "little jars"). This native of relatively high elevations in Coahuila and Nuevo León south into Queretaro has a few kissing cousins that, in the unlikely event that someone collects seed, are worth trying; these are *P. tenuifolius*, *P. vulcanellus*, and *P. saltarius*.

Penstemon ambiguus

Penstemon angustifolius is an upright plant about a foot (30cm) tall, with one or two (or three or four) stems with narrow, thick, blue-glaucous leaves. Native to much of the Great Plains, and the eastern part of the Intermountain region, this has clusters of stunning sky-blue flowers borne in late May and early June. Bluish purple, pink, and white forms exist, too. You want the blue ones. I find that var. *caudatus*, a plant of southern Colorado and New Mexico, lasts the longest in the garden; plants have been in the garden here for almost fifteen years, growing in hard-packed dry clay soil.

Penstemon arenicola is native to western Wyoming, southwestern Montana, and northeastern Utah. Despite its name (*arenicola* means "sand dweller"), this penstemon does well in clay, too. *Penstemon arenicola* is related to *P. angustifolius* and *P. nitidus*, with thick blue-glaucous leaves. The stems grow to six inches (15cm), sometimes taller, and even though they do have the upright penstemons' tendency to flop their stems about (a habit called, oddly, lodging), the clusters of brilliant electric-blue flowers in April or May are an astonishing sight.

Penstemon caespitosus is a mat-former, in some varieties growing an inch (2.5cm) by a yard (90cm) wide, the stems rooting as they grow. The blue, white-throated flowers, blooming in late May or early June, are

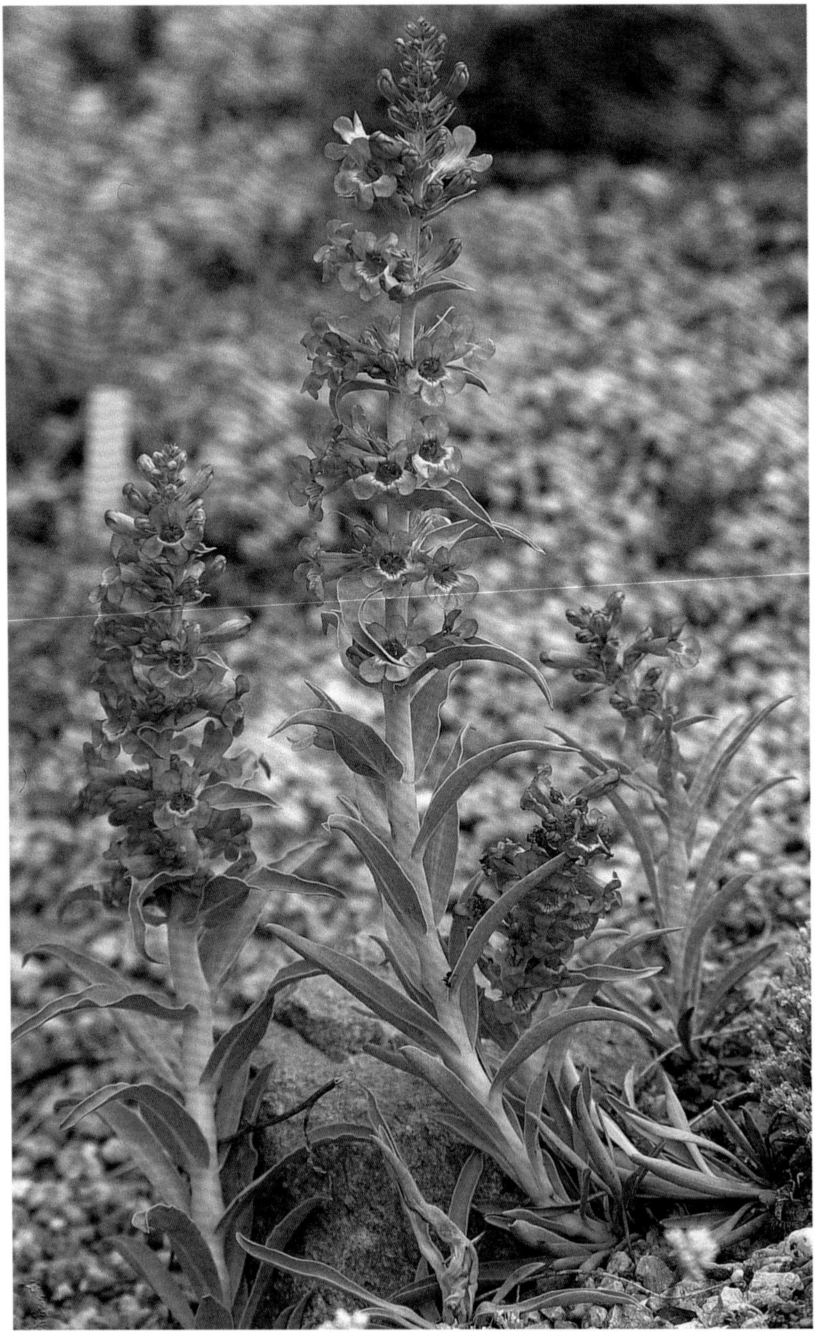

Penstemon angustifolius var. *caudatus*

held on stems barely taller than the leaves. Native to northwestern Colorado through southwestern Wyoming into Utah and Arizona. Variety *desertipicti*, from the Painted Desert, with tiny gray oblanceolate leaves, is particularly nice. *Penstemon caespitosus* is not very common in the trade (the plant labeled 'Claude Barr' has nothing to do with this species or with Claude Barr), though a fine white-flowered form is sometimes sold. *Penstemon tusharensis* is a slightly shrubby relative with gray-green leaves.

Penstemon californicus, a rare native of southern California (Riverside and San Diego counties) south into Baja California, has improbably found its way into nurseries in the Rocky Mountain region. The penstemon literature suggests that *P. californicus* can grow to a foot (30cm) tall. Maybe it can in San Diego, but in Denver it's a small mounding plant, some six inches (15cm) high and wide, with ashy-gray oblanceolate leaves about half an inch (1.25cm) long and purple, whited-throated flowers in June.

Penstemon caryi, a more or less rare native of northern Wyoming and adjacent Montana, is a multi-stemmed plant a foot (30cm) tall by as wide, when happy, with long (four inches, 10cm) linear-oblanceolate green leaves at the base, and linear leaves along the stems. The one-sided inflorescence has clusters of good-sized (one inch, 2.5cm) blue flowers in June, though sometimes starting in late May. I once saw *P. caryi* growing in a mountain garden, where possibly because of the intense sunlight and cool nights, the flowers were of the most intense midnight-blue imaginable. In my lowland garden the flowers are just blue.

Penstemon crandallii is a mounding plant, three inches (7.5cm) by eight inches (20cm) with tiny oblanceolate green leaves, in the typical variety anyway, smothered with blue, white-throated flowers in late May or early June. Native from west-central Colorado south into New Mexico and northern Arizona, and west into Utah. *Penstemon crandallii* is often confused with *P. caespitosus*, but the latter is a flat mat. A form with gray-green leaves has been called *P. teucrioides*, but there seems to be no justification for maintaining this name, though plants and seeds are frequently sold under this name. The leaves of *P. crandallii* don't seem to be overly fond of Denver's hot winter sun, sometimes burning away to nothing, but the plant quickly recovers in spring. *Pen-*

stemon ramaleyi, from mountains in southern Colorado, a more or less upright plant about six inches (15cm) high, with somewhat lax stems, is a close relative, as is *P. retrorsus*, another upright plant from western Colorado.

A couple of varieties, or subspecies, of *Penstemon crandallii* are of interest to rock gardeners. A larger-leafed, more upright form native to southern Colorado and northern New Mexico is *P. crandallii* subsp. *glabrescens* (*P. glabrescens*); this is rarely offered. *Penstemon crandallii* subsp. *procumbens* (*P. procumbens*) is less like typical *P. crandallii* than any of the other subspecies; this has nearly round green leaves on wide spreading stems, with the usual blue flowers. This one is common in the trade, always offered, bizarrely, as "*P. caespitosus* 'Claude Barr'." Even if the name is wrong, it is still worth acquiring.

Penstemon debilis is a rare inhabitant of unstable, steep slopes in oil shale country in western Colorado. A botanist friend told me that seeing *P. debilis* in the wild—sliding down shifting slopes that suddenly drop away to cliffs a thousand feet high—was the most frightening thing she had ever done. This is a penstemon with oval, leathery blue-gray leaves forming, in cultivation anyway, mounds an inch (2.5cm) high by eight inches (20cm) wide, smothered in late May with disappointingly small, pale white, pink-tinged flowers. I find *P. debilis* difficult to grow, but others have had more success.

Penstemon dolius, native to Utah and eastern Nevada, is possibly of interest only to die-hard rock gardeners, though it is a rare gem for a dry trough, an upright plant to four inches (10cm) with ashy gray-green oblanceolate leaves and a few tricolored (pale purple tubes, light blue lobes, white throats) flowers at the tips of the stems. Variety *duchesnensis*, with slightly more flowers held ever so slightly above the stems on a plant half the size of the regular variety, from the Uinta Basin in eastern Utah, is the most desirable—a plant to impress those overawed by microscopic jewels. *Penstemon pumilus*, from east-central Idaho, is similar but with much more linear leaves.

Penstemon eriantherus is a plant of heavy clay soils in northeastern Colorado, western Nebraska, and Wyoming, with varieties extending west to the dry parts of the Pacific Northwest (eastern Oregon and Washington and southeastern British Columbia). *Penstemon eriantherus*, in

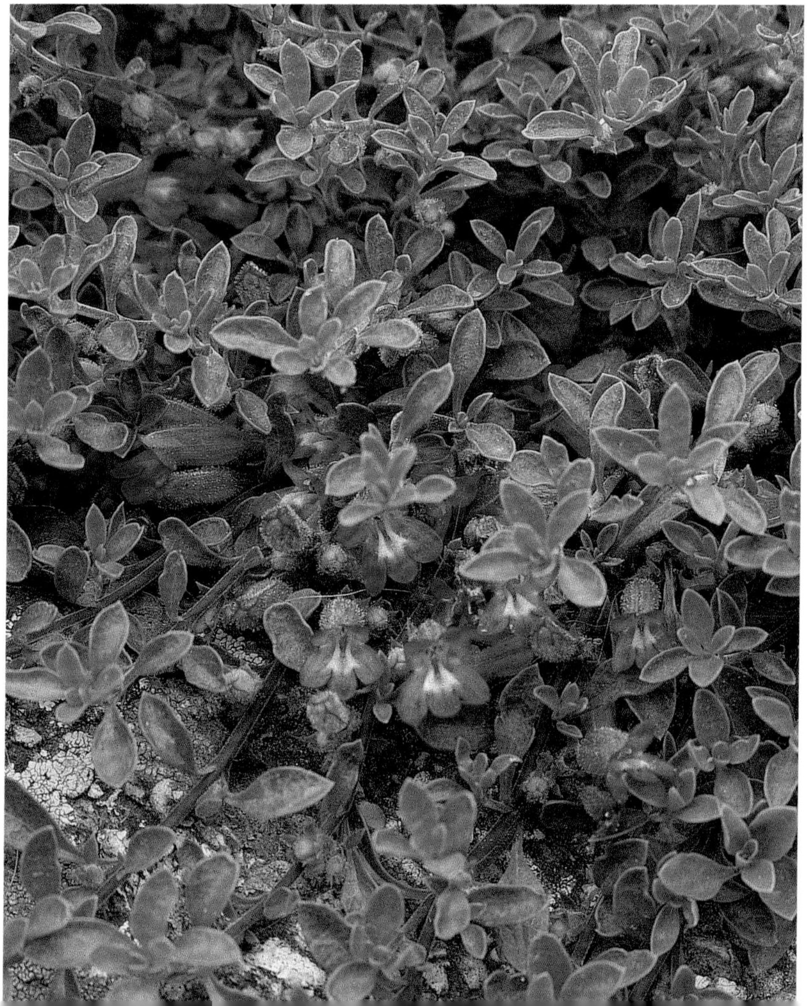

[above] *Penstemon crandallii*

[left] *Penstemon crandallii* subsp. *procumbens*

Penstemon dolius var. *duchesnensis* overawing *Eriogonum ovalifolium*

the typical, Great Plains variety, is an eight-inch (20 cm) plant with multiple stems, and clusters of good-sized pink-purple flowers with bright golden staminodes in May. The smaller western varieties, var. *redactus* and var. *whitedii*, are much less exciting. *Penstemon cleburnei*, from northeastern Utah and southwestern Wyoming (sometimes considered a variety of *P. eriantherus*, but with the throat narrower), is also definitely worth growing.

Penstemon fremontii is a native of dry hills in pinyon-juniper communities in south-central and southwestern Wyoming, also in adjacent areas of Utah and Colorado. This is a fine plant, the search for which may frustrate even the most determined rock gardeners. Seed is very occasionally available. *Penstemon fremontii* is about eight inches (20 cm) tall and wide, thanks to multiple stems, with densely ashy-gray-hairy foliage and clusters of inch-long (2.5cm) deep blue flowers all around the stems in late May and early June. *Penstemon gibbensii*, also from Wyoming and Colorado, is rather similar but with a sticky inflorescence and smooth green leaves.

Penstemon gairdneri is a fantastic little shrub with tiny linear leaves about an inch (2.5cm) long, growing to a foot (30cm) tall and wide in its native habitat in eastern Oregon and Washington, but somewhat less, in both dimensions, in the garden. The flowers are almost flat-faced like those of *P. ambiguus*, of a good lavender or bluish purple, or blue, sometimes in pale shades, produced in profusion in June. Variety *oreganus*, also found in western Idaho, has wider, opposite leaves and is surprisingly easy to grow from seed. Both *P. gairdneri* and its var. *oreganus* transplanted well, flowered, and then, a few years later—as if they didn't know how big they were supposed to get—they died. This was undoubtedly not the fault of the plants.

Penstemon grahamii is a small penstemon found growing mostly on shale (including oil shale) in the Uinta Basin in eastern Utah, also across the state line in northwestern Colorado. This one gets to six inches (15cm) in gigantic specimens, with smooth green oblanceolate leaves and clusters of large pink-purple flowers with gaping throats and golden beards in late May. *Penstemon grahamii* is an exceptionally showy miniature, for troughs; I have seen at least one nursery list it for sale. This is a short-lived plant, so be prepared. *Penstemon janishiae* (California, east of the Sierra Nevada, to Idaho) is fairly similar, with slightly smaller, though equally gaping, flowers on a longer-lived plant.

Other relatives of *Penstemon grahamii* are worth searching out, though the search will be a long and possibly frustrating one. Two of the best are *P. calcareus* and *P. monoensis*, with pink or reddish-violet flowers. Both are from the eastern reaches of the Mojave Desert in California, and will delight in dry conditions. Like the others, these dwarf jewels are probably best in a trough; they get lost in the garden.

Penstemon haydenii, from the Sandhills of western Nebraska, is similar to *P. angustifolius* but lacks basal leaves, and the sky-blue flowers are intensely fragrant. In the event that it becomes "de-listed" (it is currently endangered), this would be a highly desirable species for the rock garden. I could even replace my plant, which died a week after I planted it.

Penstemon humilis is another penstemon not too common in the trade (this isn't my fault, by the way), but easily grown from seed. Native to a large area east of the Cascades and Sierra Nevada, to Wyoming and Colorado, this has green oblanceolate basal leaves and flowering stems to eight inches (20cm), with clusters of small, intense blue flowers all around the stem in late May or early June. The variety from the Wasatch Mountains in Utah, var. *brevifolius*, is the best, with larger flowers on a smaller plant. *Penstemon humilis* is a long-lived plant, and, oh, those flowers, even if they are small.

Penstemon laricifolius (larch-leafed penstemon), native to Wyoming, is one of my favorites; this has tufts of green linear leaves, like little clumps of grass about an inch (2.5cm) tall and two inches (5cm) wide, with slender stalks about four inches (10cm) tall with clusters of good-sized flat-faced pink flowers in June, sometimes a little earlier. A very distinctive plant, easy to grow from seed, and easily transplanted. The northern Colorado variety, *exilifolius*, is somewhat smaller, with white flowers, and has a welcome tendency to seed itself about.

Penstemon leiophyllus, native to south-central Utah and Nevada, is a plant growing to over two feet (60cm) in the typical variety, but the one we want is var. *francisci-pennellii* from eastern Nevada. This has long (three inches, 7.5cm) green oblanceolate leaves and flowering stems about eight inches (20cm) tall, with a one-sided inflorescence of fat, inch-long (2.5cm) blue-purple flowers. *Penstemon leiophyllus* is reasonably easy from seed, though a few mail-order nurseries do offer plants from time to time. *Penstemon paysoniorum*, from southwestern Wyoming, is somewhat similar and equally desirable.

Penstemon linarioides is an amazingly drought-tolerant plant, having lived in the garden here for almost twenty years unfazed by the most hair-raising droughts. Native from Utah, Nevada, and Arizona to southwestern Colorado and western New Mexico, *P. linarioides* is a subshrub with linear blue-silver-gray leaves about an inch (2.5cm) long on slightly floppy stems six to eight inches (15 to 20cm) long (though it gets taller in the wild), with blue, white-throated flowers more or less all summer. *Penstemon linarioides* var. *coloradoënsis*, from the Four Corners area,

[left] *Penstemon laricifolius* var. *laricifolius*

[above] *Penstemon laricifolius* var. *exilifolius*

is the really tough one. Another variety that is worth considering is var. *sileri*, from southwestern Utah, adjacent Nevada, and at least northern Arizona; it has almost rigidly upright stems to eight inches (20 cm). In my first trial with var. *sileri* the plants winter-burned to nothing, but the second attempt proved successful. I don't know why. *Penstemon abietinus*, from central Utah, is quite similar. *Penstemon discolor*, from Pima County in Arizona, is less similar but still a close relation, with almost succulent leaves and smaller flowers.

Penstemon nitidus is easily one of the glories of the northern Great Plains (southern Alberta, Saskatchewan, and Manitoba south to Wyoming), if not of the entire temperate plant kingdom. *Penstemon nitidus* is quite similar to *P. angustifolius*, except that its blue-glaucous leaves are wider. A well-grown plant, given plenty of moisture in early spring, and not too much in the summer, can grow eight inches (20cm) tall to a foot (30cm) wide. Occasionally floppy stems notwithstanding, the profuse clusters of red buds opening to dazzling electric-blue flowers must be counted as one of the most stunning displays imaginable. *Penstemon nitidus* blooms in April in the garden here.

Penstemon nitidus

Penstemon pinifolius used to be a fairly difficult plant to find but is now as common as dirt in regional horticulture, even gracing median plantings here in Denver (with irrigation, of course). *Penstemon pinifolius* can be left to its own devices in the garden if some summer moisture falls, otherwise the plants start fading away. Subject to attack by pittosporum pit scale. Native to northern Mexico, southern New Mexico, and southeastern Arizona, *P. pinifolius* has reddish, more or less upright stems to ten inches (25cm) or so, with pineneedle-like leaves about an inch (2.5cm) long. A profusion of inch-long (2.5cm) orange-red flowers appears in August and September, the display sometimes starting earlier, sometimes lingering later into autumn, after the hummingbirds have packed up for the Yucatán.

Sports of *Penstemon pinifolius*, mostly in pale yellow, are plentiful in the trade, though the yellow forms have unattractive (to me) bright green foliage; 'Mersea

Yellow' and 'Magdalena Sunshine' are two of these. Other color forms, including orange, are also available.

Penstemon thompsoniae, native to southern Nevada, Utah, northern Arizona, and mountains in southern California, is another mat-former, related to *P. caespitosus* and *P. linarioides* but quite different in appearance. This one has round or spoon-shaped gray-blue leaves about a quarter of an inch (6mm) long on flopping stems about four inches (10cm) long, sometimes longer, with purplish blue flowers in late May. A variety with upright stems is found in southern Nevada; this var. *jaegeri* is a rare denizen of seedlists, not to mention nursery catalogs. *Penstemon thompsoniae* is perfect for a trough, and stunning in a trough mulched with white shale.

Penstemon utahensis is found along the Colorado River drainage from western Colorado to eastern San Bernardino County in California. This is an upright species to ten inches (25cm), maybe twice that with more moisture, with blue-glaucous oblanceolate basal leaves about three inches (7.5cm) long, and clusters of salverform flowers, reminiscent

Penstemon thompsoniae

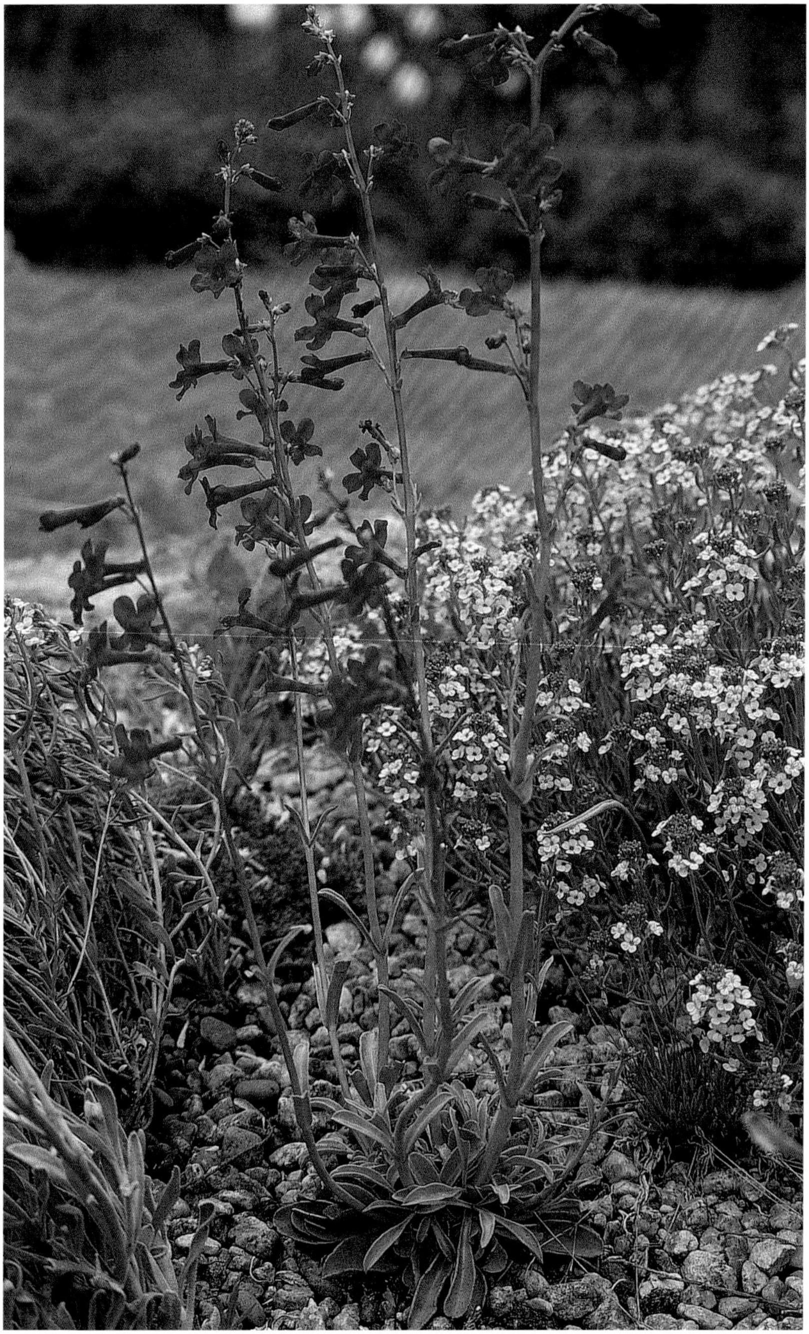

Penstemon utahensis with pennycress

of those on *P. ambiguus*, in various shades of red to pink. The really red ones are highly desirable, both for the rock garden and hummingbirds; flowering time is April to June, depending on the weather, of course.

Phemeranthus. A family of succulents in the purslane (Portulacaceae) family, formerly included in *Talinum*, and almost always sold under that name in nurseries. *Phemeranthus*, a name obviously devised by someone (Rafinesque) with no dental work in his front teeth, is differentiated from *Talinum* by having terete (circular in cross-section) leaves. The common name fameflower is also spelled "flameflower." It can't be both, so I vote for neither. Maybe flamethrower would be better.

Phemeranthuses are extremely easy to grow from seed; I sow them indoors under light, and in a few weeks the seeds are up. They transplant easily, but tiny plants set out into the garden can be subject to frost heaving. Once established the plants are generous, but not too generous, in reseeding about. Their drought tolerance is considerable.

Phemeranthus aurantiacus may be a bit large for the rock garden, to two feet (60cm) or more, sometimes shrubby, with green linear leaves about two inches (5cm) long, and solitary orange, yellow, or even pink flowers an inch (2.5cm) wide. Native to northern Mexico, Arizona, New Mexico, and Texas, flowering all summer. The yellow phase of *P. aurantiacus* used to be called, when it was a talinum, *T. angustissimum*.

Phemeranthus brevicaulis, native to Arizona, New Mexico, northern Mexico, and western Texas, is a multi-stemmed plant to about four inches (10cm), with sometimes flattened linear leaves (linear, and then stepped on) an inch (2.5cm) long, with pink, or purplish pink flowers in the axils of the upper leaves. The species formerly called *Talinum pulchellum* is now included in *P. brevicaulis*.

Phemeranthus brevifolius is a gem. This is a tiny mat-former to two inches (5cm) with congested, fat, half-inch-long (1.25cm) green leaves, on top of which sit glittering, half-inch-wide (1.25cm) sugar-pink flowers that open every second Tuesday or every fifth week during the summer, and stay open for about five minutes. *Phemeranthus brevifolius* is excellent in a trough, though probably in one where other plants are in flower at one time or another. I once grew a plant from seed labeled "*P. rhizomatus*" (I can find no reference for this name); this was a slightly

Phemeranthus brevifolius

larger plant (not that much larger, though), with blue-green leaves and larger flowers.

Phemeranthus calycinus is a plant of the Great Plains, and further east, to a foot (30 cm) or taller, branching, with leaves about three inches (7.5 cm), with inch-wide (2.5 cm) pink-purple flowers throughout the summer. This one is common in the trade but hard to keep going in the garden. (This was Barr's experience, too, so I don't feel so bad.)

Phemeranthus humilis is a tiny (about three inches, 7.5 cm), rare species from Arizona, New Mexico, and northern Mexico, with yellow flowers. Several years ago I sowed seed of this, and nothing happened. That must be why it's rare. *Phemeranthus marginatus*, also with yellow flowers, from Arizona and Mexico, is even tinier.

Phemeranthus parviflorus (sunbright) is found almost everywhere, from Alabama to Minnesota to northern Mexico to Utah. As I know it,

P. parviflorus has linear leaves two inches (5 cm) long, forming a grass-like tuft, with branching stems and small sugar-pink flowers less than half an inch (1.25 cm) wide, borne all summer. This is one of the nicest ones; as Barr says the plants will endure being heaved right out of the ground by frost and will grow normally when stuck back into the ground. *Phemeranthus confertiflorus*, from New Mexico, is sometimes considered synonymous with *P. parviflorus*. *Phemeranthus longipes*, from northern Mexico and adjacent Texas, is somewhat similar.

Phemeranthus sediformis is native to eastern British Columbia and Washington. This is a wonderful little plant for troughs; it barely makes half an inch (1.25 cm) in height, with tiny leaves, spreading to three inches (7.5 cm) or so. In June and July a profusion of small, white, yellow-tinged flowers are borne on stems about an inch (2.5 cm) tall. Examined with a hand lens, it looks dead in the winter; it usually isn't. Available as seed, and plants, from nurseries catering to the rock garden trade, as *Talinum okanoganense*, or *T. sediforme* (sometimes spelled "sedoides"), or some combination of these names. A hybrid of this species and the next, similar to *P. sediformis* but slightly larger and with good bright pink-purple flowers, is sold as *Talinum* 'Zoe'; this is a treasure.

Phemeranthus spinescens, so named because the last year's leaf midribs form spines, is a plant with clusters of inch-long (2.5 cm) leaves on tiny branched stems, and multiple inch-wide (2.5 cm) pink or red flowers on stems six inches (15 cm) or taller. Native to eastern Washington and Oregon. Both seed and plants are usually available.

Phlox. These familiar garden plants offer something for practically everyone gardening in temperate climates. I dote on the various cultivars of *Phlox paniculata*, but this is the only eastern species of phlox we still grow. All the supposedly bone-hardy cultivars of *P. subulata* that passed through the garden here are now deader than doornails, having burned right to the ground in dry, sunny winters. *Phlox bifida* only overwintered a year or two, and the forms of *P. divaricata* and *P. stolonifera* have never made it through a single winter in our garden; it seems that the climate here can never provide the requisite humidity and gentle atmosphere needed to keep these beauties happy.

For rock gardeners in the west, there are plenty of phloxes to grow, some upright, and some tight cushion plants (the "microphloxes") that will endure some serious drought, though gardeners seeing them for the first time may have to redefine the image that the word "phlox" creates in their minds. Some of the alpine species, like *Phlox condensata*, *P. hendersonii*, *P. multiflora*, and *P. pulvinata*, will tolerate dry conditions for short periods, but these plants are far happier in a watered alpine garden.

There is, to say the least, some disagreement among botanists when it comes to the taxonomy of the genus *Phlox*. The standard work on *Phlox*, by Wherry, contains vastly more species than some botanists today seem willing to admit. I take no position in this at all; I see phloxes, and I buy them. One name that continues to surface in literature, especially across the Atlantic, is *P. douglasii*. This name does not exist in floras, except as a synonym for *P. caespitosa*.

Seed of most of these phloxes is difficult to collect (seeds tend to pop out of the capsule just as it's being grabbed by overeager fingers) and therefore expensive. Phloxes germinate readily from seed sown outdoors, though, and young plants transplant easily. Once established, these taprooted plants should be left alone. (Rooted cuttings can sometimes be taken, with moderate success.) Plants of some of the species are available from rock garden nurseries.

Phlox aculeata is native to the Snake River Plain in western Idaho, also barely entering eastern Oregon. This is a dwarf, upright-stemmed phlox with linear, sticky-hairy, sharp-pointed green leaves, the stems about three inches (7.5cm) tall, with white, pink, or pink-purple lilac-scented flowers about an inch (2.5cm) wide, blooming in April in the garden. Trim the stems only after new growth begins in spring.

Phlox alyssifolia is a common dryland phlox found from southern Saskatchewan and Alberta to Wyoming and Nebraska. This is a mat- or mound-former to two or three inches (5 to 7.5cm) high by at least eight inches (20cm) wide; the oblong, thickened leaves are about a quarter-inch (6mm) long with conspicuously whitened margins. The inch-wide (2.5cm) scented flowers are white, pink, or pink-purple, blooming in April or May. In winter the plants form tangles of white stems with only the tips green; the stems should be left alone to recover by themselves. *Phlox albomarginata*, from Montana and Idaho, is somewhat similar.

Phlox alyssifolia

Phlox andicola is a low mat-forming phlox with inch-long (2.5cm, sometimes shorter) needle-like green leaves, with fragrant pink-purple or white flowers about half an inch (1.25cm) across, in April and May. This is a good ground-covering phlox for raised beds of dry clay; again the stems should be left alone until spring. Native from northwestern Kansas through eastern Colorado to Montana and South Dakota.

Phlox austromontana is common from western Colorado through the Intermountain region south to Baja California. This is another mat-former to four inches (10cm) by twice as wide, with stiff, pointed, green linear leaves about half an inch (1.25cm) long. The lightly scented flowers are white, sometimes tinged with blue, or pink ("blooms of vivid pink all over its greener, gorse-like cushions," according to Dwight Ripley, who saw the plants while traveling in the west with Rupert Barneby in the 1940s), also about half an inch (1.25cm) wide. Flowering in April and May. *Phlox jonesii* is a floppy version of *P. austromontana*, growing "festooned clumps" (in Edgar Wherry's description) in Zion Canyon in southwestern Utah; maybe, if it grows elsewhere (outside the national park, that is), it might be introduced into cultivation.

Phlox caespitosa is from an elevation higher than most of the dryland species, but it readily takes to dry conditions. Native from western Montana to British Columbia, *P. caespitosa* has linear, pointed leaves reminiscent of the eastern *P. subulata* but forms a dome four inches (10cm) by eight inches (20cm) wide, covered with inch-wide (2.5cm) white or pale purple, lightly fragrant flowers in April or May.

Phlox caryophylla is an endemic of southwestern Colorado and adjacent New Mexico, growing in woodlands. This is a woody-based upright species, with narrowly oblong leaves one to two inches (2.5 to 5cm) long, on stems eight inches (20cm) high, with inch-wide (2.5cm) pink or purple, clove-scented flowers more or less lacking the typical phlox "eye." In the unlikely event *P. caryophylla* finds its way into cultivation, it would be a good plant for dry shade.

Phlox cluteana (Navajo phlox) is another upright species, found on the Utah-Arizona side of the Four Corners area, with linear, upright leaves about two inches (5cm) long, on stems to eight inches (20cm), and clusters of small, more or less scentless purple flowers about half an inch (1.25cm) wide, in June. *Phlox cluteana* is a spreader, though not aggressively so.

Phlox gladiformis (dagger-leaf phlox) is a low, stinking taprooted thing from southwestern Utah and southeastern Nevada, with stiff, linear, sharply pointed leaves thickly clustered along the stems, on a plant six inches (15cm) tall and wide. The flowers are about half an inch (1.25cm), blooming in May. The strong stench of the plant, which comes from the glandular-sticky foliage, may be a negative feature for some people, though *P. gladiformis* is an excellent plant for a hot, dry situation.

Phlox hoodii is found throughout western North America, from the Great Plains (Saskatchewan to Colorado), and from northern Arizona to Alaska. This is a low carpeting phlox about an inch (2.5cm) tall, with tiny needle-like leaves about a quarter of an inch (6mm) long clustered on the stems, and equally small white, pink, or purple flowers scented of vanilla cake, blooming in March and April. *Phlox hoodii* var. *canescens*, mostly found in the Intermountain area, has slightly larger flow-

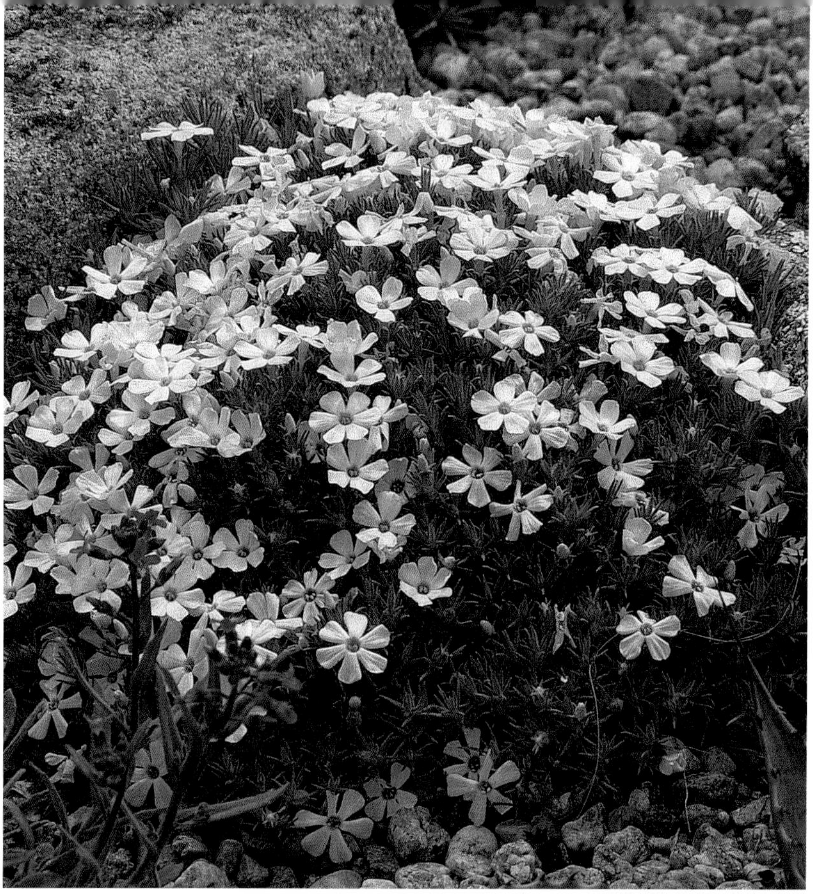

Phlox caespitosa

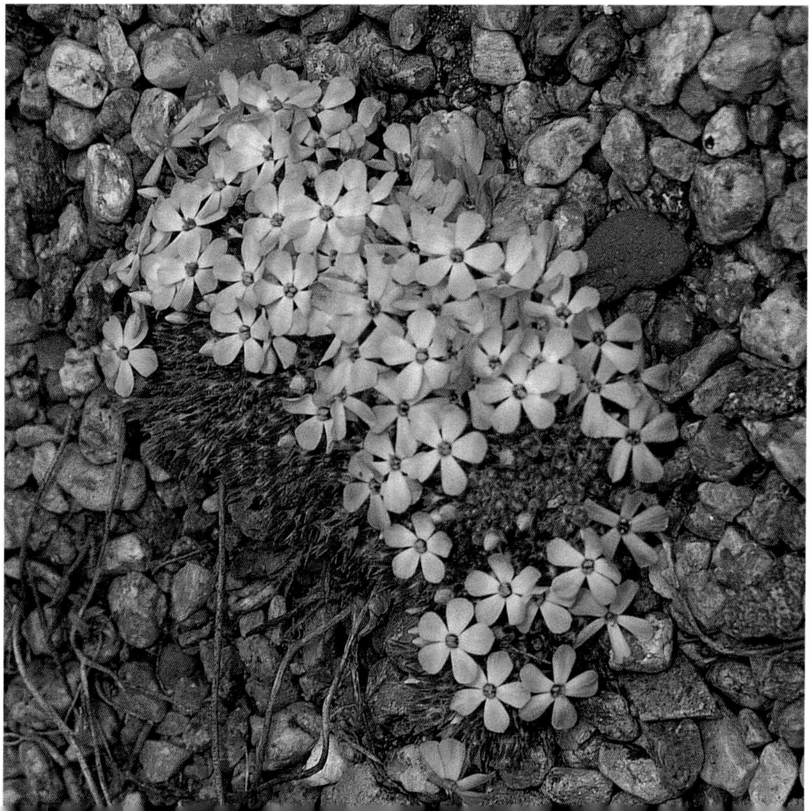

Phlox hoodii var. *canescens*

ers. Visitors to our garden have mistaken this plant for a miniature conifer. *Phlox hoodii* is an excellent plant for weaving in and out of other plants in a dry rock garden.

Phlox kelseyi (marsh phlox) is found growing in marshes and other seasonally wet areas in widely scattered locations from central Colorado to Montana west to Idaho and Nevada. This is another dome- or mound-forming phlox with linear, oddly succulent linear leaves less than an inch (2.5cm) long; the stems may reach six inches (15cm), though in a dry garden the plant is more of a pancake than a mound, and the stems may only reach two inches (5cm). The more or less fragrant flowers are an inch (2.5cm) wide, white tinged with lavender, or lavender, or light bluish purple in May and June. 'Lemhi Purple' (from the Lemhi Mountains in Idaho), a form with rich purple flowers, is common in the rock garden trade and more than worth acquiring. Despite its preference for wet, alkaline areas, these do dry out in summer and autumn, and so *P. kelseyi* will work quite well in a dry rock garden. Rumor has it that it is among the easiest to grow in the wetter, more humid climates of eastern North America. *Phlox missoulensis*, found on Waterworks Hills just north of Missoula, Montana, and possibly elsewhere, is quite similar but with stiff, nonsucculent leaves. Some botanists consider it a variety of *P. kelseyi*.

Phlox longifolia is a variable, widespread species found throughout the Great Plains and Intermountain area, with a semi-woody base and linear leaves sometimes three inches (7.5cm) long or more, sparsely arranged on upright, or ascending, stems usually about eight inches (20cm) high. The scented, white or pink flowers are slightly more than an inch (2.5cm) across, in May and June, and then again from September to November. *Phlox longifolia* moves about by roots creeping underground. Small sections of plants, with the roots, can be easily moved in the garden, though, in keeping with a number of upright-growing microphloxes, the stems are extremely brittle. The plant is semi-evergreen, with some healthy leaves persisting on seemingly dead stems, so be careful doing winter cleanup. It can also be grown from seed, though only a percentage of these seem to want to germinate.

One variety of *Phlox longifolia* especially worth mentioning is var. *stansburyi*, a much more compact plant with stiffly upright stems and

Phlox longifolia

flowers with amazingly long tubes but smaller lobes (half an inch, 1.25cm, wide, or less), hence the common name, inch-tube phlox. The flowers in this variety, native to Nevada and Utah, are not particularly fragrant, but this is a fine plant. Some botanists consider *P. grayi*, which is slightly taller and with the wider flowers of typical *P. longifolia*, to be a distinct species, but others consider it synonymous with *P. longifolia* var. *stansburyi*.

With *Phlox mesoleuca* we have a species with a much different moisture regime in the wild, spring being the dry season, the wet season (such as it is) not arriving until summer, and sometimes late in summer. So the plants would seem to have both an inherited drought tolerance and a need for moisture, depending upon when these conditions occur. It doesn't always work that way, of course; forms of *P. mesoleuca* have done quite well in gardens where the climatic conditions do not resemble the natural conditions in any way. Here, they tolerate drought to the same degree as the other phloxes, but need some summer moisture in order to bloom. *Phlox mesoleuca*, an upright species with a few inch- to two-inch-long (2.5 to 5cm) linear leaves arranged sparingly on a few foot-high (30cm) stems with large pink, yellow, white, or red flowers over an inch (2.5cm) wide, is native to southern New Mexico, western Texas, and Chihuahua.

The story of *Phlox mesoleuca* in cultivation may already have ended. A number of fantastic (maybe "improbable" would be a better word) color selections were introduced in the late 1980s and seem to have virtually disappeared. 'Tangelo' is (or was) a larger-flowered, taller plant with orange flowers with a darker orange eye; 'Denver Sunset' is orange-red fading to a yellow center; 'Alborado' is dark orange-red with a darker eye; 'Mary Maslin' is bright red with only a hint of orange; 'Paul Maslin' (named for T. Paul Maslin, the person most responsible for bringing these plants into cultivation) is a bright yellow; 'Chameleon' is white with purple markings near the eye, fading to cream the next day; 'Vanilla' is white with purple markings near the eye; 'Arroyo' is a rich pink. Only this last name appears in catalogs now.

These phloxes are propagated by root cuttings, although I did actually see one seed on a plant of 'Mary Maslin'. It turned out not to be viable. The Mexican (or Chihuahuan) phloxes are easily transplanted, but the deciduous stems are unbelievably breakable: one careless moment ripping bindweed out of the garden, and there go your Mexican phloxes. Keep the weeds down, may be the rule here (that, or don't touch your plants).

An apparent hybrid of *Phlox mesoleuca* 'Arroyo' and *P. subulata* was discovered and introduced by Homer Hill, a master propagator of the Mexican phloxes. This 'Arroyito' has the same bright pink flowers, about three-quarters of an inch (2 cm) wide, on traveling stems about six inches (15 cm). 'Arroyito' has been in our garden for many years, appearing here and there like the white rabbit, and has shown excellent drought resistance.

Phlox muscoides (*P. bryoides*) is found here and there in the Intermountain area and in Wyoming, Colorado, and Nebraska. This is one of the best microphloxes for the rock garden or trough; it forms a tight mound, or bun, one to two inches (2.5 to 5 cm) high by eight inches (20 cm) wide. The stems, densely covered with woolly cobwebs, have tiny triangular leaves arranged so that the stems look square, hence one of the common names, square-shoot phlox. The more or less scented flowers are smallish, less than half an inch (1.25 cm) wide, usually white (most of the plants in the trade have white flowers), sometimes pink, or purple. The newly described *P. opalensis*, from southwestern Wyoming, is similar, but the stems are less tightly bunched together, and the white or pink flowers are slightly larger.

Phlox nana is native to New Mexico, west Texas, and Chihuahua. This species is closely related to *P. mesoleuca*, though the stems are leaf-

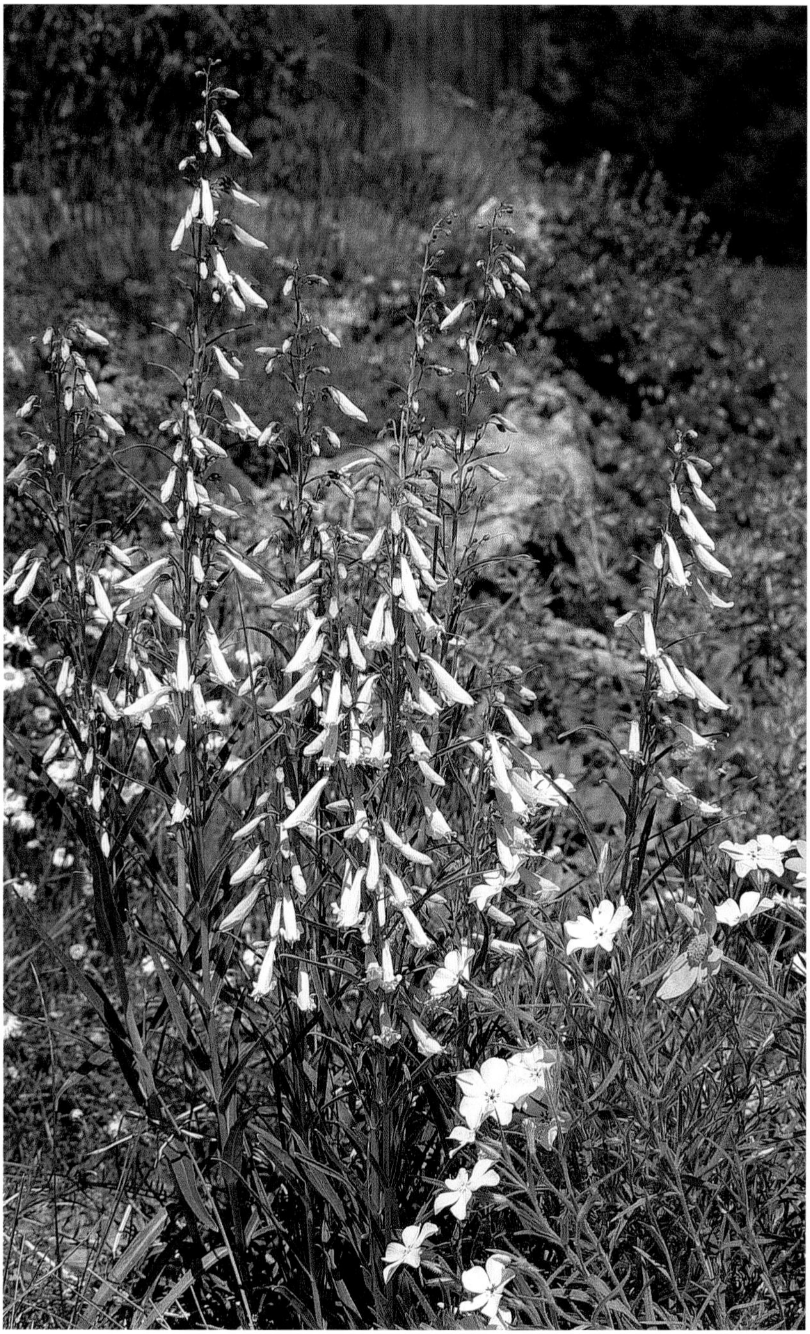

Phlox mesoleuca 'Vanilla' at foot of *Penstemon barbatus* 'Schooley's Yellow', garden of Ann and Dick Bartlett

ier, and the plant, at least in cultivation, is generally smaller. *Phlox nana* makes a nice, gray-leafed plant about eight inches (20cm) tall by a foot (30cm) or more wide, with inch-wide (2.5cm) essentially scentless pinkish purple flowers borne from midsummer onward. This can be grown either in a bone-dry garden, where it's happy but not totally thrilled, or in an occasionally watered garden. *Phlox nana* is more or less readily available in the trade, especially from nurseries catering to gardeners in New Mexico.

Phlox pungens is a rare species from the Wind River Basin in west-central Wyoming, but it seems to be on the brink of being established in cultivation. *Phlox pungens* is a loosely colonial phlox, shoots appearing here and there in no apparent pattern, about two inches (5cm) tall by six inches (15cm) wide, with tiny, sharply pointed lanceolate leaves and sticky-hairy white flowers about half an inch (1.25cm) wide in May and June. This promises to be a fine rock garden phlox.

Phlox speciosa is found from California and Nevada north to British Columbia (east of the Cascades), east to Montana, growing with sagebrush. This is a handsome, woody-based plant, with stems six inches (15cm) to two feet (60cm) tall, with a few lanceolate or linear leaves, almost three inches (7.5cm) long in some cases, sparsely arranged on the stems. The lightly scented pink or white inch-wide (2.5cm) flowers, with notched petals, bloom in May and June and are held in a loose cyme (flowering with the terminal bud first, then the lower ones) reminiscent of some of the eastern North American species. I confess to not having much success with *P. speciosa*: seed germinated and plants were set out (among sagebrush, even), but the plants died after a few years. This is one I should try again, with greater seriousness of purpose. *Phlox colubrina*, from western Idaho and adjacent areas of Washington and Oregon, is similar but lacks the notched petals.

Phlox tumulosa may be the ultimate cushion phlox. This taprooted species, from east-central Nevada and extreme western Utah, forms amazing, rock-hard mounds of light green, an inch (2.5cm) tall by six inches (15cm) wide (though it gets much wider than that in the wild—I'm here assuming that the gardener will not wait the fifty years it might take the plant to get two feet, 60cm, across), with small white flowers less than half an inch (1.25cm) wide in May and June. *Phlox tumulosa* is surprisingly easy from seed and transplants well. Astonish your rock gardening friends with this one. *Phlox griseola* is like a much looser version of *P. tumulosa*, and almost as good, with white, pink, or purple flowers projecting slightly above the cushion.

Phlox woodhousei (also spelled "woodhousii"), from northern Arizona and western New Mexico, is both taprooted and an underground creeper, with oblong basal leaves about an inch and a half (3.75 cm) long, smaller leaves higher up on the six-inch (15 cm) clustered stems, and inch-wide (2.5 cm) fragrant flowers, conspicuously notched at the ends of

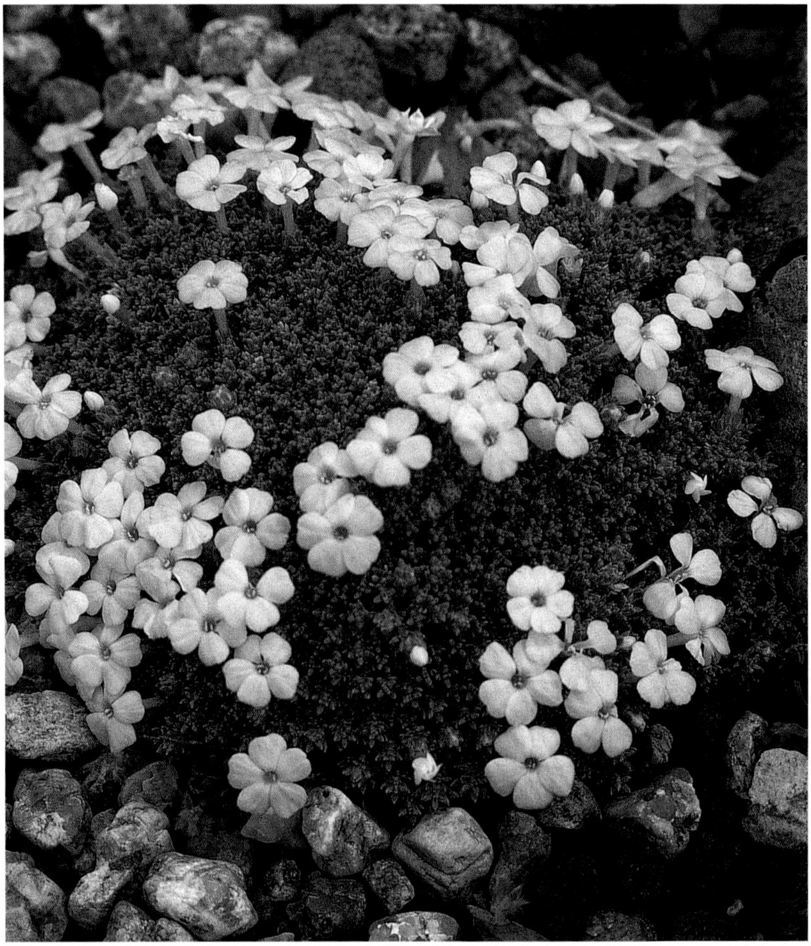

Phlox tumulosa

the petals, blooming in May, and sometimes later in the summer. *Phlox amabilis*, from essentially the same area, is quite similar.

Phoenicaulis (daggerpod). One species, *Phoenicaulis cheiranthoides*, is sometimes offered, partly because it's the only species in its genus. This member of the mustard family has a rosette of upright, gray-green oblanceolate leaves, making a plant about two inches (5 cm) high by three inches (7.5 cm) wide when extremely happy, which is not often. In May it has flowering stems to six inches (15 cm), with terminal heads of pink flowers. The long siliques are a conspicuous feature by late June. This is a tough little beauty, but, like a lot of other plants, only flowers in years with good moisture in early spring. Susceptible to attack by flea beetles.

Physaria (twinpod). An invaluable genus of mustards for the dry rock garden, with silver-gray-green rosettes lasting throughout the winter, with heads of, usually, bright yellow flowers borne on stems splaying out from the central rosette in April or May, and later bearing fat, inflated round seedpods. Farrer is better: "[The leaves] are arranged around the rosette at rare intervals, in flattened, inclined planes like the vanes of a wind-fan, which gives the plant quite sufficient charm in itself, even did not the rosette send up a spire of such handsome, clear-yellow flowers." Barr, on the other hand, was unimpressed.

Except for alpine species like *Physaria alpina* (a slightly difficult, smaller species requiring a well-watered place in the rock garden), there is much of a muchness about the two dozen species, or at least so it seems to me. Differentiation between species is often a matter of distinguishing minute characteristics of the fruits, and the species hybridize readily when they come into contact, both in the wild and in the garden. Physariophiles will no doubt want every species, but almost all have the same garden effect.

[opposite top] *Physaria chambersii*

[left] *Physaria chambersii* in fruit

[right] *Physaria vitulifera* in winter

A year-old rosette (a beautiful thing to see, as Farrer suggested) is about three inches (7.5 cm) across and about half an inch (1.25 cm) high. Mature plants are about six inches (15 cm) across, with stems three to four inches (7.5 to 10 cm) long, splayed outward from the rosette, or slightly ascending, or upright (even within the same species).

My impression is that individual plants last only three or four years,

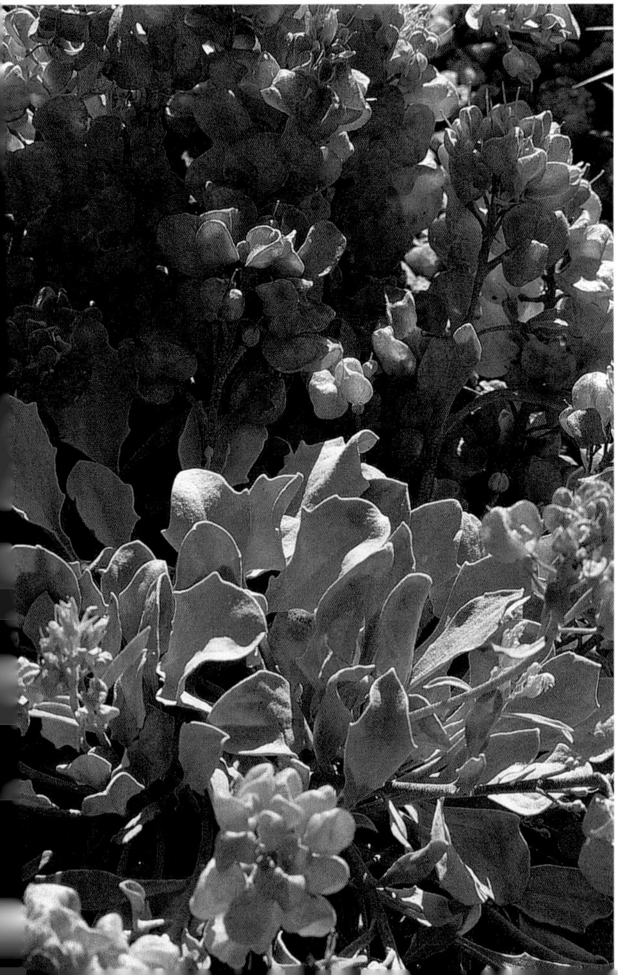

but physarias are generous with their seed. One reason their life span is so brief is that eventually they tend to grow short trunks, which in my eyes is vaguely unsightly, and so I pull them up.

They are also easy to grow from purchased seed and transplant easily. Once established, these taprooted plants die if moved. One thing to note: if the plants are on a slope, the fat, round seedpods will roll downhill, and the future generation of physarias will all be at the bottom of the slope.

Some of the plants that have been in the garden are *Physaria acutifolia*, from Wyoming, Utah, and Colorado, though unfortunately not the purple-flowered var. *purpurea*; *P. bellii*, a rare inhabitant of shale along the Front Range of the Rocky Mountains, but firmly established in cultivation and a first-rate garden plant; *P. chambersii*, especially showy in fruit, from Utah, Arizona, Nevada, Oregon, and California; *P. eburniflora*, from south-central Wyoming, with cream-colored flowers; and *P. vitulifera*, from Colorado and Wyoming, quite similar to *P. bellii* but with pandurate (shaped like a violin) leaves (this is the one species I can actually recognize, though it has hybridized with *P. bellii* in my garden).

Pulsatilla. The pasqueflowers are found throughout the northern hemisphere, especially in Central Asia. One species, *Pulsatilla patens*, is native to both Eurasia and the Great Plains, in fact almost everywhere west of the Mississippi except Arizona and California. Also known as *Anemone patens*, this is a fuzzy, furry, silky ferny-leafed plant to about six inches (15 cm) with gorgeous pale lavender, blue, or, rarely, white flowers, three inches (7.5 cm) wide and long, in April or May. Winged seedheads follow.

As with clematis, the "tail" of the seedhead is said by some to contain a germination inhibitor, so, when I obtained some seed years ago, I dutifully pinched off the feathery tails and sowed the seed outdoors in January. (I now think that indoor sowing under lights is best for this genus.) I got one tiny plant, set it out in the front yard, and nothing happened.

Then a couple of years later I almost fell over the plant in full bloom. I decided, of course, to move it, knowing full well that moving pulsatillas means killing them. It hasn't been replaced. I have to disagree with Barr, who knew the plant and its cultivation better than I do, about its requirements; here, it did quite well in a very dry place. Did well, that is, until that fatal day in spring.

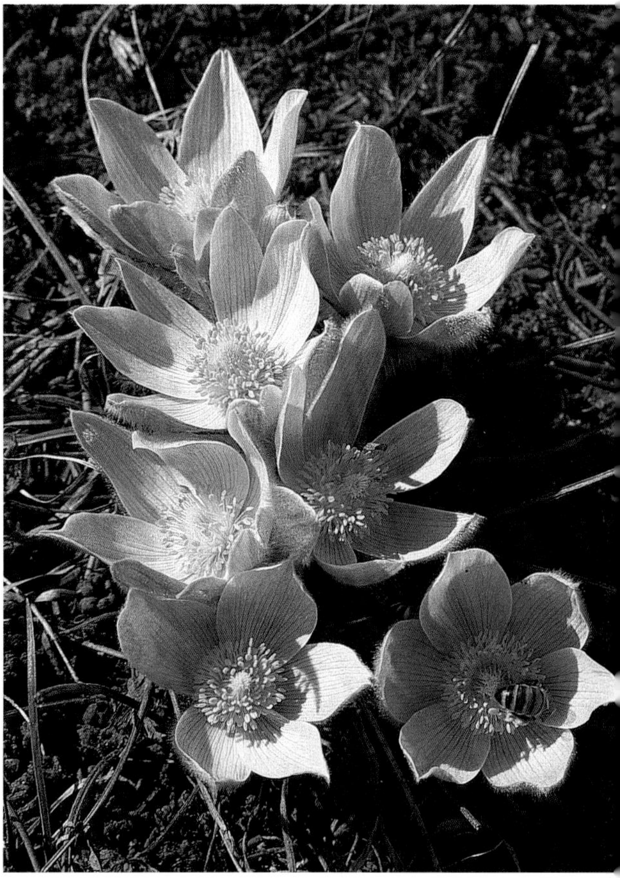

Pulsatilla patens

Scutellaria (skullcap). A large genus of plants (scoots, to those in the know) in the mint family with more or less hooded flowers vaguely reminiscent of some penstemons. Only a few native species are valuable rock garden plants. I find the aggressively spreading types to be more valuable than the upright species. (I've written off the Texan *Scutellaria suffrutescens* as being too tender to be worth growing, even if the rose-pink flowers are attractive, since it needs too much watering to get it going in its first, and only, year.)

Scutellarias are easy to grow from seed and transplant readily. Once established, the spreaders will take astonishingly dry conditions, but they do this by completely disappearing for the summer. They can be moved by digging up the shallow roots at any time of the year.

Scutellaria angustifolia is native to eastern Washington, Oregon, and parts of adjacent Idaho. Overwintering as little mats of green oblong leaves about half an inch (1.25cm) long, it sends up narrow-leafed stalks about eight inches (20cm) tall with two or three deep blue flowers about two inches (5cm) long, in the axils of the uppermost leaves. Flowering time is May to June. Then it sets seed, and disappears. *Scutellaria angustifolia* is an aggressive spreader, a fact that should be borne in mind while blithely setting out young seedlings. *Scutellaria antirrhinoides*, from the same area but also found in California and Nevada, has slightly smaller flowers, closed at the throat.

Scutellaria brittonii (New Mexico to Wyoming, also in western Kansas and Nebraska) is another spreader, not betraying its presence in winter, but sending up six-inch (15cm) stems in May, with bright blue, half-inch-long (1.25cm) flowers in the axils of the uppermost leaves. This is a beautiful plant, though the dried stems need to be removed in the summer (they can just be raked up), and you will have to resign yourself to having a bare space in the garden for eleven months of the year, or use *S. brittonii* as an underplanting for shrubs.

Scutellaria nana is, I think, the smallest of North American scutellarias, weighing in at four inches (10cm) tall by as much as it feels like spreading wide. Native to northern California and Oregon through Nevada to western Idaho, *S. nana* has ashy-gray oblanceolate leaves, with, in var. *nana*, pale purple and cream-colored flowers almost an inch (2.5cm) long, borne in May and June. This is nice in itself, but it's in var. *sapphirina* that we meet one of North America's best rock garden plants; the pale bicolored flowers are gone, and in their place are flowers of the bluest blue imaginable.

Scutellaria resinosa, from Kansas and Oklahoma south to Texas (some botanists include *S. tessellata* and *S. wrightii* in *S. resinosa*, which would extend the range to New Mexico and Arizona), used to be impossible to find but now is offered by at least a couple of rock garden nurseries. *Scutellaria resinosa* is, in Dwight Ripley's words, "an intensely woody, branched little shrub quite loaded down with its racemes of violet skullcaps, and scarcely more than six inches [15cm] high." I can only add that it is not the longest lived of plants, but keeps going by seeding around, not too far from the original location.

Senecio (groundsel, butterweed, ragwort). An enormous genus of plants distributed throughout the world, many of which have little in common with each other besides their name. The species are split off from time to time and moved around to separate genera, so much that *Senecio* has become a waiting room for plants still remaining in the genus and about to be segregated from it.

In western North America, *Senecio holmii* (*S. amplectens*) and other cremanthoid senecios from the Rockies are sometimes included in *Ligularia*, and *S. werneriaefolius* is sometimes in *Packera*. These are superior, aristocratic plants for the rock garden but are anything but suitable for the dry rock garden, belonging in a well-watered rock garden or an artificial moraine. The much larger, widely distributed *S. douglasii*, in the variety *longilobus* or any other, is a second-rate weed with tiny yellow flowers.

A couple of senecios (both of which are also called packeras) are definitely worth considering for the dry rock garden. *Senecio canus* (*Packera cana*), widespread throughout western Canada and the United States, is, in its smaller forms, an absolute delight. *Senecio canus* forms mounds of white-woolly elliptic-ovate inch-long (2.5cm) leaves, about three inches (7.5cm) high by four inches (10cm) wide, with good yellow daisies about an inch (2.5cm) wide on stems two inches (5cm) taller than the cushions. *Senecio canus* is easy from seed, transplants well, and has the pleasant habit of seeding around just enough. This is a first-rate plant for a trough.

I also grow, through no skill of my own, a dwarf form of *Senecio fendleri* (*Packera fendleri*). At least I think it's a dwarf. This is an apparently common plant found on the eastern slope of the Rocky Mountains from New Mexico to Wyoming, but I had never ever seen the plant until it appeared in one of the troughs here, from seed contained in some gravel mulch we had scooped up from a road cut on a lonely Colorado mountain byway. *Senecio fendleri*, as I know it, has silver-gray pinnate leaves, wavy edged, about two inches (5cm) long, with smallish golden daisies on stems two inches (5cm) tall. This is not a terribly long-lived plant, but its seed is viable.

Silene (campion, catchfly). Another worldwide genus, with about two dozen plants of interest to rock gardeners. Silenes have five-petaled flowers, the petals often so deeply incised as to give the impression of having dozens of petals, with conspicuous, often bloated tubes, and generally glandular (sticky) foliage, hence one of the common names. Most silenes require a well-watered situation, but a few are at home in a dry rock garden. *Silene* is a three-syllable word: expect some blank stares when you talk about "sy-*lee*-nee."

Silene californica, found west of the Sierras in California, can be grown in rock gardens in the west, though I still suspect it of being slightly tender. *Silene californica* "is loose and lax, with branches of ten inches [25cm] or so, flopping from the central rootstock, set at intervals with pairs of rather sticky oval-pointed leaves, and branching into sprays that each carry a single flower, huge and ragged, and of the most astonishing velvety scarlet, in a dark calyx" (Farrer). *Silene californica*, even though it provides bloom from midsummer onward, is a rare inhabitant of seedlists. *Silene laciniata*, from southwestern New Mexico, Arizona, southern California (where it intergrades with *S. californica*), and Baja California, is quite similar to *S. californica* but with more linear leaves. The flower color ranges from bright red to (particularly in the forms found in Arizona and New Mexico) orange-red.

Silene hookeri (Oregon and northwestern California) is the best of all silenes, superior even to the circumpolar *S. acaulis*, and one of the best of all rock garden plants. *Silene hookeri* has oblanceolate grayish green, sometimes slightly sticky leaves about an inch (2.5cm) long,

Silene hookeri

weakly ascending or decumbent stems to six inches (15cm), and fairly glorious inch-wide (2.5cm) flowers, so deeply lobed, or incised, that in some forms (subsp. *bolanderi* in particular) they appear to have hundreds of petals. Flower color is generally salmon-pink, or white. There are a number of subspecies, and a synonym (*S. ingramii*) now not recognized as distinct.

Silene hookeri is moderately easy to grow from seed. It is much less easy to transplant; the root is very brittle. I was able to get a plant going only after many attempts at trying to get the long root safely into the ground without breaking it. Siskiyou Rare Plant Nursery used to sell plants that came in long plastic tubes, with (gasp) instructions warning the gardener not to damage the root. I attribute my success to a conscious, wrenching decision to pay attention to the instructions. Young seedlings are easier to transplant, but not by much. *Silene hookeri* is an excellent choice for the north-facing side of a dry rock garden, grown in gravelly clay.

Silene wrightii, a rare inhabitant of southern New Mexico, is one of the longest-lived and most accommodating of silenes. It is certainly the stickiest. *Silene wrightii* has gray-green oblanceolate leaves, stems to about eight inches (20cm) on a plant as wide, with inch-wide (2.5cm) white flowers from midsummer onward. This one is not too profligate with its seed.

Sphaeralcea (globemallow). Hollyhock relatives widely distributed throughout western North America; the majority of species are in Arizona, southern California, Baja California, and Sonora. Plants with orange flowers are not terribly common, and sphaeralceas make valuable addition to the dry garden, especially when this unusual flower color is combined with gray or silvery leaves. Most sphaeralceas are too tall for the rock garden; the larger ones are relegated to the section on perennials, and the two little ones are found here.

Sphaeralcea caespitosa is an endemic of western Utah, growing in limestone gravel. This is a cushion plant with gray-green woolly-hairy, oval or round, barely lobed leaves, making a mound—in the rock gardens of the fortunate—about four inches (10cm) high by eight inches (20cm) wide, with luminous, inch-and-a-half-wide (3.75cm) popsicle-

Sphaeralcea coccinea with *Amorpha nana* and *Echinocereus engelmannii*

orange flowers in June. I find *S. caespitosa* completely impossible to grow from seed, but some sorcerer-propagators offer seed-grown plants. Not an easy plant to grow in the garden, though I hear, unwillingly, reports of success in some Utah gardens. *Sphaeralcea caespitosa* is highly susceptible to rust, especially if hollyhocks are grown nearby. Completely overlooked by alpine garden writers, more drought-resistant and impressive in flower than *Kelseya uniflora*, more difficult to grow than any eritrichium, this is possibly the single most desirable North American rock garden plant.

Sphaeralcea coccinea (cowboy's delight) is common throughout the Great Plains from Alberta and Saskatchewan south to New Mexico and Texas, also in Arizona and Utah. This has inch-long (2.5 cm), ovate, gray-hairy, deeply lobed miniature hollyhock leaves and stems no taller than eight inches (20 cm), though the literature suggests that it can get much taller, with inch-wide (2.5 cm) orange flowers in late May and

June. *Sphaeralcea coccinea* spreads by underground runners, sometimes forming circular colonies like fairy-rings. Even though I can easily walk to plants growing happily in the "wild," I was never able to get seed to germinate and had to resort to buying plants at a nursery. A few of the plants still live.

Sphaeromeria (chickensage). Tiny silver-leafed mat plants formerly in the genus *Tanacetum* (as far as some botanists are concerned, still in the genus *Tanacetum*) with heads of yellow tansy flowers on short stems. The species, especially the ones mentioned here, seem to be much closer to *Artemisia* than to *Tanacetum*. Only one species is generally available in the trade.

Sphaeromeria argentea is found in scattered locations from western Montana, southwestern Wyoming, northwestern Colorado, through central Idaho to northeastern and central Nevada. This has silver-gray-woolly wedge-shaped leaves ("heavily plated with silver," in Ripley's words, describing the plant he knew as *Tanacetum nuttallii*), toothed very much like *Artemisia tridentata*, but only half an inch (1.25cm) long, forming a loose cushion two inches (5cm) high, with stems to six or eight inches (15 to 20cm) tall and flat-topped clusters (corymbs) of golden yellow flowers in June, the whole group of flowers less than an inch (2.5cm) wide.

Sphaeromeria cana is a much more open, even rangy plant, shrubby, native to Nevada, California east of the Sierra Nevada, and Oregon east of the Cascades. *Sphaeromeria cana* has short, linear, silver-gray leaves mostly in threes, an inch (2.5cm) or so long, with bunches of small, off-white flowers on stems one to two feet (30 to 60cm) tall. The leaves have a pleasant scent of sagebrush.

Sphaeromeria capitata is similar to *S. argentea*, but the silver leaves are more deeply cleft, and the flowers are in tightly bunched heads. Native to northwestern Colorado (in the same places as *S. argentea*), Wyoming, southwestern Montana, and a few places in Utah. *Sphaeromeria capitata* is fairly common in the trade.

Sphaeromeria compacta, a rare native of the Charleston Mountains northwest of Las Vegas, is a cushion, or mat, to two inches (5cm) high, whose "minute leaves are trifid and densely sericeous, springing from a stout woody rootstock, while the capitula [flower heads] are borne singly above the neat silver mats" (Ripley). This "exquisite tansy from desert snows" is a highly desirable plant for a trough or pot, and is available in the nursery trade.

Townsendia (Easter daisy). A genus of invaluable plants in the daisy family with yellow disk flowers and ray flowers of white, pink, lavender, blue, or yellow, characterized by the pappus (the structure emerging from the ovary that takes the place of sepals in the Asteraceae) of bristly scales. Since some of the species are distinguished from each other by various features of the pappus, like the shape of the phyllaries (involucral bracts enclosing the flower head at the base), it's sometimes not so easy to identify the species positively. In addition, some of the species are apomictic (reproducing asexually), but they occasionally have sexual forms whose appearance closely approaches other species. Incorrectly labeled plants are rife in the trade, but this is no cause for criticism. Even botanists find the distinctions difficult to maintain over the usually wide spectrum of variables in a species.

Townsendia contains about an equal percentage of perennials and biennials, though both may behave like short-lived perennials. Some species can be either biennial or soundly perennial; there is an obvious way to tell one from another, unless the perennial plant dies. No matter; the plants are normally generous with their seed and self sow in a gratifying way.

Townsendias are very easy to grow from seed, collected from the plants or purchased from collectors; even older, stored seed is viable. Plants are sometimes available too, though not of every species, of course. Townsendias are best grown in sunny, dry sites; even many of the higher-elevation species will flourish in desert-like conditions. (*Townsendia formosa*, an unusual species with spoon-shaped basal leaves and tall stems with a single flower, native to mountains in eastern Arizona and southern new Mexico and definitely preferring a moister situation, is excluded here, as is *T. rothrockii*, a high-elevation cushion plant from southwestern Colorado, with thick spoon-shaped leaves and blue flowers, blooming as the snow melts.)

Only a few are really rare plants (the small, yellow-flowered *Townsen-*

dia aprica, from central Utah, is listed as threatened under the Endangered Species Act); and there are some others so recently described that their status both in botany and horticulture is uncertain (to me, anyway), like *T. gypsophila* and *T. microcephala*. There is also a local, unusual species in northern Arizona, *T. smithii*, which I have not seen, let alone grown.

Townsendia annua is an annual, and one of the larger townsendias, with oblanceolate inch-long (2.5cm) basal leaves, withering away at flowering time, and also with a few leaves on the stems, which can reach eight inches (20cm). The inch-wide (2.5cm) flowers are white, pale lavender, or pink. Native to sandy desert soils in Utah, western Colorado, Arizona, New Mexico, and western Texas. *Townsendia annua* is a good choice for a spectacular display of flowers in spring. The biennial *T. strigosa* is closely related, somewhat smaller, with white or pink flowers, native to southwestern Wyoming and eastern Utah (the Uinta Basin).

Townsendia condensata is a rare inhabitant of northwestern Wyoming, western Montana, central Idaho, south-central California (the White Mountains and elsewhere), and the Tushar Mountains in south-central Utah. A truly bizarre distribution range (why not in Nevada?). *Townsendia condensata* is a rosette-forming short-lived perennial, with more or less silver-gray-woolly spoon-shaped leaves, less than an inch (2.5cm) wide, forming a golfball-sized plant, sometimes branching at the base to make one or two more golfballs, but usually a solitary rosette, with large (almost two inches, 5cm, across) white, pink, or lavender flowers in May. The flowers sometimes form spectacular crests. Most, if not all, of the material in cultivation (and seed from various collectors) is of high-elevation, apomictic plants; lower-elevation plants are often sexual, with smaller flowers and a tendency to produce multiple flower heads. These are sometimes called *T. condensata* var. *anomala* and are frequently confused with *T. spathulata*.

Townsendia eximia is a somewhat variable species from northern New Mexico and southern Colorado, on the eastern side of the Continental Divide. *Townsendia eximia* is usually a biennial, but sometimes perennial, sometimes with a few stems, sometimes with multiple stems. The oblanceolate, pointed-tipped basal leaves can be three inches (7.5cm) long, or longer; the stems often have a reddish purple tinge and can be a

Townsendia exscapa

foot and a half (45 cm) tall. The flowers are blue, about two inches (5 cm) wide, opening in May or June. *Townsendia eximia* is a much shorter plant in our garden, only about six inches (15 cm) tall, and not incredibly long-lived. It might want slightly more moisture than I think it does.

Townsendia exscapa is a widespread species, found almost throughout the Great Plains (British Columbia to Manitoba, south to Texas, New Mexico, and Chihuahua, and also in Arizona), blooming as early as mid-March or April, giving the genus its common name. This is a perennial, with a few oblanceolate-linear basal leaves about two inches (5 cm) long, with stemless white, sometimes pink-tinged flowers an inch and a half (3.75 cm) wide. The flowers often have darker pink stripes on the underside. The opening of *T. exscapa* along the eastern side of the Continental Divide usually means that spring has arrived.

Townsendia fendleri is another large species, similar in some ways to *T. annua* and *T. eximia*, with a tendency to be biennial in the southern part of its range (northern New Mexico) and perennial in the northern part (southern Colorado), east of the Continental Divide. This is a species with multiple sprawling stems to one foot (30 cm), narrowly oblanceolate leaves, and white flowers about an inch (2.5cm) wide, sometimes with pink or purplish stripes on the underside, flowering in May and June. A somewhat inelegant plant, considering the rest of the species, but still worth growing.

Townsendia florifer (or *florifera*) is a biennial, sometimes living a little longer, native to dry areas in eastern Washington and Oregon through southern Idaho and south to western Utah, with two-inch (5cm), or longer, spoon-shaped hairy leaves, and a few stems to six inches (15cm) or so with solitary white, sometimes light purple, flowers about an inch and a half (3.75cm) wide, in April and May.

Townsendia grandiflora

Townsendia glabella is endemic to shale in southwestern Colorado. This is a species with two-inch-long (5cm) shiny green spatulate leaves lolling on the ground, with white or pale purple flowers about an inch (2.5cm) wide on stems two to three inches (5 to 7.5cm) long. Good in a shale trough.

Townsendia grandiflora is a biennial from the Great Plains, mostly growing along the eastern foothills of the Rocky Mountains, from northern New Mexico to eastern Wyoming, and western Nebraska and South Dakota. This is a plant with green leaves and stems sprawling on the ground, the stems about three inches (7.5cm) long, with equally wide white flowers, usually with pink or purple stripes on the underside. One year, from seed collected from plants in our neighborhood, the whole of one of the raised beds was smothered in white, a nice effect , but not to be repeated the next year. *Townsendia texensis* is a biennial from the Texas Panhandle and adjacent areas of Oklahoma, quite similar to *T. grandiflora*, but with blue, rarely white, flowers.

Townsendia hookeri (central Colorado and northeastern Utah through Wyoming, western South Dakota, barely into eastern Idaho, southwestern Saskatchewan, Alberta, and British Columbia) is one of the all-time great rock garden plants, long-lived, extremely drought-tolerant, and easy to grow. *Townsendia hookeri* has inch-long (2.5cm) gray-green linear leaves, and inch-wide (2.5cm) flowers nestled among the leaves and almost covering the cushion in March. This species is generous with its seed, which can be quite successfully sown in situ. Forms with somewhat less linear leaves and differences in the pappus of ray and disk flowers are sometimes called *T. nuttallii*. *Townsendia mensana*, a species found in the Uinta Basin and adjacent parts of Utah, is similar (also similar to *T. montana*) and equally desirable, forming an even tighter cushion. *Townsendia leptotes*, found from southwestern Montana south to western Colorado and west to southeastern California, is a variable species growing at higher elevations, quite similar to *T. hookeri*, *T. mensana*, and *T. exscapa*.

Townsendia incana is found in northwestern New Mexico, northern Arizona, Nevada, Utah, and Wyoming. This is a loose-growing, open cushion, sometimes biennial, sometimes perennial, with gray-woolly oblanceolate leaves, one to three inches (2.5 to 7.5cm) long, with strikingly white-woolly stems to six inches (15cm), with white, pink-backed flowers about an inch and a half (3.75cm) wide, in May or June. *Townsendia incana* can have a slightly disheveled look after flowering, but nobody's perfect. Otherwise good for a very dry location.

Townsendia jonesii (Nevada, Utah, and northern Arizona) is another cushion plant with variably oblanceolate or linear or spoon-shaped leaves a little over an inch (2.5cm) long, with inch-wide (2.5cm) white or even light straw-colored flowers nestled among the leaves, blooming, sort of, in June. A form in southeastern Nevada with more widely spatulate or even elliptic leaves, and flowers on stems held above the cushion of leaves, is sometimes called var. *tumulosa*. The flowers of *T. jonesii* occasionally have the curious habit of not opening completely, especially during the odd sunless, stormy Denver summer.

Townsendia mexicana is a smaller species, the only townsendia with lobes (minute though they may be) on the leaves. This has the usual white flowers, with pink stripes on the underside. Native from Coahuila south

[above left]
Townsendia hookeri

[above]
Townsendia incana

[left]
Townsendia jonesii

to Mexico City, at high elevations. I have not grown this species, and have never seen it offered for sale. It would be interesting to test it for hardiness.

Townsendia montana, from higher elevations, is a beautiful perennial species from mountains in eastern Oregon through Idaho and Utah to Montana and Wyoming, with oblanceolate green leaves about an inch (2.5cm) long clustered at the base and white, blue, or pink flowers about two inches (5cm) wide, in May, June, or July, on stems about an inch (2.5cm) taller than the leaves. The pink-rayed flowers are generally confined to the Wasatch Plateau region in central Utah and are sometimes called var. *caelilinensis*. There is a considerable amount of disagreement in taxonomic circles over whether the name *T. alpigena* takes priority over the name *T. montana*; both names are seen in seedlists. A smaller version, with thicker leaves and pale pink flowers, from south-central Utah, is sometimes called *T. minima*, when it isn't called a variety of *T. montana* or *alpigena*; of this one, Ripley wrote, "easily the tiniest of its race—minute, spoon-shaped leaves arrange themselves . . . around a woody stock [but] the less said about the flowers, the better."

Townsendia parryi is a biennial or short-lived perennial with spoon-shaped or oblanceolate basal leaves up to four inches (10cm) long, stems to a foot (30cm) tall when ecstatic, and lavender or bluish purple flowers about three inches (7.5cm) across. Found at higher elevations in Wyoming, western Montana, Idaho, Alberta, British Columbia, the Wallowa Mountains of eastern Oregon, northeastern Nevada, and also claimed for California. In a dry garden *T. parryi* functions almost exactly like *T. grandiflora*, blooming in May, forming colonies, reseeding, dying out here and there, and so on. If you modify H. Lincoln Foster's often-repeated statement about what might not have been *T. parryi* with a "not," "definitely not perennial wherever it can remain dry in summer," then you get the picture.

Townsendia spathulata and *Dactylotum bicolor*

Townsendia scapigera is a biennial from Nevada and California east of the Sierra Nevada (White and Sweetwater Mountains, etc.), with gray spatulate leaves about an inch (2.5cm) long, forming a mound not much higher than that, with white, pink-backed flowers about an inch and a half (3.75cm) wide, carried on short stems, so that the flowers are held slightly above the leaves. Very nice in a trough, blooming in May or June.

Townsendia spathulata is a cushion plant less than an inch (2.5cm) high, and about six inches (15 cm) across, with silver-gray-woolly spoon-shaped leaves, and a relatively massive display of inch-wide (2.5 cm) pink, lavender, or buff-colored flowers, sometimes opening in the garden as early as mid-February. Native to central and northern Wyoming and southern Montana. Small plants of *T. spathulata* have been frequently confused with *T. condensata*, particularly var. *anomala*. *Townsendia condensata* is a short-lived perennial with acuminate phyllaries; *T. spathulata* has acute phyllaries and lives for years.

Trifolium (clover). The dwarf clovers do not contribute as much to the rock garden as *Astragalus*, *Oxytropis*, and other members of the pea family, but there are a few adapted to dry conditions that are worth pursuing, though only through private seedlists. Some very tiny clovers, *Trifolium andinum* for instance, might grace a trough devoted to real miniatures, though I have never tried this one.

Trifolium andersonii is found in Nevada, southeastern Oregon, western Utah, and southeastern California. This is a small clover with silver-gray leaflets maybe growing to three inches (7.5 cm) and inch-wide (2.5 cm) heads of reddish purple flowers. *Trifolium andersonii* var. *beatleyae* (*T. monoense*), from Nevada and Mono County, California, is a nice variety for the rock garden, with five leaflets and a considerable taproot that snaps right off when you try to move the plant.

Trifolium macrocephalum is a larger clover with green-yellow leaflets in fives (or more) and large heads of pink-purple and white flowers almost two inches (5 cm) across, and as long, or longer, on stems a foot (30 cm) tall, more or less. Native to eastern Washington and Oregon, California east of the Sierra Nevada, Idaho, and Nevada, flowering in April or May, and disappearing for the summer.

Trifolium owyheense is a rare native of the Owyhee Desert in eastern Oregon, and also in adjacent Idaho. This is a clover about six inches (15 cm) tall, with a serious taproot, round, glaucous leaflets, and solitary heads of pink-purple and darker purple flowers two inches (5 cm) across, in May and June.

Viola (violet). A few western violets make valuable, if impermanent, additions to the dry rock garden. Most of the dryland violets disappear

[left] *Viola pedatifida*, seedling

[above] *Viola pedatifida*, white form

after flowering, something to think about in the unlikely event you actually acquire some of these. Rock garden nurseries do offer plants from time to time, and seed is available every hundred years or so. Viola seed has a reputation for not being viable for too long, so seed should be sown as soon as it's received, and left outdoors to germinate, eventually. The dryland violets have long roots that need care in transplanting.

Viola beckwithii, found in scattered locations throughout the Great Basin, is about four inches (10cm) tall, with deeply and multiply incised basal leaves and pansy flowers about an inch (2.5cm) across, with the two upper petals deep blue and the three lower petals white or light blue with purple veins, yellow at the base. *Viola beckwithii* flowers in May or June, sets seed, and then goes dormant.

Viola nuttallii is a widespread, variable species found throughout western North America (Minnesota to California, New Mexico to British Columbia). As I know it, *V. nuttallii* is about three inches (7.5cm) high, with two-inch-long (5cm) oblanceolate green leaves and bright yellow flowers less than half an inch (1.25 cm) across, in May. After rare, wet early springs, the violet makes spectacular displays in the eastern foothills of the Rockies. One spring I tried to dig up a plant growing in a hard-packed dirt road and a little worse for having been driven over, but I gave up trying to find the roots. After setting seed, *V. nuttallii* disappears for the rest of the year.

Viola pedatifida is another widespread violet, found throughout the Midwest and the Great Plains, but becoming less common as it moves further west (scattered locations in eastern Colorado along the foothills of the Rocky Mountains, northeastern Wyoming, and eastern Montana). *Viola pedatifida* (not to be confused with *V. pedata* of eastern North America) has palmately dissected leaves, sometimes only two or three, grows to two inches (5 cm), in my garden anyway, with blue-purple flowers about half an inch (1.25 cm) across. A beautiful white form exists, too. I find this a difficult violet to get established, but when happy it reseeds freely, even into dry parts of the rock gardens. *Viola pedatifida* retains its leaves after blooming.

Zinnia. Two species of *Zinnia*—looking absolutely nothing like regular garden zinnias—are worthy of the dry rock garden. These two little subshrubs are available as plants in the nursery trade, are relatively easily grown from seed, and are short-lived unless given ample moisture in summer (in excess of normal rainfall, that is).

Zinnia acerosa (desert zinnia; Arizona and New Mexico south to Zacatecas and San Luis Potosí) is a branched, greenish gray mound six inches (15 cm) tall with hairy needle-like (acerose) leaves half an inch (1.25 cm) long, smothered with white, or yellowish, flowers not quite an inch (2.5 cm) wide, borne all summer. In climates where winter temperatures regularly dip below –10F (–23C) for extended periods, *Z. acerosa* will be happier in a protected spot in the garden (next to a south-facing wall, for instance).

Zinnia grandiflora (Rocky Mountain zinnia) is a branched green mound, to eight inches (20 cm), with narrowly linear leaves about an inch (2.5 cm) long, also smothered with inch-wide (2.5 cm) flowers borne all summer, but this time the flowers are bright yellow. Maybe when

Nuttall coined the specific epithet "grandiflora" he was referring to the number of flowers rather than the size. In any case this, "the golden gem of the southern plains" (Barr), is a highly desirable plant. *Zinnia grandiflora* is found from Kansas and Oklahoma south to Coahuila and Zacatecas, and west to Arizona and Sonora.

Zinnia grandiflora

CHAPTER SIX

Cacti

Few kinds of plants are as redolent of "the old west" as the various kinds of cacti; combine an old wagon wheel, a cow skull, and a few cacti, and you have an instant Western Garden. As Barr said, the flowers provide "a major floral spectacle" on the Great Plains, and as we move further southwest into New Mexico, western Texas, and Chihuahua, the number of cacti amenable to cultivation in cold-winter climates increases, as do the chances of magnifying the floral spectacle into something quite amazing.

The chances of being heartbroken, if you take the deaths of plants seriously, are also considerable since a number of the more southerly distributed (south of the New Mexico–Chihuahua border) can't be considered to be reliably hardy under all possible horrible winter conditions. But taking chances is part of the gardening experience, and so is death.

Of course there are plenty of cactus fanatics in this country, and a good number of them have turned this obsession into a business, so it's quite easy for other cactus fanatics (like me) to get most of the cacti listed here. If not, they can be grown from seed. Except for opuntias, which seem to be best germinated indoors under lights, most cold-hardy cacti can be easily germinated sown outdoors in late winter. The young seed-

Echinocereus triglochidiatus var. *mojavensis*

lings need to be lightly shaded during their first year, and possibly their second. By the third year they can be set out into the garden after hardening them off to sunlight first, gradually moving them out into the sun for a few hours each day until they can stand out in the sun all day without turning red (a fatal sign in cacti, more so than in humans).

As most people know, cacti can also be grown from cuttings. The pads of opuntias can simply be broken off (the sophisticated way is to use a pair of pruning shears) and the pad left in partial shade, or even full sun, to allow the wound to develop a callous, which takes two or three days. This can then be dusted with sulfur if you so desire. The pad can then be set into the ground, on edge (I prefer not to plant the cut end of the pad), an inch (2.5cm) or so deep. I find using a couple of bamboo skewers (the kind used for grilling), placed on either side of the pad, prevents the pad from falling over.

Barr preferred July for rooting cacti; I see no reason not to recommend doing it then, though you can also root cacti much earlier, even in plastic pots.

Ball and barrel cacti, and chollas with woody stems, are much less easy, and sometimes even impossible to root. Chollas with nonwoody stems (stems only one or two years old) may be rooted simply by laying a branch, or a piece of a branch, on the ground, or by digging a small hole, setting the piece in upright, and bracing the cholla branch any way you see fit. The hole can be filled in slowly, after the branch has rooted.

Plants purchased from mail-order nurseries (even from nurseries in Arizona) may need to be shaded during their first summer. Spraying the plants with an antidesiccant is even more effective; my preference, right now, is for Cloud Cover™, a plastic polymer that seems to work wonders against sudden drops in temperature and blazing winter sun.

As you will notice, quite a few cacti are listed as threatened or endangered under the Endangered Species Act. Some years ago I spoke with officials of the U.S. Fish and Wildlife Service about this, and I gather that officials feel strongly that the law pertains to both wild and *cultivated* "parts" of the plants. A federal permit is required to distribute (i.e., sell) "parts" (seeds or plants) of species, subspecies, or varieties listed as threatened or endangered.

The Endangered Species Act not only gives the U.S. government authority over plants growing on public land (unlike animals, which are not stationary), but also authority over interstate trafficking regardless of the source of the plant "parts." Cacti are among the most exploited of all plants, and there is still demand for plants illegally removed from their wild habitat. This is especially true in Mexico, where whole populations of plants have been wiped out by collectors digging the plants up, for sale to collectors in other countries. Cacti are mostly easily grown from seed, and to me this whole situation is simply grotesque. Still, it does explain why cacti grown from cultivated seed should be subject to regulation. You can purchase seed or plants of threatened or endangered species from nurseries with a government permit.

Almost all the cacti mentioned here can easily be grown in plain clay soil, but I now prefer to have the plants with their roots in clay, preferably on a slope, with about an inch (2.5 cm) of fine gravel as a mulch, to help prevent frost heaving. A more porous soil allows cold to penetrate too easily and makes supplemental irrigation necessary during periods of prolonged drought.

It is normal for cold-hardy cacti to shrivel at the onset of winter. Moisture loss in the plants' cells allows the plants to remain alive without the internal moisture freezing and causing the cell walls to burst. As a general rule, dark discoloration of the epidermis is acceptable, while light discoloration is usually a fatal sign. A cactus whose epidermis becomes transparent at the onset of cold weather is a tender cactus, and soon to be a dead one.

Snow cover over dry soil, lack of prolonged, constant subfreezing temperatures (day and night), and protection from high winds are aids to the survival of cacti that might otherwise be considered marginal. Probably about ninety-nine percent of the cacti mentioned here are completely hopeless in climates with wet winters.

No family of plants has been subjected to as much nomenclatural change as has the cactus family, many of whose members display extreme variability. Some species have a dozen or more synonyms. Generic names are changed, species become varieties, the varieties disappear, and on and on. Species have been described when briefly glimpsed from a moving train. One seedpod of a particular species may yield twenty slightly different plants, all of which have been described as species. Every serious work on cactus has different names, or combinations of names, for the various taxa.

There is a real danger for compulsive collectors of cacti (again, like me) winding up buying five examples of the same plant with five different names. Such is life. The names given here (mostly following the names in Edward F. Anderson's *The Cactus Family*) are the ones I like. The dimensions are those of typical plants growing in the garden here; severe drought will dwarf the plants, while rainy springs and summers will make them swell up like spiny green balloons.

Coryphantha. Ball cacti with flowers at the tops of the plants in spring and sometimes interlocking, rather than protruding, spines, making them easy to pick up with tough fingers (required of all cactophiles). Species with nectar-secreting glands and other microscopic characteristics have been segregated out of *Coryphantha* into the genus *Escobaria*, subsumed back, segregated out, etc. Since most catalogs call them escobarias, I will too.

Coryphantha compacta is a tiny (two by two inches, 5 by 5cm) solitary (nonclustering) ball with nice yellow flowers about three-quarters of an inch (2cm) across and yellowish interlocking spines, from Chihuahua and Durango (*C. palmeri*, considered by some to be a synonym, extends the range to Zacatecas, San Luis Potosí, Nuevo León, and Tamaulipas). Good in a trough or pot. Has survived −6F (−21C) with only a little damage.

Coryphantha delaetiana (*C. laui*), three inches (7.5cm) tall and wide, with inch-and-a-half-wide (3.75cm) yellow flowers and red or black spines, from Coahuila, sometimes forms clumps after a few years. This is happier buried under pine needles in winter.

Coryphantha echinus is a larger one, potentially anyway, six inches (15cm) tall by two inches (5cm) or more wide, forming clumps with age, smothered with interlocking white spines, and sulfur-yellow flowers two inches (5cm) wide. *Coryphantha echinus* is found in Coahuila and western Texas, and seems to be hardy to about −10F (−23C), at least.

Coryphantha macromeris (southern New Mexico to Tamaulipas) has never survived temperatures below 0F (−18C) in the garden here; the enlarged, conspicuous, watered-filled tubercles just seem to be asking for trouble. And they get it. *Coryphantha macromeris* var. *runyonii*, a more compact variety, found at lower elevations along the Rio Grande, is hopeless.

Coryphantha robustispina (*C. scheeri*), from southern Arizona and Mexico, western Texas and Chihuahua, is a widely variable species; the specific epithet reflects the priority of Schott's name over Lemaire's name, *scheeri*. The typical species (now) may be six inches (15cm) or more tall by four inches (10cm) wide, densely spined, with yellow, reddish-tipped spines, the central spine curved into a hook (making this species much less pleasant to pick up with the fingers), with yellow flowers about two inches (5cm) across. This is the form from southern Arizona and, as *C. scheeri* var. *robustispina*, is listed as endangered under the Endangered Species Act. Variety *uncinata* also has hooked spines; var. *scheeri* has straight spines and is a smaller plant. *Coryphantha robustispina* var. *scheeri* seems to be at least reasonably hardy in the garden here, to about −10F (−23C).

Cylindropuntia (cholla, pronounced "*choy*-a"). Upright, tree-like cacti with cylindrical stems eventually forming woody trunks. The cold-hardy varieties are broken by heavy, wet spring snows and have to start again, which they do quickly. Nothing differentiates a western garden from gardens in wetter climates more instantaneously than a large clump of chollas in the front yard.

Not too many are available in the trade, but a visit to a plant sale sponsored by the local cactus club might yield no end of treasures.

Chollas are no fun to fool around with, requiring a long-handled set of tongs and a considerable amount of circumspection when being transplanted or pruned, or tied up. Because I am incredibly tough, I don't mind being jabbed now and then; chollas are some of my favorite garden plants. Propagation is by seed (slow) or by simply removing nonwoody joints, allowing the cut area to form a callus (this takes two or three days), and then setting the joint in a pot of sand, or even just in the dirt somewhere. Even very large sections of a cholla can be rooted in this way. Joints with too much wood in them are difficult to root, but sometimes rooting is successfully accomplished by dropping the joint on the ground and waiting. This is what nature does, after all.

Winter snow on *Cylindropuntia imbricata*

I recently learned something that I think is amazing and which should be shared with all chollaphiles gardening in places beset by wet spring snow. Mikl Brawner, owner of Harlequin's Gardens in Boulder, Colorado, and an expert arborist, lops off the top six inches (15cm) or so of the tips of all the branches on his chollas. He does this even as late as December. The effect is incredible. Instead of having a group of wand-like branches ready to snap off at the slightest provocation, the plant makes thick, heavy-looking branches that he says are never affected by snow. The proof is visible since his chollas look like no others in the area.

Cylindropuntia davisii (*Opuntia tunicata* var. *davisii*), from Oklahoma, Texas, and New Mexico, is a seriously spiny thing, looking like it has been stuck all over with toothpicks. The plants may reach two feet (60cm) or more, the stems about one inch (2.5cm) thick, becoming woody at the base with age. The spines are generally golden-yellow and two to three inches (5 to 7.5cm) long. The flowers are not much, about an inch and a half (3.75cm) wide, vaguely yellow or greenish yellow or yellow tinged with red, in June. A spectacular little cholla.

Cylindropuntia echinocarpa (Nevada to California and western Arizona, southwestern Utah, Baja California and Sonora) is a pale green-stemmed cholla with silvery spines (some forms apparently have golden spines) two to three feet (60 to 90cm) tall, with yellow-green, red-tinged flowers about two inches (5cm) wide, in June. *Cylindropuntia echinocarpa* can do a first-rate impression of a long-dead spiny piece of wood, all the while actually growing. *Cylindropuntia acanthocarpa* is similar

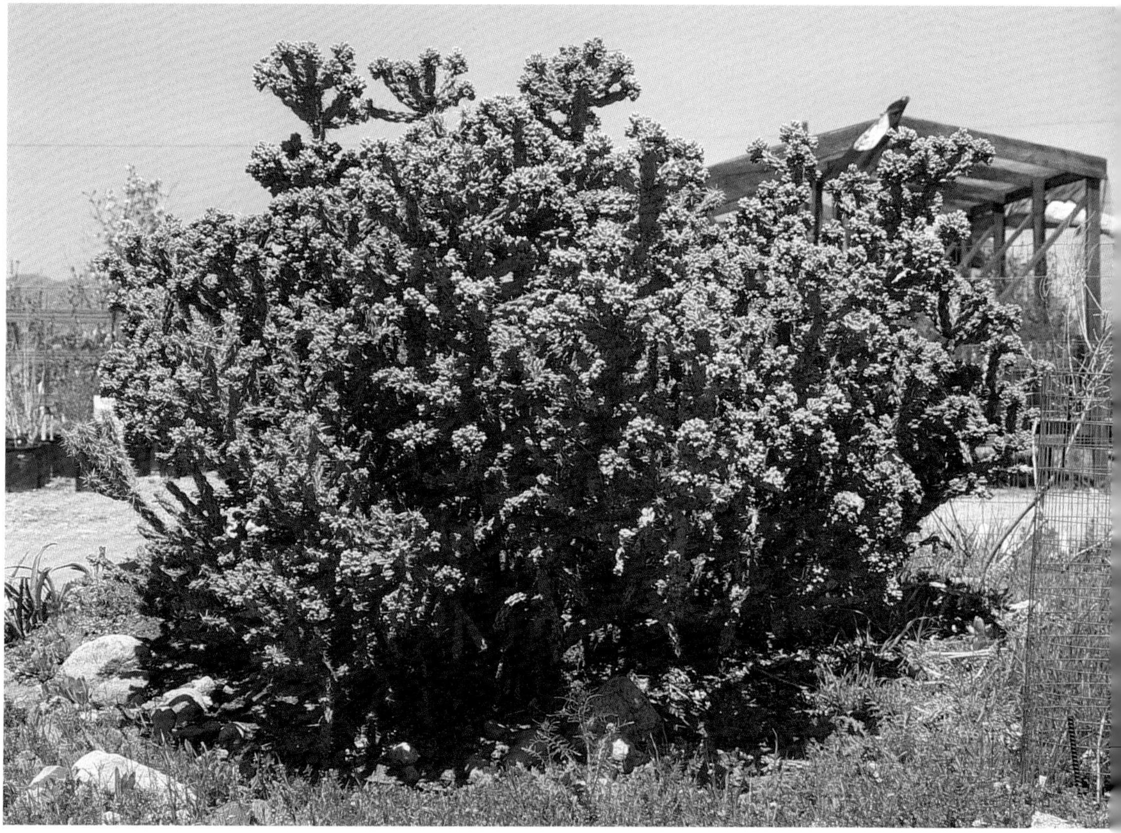

Cylindropuntia imbricata, expertly pruned by Mikl Brawner, Harlequin's Gardens

but with larger, or longer, tubercles, and with more or less the same distribution as *C. echinocarpa* but extending into the low deserts of Arizona; I have not been successful with this one but will try again.

Cylindropuntia imbricata (southern Colorado to Chihuahua and Coahuila) can grow to six feet (1.8m) before being broken to pieces by a spring snow, but, as said before, it quickly grows again. The woody stem can be six inches (15cm) across at the base. *Cylindropuntia imbricata* has usually yellow (silver in var. *argentea* from western Texas) spines and noticeably large tubercles, and glowing magenta or purple flowers about four inches (10cm) across, in June. There is a much-sought-after white-flowered (really, greenish white) form. This is a curious creature, a more compact, slower-growing plant (instead of just being a color form)

[above] *Cylindropuntia echinocarpa* at Denver Botanic Gardens

[right] *Cylindropuntia echinocarpa*

easily distinguished from the regular purple-flowered plants. Rumor has it that there is also a white-flowered form with a purple center. Be still, my heart . . .

Cylindropuntia kleiniae is an upright, sprawling cholla with stems less than an inch (2.5cm) in diameter, becoming woody at the base, but it has some difficulty standing up as it gets taller and is easily broken by snow. The flowers are about an inch (2.5cm) across, not much to look at. As with most chollas, the sheer architectural beauty of the plant saves

[left] *Cylindropuntia imbricata*

[above] *Cylindropuntia imbricata*, greenish white form

the day. Best when allowed to lean against a wall. *Cylindropuntia kleiniae* is native to New Mexico and Texas to Chihuahua, Durango, Coahuila, and Nuevo León. Hybrids with *C. imbricata* make more satisfactory garden plants, since they stand up by themselves with no trouble; these have stems about half an inch (1.25cm) wide, with white spines spaced about an inch (2.5cm) on the stems.

Cylindropuntia leptocaulis, the Christmas cholla, pencil cholla, or tesajo, gets its first common name from the massive clusters of bright red

Cylindropuntia kleiniae

fruits, and its second name from the pencil-thin stems. *Cylindropuntia leptocaulis* grows to about two feet (60 cm), though in climates with little snow it can grow taller, and forms a patch two to three feet (60 to 90 cm) or more wide. This is a wickedly spined plant, the spines up to two inches (5 cm) long, arranged sparingly, but sufficiently, on the stems. The flowers are about two inches (5 cm) wide, yellowish green, in June. *Cylindropuntia leptocaulis* can be wiped out by heavy snows, but it comes back, just as it does in the wild. Native to southern Arizona, New Mexico (where it reaches far enough north to experience cold winters), Oklahoma, Texas, and in Mexico from Sonora to San Luis Potosí and Tamaulipas.

Cylindropuntia ramosissima (diamond cholla) has been in the garden here for several years but, as it is, is not exactly the sort of thing I would point out to visitors. In the wild this is a shrub to six feet (1.8 m) with diamond-shaped tubercles on cylindrical stems not half an inch (1.25 cm) wide, with grayish spines about two inches (5 cm) long, and small copper-red flowers, in June. My plants look like green snakes slinking along the ground, but I still have hope. Native to southern Nevada, southern California, Arizona, and Sonora.

Cylindropuntia spinosior is similar to *C. imbricata*, but the tubercles are more numerous, smaller and less prominent. This would grow to about six feet (1.8 m) before getting knocked down by snow (I've only grown this for a few years); the flowers are purple, or yellow or red (white forms are also reported), about three inches (7.5 cm) wide, in June. Native to Arizona and New Mexico, Sonora, and Chihuahua. Plants are recorded growing on the Navajo Reservation in northeastern Arizona and northwestern New Mexico, so this species should have good cold tolerance.

Cylindropuntia whipplei (Utah, Arizona, Colorado, New Mexico, and maybe Nevada), sometimes called the rattail cholla for reasons unknown to me, is a semi-upright cholla with prominently bumpy tubercles and white spines about an inch (2.5cm) long, or longer. A pair of pliers (not tweezers) is required should a spine become inadvertently lodged in the skin. The flowers are greenish yellow, about an inch across, borne in June. Plants can grow to two feet (60cm), forming a woody trunk. There are also a number of highly desirable smaller forms, some only an inch or two (2.5 to 5cm) wide, spreading two to three feet (60 to 90cm) wide. Some forms are extra spiny, some are not. These are rather hard to find in the trade, but every so often plants are available. Do remember to get a pair of pliers, too.

Cylindropuntia ×viridiflora, a naturally occurring hybrid between *C. whipplei* and *C. imbricata* found near Santa Fe, New Mexico, has a habit like *C. imbricata* but smaller, and with a greenish flower. It is extremely slow-growing.

Echinocactus. Barrel cacti distinguished by heavily ribbed stems, spine-like tips on the sepals, and extremely business-like spines. *Echinocactus grusonii*, the golden barrel cactus, is one of the most familiar cacti of all (but not hardy). Slow from seed, at least for me, but plants are not hard to come by. One species, *E. polycephalus*, in its var. *xeranthemoides* anyway, from northeastern Arizona, is probably hardy, but this is not one to be found in the trade; I don't know why. These are truly memorable members of the plant kingdom. The species that follow are both called mancacaballo in Spanish; in English, horse crippler.

Echinocactus horizonthalonius is a plant of the Chihuahuan Desert, from New Mexico south to San Luis Potosí, six inches (15cm) tall and wide, with a gray-green ribbed body and heavy, gray-black reptilian spines down the middle of the ribs, with downward-curving (sometimes straight) central spines an inch (2.5cm) long. The rose-pink flowers are produced at the top of the plant in June and are about two inches (5cm) wide. The variety from Arizona and Sonora, var. *nicho-*

lii, is probably not hardy. Plants are occasionally available from cactus nurseries.

Echinocactus texensis is a squat, baleful thing about six inches (15 cm) high by a foot (30 cm) wide, gray-green, heavily ribbed with deep furrows, and thick gray rattail spines, the central one curving downward and at maturity about three inches (7.5 cm) long. The rose-pink flowers, opening in June, are about two inches (5 cm) wide. Native to southern New Mexico, western Texas, Coahuila, Tamaulipas, and Nuevo León. Larger plants are easier to establish through their first winter than smaller plants, and are easily (and inexpensively) obtainable.

Echinocereus. A popular genus of cacti grown, in part, for their ravishing flowers (as with other cacti whose names end with "-cereus", the flowers are among the most beautiful in the plant kingdom) and neat, though spiny, appearance. Fortunately most of these are readily available from nurseries specializing in cacti, and seed is usually readily available. Echinocerei take about five years from seed to flower.

Echinocereus adustus is a small one, a little over two inches (5 cm) tall, and almost as wide, with black-brown spines (the specific epithet means "scorched"), and pink-purple flowers about two inches (5 cm) across, in June. Native to Chihuahua, at high elevations. Variety *schwarzii*, from Durango, at slightly lower elevations, is a somewhat taller plant with larger flowers; I have not grown this one, though it is reportedly hardy in Denver. I have not seen the other variety, var. *bonatzii*.

Echinocereus coccineus is often included in *E. triglochidiatus*, though apparently there are enough differences, in flower shape and other features, to warrant retaining this old name. Most importantly for gardeners, many of the cactus nurseries use the name *E. coccineus* as well as *E. triglochidiatus*. Widespread throughout the southwestern United States and northern Mexico, *E. coccineus* is a round (particularly when young; seed-grown plants are especially fat) or cylindrical plant, anywhere from four to well over twelve inches (10 to 30 cm) tall and one to six inches (2.5 to 15 cm) wide. Plants can have hundreds of stems (don't expect this to happen in the garden unless you live to a great age) and form a cluster three feet (90 cm) wide. The orange-red (more red than orange) flowers, about two inches (5 cm) across and less tubular than those of *E. triglochidiatus*, are borne in May, and visited by hummingbirds.

Echinocereus coccineus is an extremely variable species in size and spination. At least half a dozen varieties have been described, mostly as varieties of *E. triglochidiatus*; all are worth acquiring. Some varieties of *E. coccineus* common in the trade are var. *gurneyi* and var. *paucispinus*; both have only a few stems (instead of forming monstrous clumps), and neither name is now recognized. A form from White Sands, New Mexico, is said eventually to become knee-high, or higher, and is floating around the nursery trade as "White Sands form." Like the erstwhile var. *gurneyi*, this turns a rich purple in winter. One variety (or subspecies), var. *arizonicus*, is listed as endangered under the Endangered Species Act, though only if the varietal distinction is recognized.

Echinocereus dasyacanthus (*E. pectinatus* var. *dasyacanthus*, *E. pectinatus* var. *neomexicanus*) can grow to a foot (30cm) high by four inches (10cm) wide, with irregularly arranged interlocking spines, the spines less tightly pressed against the body than regular *E. pectinatus* (and therefore less friendly to fingers). The flowers, borne in June, are usually a particularly gorgeous yellow, four inches (10cm) across, though the flower color can range from orange to white to pink. Native to southern New Mexico, western Texas, Chihuahua, and Coahuila.

Echinocereus engelmannii does not get as large in my garden as some of the literature suggests; as I know it, in var. *chrysocentrus*, *E. engelmannii* is a clumping plant about six inches (15cm) tall by two inches (5cm) wide, covered with spines, the white central spines about an inch (2.5cm) long, pointing downward. The flowers are purple, three inches (7.5cm) across, borne in June. *Echinocereus engelmannii* var. *chrysocentrus* is native to southern Nevada and adjacent areas of southern California, and western Utah and Arizona. *Echinocereus engelmannii* var. *variegatus* (southeastern Utah, northern and western Arizona) is also hardy, with red or black spines, white central spines, and flowers about two inches (5cm) across.

Echinocereus fendleri is a squat thing about five inches (12.5cm) tall by three inches (7.5cm) wide or more, with six or so gray, curving, inch-long (2.5cm) spines, the central curving downward, in each areole. The gorgeous flowers are huge, over four inches (10cm) across, bright pur-

Echinocereus fendleri var. *fendleri*

ple, opening in June. Native from southern Colorado to Arizona and Sonora, and New Mexico, western Texas, and Chihuahua. As usual, there are some varieties currently not recognized by some botanists. *Echinocereus fendleri* var. *rectispinus* (southeastern Arizona, Sonora, southwestern New Mexico, possibly northern Chihuahua, and western Texas) is a more cylindrical plant, with the central spine sticking straight out, whose hardiness is unknown to me. *Echinocereus fendleri* var. *kuenzleri* is a rare inhabitant of the Sacramento Mountains in southern New Mexico; this is similar to typical *E. fendleri* but lacks central spines and has conspicuously thick, corky, radial spines. *Echinocereus fendleri* var. *kuenzleri* is listed as endangered under the Endangered Species Act.

Echinocereus knippelianus is a rather peculiar-looking echinocereus, a semi-squishy green cactus with five to seven ribs and half-inch-long (1.25cm) yellow spines, often only one per areole. The plant is about three inches (7.5cm) across, and the same height, sometimes forming clumps, pulling its soft green body down into the soil for winter. The flowers, opening in June, are the usual echinocereus flowers, pink, purplish, or white, about two inches (5cm) wide. *Echinocereus knippelianus* is native to high elevations in Coahuila; a couple of varieties have been described but are not recognized by all botanists. This is definitely one wanting an especially warm place in winter; do not site it on a north slope in cold shade.

Echinocereus laui is a clumping plant, native to oak woodlands in eastern Sonora, each stem about four inches (10cm) high by three and a half inches (9cm) wide, covered with white spines about a quarter of an inch (6mm) long, with red-brown central spines slightly longer, and nice two-inch (5cm) flowers in June. *Echinocereus laui* does well if lightly shaded in summer; this is one best considered marginal at temperatures below about −5F (−20.5C) and given a site where it can be protected from the worst winter winds.

Echinocereus longisetus, native to Coahuila, is a spiny column six inches (15cm) tall, though it can get taller, and three inches (7.5cm) wide, sometimes with a few stems, with white, downward-pointing spines, the central spines about two inches (5cm) long in some plants. The flowers are about two inches (5cm) across, pinkish purple, with white centers, in June. Variety *delaetii* (*E. delaetii*) is an unkempt-looking cactus with shaggy white spines swirling around the stem. Hardy only to about 0F (−18C), unless protected from wind and ice.

Echinocereus pectinatus is another cactus with a lot of not-too-scary spines, a cylindrical plant, about five inches (12.5cm) by two and a half inches (6.25cm), though it can get over twice that large in both dimensions. The dense spines, sometimes arranged like the teeth on a comb (pectinate), cover the stem; the flowers, borne in June, are about four inches (10cm) across, pink or purple, and gorgeous as usual. Native to southern Arizona, New Mexico, western Texas, Sonora, Chihuahua, Coahuila, San Luis Potosí, and maybe elsewhere in Mexico. *Echinocereus pectinatus* subsp. *wenigeri* has fewer spines and is found along the Rio Grande in Texas and Coahuila, and may not be too hardy.

Echinocereus reichenbachii, native to southern Colorado, New Mexico, Oklahoma, Texas, Chihuahua, Coahuila, and Tamaulipas, is a variable, and variably hardy, species. It is apparently differentiated from *E. pectinatus* by having thinner and more flexible spines on the flowering stem but is otherwise similar to that species, with enormous, stunning yellow-centered pink flowers about five inches (12.5cm) across, in June. It is also easier to get *E. reichenbachii* to grow almost a foot (30cm) tall, at which point it is easily knocked over by the weather, but generally it's safer to think of this as a clumping plant about four inches (10cm) tall by two inches (5cm) wide.

The subspecies of *Echinocereus reichenbachii* native to the Great Plains are completely hardy, of course. *Echinocereus reichenbachii* subsp. *perbellus* has no central spines, or a minute one at best, and less than twenty ribs; subsp. *baileyi* has two or three (the now extinct varieties *albispinus* and *caespitosus* are forms of subsp. *baileyi*, and are

Echinocereus reichenbachii subsp. *baileyi*

definitely worth acquiring even if their names are no longer recognized). *Echinocereus reichenbachii* subsp. *reichenbachii* also has no central spines, but sometimes twice as many ribs as subsp. *perbellus*; forms of this from southern Texas may not be hardy.

The Mexican subspecies *Echinocereus reichenbachii* subsp. *armatus* seems not to care too much about bitter cold winds and temperatures of −8F (−22C), but subsp. *fitchii* seems barely hardy at the same temperatures. This latter taxon, as *E. reichenbachii* var. *albertii*, is listed as endangered under the Endangered Species Act.

Echinocereus ×*roetteri* (*E. lloydii*) is a naturally occurring hybrid of *E. coccineus* and *E. dasyacanthus*, found in southern New Mexico and western Texas, and probably in Chihuahua, about six inches (15cm) high by three inches (7.5cm) wide, with gray spines and red central spines. The flowers are about two inches (5cm) across, orange, red, yellow, or varying shades in between, opening in June. *Echinocereus* ×*roetteri* was formerly listed as endangered (as *E. lloydii*) under the Endangered Species Act but has been "de-listed" due to reports that it was only found where populations of *E. coccineus* and *E. dasyacanthus* grew in close proximity.

Echinocereus russanthus is one of the smaller-flowered echinocerei, native to western Texas and possibly Coahuila, about five inches (12.5cm) high and two inches (5cm) wide, covered with handsome rust-colored spines about half an inch (1.25cm) long. June brings red flowers about an inch (2.5cm) wide, the flowers sometimes not opening completely, clustered about three-quarters of the way up the stem, but the spines, backlit by the summer sun, are the thing. *Echinocereus russanthus* is sometimes considered synonymous with forms of *E. viridiflorus*.

Echinocereus stramineus (strawberry cactus) is a widespread cactus found in Chihuahua and Coahuila south to Durango, Zacatecas, and San Luis Potosí, and north into southern New Mexico and western Texas. Although it can form mounds as much as six feet (1.8m) across in the wild, in colder climates it can be a modestly clumping plant with stems six inches (15cm) tall by three inches (7.5cm) wide, the stems covered with straw-colored (the specific epithet means "made with straw") spines, the radial spines about an inch and a half (3.75cm) long, the central spines almost four inches (10cm) long. The red-purple flowers are huge, over four inches (10cm) across, opening in June in cold-winter gardens. The fruits are edible and taste like strawberries, giving the plant its common name.

Echinocereus triglochidiatus (claret cup) is another widespread species, with stems about four inches (10cm) tall and two inches (5cm) wide, with a few to many spines, usually pale yellow, though sometimes darker, and forming clumps four feet (120cm) wide, with, in a good year, hundreds of tubular, funnel-shaped red or orange-red flowers in May. The flowers stay open for a few days and are visited by hummingbirds. *Echinocereus triglochidiatus* is reasonably easy to grow from seed. Occasionally field-dug clumps are available (from people who dislike cactus on farm or grazing land), but these do not always transplant well unless

Echinocereus triglochidiatus

every possible air pocket is removed when the clump is settled into the ground. Adding sand, which attracts ants, is a fairly bad idea.

Echinocereus triglochidiatus is native to Colorado, south through western Texas to Coahuila and Durango, and from Utah to Arizona and California. The form with curving spines sometimes called *E. triglochidiatus* var. *mojavensis* is considered by some to be a distinct species, *E. mojavensis*. Other varieties, except var. *melanacanthus*, which seems to have vanished utterly, have been removed to *E. coccineus*. The spineless form of *E. triglochidiatus* is listed as endangered, as var. *inermis*, under the Endangered Species Act, even though it isn't a botanical entity at all (writing here as a non-botanist); seedlings of the spineless forms can have any number of spines, including none.

Echinocereus viridiflorus is found throughout the Great Plains and parts of the Chihuahuan Desert (South Dakota to western Texas, Coahuila, and Chihuahua). *Echinocereus viridiflorus* is oval-shaped, with whitish, red, or brown central spines, the plants clumping with age, about two inches (5cm) high by an inch (2.5cm) wide, with green flowers about an inch (2.5cm) across, flowering in May, sometimes even earlier. Barr wrote that during rainy periods the flower can be almost traffic-signal green, but, not experiencing too many rainy periods when the cacti are blooming, I have never noticed this. *Echinocereus viridiflorus* var. *chloranthus* is a cylindrical form about four inches (10cm) tall from western Texas and southern New Mexico; var. *cylindricus* is similar to this, with a similar range, but has purplish red flowers; var. *correllii*,

Echinocereus triglochidiatus var. *inermis*, only partly spineless

Echinocereus viridiflorus var. *davisii*

from western Texas, is also cylindrical, or oval-shaped, with green-yellow and white spines arranged in bands around the stems, with yellowish green flowers. *Echinocereus viridiflorus* var. *davisii* is a little white-spined golfball with yellowish green flowers from western Texas; it is listed as endangered under the Endangered Species Act.

I also have a plant of *Echinocereus viridiflorus* var. *canus*, which I have been too chicken, so far, to plant out. This too is from western Texas and may prove hardy; it has clusters of white, not-too-threatening spines (the plant can be handled by gently grabbing the spines) and white wool on the lower stem.

Some gardeners able to provide more protected locations for some of the marginal cacti have been able to overwinter *Echinocereus bonkerae* and *E. boyce-thompsonii*, but these have not been hardy for me.

Echinomastus intertextus, Kelaidis garden

Echinomastus. A genus of ball cacti with spiny tubercles. A number of these may be potentially hardy (e.g., *Echinomastus mariposensis*, listed as threatened under the Endangered Species Act, and *E. warnockii*, both from the Big Bend area of western Texas and adjacent areas in Coahuila) but would probably need a protected site in winter.

Echinomastus intertextus is a completely hardy species about four inches (10cm) high by two inches (5cm) wide, covered with white spines, about half an inch (1.25cm) long, and silver-white to pale pink flowers, about an inch (2.5cm) wide, in May or June. This poor cactus has been, at times, in *Neolloydia*, *Pediocactus*, and *Sclerocactus*. Native to northern Sonora, Chihuahua, Coahuila, southeastern Arizona, southern New Mexico, and western Texas. I find *E. intertextus* difficult to grow from seed, but plants are sometimes available.

Epithelantha. Little gray-white golfballs with tiny spines and tiny clusters of pink flowers at the tops of the golfballs. There are two species, *Epithelantha bokei*, from the Big Bend area of western Texas and possibly Coahuila, and *E. micromeris*, from Arizona, New Mexico, western Texas, Coahuila, and Nuevo León. Three subspecies of *E. micromeris* are currently recognized, but probably only subsp. *micromeris* is of interest to us. Occasionally a clumping plant, subsp. *micromeris* bears its flowers in June, with tiny half-inch (1.25cm) clusters of red fruits later. This requires a protected location, possibly wedged between some rocks on a south-facing slope.

Escobaria. A genus of mostly ball cacti sometimes included in *Coryphantha*. Most cactus nurseries list them as escobarias.

Escobaria dasyacantha is native to Zacatecas and is probably not hardy. *Escobaria dasyacantha* subsp. *chaffeyi* is native to Chihuahua, Coahuila, southern New Mexico, and western Texas, and is fairly hardy. In a cold-winter garden it makes a plant about two inches (5cm) tall and wide, covered in white spines, with small brownish pink flowers rarely opening fully, in June. *Escobaria duncanii*, from western Texas and southern New Mexico, is similar but slightly smaller, with pink flowers. *Escobaria orcuttii* (*Coryphantha strobiliformis* var. *orcuttii*) is also similar, but a larger, more cylindrical plant, native to New Mexico and southeastern Arizona.

Escobaria hesteri is a green-bodied (not obscured by spines) cactus with conspicuous tubercles like anti-ship mines, and white spines forming stars on the tubercles. The plant is about two inches (5cm) tall by an inch (2.5cm) wide, with flowers about half an inch (1.25cm) wide, in June. *Escobaria hesteri* forms mounds in its native habitat, the Big Bend area of western Texas; in my garden it grows but slowly.

Escobaria minima, as the name suggests, is a tiny thing, a ball of dense white spines about an inch (2.5cm) in diameter and as high, forming clusters, with half-inch (1.25cm) brilliant red-purple flowers in June. Native to western Texas, *E. minima* is listed as endangered under the Endangered Species Act. This is a spectacular miniature, good in a trough, and relatively easy to grow from seed.

Escobaria minima

Escobaria missouriensis (*Neobesseya missouriensis*) is found scattered throughout the Great Plains (North Dakota to Texas, even in Arkansas and Louisiana) and also in Montana, Idaho, southern Utah, and northern Arizona. This is another small cactus, with prominent tubercles, usually with no central spines, forming a ball or a bun about an inch (2.5 cm) tall and wide, though sometimes growing two or three times that wide, and sometimes forming clumps, with straw-colored (sometimes orange-tinted) flowers an inch (2.5 cm) wide, in May or June. Attractive bright red pea-sized fruits follow. Besides typical *E. missouriensis*, a couple, or several, subspecies or varieties are sometimes recognized. Subspecies *asperispina* (*Neobesseya asperispina*) is from Coahuila and Nuevo León and may not be hardy; subsp. *navajoensis* is from northeastern Arizona and has veined flowers. Other varieties differentiated by microscopic, trivial attributes (no longer recognized as distinct

Escobaria missouriensis

though still worth acquiring) are sometimes offered for sale; these are var. *caespitosa*, with flowers two inches (5 cm) wide; var. *marstonii*, with flower petals gradually tapering to a point; and var. *robustior*, without fringed sepals.

Escobaria organensis is from high elevations in the Organ Mountains in southern New Mexico. As a young plant *E. organensis* is white-spined ball, with yellow central spines, about an inch (2.5 cm) across, and it stays that way for many years. Eventually it grows into a cylinder four inches (10 cm) high, with clusters of pink flowers half an inch (1.25 cm) across.

Escobaria sneedii is similar to *E. organensis*, but in the garden, at least, it forms clumps much more quickly, growing to a foot (30 cm) across in just a few years. *Escobaria sneedii* is cylindrical, three inches (7.5 cm) high and one inch (2.5 cm) wide, on older stems. The flowers are

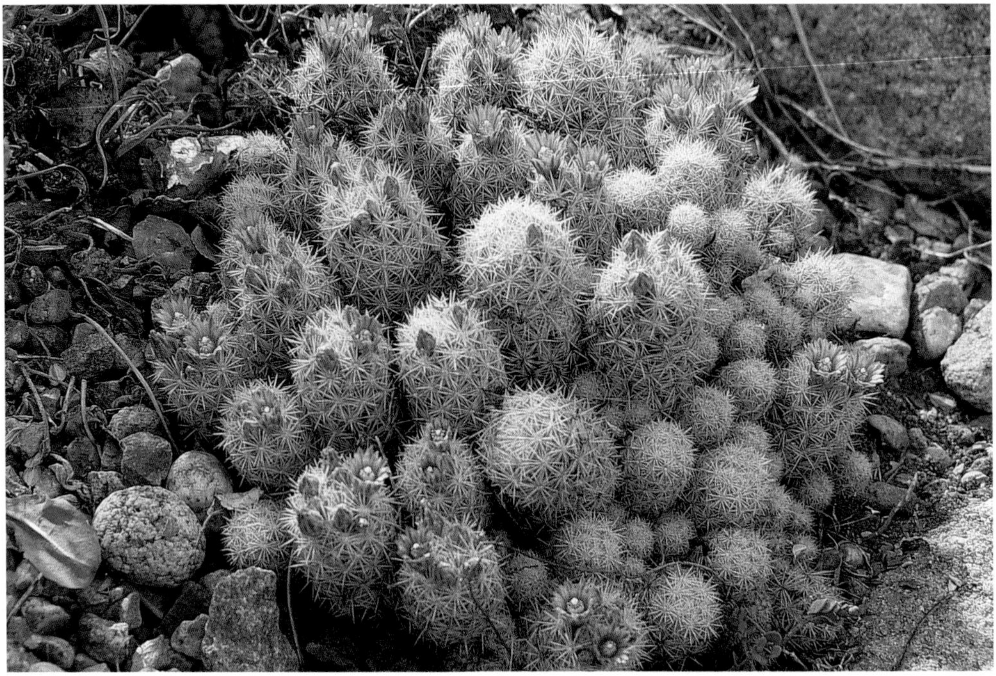

[above]
Escobaria sneedii var. *sneedii*

[right]
Escobaria vivipara

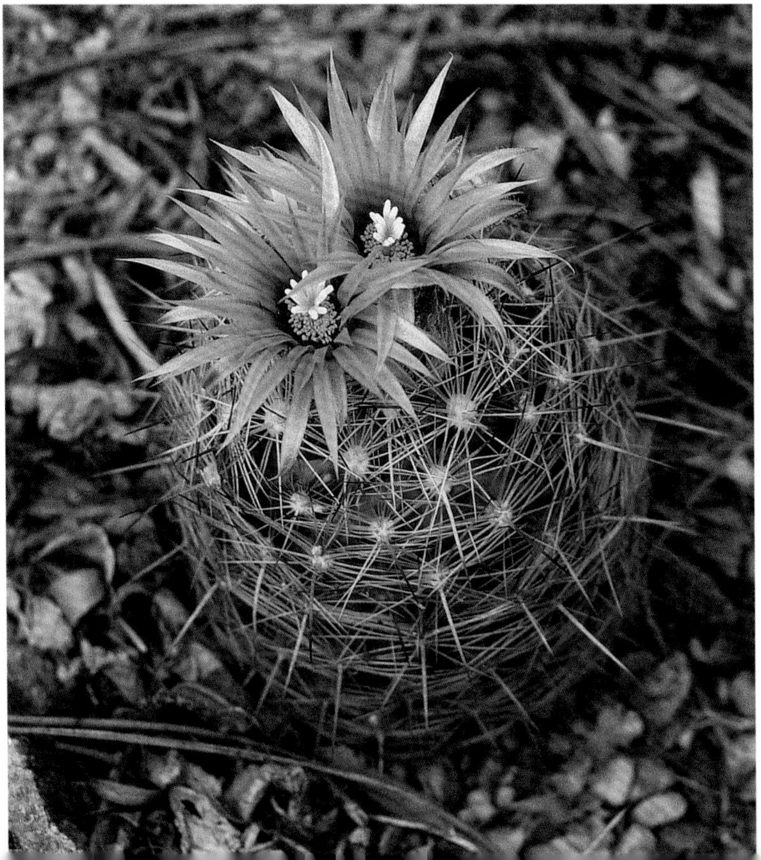

white with pink or darker pink veins, half an inch (1.25cm) or so wide, in clusters, opening in June. There are two varieties. *Escobaria sneedii* var. *sneedii* is found in the mountains of extreme southeastern New Mexico and adjacent Texas, and is listed (as *Coryphantha sneedii*) as endangered under the Endangered Species Act. *Escobaria sneedii* var. *leei*, with backward- and downward-pointing spines, is found only in the Guadalupe Mountains in southeastern New Mexico, and is listed as threatened under the Endangered Species Act.

Escobaria vivipara is a ball cactus, usually (but not always) clumping after several years (especially after a good rainy spring and summer), found throughout the Great Plains from southern Alberta, Saskatchewan, and Manitoba south to Texas, Coahuila, and Chihuahua, and from Montana to eastern Oregon south to the Mojave Desert region of California. The basic plant is about three inches (7.5cm) in diameter with prominent tubercles with starfish spines and showy clusters of pink to purple flowers, about two inches (5cm) across, in June. *Escobaria vivipara* is an extremely satisfactory plant in the garden and gratifyingly easy to grow from seed. There are the usual varieties, distinguished by the usual similarities, that some botanists prefer not to recognize. Most nurseries offer (sometimes as *Coryphantha*) *E. vivipara* var. *vivipara*, var. *arizonica*, var. *bisbeeana*, var. *radiosa*, and var. *rosea*. Other varieties are now considered species in their own right: *E. vivipara* var. *alversonii* (*E. alversonii*) and var. *deserti* (*E. deserti*), neither of which has been hardy for me.

Grusonia. A genus of plants formerly included in *Opuntia*, and still kept there by some botanists, though none of the species I know looks even remotely like an opuntia.

Grusonia clavata (*Opuntia clavata*; club cholla), from north-central to south-central New Mexico, forms mats of club-shaped stems about four inches (10cm) high and an inch (2.5cm) in diameter, with wonderfully wicked-looking, dagger-like spines, flattened and white and an inch (2.5cm) or so long. The bright yellow flowers are about two inches (5cm) across. *Grusonia clavata* has a reputation for refusing to flower in gardens, though it does happen from time to time.

Grusonia emoryi (*Opuntia stanlyi*; devil cholla) is a cactus about six

Grusonia clavata

inches (15cm) high by maybe eight inches (20cm) wide, though in the wild it can grow to many times that width. Cold winters tend to prune off bits here and there (which you need to remove with tongs). *Grusonia emoryi* has green, egg-shaped joints, covered with stiff, tan or brown, two-inch-long (5cm), deadly serious spines. The two-inch-wide (5cm) yellow, green-tinged flowers open in June. Native to southeastern Arizona, southern New Mexico, Chihuahua, and western Texas (var. *parishii*, native to California, is now its own species, *G. parishii*).

Grusonia pulchella (*Opuntia pulchella*; sand cholla), is native to Nevada and western Utah, and is a rare inhabitant of cactus nursery catalogs. *Grusonia pulchella* is a tiny, stemmed plant rising from a sweet-potato-like root, the stems with cylindrical joints about two inches (5cm) high, though taller stems are recorded, and forming mats a foot (30cm) wide. The downward-pointing spines are two inches (5cm) long; the flowers, which open in May or June, are about two inches (5cm) wide and of a beautiful rose-pink. Seed of *G. pulchella* (as *O. pulchella*) is rarely offered; this would be an excellent choice for a trough or a pot.

Mammillaria. A variable genus of well over a hundred species, almost entirely Mexican, and favorites of collectors, including me. Only two species, that I know of, have any tolerance to cold, and these seem to require absolutely dry conditions during winter in order to survive temperatures below 0F (−18C).

Mammillaria heyderi is native to southeastern Arizona, New Mexico, Texas, Oklahoma, south to Sonora, Chihuahua, Coahuila, Nuevo León, Zacatecas, San Luis Potosí, Tamaulipas, and even further south. As usual there are a number of subspecies, but I think we can safely ignore those found in the southern part of the range, like subspp. *gaumeri*, *gummifera*, *hemisphaerica*, and *macdougalii* (I tried subsp. *hemisphaerica* outdoors, once; it lasted until midwinter, and then that was that). *Mammillaria heyderi* subsp. *heyderi* is a flattened ball about an inch (2.5cm) high by three to four inches (7.5 to 10cm) wide, with conical tubercles tipped with spines. The two-inch-wide (5cm) pink or white flowers are borne at the top of the plant, in June. The plant typically just barely grows above the soil surface; its presence is not outstandingly obvious at all times of the year and can be a bit of a surprise to gardeners moving through the garden on their hands and knees. Subspecies *meiacantha* is found as far north, almost, as the New Mexico–Colorado border and should be the hardiest if given the requisite dry site in winter; it has a more hemispherical body than subsp. *heyderi*, with slightly larger flowers. The flat pancake *M. heyderi* var. *bullingtoniana* has apparently disappeared from the cactus literature; this one has the same hardiness requirements. Forms of *M. heyderi* are probably best grown in light shade.

Mammillaria wrightii is another flattened ball, two inches (5cm) high by three inches (7.5cm) across, with the same tiny-spine-tipped tubercles as *M. heyderi*, but in *M. wrightii* the central spines are inch-long (2.5cm) fishhooks, making this plant a little less fun to pick up with the fingers. It is, in fact, a lot less fun to pick up; this is one to handle with tongs. The flowers are purple and about an inch (2.5cm) wide, opening in June. Native to New Mexico, southeastern Arizona, Sonora (these plants would be subsp. *wilcoxii*, a plant with fewer spines, bright purple flowers, and probably much less hardy), Chihuahua, and western Texas.

Opuntia (prickly pear, nopal). A large number of cold-hardy opuntias are available for those who like effortless gardening. I confess to an inordinate fondness for these plants, but they do take up quite a bit of room. It's also difficult to find volunteers to weed among the opuntias.

The biggest drawback to opuntias, aside from the spines you brush into while doing the weeding no one else wants to do, is the glochids,

Opuntia sp.

tiny barbed hairs that detach from the pads with only the slightest provocation. Glochids can be removed with duct tape (use the sticky side), though this is not too much fun, or with tweezers. Tweezers with pointed tips are especially effective.

Aside from the handsome architectural feature that a well-grown patch of opuntias can add to a garden (opuntias are especially good grown in buffalograss), they have stunningly beautiful flowers in June and attractive, often edible fruits called tunas (make absolutely sure that the skins, with their spines and glochids, are removed, and the seeds need to be removed, too). The pads of some opuntias are used in Mexican cooking.

Fortunately for gardeners, there are some named selections of opuntias available, most selected for color form, but some selected for the color, usually purple, of the pads in winter.

Propagation of opuntias is easy. A single pad, or a group of pads, can be rooted simply by detaching them from the parent plant, allowing two or three days for the cut end to callus, and setting them on edge on the garden. The edge should be free from spines, and a wooden stick set on each side to prevent the plant's tipping over. The pad will root in about a week or ten days. Burying the pad deeper, or planting the cut end, may result in rotting.

Opuntias prepare themselves for winter by losing most of the water in their cells and shriveling; as a rule if the pads do not shrivel, the plant is doomed. There are exceptions, of course, which mystify me, though it occurs to me now that the opuntias I thought were braving the winter in a fully upright position might actually be frozen to death and just waiting for spring to fall into a pile of mush.

The descriptions that follow may safely be considered broad generalizations.

Opuntia aurea (*O. basilaris* var. *aurea*), apparently found only in southern Utah, is a spineless, beavertail type (the term needs no explanation), the pads about six inches (15 cm) tall and four inches (10 cm) wide, green, or at least greener than *O. basilaris*, with yellow flowers about four inches (10 cm) wide, in June. *Opuntia aurea* tends to form chains of pads instead of clusters, not a terribly attractive tendency in the garden but one that can be curbed by planting this species between rocks, timbers, or other barriers. A fine purple form also exists; it holds its color well, especially in winter.

Opuntia basilaris is found in southwestern Utah, southern Nevada, western Arizona, southern California, northern Baja California, and Sonora. This is a beavertail with blue-green, or blue, pads six inches (15 cm) tall by four inches (10 cm) wide, usually completely spineless (but still with glochids), forming clumps six feet (1.8 m) wide, with pink, red, or yellow flowers in June. Rare forms with white flowers are sometimes offered; the flowers are a good clean white. Some varieties (var. *brachyclada*, var. *longiareolata*, var. *treleasei*) are native to lower elevations in southern California and are probably not hardy, but I could be wrong. Variety *treleasei* is listed (as *O. treleasei*) as endangered under the Endangered Species Act. *Opuntia basilaris* is one of the best, but it needs room.

Opuntia aurea, purple form, in winter, at Denver Botanic Gardens

Opuntia chlorotica can become something of a tree but probably not in climates where the temperature drops to below −5F (−20.5C). I still have hope, though the thing grows so slowly my visions of a six-foot-tall (1.8m) opuntia skyscraper will probably never be realized. As I know it, *O. chlorotica* has light green round pads about eight inches (20cm) in diameter, covered with yellow spines about an inch and a half (3.75cm) long. The flowers are reported to be yellow and about two inches (5cm) across. Native to southern Utah, southern Nevada, southern California, Baja California, Arizona, southwestern New Mexico, Sonora, and Chihuahua.

Opuntia cymochila is native to eastern New Mexico and adjacent Texas. This is a low, creeping cactus, with round green pads six inches (15cm) across, a few pale spines an inch (2.5cm) or so long, and two-

Opuntia basilaris

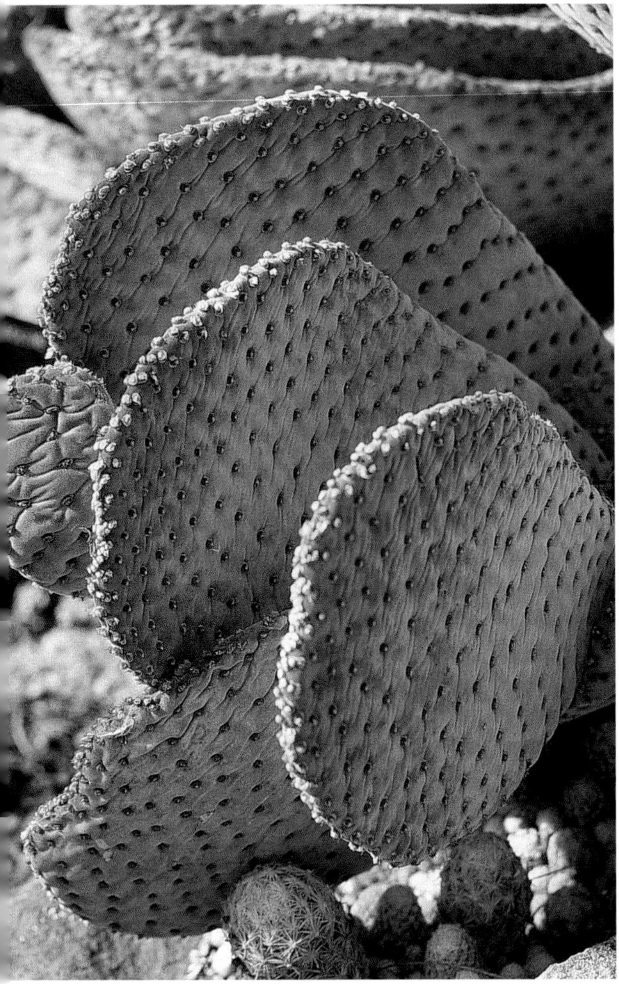

Opuntia basilaris in winter

inch-wide (5cm) yellow flowers in June. This makes a plant about three feet (90cm) wide.

The name *Opuntia engelmannii* brings visions of huge opuntia shrubs ten feet (3m) tall, but growing this species in cold-winter climates brings horrible reality, in the form of a completely collapsed, yellowed mass of despair. And yet there are some forms that do moderately well. Native from southern California to Texas and south into San Luis Potosí and Tamaulipas, *O. engelmannii* has round, green or bluish green pads ten inches (25cm) across, yellow spines about an inch and a half (3.75cm) long, with yellow flowers about two inches (5cm) across, in June. So depending on the previous winter, *O. engelmannii* may be a small plant with two or three pads, or a larger one with ten pads, but never a tree. There are several varieties, some of which (var. *cuija*, var. *flavispina*, and var. *flexospina*) are probably not hardy since they are found in the southern parts of the range of *O. engelmannii*. A huge sprawling thing against our basement window, where it gets some heat reflected off the western side of the house, is a plant of what I believe is *O. engelmannii* var. *lindheimeri* (*O. lindheimeri*), this has green pads ten inches (25cm) long and six inches (15cm) wide; it has never flowered. Some gardeners have reported success with var. *linguiformis* (cow's tongue cactus); this is a weirdly elongated form with pads sometimes over a foot (30cm) long.

Opuntia fragilis is found throughout the Great Plains and elsewhere, from fairly far north in British Columbia to Michigan, south to California and Texas. *Opuntia fragilis* has round green joints an inch (2.5cm) or so across, spines half an inch (1.25cm) long, and yellow flowers an inch and a half (3.75cm) wide, in June. This is a creeping plant, forming a mat a foot (30cm) or more across. A virtually spineless form turns brown-purple in winter; this so-called potato cactus is an attractive plant for a pot. *Opuntia fragilis* perpetuates itself by means of the readily detachable joints; the spines can get entangled in the coats of dogs and cats, or in the soles of tennis shoes, so be careful to plant this one away from a well-trodden path. 'Smithwick', a vigorous hybrid of *O. fragilis* and the eastern *O. humifusa*, about twice the size of *O. fragilis* itself, with flatter joints, was introduced by Claude Barr and is sometimes available from nurseries.

Opuntia macrocentra is a native of southern Arizona and New Mexico, western Texas, Sonora, Chihuahua, and Coahuila. It has round pads

Opuntia fragilis

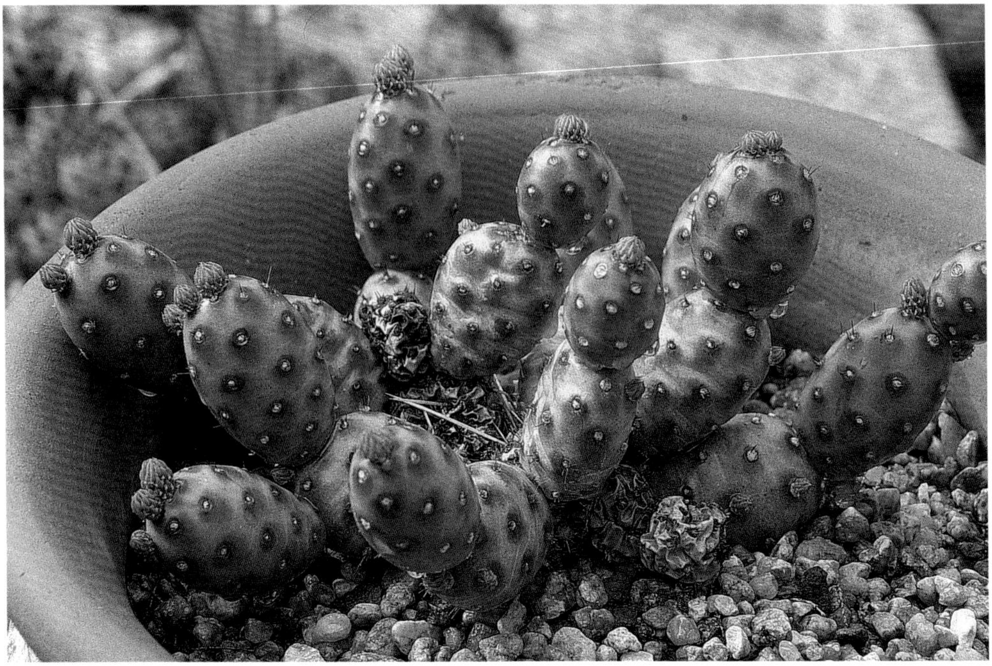

Opuntia fragilis, "potato" form

six inches (15cm) in diameter, dark green but often with a strong purplish tint, black spines two inches (5cm) or more long, and flowers two and a half inches (6.25cm) wide, yellow with red centers, opening in June. Variety *minor* has slightly smaller, bluer pads. *Opuntia macrocentra* is offered by nurseries every now and then (often as *O. violacea* var. *macrocentra*) as the "poor gardeners' version of *O. santa-rita*," poor gardeners in this case being ones unlucky enough to live in climates with bitterly cold winters where the dazzlingly purple *O. santa-rita* is not hardy. But, alas, even poorer me, a particularly purple form of *O. macrocentra* did not survive one winter for me. I should try again.

Opuntia macrorhiza is found throughout the Great Plains, even in southern Wisconsin and Minnesota, south to Coahuila and Tamaulipas, and west to Washington, California, and Sonora. *Opuntia macrorhiza* has more or less round, bluish green pads six inches (15cm) in diameter, with whitish two-inch-long (5cm) backward-pointing spines mostly at the tops of the pads, and yellow flowers with red centers, two inches

(5cm) wide, in June. Clumps may be as wide as six feet (1.8m) across. *Opuntia macrorhiza* has, as the name suggests, an enormous root, which makes a large clump difficult to transplant. *Opuntia macrorhiza* var. *pottsii* is a smaller form with blue pads and red flowers. A number of selected color forms, with flowers of salmon, pink, purple, or white, exist precariously in the trade. Just make sure you plant them where they can live happily for many years.

Opuntia microdasys (bunny-ear prickly pear), native to the Chihuahuan Desert in Mexico, has oblong pads five inches (12.5cm) long by four inches (10cm) wide, usually completely spineless but liberally endowed with golden glochids. The flowers are two inches (5cm) wide, yellow, tinted with red, blooming in June. I am growing a form with strongly purple-tinted pads that seems to be fully hardy, though it falls over alarmingly at the onset of cold weather. *Opuntia microdasys* is related to *O. rufida* (blind prickly pear; western Texas, Coahuila, and Chihuahua), but the glochids of *O. microdasys* fly off the pads less easily, and, for me, anyway, *O. microdasys* is the hardier species.

Opuntia phaeacantha is found from Colorado south through Oklahoma, Texas to Nuevo León and Tamaulipas, and west to California and Baja California. *Opuntia phaeacantha* has oblong pads eight inches (20cm) or more long, maybe six inches (15cm) wide, or wider, with variously colored (whitish to brown) spines, two inches (5cm) long, more or less, usually covering the pads, straight or pointing in practically any direction, with three-inch-wide (7.5cm) flowers in June, usually yellow, sometimes with red at the center. A number of selected color forms flit in and out of the trade. This is another one that can form large clumps, six feet (1.8m) wide, or more. Possibly fewer than ten thousand varieties have been described.

Opuntia polyacantha is a spiny thing with green pads four inches (10cm) long by three inches (7.5cm) wide, the spines white and two to four inches (5 to 10cm) or more long, pointing every which way. The flowers are yellow, three inches (7.5cm) across, borne in June. *Opuntia polyacantha* is native to practically everywhere in western North America, and as a result of the ensuing variability there are dozens of synonyms. Varieties include var. *arenaria* (*O. arenaria*), found along the Rio Grande in southern New Mexico, western Texas, and northwest-

Opuntia polyacantha

ern Chihuahua, a creeper with pads three inches (7.5cm) long and only an inch (2.5cm) wide; var. *erinacea* (*O. erinacea*; eastern Washington and Oregon south to California and New Mexico), covered with long white spines; var. *hystricina* (northern Arizona and northwestern New Mexico), covered with longer white spines; and var. *nicholii* (*O. nicholii*; southern Utah and northwestern Arizona, along the Colorado River drainage), covered with even longer white spines. The long spines of the different varieties can make for an untidy plant that catches leaves and other debris, something to think about when contemplating purchase of these plants, since you won't find volunteers to clean up the clusters of pads. A few other names, like *O. rhodantha* and *O. rutila*, linger in the trade, the latter emerging in Barr's selection, 'Super Rutila', a form with bright pink flowers.

In fact, Barr had a hand in introducing several fine color forms of *Opuntia polyacantha*, and forms with orange, chartreuse, and red flowers are associated with his name, as is 'Crystal Tide', with large white,

Opuntia polyacantha 'Crystal Tide'

pink-centered flowers. A number of other selected color forms are in the trade, including 'Dark Knight', whose pads turn to rich purple in winter.

Pediocactus. Pediocacti are mostly miniature ball cacti ideally suited to trough or pot culture. As usual, someone proposes name changes in this genus or recombinations of names about every three months. Eventually the names go back to where they started. Only *Pediocactus simpsonii* is available in the trade, and even that is pretty uncommon. Seed is usually available, but it can take five or more years from seed to flower. Grafted plants are sometimes sold by cactus nurseries, but these are only for indoor culture.

Pediocactus bradyi is a green ball, two inches (5 cm) in diameter, covered with tiny white or pale yellow radial spines; there are no central spines. The areoles are oddly elongated, about 2 mm long, giving the impression that little bugs are crawling over the plant. The flowers can be pink to straw-colored, or shades in between, an inch (2.5 cm) wide, opening in April or May. In summer the plants pull themselves down to soil level, where they remain until the following spring. Native to a commensurately tiny area in northern Arizona, *P. bradyi* is listed as endangered under the Endangered Species Act. This is one of the more difficult species to grow from seed. The similar *P. despainii*, sometimes considered a subspecies of *P. bradyi* and also endangered, is native to a small area in central Utah.

Pediocactus knowltonii is another tiny green golfball, about an inch (2.5 cm) across and high, if that, when it pulls itself toward the sun in spring in order to flower. The tubercles are tipped with tiny areoles from which tiny white radial spines emerge (there are no central spines); the flowers are pink, and an inch (2.5 cm) wide, in April. *Pediocactus knowltonii* is native to a small area in either northwestern New Mexico or southwestern Colorado, depending on where people think the state line is, and is listed as endangered under the Endangered Species Act. The population is now under the care of The Nature Conservancy. I understand that some years ago about four dozen plants were removed from this area, apparently to satisfy the demand for wild-collected plants. There must be no limit to the greed and stupidity of some people. In my experience *P. knowltonii* is the easiest of all cacti to germinate from seed, and very easy to grow; in captivity, new seedlings cluster around the parent plants every year.

Pediocactus paradinei, on the other hand, is not listed under the Endangered Species Act, but it is restricted to a relatively small area in northern Arizona. This is yet another green golfball, about an inch (2.5 cm) wide and high, with tiny thread-like central spines, with inch-wide (2.5 cm) pink to pale yellow flowers in April or May. *Pediocactus paradinei* pulls itself down to soil level after flowering, and sits there until the next spring. It is fairly easy to grow from seed.

Pediocactus peeblesianus is also from northern Arizona, and is another little cactus, one to two inches (2.5 to 5 cm) across and sometimes actually appearing above ground, though not by much. This has heavier spines than most pediocacti, about half an inch (1.25cm) long, curving slightly, occasionally with a central spine. The flowers are yellow, or a shade of yellow, about an inch (2.5cm) wide, in April or May. Definitely one for a trough or pot. *Pediocactus peeblesianus* is listed as endangered under the Endangered Species Act. Seed is relatively difficult to germinate.

Pediocactus simpsonii is the largest pediocactus, the easiest to grow, and the most widespread (central Washington to New Mexico). *Pediocactus simpsonii* may grow to almost six inches (15cm) wide (eventually) and as high (eventually). The tubercles are tipped with both central and radial spines less than half an inch (1.25cm) long, variously colored from light to dark. The flowers are about an inch (2.5cm) wide in var.

Pediocactus simpsonii

simpsonii, white, yellow, pink, or magenta, scented of old roses, opening in April. There are two varieties: var. *robustior*, a smaller plant with a tendency to clump, with more erect spines and the largest flowers (to two inches, 5cm, wide), found in the northwestern part of the range of *P. simpsonii*, and var. *minor*, again a smaller plant, with smaller flowers (about half an inch, 1.25cm, wide), found at high elevations, even subalpine elevations, in Wyoming, Colorado, and New Mexico. It takes about four years to flower from seed.

Pediocactus winkleri brings us back to the tiny pediocacti, this time a plant about half an inch (1.25cm) wide and as tall, sometimes clustering (one plant in the trough here has three stems), usually single, very slow-growing, with no central spines, and downward-pointing radial spines. The flowers are an inch (2.5cm) wide, opening in April or May. Native to a small area in south-central Utah, *P. winkleri* is listed as threatened under the Endangered Species Act.

Sclerocactus. A genus of spiny cacti with a bewildering (or just plain annoying) array of synonyms. A number of these are quite difficult to grow from seed, while others are fairly easy. Aftercare in the garden seems to be just as dependent on how the planets are aligned as on skill, so if you decide to start growing sclerocacti, expect some disappointment. Cultivation in a trough or pot, in gritty soil, seems to be the best way to grow them, though plants seem unduly difficult to establish. Do remember to shade little plants (a burlap tent, a plastic pot cut in half lengthwise and propped over the cacti with a stick, or a polymer spray like Cloud Cover™) for their first summer.

I have written off a few of these as being hopelessly tender: *Sclerocactus brevihamatus* (*Ancistrocactus*, *Ferocactus*, or *Pediocactus brevihamatus*) and its subspecies *tobuschii* (*A.* or *F. tobuschii*); *S. polyancistrus*; *S. scheeri* (*A.*, *F.*, or *P. scheeri*); and *S. uncinatus* (same synonyms times fifty) and its subspecies *crassihamatus* and *wrightii* (not to be confused with *wrightiae*). Since I like to put a lot of information on my plant labels, maybe my plants died because the labels fell on them.

I have not grown the recently described species from southern Nevada, *Sclerocactus nyensis*.

Sclerocactus glaucus (*S. brevispinus*, *S. wetlandicus*) is native to western Colorado and eastern Utah. This is a plant about three inches (7.5cm) high by two inches (5cm) wide, with whitish spines, the central spine about an inch (2.5cm) long, straight or curving but not hooked (usually), the radials somewhat shorter. The flowers are pink, an inch and a half (3.75cm) wide, opening in May. Listed as threatened under the Endangered Species Act, *S. glaucus* is difficult from seed, but semi-reasonably easy to grow as a plant, once established.

Sclerocactus mesae-verdae is native to the area around Mesa Verde, southwestern Colorado and northwestern New Mexico, and is listed as endangered under the Endangered Species Act. This is a grayish green golfball, sometimes flattened on top, with rounded tubercles and tiny gray spines, usually with no central spine, and yellow or pale yellow flowers usually less than an inch (2.5cm) wide, in April or May. Very difficult to grow from seed, but it can be done. Young seedlings need the most tender loving care.

Sclerocactus papyracanthus (*Toumeya papyracantha*) is a cactus with a difference. This is a plant about an inch or two (2.5 to 5cm) high, and an inch (2.5cm) wide, with tiny grayish radial spines and inch-long (2.5cm) flat, gray-white central spines, curving and twisting upward, obscuring the stem, looking exactly like dry blades of blue grama (*Bouteloua gracilis*), the grass it hides in, in New Mexico and western Arizona. The May-blooming flowers are white, about an inch (2.5cm) wide. *Sclerocactus papyracanthus* (almost always sold as *Toumeya*, though apparently DNA research suggests it's a sclerocactus) is probably best grown in a trough or pot, instead of in blue grama, where you would never see it.

Sclerocactus parviflorus is a furiously spiny thing that can grow eight inches (20cm) tall by four inches (10cm) wide, or more, in both dimensions, over time, of course. The central spines are hooked, and two inches (5cm) long. Flower color can be anything in the usual color range, from white or yellow to rose or pink. The flowers are about two inches (5cm) wide, though often less so, opening in May. There are a few subspecies, subsp. *havasupiensis*, subsp. *intermedius*, and subsp. *terrae-canyonae*, mostly distinguished by the spines, but these are rarely available from cactus nurseries. Regular *S. parviflorus*, though, is one of the most common sclerocacti and the most commonly available, relatively speaking. Native to northwestern New Mexico, western Colorado, eastern and southern Utah, and northern Arizona. Suitable for a trough or pot, or the rock garden.

Sclerocactus pubispinus, so called because of the pubescent spines on young plants, is native to eastern Nevada and western Utah, growing to about five inches (12.5cm), and as wide, though it's usually a more cylindrical plant. The radial spines are whitish; the centrals are dark, as much as two inches (5cm) long, and hooked. The flowers are an inch (2.5cm) wide, more or less, in shades of yellow, green, or light purple, opening in May.

Sclerocactus sileri (*Pediocactus sileri*) can be a cylindrical plant eight inches (20cm) tall by four inches (10cm) wide, though usually it's a spiny golfball that grows at glacial speed. The radial spines are white, the centrals are dark brown, not hooked. The flowers are yellow, an inch (2.5cm) wide, opening in May. *Sclerocactus sileri* is almost always offered as a pediocactus, and this only as seed that germinates erratically; as *P. sileri* it is listed as endangered under the Endangered Species Act. This one is as difficult to grow in the garden as any plant could possibly want to be.

Sclerocactus spinosior is a fattish cylinder native to western Utah, four inches (10cm) high by three inches (7.5cm) wide, horribly beset (as the name suggests) with spines, the white centrals two inches (5cm) long. The lower central spines are dark and hooked. The flowers are various shades of purple, an inch (2.5cm) or so wide, opening in May. Subspecies *blainei*, from eastern Nevada, has white lower centrals. *Sclerocactus spinosior* is the easiest sclerocactus to grow from seed.

Sclerocactus whipplei, graced with common names that include the words "devil's claw" (meaning, get out the tongs), is native to northeastern Arizona, northwestern New Mexico, southwestern Colorado, southern Utah, and eastern Nevada (the usual sclerocactus range, in other words). This is a cylindrical plant five inches (12.5cm) high by four inches (10cm) wide, covered with spines, the centrals white, or darker, an inch (2.5cm) or more long, the upper ones flattened, the lower ones hooked. The flowers are yellow, opening in May, and about a quarter of an inch (6mm) wide. *Sclerocactus whipplei* is slow from seed.

Sclerocactus wrightiae is a deadly golfball, two inches (5cm) in diameter, covered with spines. The white centrals can be well over an inch (2.5cm) long, with the lower ones hooked. The fragrant flowers are yellow or pink or white, an inch and a half (3.75cm) wide, opening in May. Native to a small area in central Utah, *S. wrightiae* is listed as endangered under the Endangered Species Act. Use tongs when transplanting this species; getting the hooks caught in your fingers is not what you would call fun. The first inclination is to get rid of the cactus by a swift flick of the wrist, which results in a serious tear in the skin, and a rare cactus flying through the air. It will usually land on the dog.

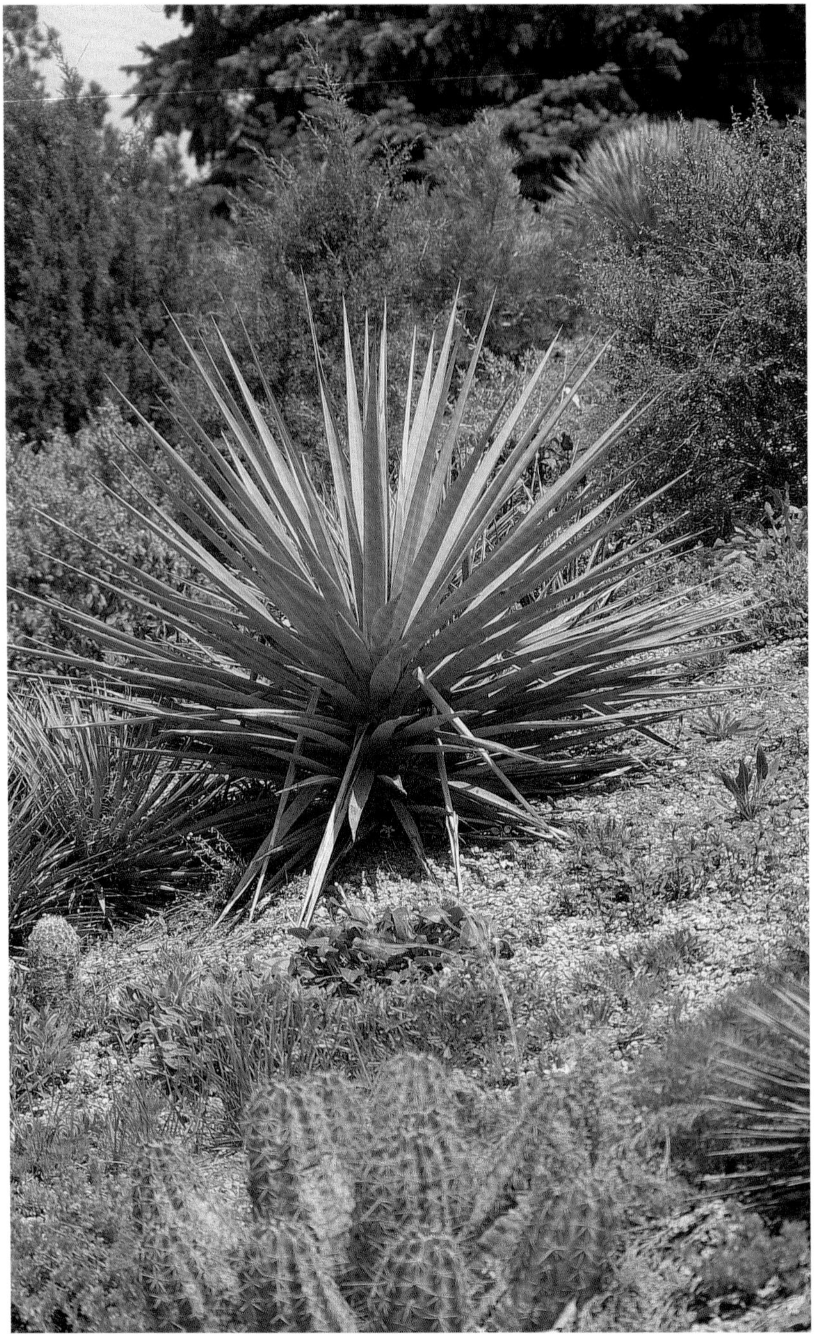

CHAPTER SEVEN

Yuccas, et cetera

Rosette-forming woody plants evoke the desert as few other plants do; their shock value in cold, dry gardens is so good that, even if the yucca or agave dies the minute frost comes to the garden, it's worth buying larger specimens of the more marginal varieties just to see the expressions on the faces of garden visitors. If you know where to look, some nurseries sell plants slightly smaller than Volkswagen beetles for surprisingly little money. You can say you're testing this one for hardiness. It might even live.

Their flowering, mostly, is as spectacular a thing as the plant kingdom has invented; the inflorescence of *Agave neomexicana* (*A. parryi* subsp. *neomexicana*), to take just one example, is about twenty feet (6 m) tall, widely branching at the top. Even as it grows, resembling nothing so much as a gigantic asparagus, it's something to see.

These plants are traditionally placed in the lily family (Liliaceae), though most of the genera have had their own families from time to time (Agavaceae, Nolinaceae, etc.) No matter. With some exceptions, the actual names of the plants have not changed much.

Most of the species mentioned here are from the mountains of Arizona, New Mexico, western Texas, Sonora, Chihuahua, and Coahuila; only a few are from the Great Plains or Great Basin.

Yucca schottii, Kelaidis garden

Agave parryi in snow

Once the "woody lilies" (to use Yucca-Do Nursery's perfect term for them) are established, summer water needs are very low, though extra water is of course appreciated. In the wild some of these plants, especially the ones from Arizona and Mexico, depend on late-summer moisture from the Mexican monsoon season, a point worth remembering after weeks of drought. The moisture from summer storms is usually sufficient to keep these plants happy, and though they will not die if they receive no moisture, it seems churlish not to give them a little water if restrictions allow it and no rain has fallen for two or three months. Water once for fifteen minutes in late July, again in mid-August, and in mid-September, but not after that time.

They benefit from a high-calcium water-soluble fertilizer (usually labeled cactus fertilizer; there are a number of good products on the market) applied once a week from June until August.

The plants will take clay soil, which is what I grow them in, but where the soil is exceptionally heavy they prefer being on a slight slope with a gravel mulch around the crown to keep the crown dry during the occasional thaw in winter and spring. Prolonged cover with organic matter (dead leaves, etc.) is almost certainly fatal.

Plant these away from areas where children might be playing, and be careful of them when you work in the garden.

Keep the light intensity of your garden in mind when unpacking mail-order plants grown in places where they think they have sun. An agave or yucca grown outdoors in Phoenix and planted directly out under Denver's sun will be dead within a week. To be safe, use an antidesiccant spray, or cover the plants with burlap for a few weeks.

All woody lilies are extremely easy to grow from seed, sown under lights, but somewhat less easy to move out into the open garden. The plants should be kept for at least two years before transplanted outside. Again, use an antidesiccant spray to protect them for the first few months. Larger plants, set out as early as possible in spring, usually do much better than smaller plants.

Rumor has it that larger plants are easier to overwinter than smaller plants. This is especially true if plants are very small, but larger plants aren't cheap, so protecting smaller ones might be a good idea for a few winters.

Winter hardiness varies with the species; some benefit from application of an antidesiccant spray, like Cloud Cover™, at least for the first winter. Plants prefer open, sunny winters, where they are indifferent to the occasional cold snap, even temperatures dipping below −20F (−29C); the killers are prolonged light snow cover and cool daytime temperatures, where moist soil remains near the crown for days or weeks on end. (I've seen rain in winter in Denver maybe twice in forty-five years, so the phrase "winter wet" has no meaning for me.) Many of these plants can be damaged, if not killed outright, by extremely cold winds, and should be sited accordingly.

Hardiness of some of these plants has probably been exaggerated in horticultural texts, both under- and overestimating the amount of cold these plants will endure, especially so since much of our region has not been subjected recently to the extremely cold temperatures that make people claim the major cities in the Rocky Mountain region are "in" a particular USDA hardiness zone when they really are not. The hardiness estimates here are pretty conservative ones, but they reflect bitter experience in the garden here. In general, yuccas are the hardiest, followed by agaves, then dasylirions and nolinas. Only yuccas, and just a few of those, actually experience reliable (if that's the right word), severe cold in their native habitat, and so the rest should be considered experimental in climates where winter temperatures regularly drop below –10F (–23C). The exceptions to this, like *Hesperaloe parviflora*, which has demonstrated complete winter hardiness to temperatures below –25F (–32C), prove the rule that long-term garden performance is the only way to evaluate plants.

As you go further south, into New Mexico and Arizona, the winter temperatures become less extreme, of course, even at high elevations. Snow may fall, but the presence of snow is not an indicator of serious cold weather; it can snow when the temperature is 25F (–4C), which is hardly characteristic of a cold climate. It has snowed in Malibu, where winter hardiness is something no one talks about.

The coldest region in the southern part of our area is probably the Chihuahuan Desert, which stretches roughly from southeastern Arizona to New Mexico, where it ranges northward up the Rio Grande to Albuquerque, through Chihuahua, Texas west of the Pecos River, to Coahuila, and barely entering Zacatecas, San Luis Potosí, and Nuevo León where these three states meet. Temperatures as cold as –22F (–30C) have been recorded in the city of Ahumada, Chihuahua (Brown 1982), but not every winter. The climate is certainly one that suggests a wide range of plants might be available for gardeners, since this is a cold desert, but there is a problem with this notion.

For one thing, the Chihuahuan Desert isn't a cold desert in the same sense as the Red Desert in southwestern Wyoming is. Plants native to the Red Desert (all three of them) are perfectly hardy in Denver. But only some plants native to the Chihuahuan Desert are perfectly hardy; others must be considered marginal, or hardy in just the right situation. (*Agave havardiana*, for instance, is completely hardy, but *A. scabra*, which grows next to it in some areas, is not.) There is a big difference between

Yucca glauca at Denver Botanic Gardens

a climate that experiences record cold temperatures (the aforementioned Malibu), and a climate that experiences the same cold temperatures on a more or less regular basis.

So, except for stalwarts like *Yucca glauca* and a few others, I would consider these recommendations tentative until you get a good feel for what works in your garden and what doesn't. Or go all out, buy everything, and see how much fun you can have.

As with cacti, turning red in winter is acceptable; a yellow or white discoloration is a sign of impending death (if not of the plant, at least of the leaf so colored).

Almost all these plants are, of course, much larger and exponentially more spectacular in mild-winter climates; all we can do is try to evoke those climates with smaller plants.

Agave parryi, just starting to bloom, and a host of other succulents, garden of Kelly Grummons

Agave (century plant). A genus of a hundred or so species, most of them hopelessly tender. Their leaves, mostly, are tipped with lethal spines. It is probably worth moving further south in order to grow these wonderful plants, but gardeners in cold-winter climates can satisfy their desires with a number of species that give the impression of having taken the wrong turn off the evolution highway and parked themselves at relatively high elevations in the dead of a cold, snowy winter. And there are also some surprises; again, nature sometimes cloaks the hardiness of plants in the guise of an unlikely winter environment.

Most of the agaves considered here "pup" like there was no tomorrow. New plants sprout from adventitious buds on the thin, icicle-like roots that snake just under the soil surface. Even if a plant is killed or dug up, new plants will emerge a few years later. And you'll have dozens to give to friends.

Agave havardiana, from Coahuila, Chihuahua, and west Texas, is the heavyweight contender in the class of cold-hardy agaves. Distinguished by the width of the leaf at the base (six inches, 15cm) and reasonably vicious-looking, backward-pointing teeth on the leaves, this one can get almost three feet (90cm) tall and wide, though it rarely does where winters dip below −5F (−20.5C). Success seems to hinge on it being planted in soil that stays extremely dry in winter. *Agave havardiana* spreads by suckers. I had a basketball-sized plant killed by an unusual winter where ice and snow lay on the ground for three months; a dozen new plants grew from the roots, spread out like the rays emanating from a dead sun. *Agave neomexicana* (*A. parryi* subsp. *neomexicana*; southwestern and south-central New Mexico) is similar to *A. havardiana*, but the leaves are half as wide, and the plant is smaller. This is again a suckering plant; one will get you ten in just a few years. *Agave neomexicana* is one of the most likely to flower in cold-winter climates.

Agave lechuguilla, a typical plant of the Chihuahuan Desert flora (Puebla north through San Luis Potosí and Nuevo León to Coahuila, Chihuahua, western Texas, and southern New Mexico), is a more open-growing agave with stiff green leaves, lethally pointed at the tips, and intensely serious spines. With me it is about two feet (60cm) high and as wide, slowly suckering. It is hardier than most, possibly because the leaves have less water in them. Not as architectural as some of the others, but still wonderfully dangerous in appearance. *Agave gracilipes*, a putative hybrid of *A. lechuguilla* and *A. neomexicana*, is a species of Chihuahua, western Texas, and southeastern New Mexico, and is said to be as hardy as *A. lechuguilla*. I've never grown it, but there is a splendid plant (which should be mine . . .) in a garden less than a mile away.

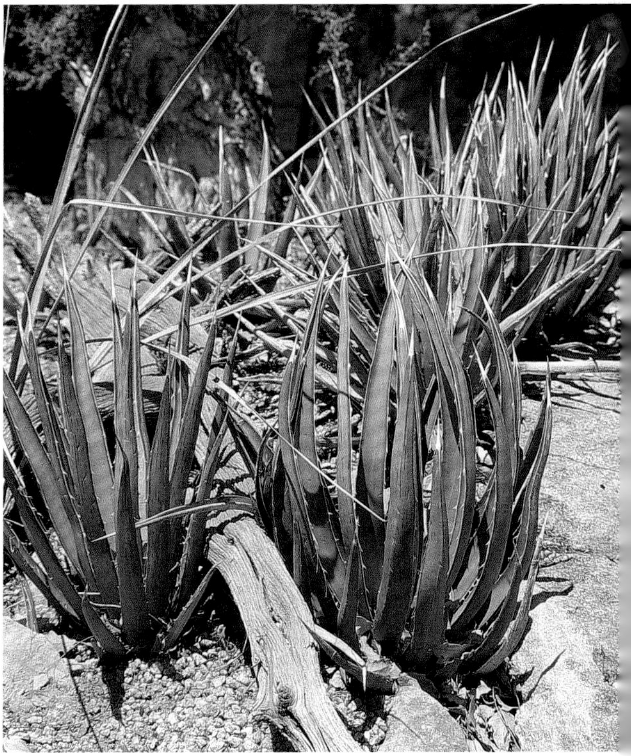

Agave lechuguilla at Denver Botanic Gardens

Agave parryi, one of the most beautiful of the smaller agaves, is a riotously suckering plant with broad, short, blue-glau-

Agave gracilipes, garden of Neal Lundquist

cous leaves that form a wicked-spined rounded rosette about eighteen inches (45cm) high and wide. It has a wide distribution, from north-central Arizona to southwestern New Mexico, Chihuahua, and Durango. Northern populations of this plant experience temperatures below 0F (−18C) (Gentry 1998), but the larger southern var. *huachucensis* (from the Huachuca Mountains in southeastern Arizona) is just as hardy in the garden. The candelabra-shaped inflorescence of *A. parryi* tops out at about fifteen feet (4.5m); you only have to wait about twenty years for this to happen.

Agave parryi var. *couesii* is about two-thirds the size of typical *A. parryi*; this is found in central Arizona and seems to be hardy. *Agave parryi* var. *truncata* (*A. patonii*) is from the Durango-Zacatecas border; it does not seem to be reliably hardy. One plant made it through −6F (−21C) but gave up the ghost later in spring, while a second, a cut-

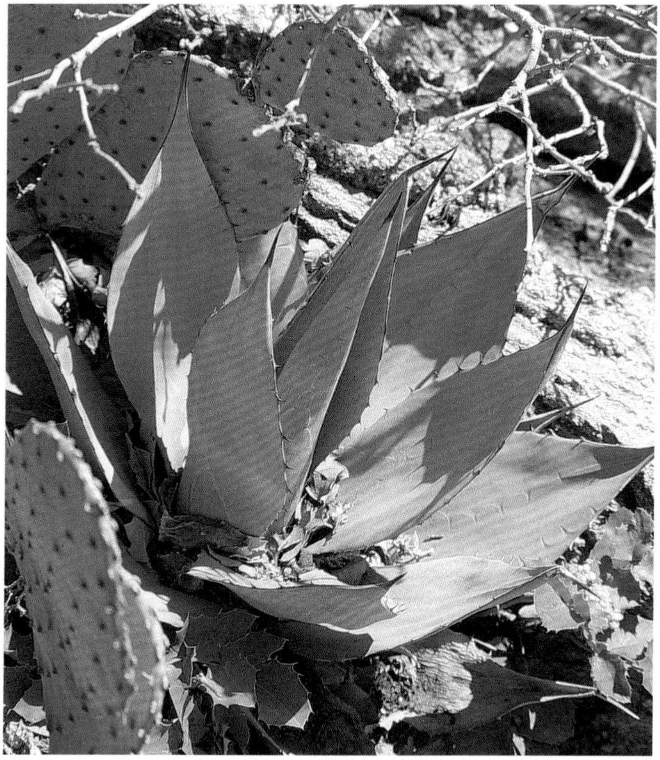

[left] *Agave parryi* var. *huachucensis* at Denver Botanic Gardens

[below] *Agave parryi* at Denver Botanic Gardens

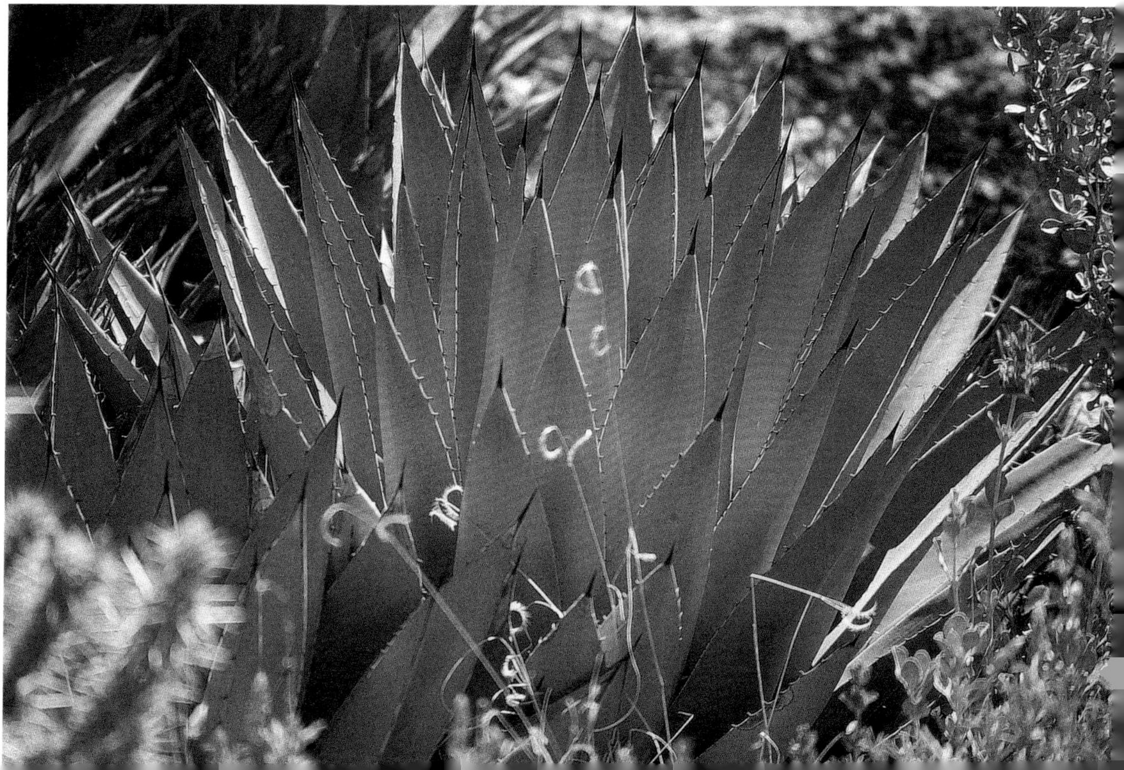

ting from the original type collected by Gentry (HBG 23389) I killed by planting it out after thoughtlessly allowing the center of the plant to rot while it was sitting in a pot; exposure to sun and dry conditions simply finished it off.

Agave utahensis is a small species with upward-curving blue-gray leaves tipped with long spines. This is a clustering, but not suckering plant that grows in congested clusters and looks best in a rock garden. *Agave utahensis* is the hardiest of all agaves, perfectly hardy to −20F (−29C). The typical variety is about eight inches (20 cm) high and spreads very slowly (a plant almost twenty years old here is about two feet, 60 cm, wide, with no supplemental irrigation or fertilizing).

Agave utahensis has three varieties, *kaibabensis* (northern Arizona), larger than the type, with green leaves, growing singly instead of in clusters; var. *nevadensis* (southeastern California and adjacent areas in southern Nevada), smaller with longer spines (especially at the leaf tips); and var. *eborispina*, found just north of var. *nevadensis*, with beautiful, wicked-long white spines. Any one of these, or all of them, will do nicely.

And then there are some surprises. *Agave deserti* does not seem to realize that cold temperatures are upon it; it even showed no response when there was a sudden drop in temperature in our garden from 70F (21C) to 0F (−18C) one November, an event that carried away some of the more "experimental" succulents. *Agave deserti* is native to southeastern California, western and southern Arizona, and northwestern Sonora. In our garden it is about eight inches (20 cm) high and wide. There are other varieties of *A. deserti*, but their native range suggests a total lack of resistance to cold, so I haven't tried them. I have also not tried its relative *A. mckelveyana* (from northwestern Arizona, south of the Grand Canyon) because I gave away all the plants I raised from seed. (I see now that this was a mistake.)

I am not entirely certain of the garden value of *Agave scabra* (known in some quarters, because the epithet was already used for a species of *Manfreda*, as *A. asperrima*), another large one on the havardiana scale of things. This species has thick, rigid leaves, curved inward at the edges, but it seems somewhat unhappy where I have placed it. A warmer location next to a south-facing wall would probably suit this, a companion

Agave utahensis var. *eborispina* at Denver Botanic Gardens

of *A. lechuguilla* and *A. havardiana* in the wild, better. It seems to be killed outright at temperatures below –8F (–22C).

I bought, and planted, a compact-car-size plant of *Agave scabra* × *A. havardiana* (or maybe it was the other way around) just in time for visitors to gawk at it during a major rock garden conference. I'm not sure that every visitor approved of it. Unfortunately the entire plant turned to mush after the temperature drop just mentioned.

Agave toumeyana var. *bella* is a smaller, softball-sized species with myriad leaves (var. *toumeyana*, also hardy, has fewer leaves) with conspicuous bud-prints (white lines left from the impression of leaves as they separate from the inward ones). It grows only in the mountains of central Arizona and never experiences the kind of cold that it is forced to experience in my garden. So long as it never learns this, maybe it will be fine. Small plants are surprisingly easy to overwinter if sprayed with an antidesiccant. Exposed leaves are damaged at temperatures below –5F (–20.5C), and the plant looks so hideous that it is well worth planting this close to the house for the extra heat, where it does quite well. The inflorescence is a three-foot-tall (90cm) pencil with tiny flowers, but never mind. It's an agave *blooming* in your garden.

Agave parviflora, from the Pajarito Mountains in southern Arizona, is quite similar to *A. toumeyana*, with the same bud-prints on the leaves but smaller flowers, and may be as hardy. So far my small plant has not died, though another plant of the same size was killed by exposure to Colorado's sun before it was completely hardened off. (Even though I strongly recommend use of antidesiccants in transplanting, I don't always practice what I preach.)

Agave schottii (southern Arizona, extreme southwestern New Mexico, and Sonora), another relative of *A. toumeyana* but lacking the bud-prints, is a plant about eight inches (20cm) high and wide, with narrowly linear green leaves. *Agave schottii* is not incredibly attractive, but since it can be grown in cold-winter gardens it has its own blasé charm. Hardy to about –10F (–23C).

Though visitors may suspect you of accidentally trying to grow a familiar houseplant outdoors, *Agave victoriae-reginae* has a secret history of winter hardiness in the Rocky Mountain region. This Mexican species, with even more noticeable bud-prints than *A. toumeyana*, no teeth on the leaves, and a black, blunt spine at the leaf-tip, seems to like being stuck outside, wedged in a crevice between two rocks. It does not like being covered with fallen leaves during the winter, so pay attention to this more than I did. (The lower leaves of the agaves rotted under what I thought might be a beneficial mulch.) *Agave victoriae-reginae* is from fairly high elevations in Coahuila, Durango, and Nuevo León and is hardy to about –10F (–23C).

Dasylirion (desert spoon, sotol). Think of these as yuccas with teeth, though the inflorescence looks more like a dried stalk of mullein from a distance (it could just be my imagination). The leaf tips are relatively harmless, but the leaf edges have varyingly sharp teeth, depending on the species.

You can grow these from seed (and wait ever so patiently for them to get large enough to be set out into the garden, and then suffer the heartbreak of watching them die in twenty-four hours from overexposure to the sun), or you can buy large plants (cheaply!) from nurseries in Arizona.

We can be tempted by at least three species. *Dasylirion texanum* is the hardiest species, so far proving itself completely undamaged at temperatures to at least −10F (−23C). A handsome thing it is, too. *Dasylirion texanum* has stiff green leaves with forward-pointing teeth, which you will notice if you grab a leaf by mistake. *Dasylirion texanum* is a plant about three feet (90cm) tall and wide in cold-winter climates. The flowering stalk is about six feet (1.8m) tall. This is native to Texas, of course, and Coahuila. Plants are available in the trade, and they establish quite easily. *Dasylirion leiophyllum* (southern New Mexico, western Texas, Chihuahua, and Coahuila) is quite similar to *D. texanum*, but the teeth on the leaves point backward. If you want this one, you'll have to grow it from seed.

Dasylirion wheeleri has waxy, light gray or bluish silver leaves with forward-pointing teeth, and makes, if you're lucky, a plant five feet (1.5m) high and wide. *Dasylirion wheeleri*, native to Chihuahua and extreme western Texas (around El Paso), west through extreme southwestern New Mexico to Arizona and Sonora, is the problem child among the hardy dasylirions. It seems to be safely hardy to about −5F (−20.5C), but placement in the garden is critical unless you are one of those gardeners with an unusual amount of luck. The drier the soil in winter, the better; winter shade and protection from cold wind also help winter hardiness. The suggestion has been made that plants from the Chihuahuan Desert are hardier than plants from the western area of the species' range.

Hesperaloe. The "western aloes," once unheard-of in cold-winter gardens, have now become so common that you see them in highway median plantings in Denver suburbs (heavily watered, of course). Well, almost common: only one species, *Hesperaloe parviflora*, is well known. This has clusters of stiff, folded, narrow, curving yucca-like leaves, making a clump about two feet (60cm) high and as wide or wider, and pink-red flowers on three-foot-tall (90cm) spikes. *Hesperaloe parviflora* blooms from June, given sufficient moisture early in the season, until autumn, sometimes even to the end of October. A form with beautiful pale yellow flowers is less common in the trade. The distribution of *H. parviflora* in the wild, Coahuila and Texas (the Big Bend area, and northeast almost to the Oklahoma border), is worth contemplating for those who believe that habitat always determines hardiness.

Two other species are worth trying, and are available in the trade. *Hesperaloe campanulata*, native to a small area in Nuevo León, has larger pink flowers and is almost as hardy; *H. funifera*, my favorite, has stiff, strap-like leaves almost six feet (1.8m) long, with strands of white fiber peeling from the edges (giving the plant its epithet, which means "fiber-bearing"). The greenish flowers are okay, but with this species, the leaves alone are enough. This is native to western Texas near the Big Bend south to Nuevo León and San Luis Potosí. A plant near the main entrance at Denver Botanic Gardens has done well; this is an area almost completely protected from cold winter winds and benefits from reflected heat from the building. Plants grown in exposed areas are much more susceptible to damage, and rating this plant as hardy only to –5F (–20.5C) seems reasonable to me, though the plant will grow back from the roots. This is cold comfort to me.

Nolina (beargrass, sacahuista). Nolinas are similar to yuccas but have more leaves; the inflorescences are similar too, but, since the flowers are smaller, they are less spectacular. (I wouldn't worry too much about having unspectacular flowering nolinas in your garden, though.) The hardy nolinas are not unbelievably exciting plants, some looking for all the world like overgrown clumps of a second-rate ornamental grass. At least two species may be safely tried where temperatures do not regularly fall below about –20F (–29C). All the nolinas mentioned are obtainable as plants in the trade.

Nolina microcarpa (Chihuahua, Arizona, and New Mexico) is an enormous yucca-like thing, about five feet (1.5m) high and wide, with a pretty good history of winter hardiness in cold, dry-winter climates, but tree-sized specimens remain but a dream.

Nolina texana is a clump of wiry green leaves a foot (30cm) tall and wide, native from Coahuila to extreme southeastern Colorado and the Oklahoma pandhandle. It's an extremely unimpressive grassy-looking thing, but still different enough to be grown in gardens that yearn to be different. I no longer grow it. Some botanists consider the northern forms of *N. texana* to be a separate species, *N. greenei.*

Some others, like *Nolina erumpens* (Coahuila and Texas near the Big Bend), and *N. lindheimeriana* (Texas) have overwintered in the garden here but seem to call out for special protection from hot winter sun. I also tried *N. nelsonii* (tree nolina; Tamaulipas), since the label said "cold hardy." It is not. Two separate plants in two winters were killed outright at 5F (−15C).

Yucca. A thoroughly detested plant over much of its range, loathed by ranchers and farmers (though an abundance of yuccas is a sure sign of overgrazed land), yet loved by English gardeners. William Robinson writes, of the southeastern yuccas to be sure, "though the stiffest of garden plants, it has grace and elegance, under all conditions, if the plant is not cramped for room. Yuccas seem fitted for various uses, as a single plant may stand alone on a lawn, or in the centre of a bed, or numbers may be grouped with other plants, or form a bed by themselves."

Contemplating the taxonomy of the genus *Yucca* involves much rolling of the eyes. Fortunately, nursery-grown plants are almost always correctly labeled, so it's unlikely that you will get a frost-tender yucca by mistake.

Yuccas are easily grown from seed, though plants are also available, and they tolerate dense clay soil, if the soil is kept dry, as usual. Occasionally they object to heavy snowfall. The plants may be hideously splayed and take up to a year to recover, but recover they do. The spectacular flowers are, of course, an added attraction in the garden, mostly appearing in May or June.

Yucca angustissima (Arizona, Utah, and New Mexico) and *Y. baileyi* (same distribution: a botanist friend says that reports of *Y. baileyi* in Colorado are mistaken) are fairly similar in appearance, but *Y. angustissima* has a flowering stalk much taller than the leaves, with more open, bell-shaped flowers, while *Y. baileyi* (*Y. navajoa*) has a stalk not much taller than the leaves, with larger, less open flowers. At least, this is the way some people think it goes. Buy both and see what happens. *Yucca angustissima* has long, very narrow leaves half an inch (1.25cm) wide with a silver edge; the rosette is about three by three feet (90 by 90cm). Two varieties of *Y. angustissima* from southern Utah, var. *toftiae* and var. *kanabensis*, are sometimes available as seed, or even as plants; each has been considered a separate species, though they seem to be not much more than progressively larger versions of the basic species.

Though planting it in a lawn may be asking for trouble, *Yucca baccata* (banana yucca, datil) is a spectacular plant that can take very cold temperatures, to −30F (−34C). This is found from extreme eastern California through southern Nevada, southern Utah, western Colorado south to Arizona and Sonora, and New Mexico, western Texas and Chihuahua. *Yucca baccata* grows to about four feet (120cm) with equally long, thick, fairly rigid leaves, tipped with vicious spines that can inflict serious pain. Snipping these tips where they are close to traffic is not only a friendly gesture, it can save you some agony. Since I would not want to be without this plant, and also want to appear to be at least moderately friendly, I snip my plants where they face the street.

The flowering stalk of *Yucca baccata* is usually hidden within the huge thicket of leaves, which is a disappointment since the flowers are so nice. The seedpod is a four-inch-long (10cm) green banana.

Yucca brevifolia var. *jaegeriana* is the hardy one to look for in seed catalogs (since it is almost never available as a plant). Yes, this is the Joshua tree; though not much of a tree (actually, not much of anything) in climates where temperatures regularly drop below about −5F (−20.5C); still, it will be something to show off to visitors, who might have difficulty being persuaded that the tiny yucca-like things you're so proud of are any relation to the Joshua tree. So what if you're the only one who cares. *Yucca brevifolia* var. *jaegeriana* used to be considered to be the dwarf version of the Joshua tree found from southeastern California to southwestern Utah, but botanists no longer recognize varieties within *Y. brevifolia*.

I would be hard pressed to give an answer to gardeners who might wonder why a dwarf variety that had a botanical name is considered hardy, but the larger version is not considered hardy when the varietal name distinguishing the two disappears. Maybe *Yucca brevifolia* itself is hardy in the same way; that is, it can be grown in cold-winter gardens, but doesn't make much of an impression.

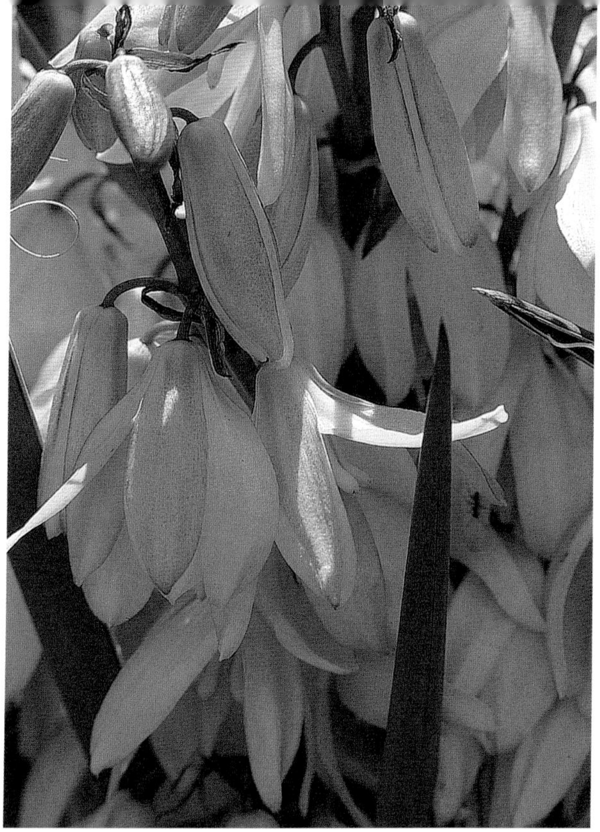

[left] *Yucca baccata*

[below] *Yucca baileyi* at Denver Botanic Gardens

Yucca faxoniana at Denver Botanic Gardens

Yucca elata, the state flower of New Mexico, can be a tree, to ten feet (3 m), flowering stalk included, even in Denver. Imagine a yucca glued to the top of a palm tree, and you get the idea. Just one of these, after a dozen years' worth of growth, will slow down, if not stop, traffic. For some bizarre reason, *Y. elata*, which should be considered completely hardy to −30F (−34C), is uncommon in the trade. *Yucca elata* is native from southwestern Utah and northwestern and eastern Arizona, south to Sonora, Chihuahua, and Coahuila, and east through western and southern New Mexico to western Texas. It is a glorious plant. Nonarborescent forms of *Y. elata* found in Utah, Nevada, and Arizona are sometimes called *Y. utahensis*.

Yucca faxoniana (Texas, Chihuahua, and Coahuila) is a monster tree yucca to about eight feet (2.4 m), not including the flowering stalk, which can add another one to two feet (30 to 60 cm) to the overall picture. With age this has a trunk about two feet (60 cm) wide, or wider, topped by stiff, vicious, light green spine-tipped leaves three feet (90 cm) or more long. A group of these in the front yard would definitely make a statement (I have one plant, but it's too small to talk yet). There seems to be a current fashion in my part of the world for acquiring large specimens of *Y. faxoniana* for instant effect; the plants are not exactly cheap and require planting with a backhoe. *Yucca faxoniana* is rather susceptible to damage from heavy, wet spring snow. Otherwise it seems hardy, though its tolerance for really low temperatures is still unknown; −10F (−23C) seems to be a safe estimate.

Yucca faxoniana is often called *Y. carnerosana* in older texts dealing

Yucca glauca

with the Chihuahuan Desert flora. Some botanists now consider these two species to be distinct, *Y. carnerosana* being the exclusively Mexican species found in Coahuila, Nuevo León, Zacatecas, and San Luis Potosí. Young plants of *Y. faxoniana* seem to me to have much thicker, stiffer leaves, reminiscent of *Y. baccata*, than do even much larger specimens of *Y. carnerosana*.

Yucca glauca is the ubiquitous yucca of the Great Plains (Alberta to New Mexico and Texas). The blue foliage by itself is attractive, though reading Claude Barr's account of this plant's potential to have entirely red-sepaled or entirely black flowers, and then contemplating the total absence of red-flowered forms of *Y. glauca* in regional nurseries, does more to illustrate the negative effects of conservative gardening practices in the west than possibly anything else. (I believe the flowers become completely white when fully opened.) *Yucca glauca* is a clustering plant with rosettes two feet (60cm) tall and wide. The white-flowered plants are admittedly quite beautiful. This is the hardiest yucca, easily taking temperatures to –40F (–40C). I am currently trying a dwarf form (I almost killed the two plants, which would have been humiliating since the species grows within a few minutes' walking distance of my house), said to be eight inches (20cm) high, offered by Huntington Botanic Gardens (HBG 94020, clone 30), which promises to be an ideal plant for dry rock gardens.

A naturally occurring hybrid between *Yucca glauca* and *Y. angustissima* is sometimes called *Y. intermedia*; this is a native of New Mex-

Yucca harrimaniae

ico and is said to form a plant about two feet (60cm) high and wide, with greenish flowers. I have never seen this name mentioned anywhere but in *Flora of North America*. Another hybrid of *Y. glauca*, this time with *Y. faxoniana*, is occasionally offered as seed. (*Yucca pallida*, a wider-leafed version of *Y. glauca*, is native to east-central Texas and thus outside the limits of our area.)

Given its hardiness, hybrids involving *Yucca glauca* have an intrinsic value for the dry garden; it's disappointing that so few (in fact, none) are common in the trade. At the Chatfield Arboretum southwest of Denver, there is a small garden with three or four handsome hybrids with obvious *Y. glauca* genetic material in them; it would be nice if someone made these available to the trade, or just to me.

Plants labeled *Yucca harrimaniae* in nurseries are almost always likely to be dwarf, clustering plants, some small enough to hide under a baseball cap. Buying plants from local and mail-order nurseries will most likely give you a wide variety of plants that may or may not be the real *Y. harrimaniae*, but after poring over botanical treatments of this species, I am not exactly sure what the real species is supposed to look like. Some plants have more or less linear light green leaves, some have more lanceolate leaves, the margins peeling away to varying degrees. In some forms this is a very attractive characteristic and adds a great deal to the appearance of the plant. The tiniest versions of this may be the plants sometimes called *Y. nana*. *Yucca harrimaniae* has greenish flowers on a fifteen-inch (38cm) stalk; it is found from Nevada and Arizona to Colorado and New Mexico and is hardy to at least −30F (−34C). The typical forms of *Y. harrimaniae* are suitable for the rock garden, and the smallest forms are suitable for troughs, or Lilliputian gardens.

Yucca rostrata at Denver Botanic Gardens

Larger forms of *Yucca harrimaniae* are sometimes called *Y. neomexicana*. Forms the same size as larger forms of *Y. harrimaniae* are also called *Y. neomexicana*. Some botanists consider this merely a variety, others a species. *Yucca neomexicana* is said to have more linear leaves and white flowers. It will, of course, be found in nursery catalogs under *Y. neomexicana* . . . or *Y. harrimaniae*.

Yucca rostrata is a tree yucca from Coahuila and western Texas, in the Big Bend region. It is said to be the largest cold-hardy yucca; I know of no plants in any garden larger than some examples of *Y. faxoniana*, but I haven't been everywhere, so let's say that it is. *Yucca rostrata* is an exceedingly beautiful plant: when just a few feet tall, the steel-blue leaves, three feet (90cm) long and an inch (2.5cm) or so wide, shimmer with the slightest breeze like a metal sculpture. The flowering stalk adds another two to three feet (60 to 90cm) to the picture. *Yucca rostrata* is hardy to at least −11F (−24C). Good-sized plants are available at reasonable prices from nurseries in Arizona. The dead leaves hang on the trunk in a manner reminiscent of palm trees.

Yucca rupicola either does or does not enter our area, depending on who is consulted. Maps on the University of Texas Web site suggest that it does, and since we can always use another hardy yucca, I will accept this. *Yucca rupicola* is endemic to west-central Texas and is unique among hardy yuccas in having twisted green leaves. The leaves seem to

Yucca thompsoniana at
Denver Botanic Gardens

have some difficulty remaining upright and form sort of a rosette about two feet (60cm) tall and wide, making a vaguely curious but at the same time welcoming effect for its definitely green leaves. The flowering stalk adds another two to three feet (60 to 90cm). *Yucca rupicola* has been grown at Denver Botanic Gardens for many years and has only recently become widely available in nurseries; consider it safely hardy to −20F (−29C), at least.

Yucca schottii, a yucca with a trunk, over time (though maybe not tall enough to be considered a tree yucca), is sometimes offered in the trade. I only have little plants in the garden and can make no comment, except to note that current taxonomy considers *Y. schottii*, a plant of Sonora, Coahuila, southeastern Arizona, and southwestern New Mexico, to be possibly a hybrid between *Y. baccata* and *Y. madrensis* (essentially the same distribution just mentioned) with, possibly, some genetic material from *Y. elata* thrown in. Apparently *Y. madrensis* is the preferred name for *Y. schottii* (making it a hybrid with itself). Whatever. I don't know of any reliable reports of its hardiness to −10F (−23C), but it should be tried, no matter what name it has.

Yucca thompsoniana (Chihuahua, Coahuila, western Texas) is another tree yucca, with relatively short, stiff, foot-long (30cm) green leaves. This can form a multi-trunked tree to eight feet (2.4m) or so, with flowering stalks two feet (60cm) or more higher—very impressive in a cold-winter climate where it, naturally, evokes images of warmer climes. In my part of the world, plants of *Y. thompsoniana* taller than a Great Dane may be purchased from Arizona nurseries (the climate here not being conducive to tropical-style growth), and tree-type plants of *Y. thompsoniana* are now almost common in the trade, at least where I live. My ground-dwelling plant probably has another hundred years before it reaches for the skies. *Yucca thompsoniana* is perfectly hardy to at least −11F (−24C), and probably lower.

CHAPTER EIGHT

Shrubs

Now that more and more dryland shrubs are available from western nurseries, writing about these plants is much less an exercise in futility than it was just fifteen years ago. Some plants are still only available in smaller sizes, which can be frustrating to gardeners wanting an instant effect, but at least it's quicker than growing them from seed.

The characteristic adaptations of plants growing in dry areas, most notably smaller, leathery leaves (called sclerophylly), may take some getting used to if all you know is the usual selection of plants typically grown in eastern North American gardens. A number of the western shrubs are what you might call narrow broad-leafed evergreens: their leaves are wider than those of conifers but much more narrow than those of pierises, rhododendrons, or kalmias.

Geoffrey Charlesworth's statement that he was not drawn to long-lived woody objects keeps echoing in my mind when I advocate growing western dryland shrubs. Having to chop out a shrub that took years to find in the first place is agonizing. Most, if not all, of these shrubs can't be moved once they have been established, so it's probably a good idea to take this into account before digging the planting hole. (Not that I always, or ever, pay attention to this advice.)

Mahonia fremontii and sooty-winged katydid (*Capnobotes fuliginosus*)

Not all cold-hardy dryland shrubs make fantastically exciting garden plants. Some are downright bores, blank green things that take up space. The ones mentioned below, except where obvious disparaging comments are made, are equal to almost any of the shrubs traditionally planted.

Amelanchier (serviceberry). Two species of serviceberry are found throughout western North America: *Amelanchier alnifolia*, a ten-foot-tall (3m) shrub mostly, but not always, growing in wet areas, and *A. utahensis*, a slightly smaller shrub growing in dry areas throughout the Intermountain West, with grayish pubescent leaves about an inch (2.5cm) long. Both are highly susceptible to fireblight and are not really worth growing for that reason, unless you live out in the country far from the millions of crabapples typically planted in western cities.

Amorpha canescens

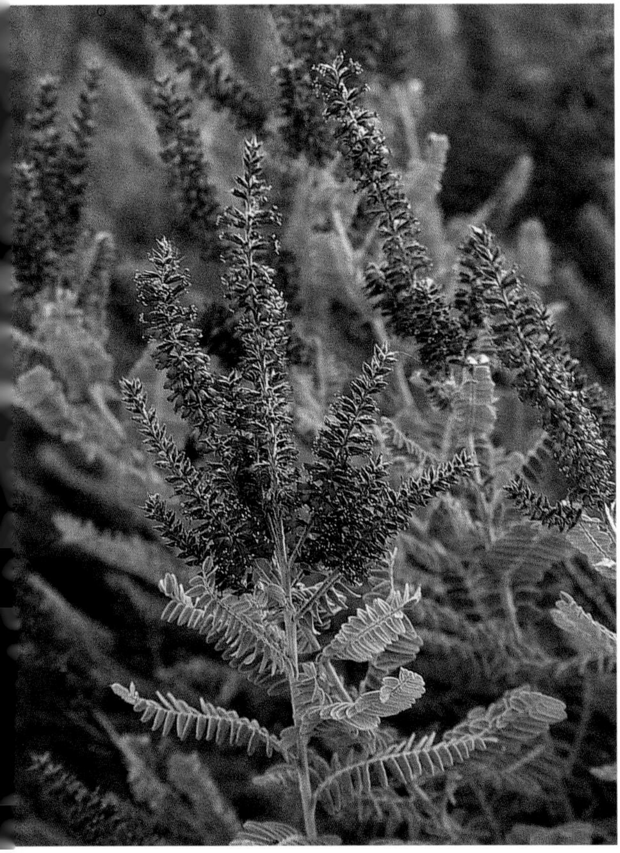

Amorpha (false indigo). Members of the pea family, mostly native to the southeastern United States. Three species are of value in the dry garden.

Amorpha canescens (lead plant) is native to a large area in the Midwest, also venturing out onto the high plains in Wyoming, Colorado, New Mexico, and Texas. This is an erect shrub about three feet (90cm) tall and wide, sometimes spreading by the roots (especially after a wet summer), with gray-green hairy pinnate leaves about six inches (15cm) long, the individual oblong leaflets about an inch (2.5cm) long. The plant leafs out late in spring from gray branches. In July, *A. canescens* throws five-inch-long (12.5cm) spires of bright purple flowers with orange stamens from the uppermost branches to create an absolutely spectacular display. A fabulous plant, good in heavy clay, with no effort required.

Amorpha fruticosa is a shrub six feet

(1.8m) tall, sometimes higher, with willowy single trunks; green pinnate leaves eight inches (20cm) long, the individual leaflets oblong or oval, about two inches (5cm) long; and spires of purple flowers about six inches (15cm) long, in June. Not as exciting as *A. canescens*, but nice. Native to practically everywhere in the United States, usually growing by streams (especially in the drier parts of the west), but quite amenable to cultivation in dry soil.

Amorpha nana is a smaller species (*nana* means "dwarf"), open branching, to two feet (60cm) by four feet (120cm), with green pinnate leaves about three inches (7.5cm) long, the leaflets narrowly oblong, half an inch (1.25cm) long. The flowers are red-pink bottlebrushes about two inches (5cm) long, borne in June. This is another easy plant for dry,

Amorpha nana

Amorpha nana in autumn

heavy clay soils. Native in scattered locales from Saskatchewan to New Mexico.

Arctostaphylos (manzanita). Brushing aside the circumpolar *Arctostaphylos uva-ursi* (bearberry, kinnikinnick), which seems to me to need more water in the garden than the plants discussed here, manzanitas are some of the most valuable—and frustrating—plants for the dry garden.

Even though a fairly large number of them grow in our garden, cultivation of manzanitas seems to be a complete mystery to me. They seem not to want an alkaline soil, to prefer light shade, to detest irrigation—but only at certain times of the year—and to be happiest when grown in the driest soil possible, with no organic matter anywhere in sight. I have killed plants by watering them after planting (the leaves get a fungus and the plants die within a few days), but have also killed them by forgetting to water them after planting. Some experts recommend only watering them once after planting, and setting a rock over the roots on the western side of the plant, but I tried this and the plants died. Discreet watering after planting, only around the root ball, seems to be reasonably safe.

Manzanitas are subject to a mysterious (naturally) dieback of the branches, the leaves suddenly drying up and falling off; but my observation is that a prolonged dry spell stops the dieback, and plants usually recover.

They do not recover from being transplanted more than once. The first planting in the garden should be the last; the roots are very sensitive to disturbance, and your chances of successfully moving a plant are pretty close to zero. Large plants are even more difficult to move, not to mention to plant successfully in the first place.

Still, there is every reason for you to want to try these plants; aside from their extreme drought tolerance, manzanitas are the best, if not the only, true broad-leafed evergreens that will endure the vagaries of cold, dry climates.

Arctostaphylos patula is a widespread, variable species, usually found growing in ponderosa pine forests, from western Colorado to California and Oregon. The basic plant is anywhere from one to two feet (30 to 60cm) tall, or taller, spreading several times that wide, with beautiful smooth reddish brown or brown bark, and leathery green oval leaves about one inch (2.5cm) long. Pale pink or white urn-shaped flowers (manzanitas are members of the heath family) appear in April. A number of selections of *A. patula* have been made, notably 'Big Red', a form with reddish flowers; these are at least as common as dragons' teeth.

Where *Arctostaphylos patula* meets *A. uva-ursi* in the wild, hybrids can result; these sometimes have the smaller leaves and lower habit of *A. uva-ursi* but the extreme drought tolerance of *A. patula*. The name *A. coloradoënsis* var. *nevadensis*, probably one of these hybrids, can be found in some of the older botanical treatments of western Colorado; some nurseries still offer plants under this name, although it has disappeared completely from the literature.

Arctostaphylos pringlei is a plant of lower elevations, from southwestern Utah to California, Baja California, and Arizona, but it seems

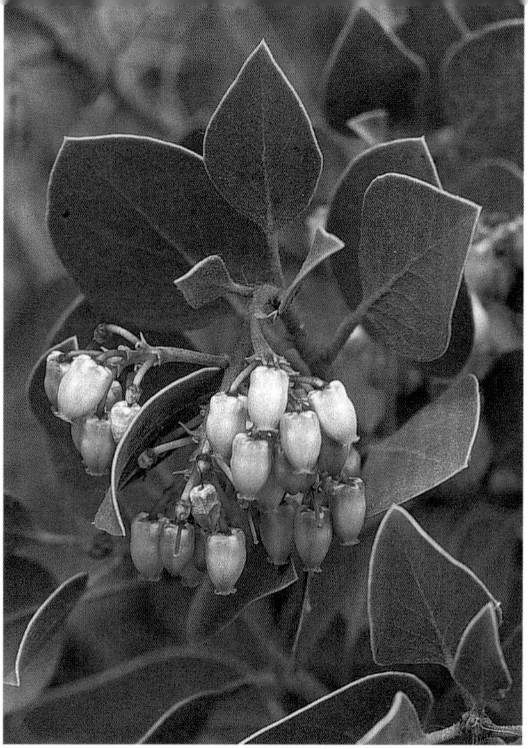

[right]
Arctostaphylos patula

[below]
Arctostaphylos patula at Denver Botanic Gardens

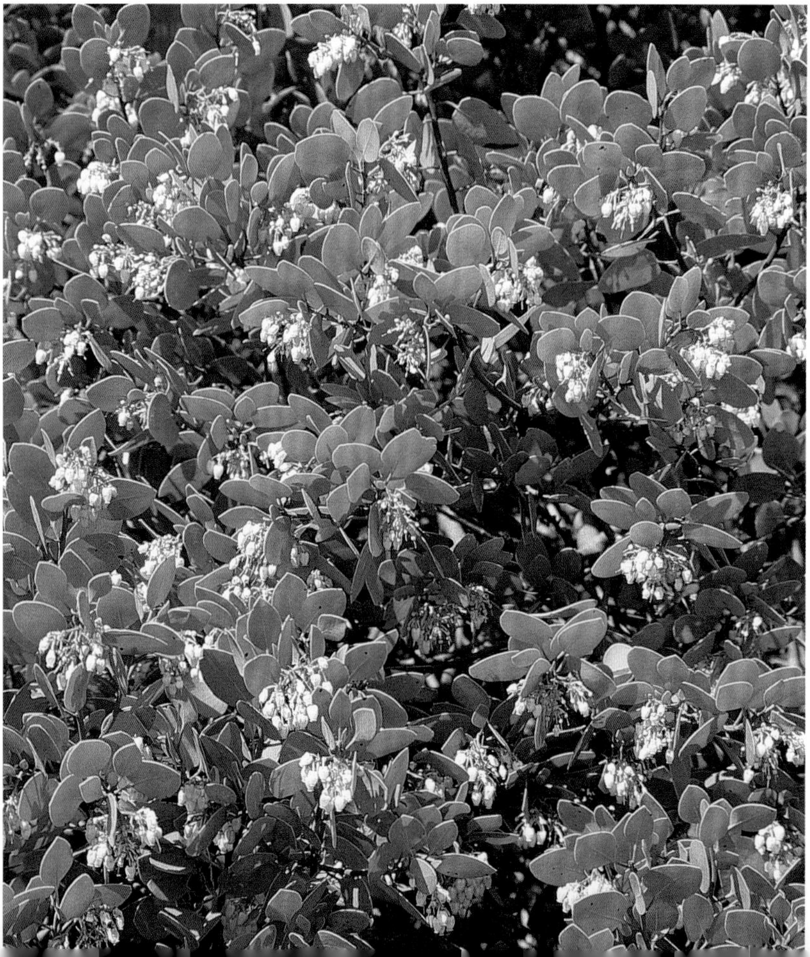

to have at least some cold tolerance, being undamaged at temperatures of −5F (−20.5C). This can be a large shrub, over six feet (1.8m) tall (I wouldn't set my hopes on it, though), with the same smooth reddish brown bark and pale pink or white flowers as *A. patula*, but with gray-hairy oblong leaves. This is definitely worth trying in a lightly shaded area of the garden, protected from winds in winter and overhead sprinklers in summer. *Arctostaphylos pungens* (New Mexico, Texas, Sonora, and Chihuahua) is rather similar but with green leaves.

There are some other manzanitas worth trying. About ninety-nine percent of the species of *Arctostaphylos* are found in California, and most of these are hopelessly tender. (A good reason to move there, I suppose.) Some forms of *Arctostaphylos glauca* and *A. parryana* are reputedly hardy and available from nurseries selling plants native to California.

Artemisia (sagebrush). A large genus of plants grown mostly for their silvery, aromatic foliage. The shrubby species of *Artemisia* are sometimes placed in the genus *Seriphidium*, though this has not caught on everywhere. The North American artemisias are, mostly, extremely common in the wild, which may account for their scarcity in regional nurseries; this is a pity, because the Eurasian artemisias found in the trade are often less drought-tolerant, and probably better associated with things like roses for a contrasting silvery effect in parts of the garden requiring more irrigation.

Artemisias are grown for their foliage, not for their flowers. The artemisias discussed here, with one tiny exception, offer the quintessential silvery effect of the true no-water garden, in which the color green is a rare feature.

Artemisia bigelovii is a wispy thing about a foot (30cm) tall by as wide, with half-inch (1.25cm) wedge-shaped silver-woolly deciduous leaves with three tiny lobes, and flowering stems twice as tall, with tiny yellowish flowers in clusters along the stems, in late summer. Nice, but not totally spectacular. *Artemisia bigelovii* is found throughout the Intermountain region (Colorado to California).

Artemisia cana is a big, spectacular shrub, six feet (1.8m) tall by ten feet (3m) wide, or wider, found throughout the northern Great Plains and Intermountain region, usually growing on heavy soils, and spreading a little from slowly wandering roots. *Artemisia cana* has two-inch-long (5 cm) linear-oblanceolate silvery gray deciduous leaves, sometimes three-lobed at the tips, and clusters of small yellow flowers on flowering stems a foot (30 cm) taller than the plant, in August. These should be removed in late winter or early spring. Little plants sprouting from the roots can be easily dug up and moved to another location, or repotted. Despite its preference for more moisture-retentive soils in the wild, *A. cana* will sail through the most severe droughts with nary a wilted leaf.

Artemisia cana with hybrid penstemons

Artemisia filifolia (sand sage) is common from Wyoming and Nebraska south into Texas and Chihuahua, and west to Utah and Arizona, growing in sandy soil, even dunes. Like most dryland plants that grow in more porous soils in the wild, *A. filifolia* is perfectly happy in unirrigated, heavy clay soils with no organic matter. In these situations it makes a plant about three feet (90cm) high and wide, though in some years, after a wet summer and the resulting exuberant growth, it may require cutting back. The leaves are silvery green, thread-like, three inches (7.5cm) long, persisting in tiny clusters through the winter. The tiny yellowish flowers are borne at the ends of the stems, in August.

Artemisia frigida is found, essentially, everywhere in western North America (and Siberia, too). This is a mat-forming plant, about three inches (7.5cm) tall, with green-silver leaves less than half an inch (1.25cm) long, clustered at the base and along the stem, and flowering stems a foot (30cm) tall, with insignificant yellow flowers in bunches along the stems, in July and August. I remember having a discussion with the proprietor of a long-defunct nursery about the desirability of *A. frigida* ("a weed you can dig up anywhere") versus *A. schmidtiana* 'Nana' (said to be the most commonly sold plant in North America). The latter, a Japanese plant, is admittedly beautiful (we grow it), but *A. frigida* is more drought-tolerant, reseeds into dry clay soil, and is an excellent host for species of *Castilleja*.

Artemisia pygmaea is a tiny thing about three inches (7.5cm) tall by four inches (10cm) wide, with microscopic green, almost fern-like leaves, and sticky yellowish flowers on spikes three inches (7.5cm) taller than the plant. *Artemisia pygmaea* is easy to grow from seed and forms an almost instant bonsai shrub for a trough; I lost my plants after five or so happy years in the garden. Native to northern Arizona, eastern Nevada, Utah, and western Colorado (barely).

Artemisia spinescens (*Picrothamnus desertorum*) is a round shrub, a foot (30cm) or so tall and wide, the old stems forming spine-like structures, with gray-hairy lobed leaves about half an inch (1.25cm) long, clustered around the woody stems. The flowering branches may be six inches (15cm) tall, or taller, with the usual yellowish flowers, but, unusually, blooming in April or May. The leaves drop in summer, something to consider when planting this little shrub. *Artemisia spinescens* is found from western Montana to eastern Oregon and California, and south into Arizona and New Mexico.

Artemisia tridentata (sagebrush) is found throughout the Intermountain region, from British Columbia to Baja California, and in the Great Plains from North Dakota to eastern Colorado, sometimes, especially in the Great Basin, growing in vast numbers—gray seas of sagebrush reaching to the horizon. This can be a big (ten feet, 3m) shrub with a thick, twisting trunk, sometimes several trunks, the bark peeling in a picturesque, gnarly way, and gray, wedged-shaped leaves an inch (2.5cm) long, depending on the variety, thickly clustered on the branches, with flowering stems a foot (30cm) or so tall in July and August, with the typical yellowish flowers. Naturally, there are some varieties which have at one time or another been species in their own right: var. *parishii*, a south-

Artemisia tridentata at Harlequin's Gardens

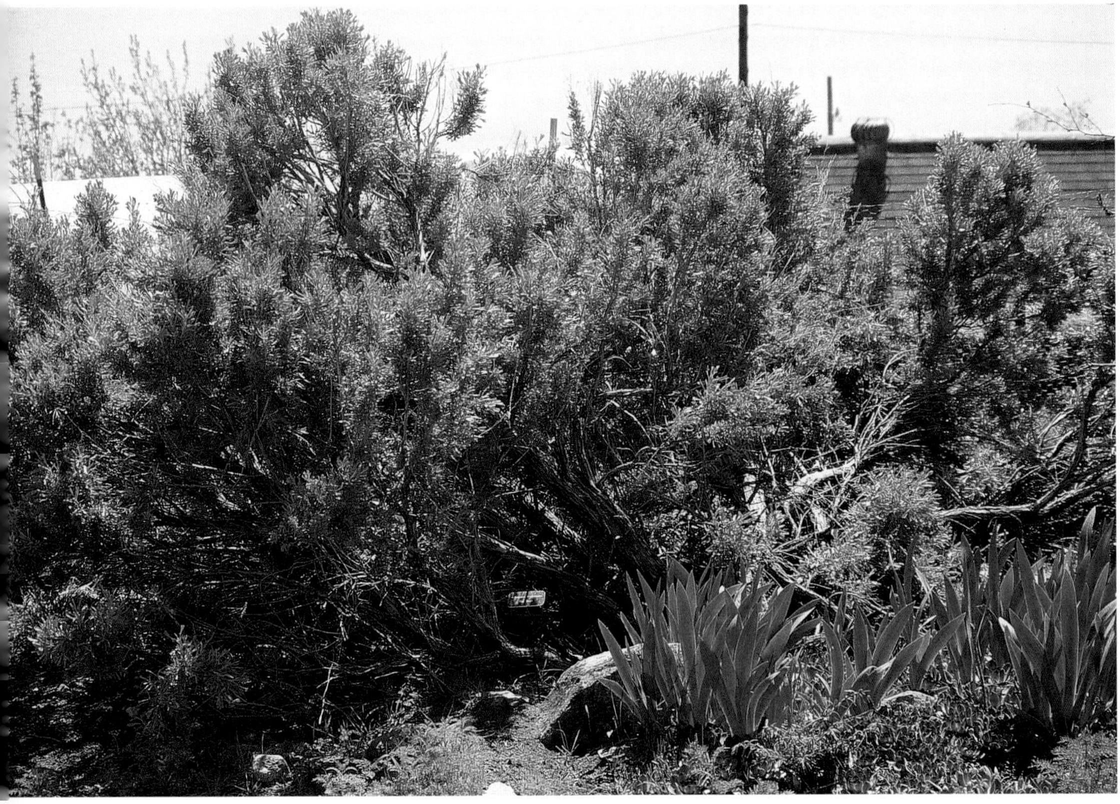

ern Californian with longer, more or less linear leaves and dubious hardiness; var. *vaseyana*, a smaller plant of higher elevations with leaves smelling of camphor (offered in the trade as *A. vaseyana*); and var. *wyomingensis*, with slightly smaller leaves.

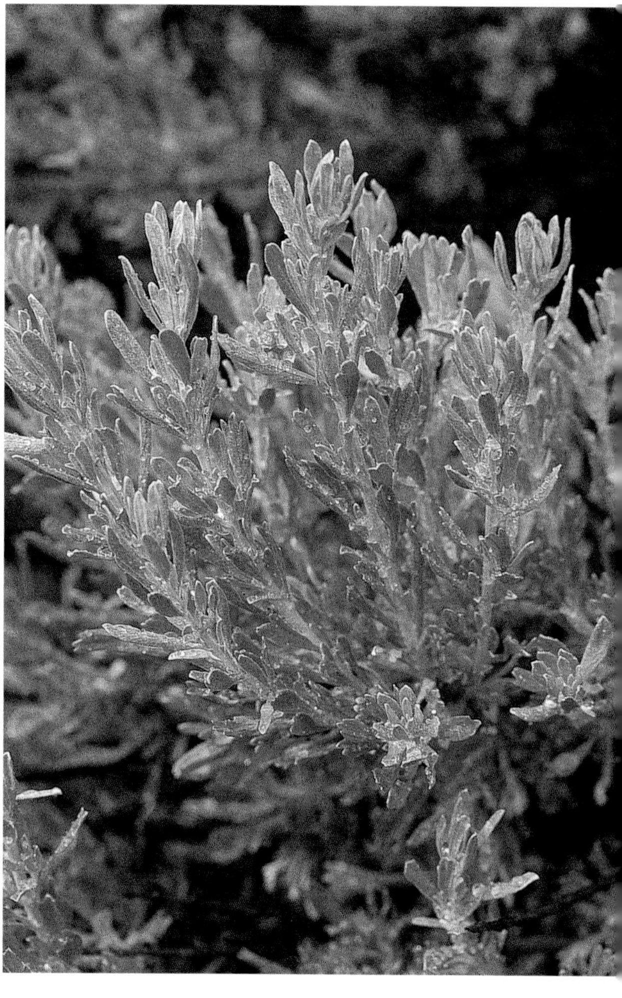

Artemisia arbuscula

If your garden or landscape can't accommodate a shrub the size of a small car, there are some other artemisias that, in garden effect, are miniature versions of *Artemisia tridentata*. *Artemisia arbuscula*, found more or less throughout the Intermountain area, about two feet (60cm) by three feet (90cm), and *A. nova* (Montana to Oregon and California), about the same size, but with darker leaves; both of these can be pruned to good effect.

Artemisia tripartita is a native of the northern part of the Intermountain region (southeastern British Columbia and eastern Washington to Wyoming); this is a two- to three-foot-tall (60 to 90cm) shrub with gray-green-silver, deeply divided leaves (whence the common name, three-tip sagebrush) and the usual flowers on stems about a foot (30cm) taller in July and August. Like *A. cana*, *A. tripartita* has a slowly running root; new plants can easily be propagated from the shoots that emerge.

In Wyoming, *Artemisia tripartita* becomes, here and there, a congested, extra silvery dwarf about four inches (10cm) tall, spreading about eight inches (20cm), a highly desirable plant for the rock garden or trough; this is *A. tripartita* var. *rupicola*, an occasional inhabitant of seedlists.

Atriplex (saltbush). Only a handful of North American *Atriplex* species are worth introducing into the garden; the rest are annual weeds, though *A. hortensis* 'Rubra' (red orache) is grown in many gardens. This is another genus grown for the foliage and not the flowers; the family resemblance between the species mentioned here is not terribly strong.

Some gardeners report middling success with *Atriplex hymenelytra* (desert holly), a tall shrub with white-silver holly-like leaves native to lower elevations along the Colorado River drainage to Baja California, but I have never grown it.

Atriplex canescens (four-wing saltbush), found throughout western North America, from southern Canada to northern Mexico, is an upright shrub three to four feet (90 to 120cm) tall and wide, with thick, scaly, linear or narrowly oblong gray-green leaves two inches (5cm) long, and similarly colored flowers, about half an inch (1.25cm) wide, with four conspicuous winged bracts, in July or August. The dried leaves remain on the shrub all winter, not the most attractive thing in the world, but in summer four-wing saltbush adds a certain something to areas of the garden with the worst soil imaginable.

Atriplex gardneri

Atriplex confertifolia (shadscale) is another widespread saltbush, found from North Dakota to northern Mexico to eastern Oregon, utterly different in appearance from four-wing saltbush. *Atriplex confertifolia* is a spiny, branching shrub, two feet (60cm) high and wide, with round, inch-long (2.5cm) grayish green leaves; the leaves are covered with scales, giving the plant a silvery look in bright sunlight. The flowers, borne in July, are of no consequence.

Atriplex corrugata, native to clay hills in Utah, western Colorado, and northwestern New Mexico, is a mat-forming shrub six inches (15cm) high by three to four feet (90 to 120cm) wide, with tiny oblong or linear silver leaves an inch (2.5 cm) or less in length, and tiny yellowish flowers in July. As the plant ages, it forms gnarled trunks snaking along the ground and may, in time, look disreputable to gardeners hoping for an ancient dwarf desert bonsai and getting instead a plant that looks like it's dying, branch by branch. *Atriplex corrugata* is nice for the first five years; mine eventually passed away after the wet summer of 2004.

Atriplex gardneri (*A. nuttallii*) is a widely variable species found from southern Saskatchewan to New Mexico, and Idaho to Utah and Nevada, with half a dozen varieties of little concern to anyone other than students of *Atriplex*. At least this is the way I see it. *Atriplex gardneri* may be an upright shrub to three feet (90 cm), or, as I know it, a low, spreading shrub about six inches (15 cm) high by two feet (60 cm) wide, with narrowly oblanceolate silver leaves and yellowish flowers in July.

Baccharis. A large genus of shrubs in the daisy family with little yellowish shaving brushes for flowers. The species native to western North America are of moderate interest (but to me, not even that); few, if any, are offered in the trade. The one species I might recommend is *Baccharis wrightii*, a native of the southern Great Plains south to Texas, Chihuahua, Coahuila, and west into Utah and northern Arizona; this is woody at the base, with green, ribbed, almost leafless stems and whitish flowers about an inch (2.5 cm) wide in June.

Berberis (barberry). It seems hopelessly retrograde not to include the hollygrapes (*Mahonia*) here, since this is what botanists call them, and I can already hear the cries of protest from my millions of readers trying to find information on plants that are always sold as mahonias. So *Mahonia* it is.

There is an actual barberry, *Berberis fendleri*, native to Colorado, Utah, and New Mexico, in no way as good as the Japanese barberries, and susceptible to wheat rust.

Brickellia. A group of not-very-exciting annuals, perennials, and shrubs in the daisy family. Still, *Brickellia californica*, a three-foot (90 cm) shrub with cottonwood-like leaves and small pale rayless yel-

Ceanothus velutinus is a widespread shrub (California to British Columbia to Saskatchewan), growing five to six feet (1.5 to 1.8m) tall, sometimes spreading as wide, with thick, three-inch-long (7.5cm), sticky resinous leaves and clusters of fragrant white flowers in June or July. But this is better described by Rowntree: "The large round-ovate evergreen leaves have a wonderful shine . . . looking as though they had been shellacked, and when crushed in the hand their spicy scent suggests a bitter cinnamon." *Ceanothus velutinus* is best in winter shade, and will accept more or less summer water, once it is established.

Cercocarpus (mountain mahogany). Naturally, the taxonomy of *Cercocarpus* is subject to some disagreement; and technically, the trees in this wonderful genus of mostly evergreen shrubs or small trees in the rose family are large shrubs, since they have multiple trunks. The common name refers to the extremely hard wood. Many of the species have small leaves reminiscent, to some, of a birch (they remind me of Siberian elms). Mountain mahoganies are grown for everything but their flowers, which are infinitesimal yellowish petal-less sprays in May or June, though quite noticeable when the whole plant is in flower, followed by winged seedheads reminiscent of a clematis. These plants are superior choices for very dry, exposed situations.

The Californian species, *Cercocarpus betuloides*, *C. minutiflorus*, and *C. traskiae*, have never been grown in the garden here. *Cercocarpus betuloides* (birch-leaf mountain mahogany) is found at moderate to low elevations through California west of the Sierra Nevada, and also in southern Oregon, Arizona, and Baja California. This is a shrub or small tree to twenty feet (6m) with elliptic evergreen leaves (apparently deciduous in Arizona), slightly toothed at the tips, hairy on the underside. *Cercocarpus minutiflorus*, from northern Baja California and San Diego County in California, is similar to *C. betuloides* but only about ten feet (3m) high, with smaller flowers and leaves smooth on the underside. *Cercocarpus traskiae* is again similar to *C. betuloides* but with thicker, woolly leaves; one of the rarest plants in the world, this is confined to Santa Catalina Island and is listed as endangered under the Endangered Species Act.

Cercocarpus breviflorus is a small tree to ten feet (3m) or more, native

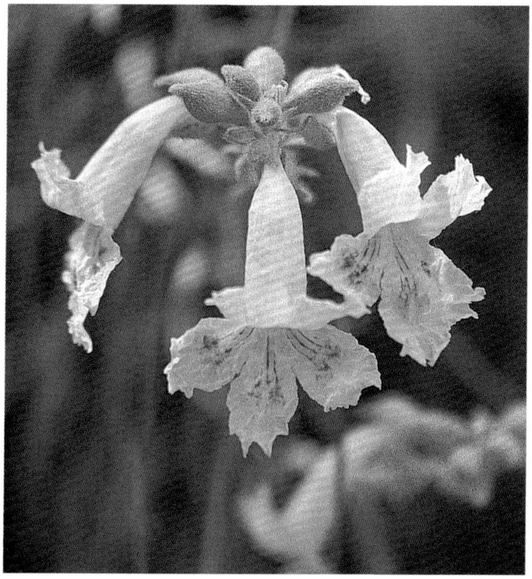

[left] *Chilopsis linearis*

[below] *Chilopsis linearis*, red-purple form

display may last for three weeks or a month; long bean pods, like those of catalpas, follow soon after.

Chilopsis linearis is the toughest shrub that can be grown in our garden. Some writers have tried to translate the desert willow's preference for growing along washes in its native habitat into a need for moisture in the garden, but surely the reason why it prefers such locations is that the seeds germinate almost instantly when exposed to water; in fact, *C. linearis* will grow either with or without summer water. I have never watered my plants. Not only that, my plants have endured −27F (−33C); been half killed in a hailstorm that defoliated every plant in the garden (and wrecked the roof and totaled the car parked in the driveway); and had all their new growth killed by a freeze the last week in May and then come back from that to bloom normally. Other color forms, particularly a dark reddish violet, are available in the trade.

Note to the worrywort (this includes me): desert willow leafs out quite late in spring, as late as the third week in May. Do not give your plant up for dead the first week in May.

Chrysothamnus (rabbitbrush). Rabbitbrushes are mostly large semi-willowy shrubs covered with golden heads of flowers just before the coming of autumn to western North America. The genus *Chrysothamnus* is described as "complex," meaning that every plant is slightly different and it's impossible to tell one from another. E. L. Greene in particular named dozens and dozens of species, but now botanists (some of whom want to place these in a different genus, *Ericameria*) prefer to reduce these to about fifteen species of which one, *Chrysothamnus nauseosus* (the specific epithet describes the feeling you get if you try to eat the leaves) is commonly available in the trade, and found almost everywhere throughout western North America. Fortunately for gardeners, this is a highly desirable plant, growing easily in very dry locations, blooming in September, October, and November. Average height and width is six feet (1.8m), with narrowly linear leaves about four inches (10cm) long. The basic plant, though, is elusive, since dozens of varieties are described. You could get a plant with green leaves and relatively green branches, or you could get one with bluish silver leaves and white-woolly branches. Maybe these are two separate species.

ers along with clusters of tiny green leaves. Ocotillos are more or less (closer to the "less" part) hardy in cold-winter climates like Denver's, especially if protected from cold winter winds. Plants are available in various sizes from Arizona nurseries. Seed is also available, but nothing has ever happened when I sowed seed. Even in their native habitat ocotillos look dead for most of the year anyway, so who is to tell if yours hasn't been alive for the last five years and ready to leaf out any moment?

Fouquieria splendens, alive, at Denver Botanic Gardens

Frankenia. *Frankenia jamesii* is a low shrub, to two feet (60 cm) high and wide, with tiny, awl-shaped linear green leaves about a quarter of an inch (6 mm) long, and tiny white flowers, a quarter-inch (6 mm) wide, in May or June. Native to gypsum shales in southern Colorado, New Mexico, and western Texas, with a disjunct population in southwestern Colorado, *F. jamesii* is not a thrilling plant, but a nice little shrub, similar in appearance to a heath. Call it semi-evergreen: it has a worrisome appearance in winter but recovers rapidly in spring. Even though it may not prefer shale, I have mine in a shale trough, just to be safe.

Fraxinus (ash, fresno). A couple of ashes are of interest here, vastly different plants from the ubiquitous green ash (*Fraxinus pennsylvanica*), which has such a bad reputation with people like me. In other words, these are not fast-growing trees that can be killed to the ground in a cold snap, but rather slow-growing shrubs, at least in cold-winter climates.

Fraxinus anomala (single-leaf ash) looks more like a cottonwood than an ash at first sight; this has ovate green leaves about two inches (5 cm) long, and slightly less than that wide, almost always simple, rarely trifoliate, on a shrub about ten feet (3 m) tall. The typical samaras give the whole thing away late in the season. Native from western Colorado and northwestern New Mexico to southeastern California. *Fraxinus anomala* will grow in frightfully dry places, though plants are difficult to get established. Propagation by seed, in my experience, is impossible, though obviously nature can do it.

Fraxinus cuspidata (fragrant ash) is found from western Texas, Coahuila, and Chihuahua to Arizona. This is a shrub about ten feet (3 m) tall, give or take, with the more typical pinnate ash leaves in groups of three or more, the individual leaflets about two inches (5 cm) long, lanceolate, and green. In May come half-inch-long (1.25 cm) fragrant white flowers. I managed to kill the one plant I tried to grow, and seed never germinated. Populations of *F. cuspidata* are reported on the North Rim of the Grand Canyon, not exactly the mildest-winter place in the world, so this is one definitely worth trying.

Garrya flavescens at Denver Botanic Gardens

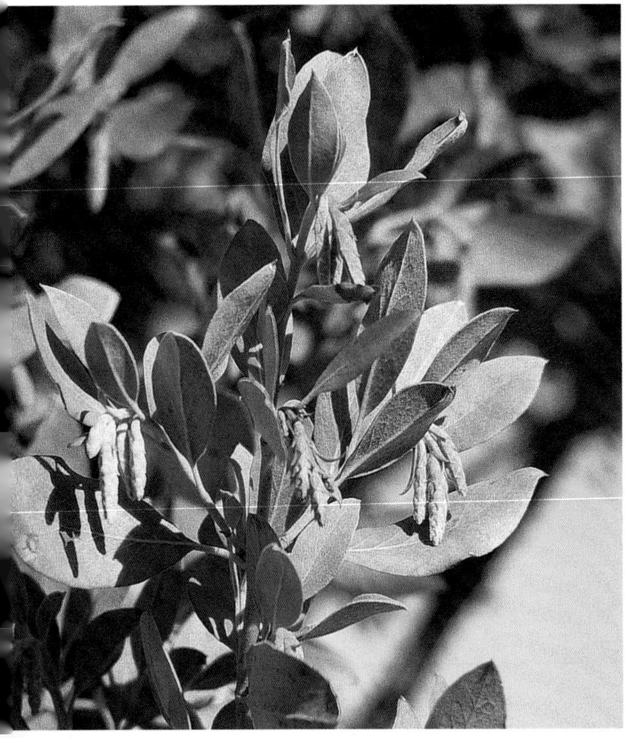

Garrya (silktassel). About a dozen species of evergreen shrubs or small trees sometimes included in the dogwood family (Cornaceae), but nowadays almost always placed in their own family, Garryaceae, with peculiar, yet somewhat charming, dangling flowers resembling, of course, tassels. The species you read about in British gardening books, *Garrya elliptica*, is a winter-blooming native of the west coast from California to west-central Oregon, and is completely and hopelessly tender. Their being evergreen works against them in cold-winter climates that have more than their share of wind and hot winter sun. *Garrya fremontii*, a smaller shrub to about eight feet (2.4 m), native from Washington to California and extreme western Nevada, has convinced me it is equally hopeless, though the repeated failures could be attributed to indifferent cultivation. *Garrya wrightii*, a summer-blooming native of Arizona, southern New Mexico, western Texas, and Chihuahua, might be possible, though it decided not to spend an entire winter in my garden in a living state. It has proven hardy in more protected gardens in Colorado.

The one species that appears to have some promise is *Garrya flavescens*, a ten-foot (3m) shrub with thick, stiff gray-green elliptic leaves two inches (5cm) long, or a little longer, with flowering tassels in May. It is not entirely hardy. A small plant in the garden here has recovered, more or less, from the stunningly brutal winter of 2005–06, and a plant at Denver Botanic Gardens was cut right to the ground after one night of −27F (−33C) back about 1990, but quickly rebounded.

Glossopetalon. Only one member of this tiny genus in the spindle tree family (Celastraceae), or in the crossosoma family (Crossosomataceae . . . I don't make these things up), is of interest here; this is *Glossopetalon spinescens*, also known in the literature, such as it is, as *Forsellesia spinescens* or *F. meionandra*. A wide-ranging (eastern Washington and Oregon to southern California, east to western Wyoming, Colorado, south and east to Oklahoma, western Texas, Chihuahua, and Coahuila), twiggy, spiny shrub to six feet (1.8m), though often lower, with tiny, quarter-inch-long (6mm) oblanceolate gray-green leaves, and equally tiny white flowers in April or May, *G. spinescens* is so far out on the fringes of western horticulture as not to exist at all; yet, if you should come across one or two, they are definitely worth considering for a very dry situation. Their dry western twigginess is their best asset.

Grayia (hopsage). Another plant rarely found in nurseries, *Grayia spinosa* (*Atriplex grayi*) is native from Montana west to eastern Washington, south to California and east into New Mexico. This is a four-foot (1.2m) shrub with brown-gray peeling bark, grayish wedge-shaped leaves about an inch (2.5cm) long, and inconspicuous, practically petalless flowers in April (not that it matters). Later, in summer, as the seedheads mature, they are encased in yellowish or greenish hop-like bracts strongly tinted with red. *Grayia spinosa* (incidentally, named for Asa Gray, not for the overall gray color of the shrub) is occasionally found in the nursery trade, though quite difficult to transplant into the garden, dying almost immediately after being planted. Plants can be grown from seed, but seedlings seem as resentful of the garden (maybe just mine) as nursery-grown plants do. Young plants look like little sticks with tiny gray balls stuck on them, until the leaves unfurl. An attractive plant for very dry locations.

Holodiscus (oceanspray, rock spiraea). A common shrub found from eastern Oregon to California, and Wyoming to Colorado to Chihuahua, *Holodiscus dumosus* is another aristocratic member of that group of indispensable dryland rosaceous shrubs. (The larger, more westerly distributed *H. discolor*, a plant of moister habitats, is not really suitable for our purposes.) *Holodiscus dumosus* grows six feet (1.8m) tall, and slightly wider, the branches arching outward, with inch-long (2.5cm), half-inch-wide (1.25cm), ovate, toothed green leaves, gray underneath, stiff in the summer, with spiraea-like sprays of creamy small flowers in June or July. More or less readily available from native plant and other nurseries. Give it at least one good drink during a rainless summer. *Holodiscus dumosus* is stunning, believe it or not, when underplanted with 'Black Prince' snapdragons.

Jamesia. A genus in the hydrangea family with two species, one of which I know. *Jamesia americana* is common from California to Wyoming, Colorado, and New Mexico (there are disjunct populations in Chihuahua and Nuevo León as well). This is a shrub growing to six feet (1.8m) and as wide with brown, peeling bark, slightly fuzzy ovate leaves an inch (2.5cm) long by half an inch (1.25cm) wide (good pink-tinted autumn color when grown in full sun), and clusters of waxy white five-petaled flowers about half an inch (1.25cm) during the summer. I have my plants in bone-dry soil on the north side of the house, where they grow slowly. The plants do tolerate sun, but I have never tried them anywhere but in shade.

Jamesia americana is a variable species, with several varieties described. One of them, var. *rosea*, with pink flowers, from southeastern California and southern Nevada, sounds nice; I have not tried, nor even

Holodiscus dumosus

seen it. There is another species, *J. tetrapetala*, with solitary, four-petaled flowers, from Utah and Nevada, which I have not seen.

Keckiella. A genus of penstemon relatives with galeate (hooded) flowers mostly native to California. A number of these are drought-deciduous, waiting out the long summer-dry period in California with no leaves at all. I had high hopes that at least a couple of species would make nice additions to the dry garden palette, but currently I am not so hopeful. Plants that are otherwise thoroughly drought-tolerant but are marginal in cold-winter climates rarely display any drought tolerance at all. *Keckiella antirrhinoides*, from southern California, Arizona, and Baja California (in its var. *microphylla*, found in older floras as *Penstemon microphyllus*) makes a little shrub about a foot (30 cm) tall in cold-winter climates, with bright yellow flowers, something like a cross between a penstemon and a snapdragon, in June. In 2004, the year it attained most of its floral glory, there was almost constant rain throughout June and August, and the plant never lost any leaves. It decided not to return the next year.

Some gardeners report success with *Keckiella corymbosa*, a plant of northern California, though its drought tolerance in cold climates must be suspect. I am presently trying to keep *K. ternata* (from southern California and Baja California) alive; only time, and the plant's ability to dodge cold winter winds sweeping down from the Arctic, will tell.

Larrea. *Larrea tridentata* (creosote bush, cenizo) is a common ingredient of the deserts of the southwestern United States and northern Mexico, in fact the dominant shrub of the Sonoran, Chihuahuan, and Mohavean Deserts. Probably the oldest living thing on the planet, the King Clone, near Victorville, California, is estimated to be 11,700 years old. (Don't count on this in the garden, though.) This is a variable (especially depending upon which desert it comes from) evergreen shrub, sticky, scented of creosote, to ten feet (3 m), densely branched (Mohavean), more openly branched (Sonoran), or sparsely branched (Chihuahuan). The leaves are green, leathery half-moons in pairs, less than half an inch (1.25 cm) long, with yellow flowers about an inch (2.5 cm) wide in April and May.

Creosote bush has some definite potential as a cold-tolerant shrub; its

Larrea tridentata at Denver Botanic Gardens

drought tolerance is of course unquestionable. I would not recommend landscaping with it in vast drifts, though, until its hardiness has been completely proved. Seed is easy to germinate but damps off with even greater ease. Plants are difficult to transplant, but with care—and not too much overly enthusiastic watering—the plants seem to establish in the first year. Creosote bush is safely hardy to at least −5F (−20.5C), possibly lower.

Lycium. A few species of *Lycium* (a genus in the nightshade family) are native to dry areas of the southwestern United States and northern Mexico; the plant growing in our garden (half of it actually growing in the driveway: we have only one car) seems to answer to *L. pallidum*, a six-foot (1.8m) shrub with arching, spiny branches and inch-long (2.5cm) or more, pale green-glaucous, semi-succulent leaves. In May or

June, the branches are festooned with hundreds of green, dark-veined trumpets almost two inches (5cm) long, followed by an equal number of bright orange, pea-sized tomatoes (I wouldn't eat them, but that's just me). *Lycium pallidum* is drought-deciduous and may drop all its leaves come August. Native to southern California, Utah, western Colorado, New Mexico, western Texas, Arizona, Sonora, Chihuahua, and Coahuila; often associated with Anasazi ruins.

Lycium pallidum and *Dynastes granti*

I was under the impression that *Lycium pallidum* traveled by means of wide-ranging roots, considering that little plants have appeared at some distance from the plant, but only in two directions; maybe these are seedlings. Other species possibly worth trying are *L. andersonii*, with smaller, pale flowers tipped with purple, and red, juicy fruit, more or less native to the same areas as *L. pallidum* but with a more westerly distribution (not in Colorado, Texas, Chihuahua, or Coahuila), and *L. torreyi*, same distribution except for Colorado, with pale whitish or greenish flowers and juicy red berries.

Mahonia. Enthusiastic or critical readers (not that there could possibly be any of the latter) will doubtless find my arbitrariness with plant names to be as annoying as my decisions were agonizing; no living botanist acknowledges the genus *Mahonia*, segregated from *Berberis* long ago. The distinctions between *Berberis* (spines on the stem) and *Mahonia* (spines on the leaves) do not hold up throughout the genus. All nurseries refer to the plants listed here as species of *Mahonia*; all, or almost all, botanical treatments place them in *Berberis*. The species included here are evergreen (or everblue), which does distinguish them from some members of *Berberis*.

Some species of *Mahonia* are susceptible to the wheat rust *Puccinia graminis* (though George W. Kelly disputed this) and are prohibited from eastern Washington, Montana, Wyoming, Nebraska, Kansas, and states east to Pennsylvania.

Mahonia aquifolium (Oregon-grape, Oregon hollygrape; the state flower of Oregon) is native from British Columbia to Idaho and California and is a commonly planted ornamental. It has a reputation for drought-tolerance in the nursery trade which it does not deserve. It is best grown, in Denver at least, in sites shaded in winter, and protected from wind; otherwise it emerges from winter looking as though it had been dragged along the interstate for several days. Trying to grow this beautiful plant like one of the desert mahonias is just plant abuse. Self-sown seedlings *do* exhibit some drought resistance, but grow so slowly as to be useless as garden plants.

Mahonia fremontii (algerita or palo amarillo, names used for any of the blue-leafed mahonias), on the other hand, will flourish in extreme drought (it also does well in England). This is native to Utah, western Colorado, New Mexico, and maybe elsewhere further south. *Mahonia fremontii* makes a shrub six feet (1.8m) tall and wide, sometimes larger than this, with beautiful, thick, stiff, blue-glaucous holly-like leaves about half an inch (1.25cm) long, the leaves in sun tinted violet in winter, those in shade remaining blue. The plant is covered with sprays of yellow flowers in May. The fruit is either black or red, but *inflated*, not juicy. *Mahonia fremontii* can be pruned to gorgeous effect, but this is a prickly business. Easy from seed, but curiously, the two twenty-year-old plants in our garden have never produced seedlings. Said to be susceptible to wheat rust.

Mahonia haematocarpa is similar to *M. fremontii*, but the terminal leaflet is two or three times as long as the rest of the leaflets, and the fruit is red, juicy, and "edible." According to a botanist friend, these species are much confused in the literature and in herbariums (apparently the specimens in New Mexico are actually *M. fremontii*), and *M. haematocarpa* is probably only native to areas south of the Mogollon Rim in Arizona, California, and maybe Baja California and Sonora. Some botanists consider this to be merely a form of *M. fremontii*. Also said to be susceptible to wheat rust. *Mahonia trifoliolata* (Arizona, southern New Mexico, western Texas, Chihuahua, Coahuila, and maybe elsewhere in northern Mexico) is similar but with only three leaflets. I have never had the opportunity to try this one, but it has made a huge shrub in a Boulder, Colorado, garden.

Mahonia haematocarpa

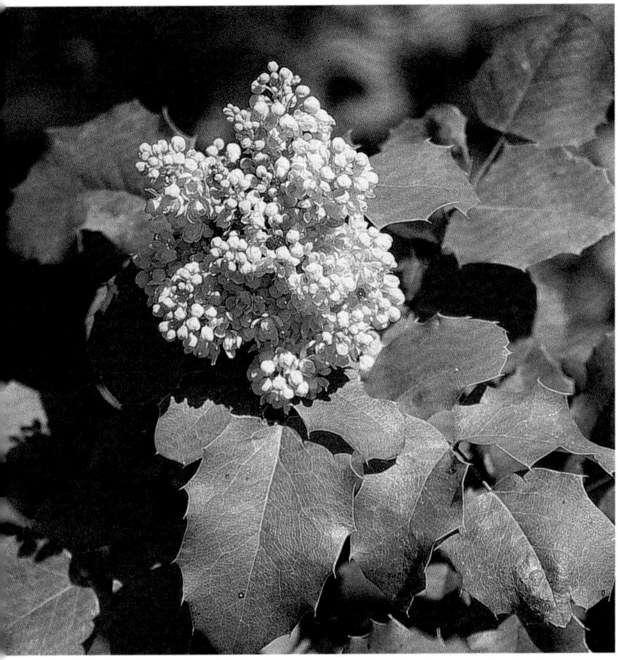

Mahonia repens

Mahonia repens (also known as Oregon-grape) is native practically everywhere in our area (British Columbia to California, Montana to western Texas); this is a low shrub to two feet (60cm), sometimes taller, spreading (hence the epithet) by the roots, but also freely seeding (the young seedlings are easily transplanted), the leaflets about an inch (2.5cm) long, glossy or matte, with clusters of fragrant yellow flowers in June (sometimes much earlier, even in winter), followed by purple grape-like fruits. This is a superior plant for dry shade, the leaves turning a beautiful maroon or purple in winter. If possible, you should buy plants in person so that you can get forms with the most attractive leaves.

Malacothamnus (bush mallow). Bush mallows are native to California and Baja California and have some potential for dry gardens in cold-winter climates. I have only tried the chaparral mallow, *Malacothamnus fasciculatus*. This native (from northern California to Baja California) makes a shrub about three feet (90cm) tall with two-inch-long (5cm), lobed, gray-green leaves, and inch-wide (2.5cm) pale pink flowers borne throughout the summer. It has the fairly alarming tendency of remaining completely green and alive late into November in Denver, which ordinarily would be a very bad sign; but eventually the stems do die down, and the plant quickly regrows from the base the next year. *Malacothamnus fasciculatus* is hardy to at least –10F (–23C). There are probably other species worth trying, but they are rarely available, except from native plant nurseries in California.

Menodora. A genus of shrubs in the olive family (Oleaceae) mostly native to southern Africa, but with a few species deciding to make their home in North America. *Menodora scabra* (southern Colorado to western Texas and Coahuila, west to southern California and Sonora) might be classed as a herbaceous perennial except for its woody base. *Menodora scabra* has a few branching stems to two feet (60 cm) with narrowly oblanceolate green leaves and yellow flax flowers about an inch (2.5 cm) wide, borne in summer. This is only occasionally available as seed, which sometimes germinates. At least one nursery offers plants from time to time, too. *Menodora spinescens* might also be tried as something different, but in the typical spiny-leafless-desert-shrub vein; this is a branching shrub about two feet (60 cm) tall, with a few tiny leaves and flowers smaller than those of *M. scabra*. *Menodora spinescens* is native to the area where California, Nevada, and Arizona meet.

Peraphyllum ramosissimum

Peraphyllum (squaw apple). A monotypic genus in the (surprise) rose family, *Peraphyllum ramosissimum* is native from northwestern New Mexico and western Colorado to eastern Oregon and California. This is a deciduous shrub to three feet (90 cm), though twice as tall with age or additional water, and as wide, with elliptic-oblanceolate leaves about two inches (5 cm) long, clusters of three-quarter-inch-wide (2 cm) white flowers in May, scented of anise (I say strongly scented; my wife—one of those benighted souls who hates licorice—says barely, if at all, scented). The flowers are followed by little apricot-colored marble-sized apples. One of my favorites. *Peraphyllum ramosissimum* is quite happy growing in bone-dry clay soil. When I acquired my plants years ago, the above-ground part was two inches (5 cm) tall, and the roots were a foot (30 cm) long.

Peraphyllum ramosissimum and cecropia moth

Philadelphus (mock-orange). The cultivated mock-oranges are of course a delight, but it's nice to think there are two native plants suitable for the dry garden. In fact, one of the species, *Philadelphus microphyllus*, is a parent of *P.* ×*lemoinei*, one of the most commonly planted ornamental mock-oranges. Unfortunately, neither of our natives is commonly available in the trade; they can be grown from seed sown outdoors in winter. Mock-oranges are commonly called syringas, which is the generic name for lilacs, but, whatever.

Philadelphus lewisii (British Columbia to eastern Oregon to western Montana and southern Alberta), the state flower of Idaho, is one of the truly outstanding plants native to North America. This is an upright deciduous shrub to ten feet (3m), with branches that become reddish brown, with cracking or peeling bark, and variably shaped (usually ovate) green leaves, two inches (5cm) long, sometimes longer. In May or June, sometimes later, the plant is smothered with two-inch-wide (5cm), four-petaled white flowers, intensely scented of pineapple (some say orange, I say pineapple); the fragrance carries throughout the garden.

I have it on good authority that, even though *Philadelphus lewisii* does grow along streams in much of its habitat, it can also be found in quite dry locations, where it is a shorter plant.

My plant is the Plant Select® introduction from the Cheyenne Botanic Gardens (the Hildreth-Howard Arboretum). Sited on the north side of the fence that encloses a "furnace garden" (too hot to stand in in any month except January), in terrible soil, this mock-orange seems to have considerable drought resistance, though the flowers, most years, are only about half an inch (1.25cm) wide.

Philadelphus microphyllus (littleleaf or desert mock-orange) is native to southern California and Baja California, to Utah, Colorado, and extreme southwestern Wyoming, through Sonora, Chihuahua, and Coahuila to western Texas. This is an arching, deciduous shrub to about six feet (1.8m), though shorter in cold-winter gardens when grown without irrigation. The red-brown bark peels with age, so that the straw-colored bark beneath looks as though it had been shellacked years ago and needed attention. The straw-colored bark eventually peels to some extent (why does nature do this?). The leaves are green, oblanceolate, an inch (2.5cm) long; the inch-wide (2.5cm), four-petaled white flowers, (definitely) scented of pineapple, are borne in May, June, or July.

Physocarpus (ninebark). There are half a dozen species in the rosaceous genus *Physocarpus*; these have bark peeling in layers (hence the common name), lobed leaves, and corymbs of white, sometimes pinkish flowers throughout the summer. The eastern North American species, *P. opulifolius*, is the commonly planted ornamental, with cultivars having yellow or purple leaves—and zero drought tolerance. All but two of the western North American species have similar requirements. *Physocarpus alternans* (California, Nevada, Idaho, Utah, and Colorado) is about four feet (1.2m) high and wide; *P. monogynus* (South Dakota to Texas) is half that size. Both are rare in the trade.

The ninebarks do not represent, to my eyes, the pinnacle of horticultural excitement. In fact, after years of searching for *Physocarpus monogynus*, I found one, planted it, and a few years after that, I dug it up.

Potentilla (shrubby cinquefoil). There are probably more plants of *Potentilla fruticosa* than people in the United States, yet you can still bring these into the garden and not have it feel like an industrial park

Philadelphus lewisii

Philadelphus microphyllus

or highway median. I would hope this species needs no description. *Potentilla fruticosa* is native to practically everywhere in North America except the southern United States (and is also found in Eurasia). The type, in North America anyway, has somewhat paler yellow flowers than the garishly bright-flowered plant so beloved of landscapers. It favors meadows and other sites with more moisture than a plant as drought-tolerant as this would lead you to believe; and yet, it is extremely tolerant of drought and dry clay soil, flowering all summer.

But which of the numerous cultivars are derived from native plants, and which from their Eurasian cousins? Purists, of which I am not one, will shy away from these, thinking their pedigree is suspect. Maybe so. If you like, you can acquire plants from a native plant nursery (Mt. Tahoma Nursery in Washington offers a prostrate form from the Pacific Northwest which is ideal for rock gardens), or just buy whatever you like and pretend it's a native plant.

Botanists have decided to segregate the shrubby species out of the genus *Potentilla* (incidentally, the name is pronounced like it looks, not as though it were Spanish and rhymed with "tortilla"); *P. fruticosa* is now *Dasiphora fruticosa* or even *Pentaphylloides fruticosa* (or *floribunda*, if you think the Eurasian species' different chromosome numbers warrant this distinction); but it's still *P. fruticosa* in nurseries everywhere.

Prosopis (mesquite, algaroba). At least one species, *Prosopis glandulosa* (honey mesquite), can be grown in cold-winter dry gardens. Honey mesquite is native from southern California to southern Kansas, and throughout northern Mexico. This is a small tree about twenty feet (6 m) high, or a shrub two feet (60 cm) high, with bipinnately compound green leaves, the leaflets narrow, oblong, about two inches (5 cm) long. Older branches have impressive white spines, an inch (2.5 cm) long. The pale yellow, scented flowers are borne in spikes, two inches (5 cm) or more long, all through the summer. The long seedpods only occasionally form fully in cold-winter gardens; do not expect an annual show.

Honey mesquite is hardy to at least −10F (−23C). It needs copious amounts of water the first year in order to get established; use of the new mycorrhizae may help.

Prunus (cherry, chokecherry, peach, plum). While the western chokecherry, *Prunus virginiana* var. *melanocarpa*, will tolerate quite dry conditions and a variety of fairly terrible soils, and perfumes the garden with its scent in late April, I am unable to recommend this horrific weed to anyone but the masochistic gardener. Chokecherries produce thousands of seedlings a minute; birds eat the fruit and drop purple stains all over the place; and the plants are susceptible to black knot (caused by a fungus, *Apiosporina morbosa*), which eventually kills branches. One day I will cut down the chokecherries in the garden here; some are trees twenty feet (6 m) tall.

Prunus andersonii

A few native members of the genus *Prunus* are actually worth introducing into the dry garden.

Prunus americana (wild plum) is native to practically everywhere east of the Continental Divide; this is a thicket-forming shrub to six feet (1.8 m), at least as I know it in Colorado, with scented white flowers in early May (their fragrance means Spring in Colorado to me), followed by extremely edible rose-colored plums (making a superior jelly), which the raccoons eat in the garden here, and good autumn color (yellow, orange, and pink tints). I believe *P. americana* is also susceptible to black knot, but not terribly so. Not a common plant in the nursery trade.

Prunus andersonii (desert peach), native to Nevada and California east of the Sierra Nevada, is a spectacular plant for the dry garden; this is a shrub to eight feet (2.4 m), with silver-gray bark on older branches, glaucous red-brown on newer branches, with spiny lateral branches,

Prunus besseyi

and clusters of half-inch-long (1.25cm) oblanceolate green-blue leaves. In late April the plant is covered with half-inch-wide (1.25cm) pink flowers, a few of which form hard, inedible fuzzy peaches about half an inch (1.25cm) long. The only drawback to *P. andersonii* is its tendency to fall apart, structure-wise, under heavy, wet spring snows.

Prunus besseyi (*P. pumila* var. *besseyi*; sand cherry), native to much of the northern Great Plains (Minnesota to Wyoming, Colorado, and Kansas), is a somewhat variable shrub to three feet (90cm), spreading to twice as wide, with oblanceolate green leaves, a profuse display of white cherry flowers about half an inch (1.25cm) across, in early May, and handsome black cherries, juicy and edible (hurry, or the birds will get them all), later in summer. Sand cherry (obviously, per its common name) will thrive in extremely dry situations. The low-growing form introduced by Plant Select® from the Pawnee Buttes in northern Colorado is widely available in nurseries; prostrate forms are sometimes available.

Purshia. A genus of seven species in the rose family, of which three concern us here, though only two are available in the nursery trade, and then only marginally so.

Purshia stansburiana (cliffrose) is sometimes sold, when it's sold at all, under the old name *Cowania mexicana*, or sometimes under the older, original name, *C. stansburiana*. Apparently some horticulturists seem to prefer to cling quixotically to names of plants that practically no one grows; the differences between cliffrose and bitterbrush (*P. tri-*

dentata) are not as great as some people suggest.

Names aside, the cliffrose is native to western Colorado and New Mexico, Chihuahua, Sonora, Arizona, Utah, southern Nevada, and southeastern California; it grows to ten feet (3m) and as wide (though a twenty-year-old plant in the garden here is half that height, having been flattened by five feet, 1.5m, of heavy, wet snow in the blizzard of 2003), with peeling gray bark (red-brown on younger branches) and tiny (less than a quarter of an inch, 6mm, in length) palmately lobed evergreen leaves. In June comes a massive display of inch-wide (2.5cm), pale yellow, intensely fragrant flowers, followed by plumose seedheads reminiscent of mountain-mahogany, clematis, and pulsatilla. *Purshia stansburiana* is one of the glories of the western North American flora, and one of the most beautiful, and drought-tolerant, shrubs for the dry garden. I just love it.

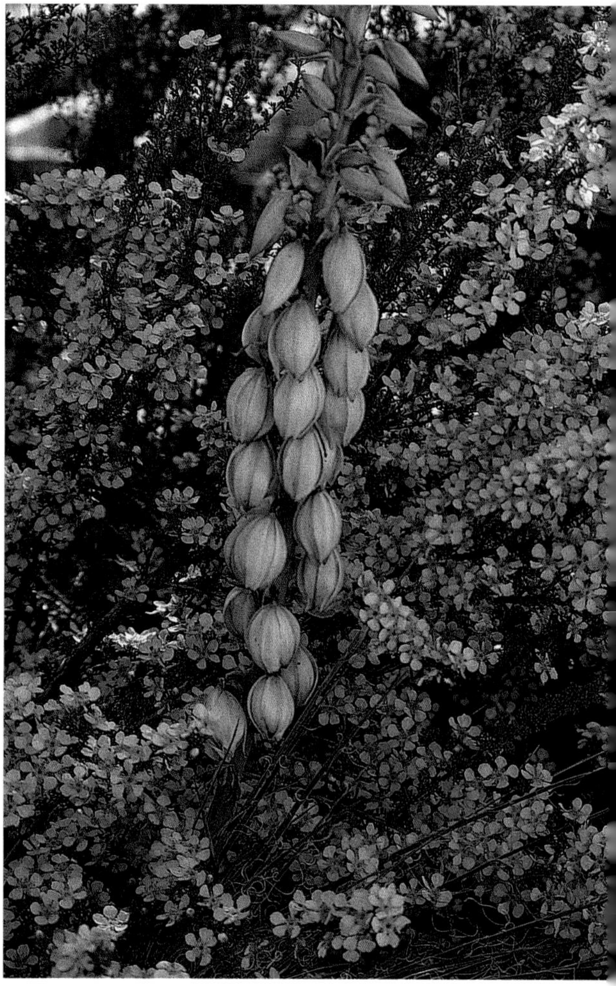

Purshia stansburiana and Yucca angustissima

Purshia tridentata (bitterbrush; Montana to New Mexico, British Columbia to California) is a three-foot (90cm) shrub, spreading, sometimes, to twice as wide, with deciduous green three-lobed leaves less than a quarter-inch (6mm) long and a massive display of half-inch-wide (1.25cm) pale yellow flowers, without scent, in late April. The seedheads lack the feathery styles of the cliffrose. Bitterbrush is even less common in the nursery trade than cliffrose, which is a pity since it has many admirable qualities.

Putative hybrids between *Purshia tridentata* and *P. stansburiana* are called *P. glandulosa*; this is about twice the size of *P. tridentata* but evergreen. It ought to be made available. There is also *P. subintegra*, a three-

Purshia tridentata

foot (90 cm) shrub with white-woolly, nearly entire leaves, but this is listed as endangered under the Endangered Species Act. (*Purshia subintegra* is thought by some to be a naturally occurring hybrid between *P. stansburiana* and the newly described Arizona species *P. pinkavae*, about which I know nothing.)

Other purshias worth testing for cold-hardiness—if you can find them—are the original Mexican species, *Purshia mexicana* and *P. plicata*, from Nuevo León, and *P. ericifolia*, from western Texas.

Quercus (oak, encino, roble). The southwestern United States and northern Mexico are especially rich in oaks, many of which are adapted to drought. These western oaks are variable, evergreen (encino) or deciduous (roble) trees or shrubs, with large or small leaves.

Unfortunately, this profusion of species is not reflected in the inven-

Quercus gambelii

tory of most nurseries, no doubt because horticulture has always fixed its eyes eastward in the search for desirable garden plants. So, if you happen on one of these in a local nursery, buy it, plant it in ordinary clay soil, water it the first year, and, in the dry garden, leave it alone after that. (These oaks will also accept summer watering.) Or, if you know one of those planthunter-gatherers who has a passion for oaks, you might be able to acquire some acorns or—better yet—small plants.

Quercus gambelii (Wyoming to western Texas, Utah, and Nevada) is a gray-barked shrub to ten feet (3 m) without supplemental irrigation, or a tree three times that height with a regular supply of moisture. The leaves are green, deciduous, deeply lobed, about four inches (10 cm) long, though the shape is so wildly variable that the oak sometimes can't be identified by leaf shape alone. Autumn color is yellow. Squirrels usually get all the acorns, but some inevitably drop, and eventually you will have tiny oak seedlings under the larger plant. These can be moved, but only in the first few years.

Natural hybrids between *Quercus gambelii* and *Q. macrocarpa* (bur oak) are known from northeastern New Mexico and other areas where the two species meet. I purchased a small plant at a nursery some years ago in autumn, with enormous, dazzling dark red leaves. I thought it would be a shrub with huge leaves; I was later told that it would be a tree, the size of a bur oak (larger than the house) in not nearly as many years as I thought, though it would be quite drought-tolerant. After shedding a tear or two, I gave the plant away.

Quercus turbinella (western Colorado and New Mexico through Utah and southern Nevada to Arizona, southern California, and Baja California) is evergreen (hence the sometime common name, shrub live oak) in mild winter climates, and at least partly deciduous in my garden. This highly desirable oak is a shrub (slow to ten feet, 3m, without irriga-

Quercus turbinella

tion) with inch-long (2.5 cm) blue-gray-green holly-like leaves and little acorns, but middling, if any, autumn color. One plant in the garden here was planted when it was four inches (10 cm) tall; it has grown no taller in over ten years, but this must be an exceptional dwarf.

Quercus ×undulata (wavy-leaf oak) is the name given to the offspring of natural crosses between several species of oaks. Like *Q. turbinella*, which contributes some genetic material, this is a slow-growing shrub (fifteen feet, 4.5 m, in twenty years in our garden) with wavy, sometimes deeply serrated (or lobed) blue-gray-green leaves about three inches (7.5 cm) long; foliage is shrimp-pink when new in spring and a good pinkish red in autumn. Some winters the brown leaves remain until spring. This is another highly desirable oak, unfazed by any of the endless series of weather horrors experienced in Denver-area gardens.

Quercus ×undulata and *Cylindropuntia imbricata* in autumn

I am also growing *Quercus mohriana*, native from the Oklahoma panhandle south into Coahuila, which is vaguely similar to wavy-leaf oak but with green leaves, white underneath, with a scattering of teeth along the margins. This oak, which I received as a gift, has only been in the garden a few years, but it did survive the brutal winter of 2004–05. I have killed *Q. vacciniifolia* (huckleberry oak) twice; this oak, an understory shrub from the Sierra Nevada, is reputedly hardy but has never made it through more than one winter here.

A number of other oaks are worth acquiring: gray oak (*Quercus grisea*), Emory oak (*Q. emoryi*), silver-leaf oak (*Q. hypoleucoides*), and so on. Why these shrubs are not in commerce is anyone's guess, since people seem to get all doe-eyed over oaks in general.

I might conveniently mention here a tree from western Texas, *Quercus tex-*

Quercus ×*undulata* and
plains lubber grasshopper
(*Brachystola magna*)

ana, said to be like *Q. shumardii* but tolerant of alkaline soils. It is a beautiful tree, with (once again) pink new growth, shapely branches, and good autumn color. I don't grow it, since I've never seen one for sale. The aforementioned bur oak (*Q. macrocarpa*) will also tolerate dry conditions, especially when older, but it becomes a gigantic tree, blocking out the sun even in winter.

Rhamnus (buckthorn). A number of buckthorns are native to our area; these are apparently plants of interest to native plant gardeners, but not to me. I once grew *Rhamnus smithii*, a six-foot (1.8m) deciduous shrub with glossy green leaves, tiny white flowers, and black fruit. It died, and the place where it grew is now bare dirt, which has more character.

Rhus (sumac). Sumacs are members of the cashew family and provide, in *Rhus typhina* (staghorn sumac), a superior ornamental with fantastic autumn color. The native *R. glabra* is similar but without the fuzzy staghorns; like its cousin it prefers a more traditional cultivation with fairly regular irrigation. I have never tried the more southerly distributed sugarbush (*R. ovata*) and always assumed that the evergreen *R. choriophylla* was hopeless, but what do I know. Seed of these last two is usually available; sumacs germinate with some success sown outdoors in winter.

Rhus microphylla (little-leaf sumac; eastern and southern New Mexico, western Texas, Coahuila, Chihuahua, Sonora, and southern Arizona) is a six-foot (1.8m) deciduous shrub, growing as wider or wider, with slightly spiny branches and light green silky-hairy compound leaves, the leaflets maybe half an inch (1.25cm) long. Tiny yellowish flowers appear before the leaves in April; the fruits are pea-sized, in clusters, reddish orange. I find this a very attractive shrub, with a nice, open look to it, but it should probably only be considered semi-hardy over the long run. As far as I know, little-leaf sumac is not available anywhere, except in the wild. The seed is slow to germinate.

Rhus trilobata (*R. aromatica* var. *trilobata*) is found throughout western North America, the distribution depending on what name is given to this highly variable plant. My concern is with three-leaf sumac, plain *R. trilobata* (though, perversely enough, there is a single-leaf three-leaf sumac, *R. trilobata* var. *simplicifolia*); this is a highly attractive deciduous shrub about six feet (1.8m) tall by ten feet (3m) wide, with green lobed trifoliate leaves about an inch and a half (3.75cm) long. The tiny yellow flowers appear before the leaves, usually, and are of no consequence. Red, hairy, pea-sized fruits follow. Autumn color is a good yellow or, in some plants, a beautiful deep red. The plant has an odd smell about it, which you will discover when pruning it, or if you brush up against it—a sort of clinging scent reminiscent, to my nose, of some unsweetened breakfast cereals, but slightly more rank. The common name skunkbush is fairly appropriate. *Rhus trilobata* is available in the nursery trade and will grow, blissfully, with no supplemental irrigation at all.

Ribes aureum

Ribes. In this genus, species with thorns are gooseberries; those without thorns are currants. A large number of currants are native to western North America; I don't by any means know them all, and I am interested in only one. I am aware of the existence of *Ribes cereum* (wax currant), native from British Columbia to California to South Dakota and Oklahoma, but this holds no real fascination for me.

Ribes aureum (golden, clove, or buffalo currant) is the currant of my dreams, and an utterly wonderful thing it is. Native from western Texas to Saskatchewan to Washington and California, this is one of the glories of the North America flora, and if you don't have one, well, get one. It is a plant that will flourish in extremely dry situations, or accept any amount of water you may give it, growing to about five feet (1.5m) and as wide (larger with more moisture), smothered with half-inch-long (1.25cm) golden yellow flowers, intensely scented of cloves, in March or April, turning orange later; these are followed by edible (the birds will prove it) reddish black fruit in late July or August. Autumn color is a fine red, the leaves turning earlier than most, in September. The currants, if you can harvest them, make delicious raisins. One shrub in flower will perfume an entire small garden.

Some botanists maintain that the Great Plains phase of *Ribes aureum*, a slightly smaller plant with smaller flowers and downier foliage, is a separate species, *R. odoratum*. Other botanists prefer to call this phase *R. aureum* var. *villosum*. This latter idea makes more sense to me.

Curiously, some plants seem to have no fragrance at all. Those with scentless flowers all seem to have petals with a red tint as they age. The Jepson Manual lists a variety of *R. aureum*, var. *gracillimum*, that answers this description, including the lack of scent. I think it is more than probable that a number of these scentless Californians were introduced into western states by the nursery trade and have naturalized outside of California. The moral of this, I guess, is that you want to buy your plants in flower; just follow your nose.

Robinia. The New Mexican locust, *Robinia neomexicana*, is native from southern Colorado to western Texas, west to California. This is a deciduous shrub, or small tree, about fifteen feet (4.5m) tall, with compound pea leaves about eight inches (20cm) long. The stems are armed with half-inch-long (1.25cm), slightly curved, very nasty thorns (I once got one stuck in my knuckle, and the whole neighborhood knew it). In May or June the plant is covered with large clusters of pink pea flowers, followed by pods later in the summer. This is a pretty attractive plant, but the thorns might be considered a drawback; its freely suckering habit could also be considered a drawback, but this can be somewhat curtailed by growing the plant without supplemental irrigation. *Robinia neomexicana* can be grown from seed; nick seeds opposite the hilum and sow indoors or out.

Rosa (rose). This is where I get myself into trouble, if I haven't already, with readers expecting a thorough review of every species of everything everywhere. The North American rose species are simply not all that exciting. I once grew what was purported to be a white form of *Rosa*

Rosa stellata

arkansana; it turned out pink, and took up space. I don't know Barr's double form of this, 'J. W. Fargo', which may be out of commerce. The other species, *R. woodsii* (*R. fendleri*), *R. gymnocarpa*, and so on, may be fascinating to native plant enthusiasts, but to a rose lover, like me, they aren't worth the garden space.

Rosa stellata, on the other hand, is something else entirely. Native to New Mexico and western Texas, with disjunct populations on both rims of the Grand Canyon, this is a rose, deciduous, of course, growing to three feet (90 cm) or slightly more, with stiff stems bearing serious prickles, leaves with three, sometimes five, leaflets, and three-inch-wide (7.5 cm) pink-magenta scentless flowers in June, followed by bristly dark red hips. The hips have an unpleasant odor when crushed to extract the seed (I grew my plants from seed). Plants regularly bearing five leaflets are sometimes called var. *mirifica* (the Sacramento rose, named after the mountains in New Mexico, celebrated by Graham Stuart Thomas, from whose books I learned about this plant). *Rosa stellata* is slow-growing in very dry soil, with some winter dieback in cold winters, from which it quickly recovers.

Rubus (blackberry). *Rubus deliciosus* (boulder raspberry) is a glorious shrub adaptable to both dry and watered gardens. Like other raspberries, it produces sterile primocanes the first year, and floricanes the second year. It has fuzzy, three-lobed, maple-looking deciduous leaves about an inch (2.5 cm) long and wide, scattered on arching branches. In May comes a massive display of two-inch-wide (5 cm) white single flowers, followed by "edible" reddish purple raspberries, which, if the birds don't get them, will provide plenty of new plants. Autumn color is, briefly, yellow. Somewhat susceptible to rose stem girdler. *Rubus deliciosus* is native to southern Wyoming, Colorado, and New Mexico.

A cross between *Rubus deliciosus* and the Mexican *R. trilobus*, from high elevations in Veracruz and probably elsewhere, was made by Collingwood Ingram in his garden in Benenden in Sussex in the last century. This *R.* ×*tridel* 'Benenden' (or some similar permutation) is a slightly larger shrub with flowers half again as large as the pollen parent, *R. deliciosus*, which it otherwise strongly resembles. I am currently "testing" (trying to keep alive) a small plant; it may have the same drought resistance as *R. deliciosus* and is occasionally available in the nursery trade.

Rubus deliciosus

Salvia (sage). The genus *Salvia* offers gardeners living in subtropical climates an awesome array of unbelievably gorgeous plants. Gardeners in cold-winter climates—after spending perhaps a few minutes pondering why they live in such unforgiving, desolate, merciless, soul-destroying places—have, aside from a wide range of Turkish salvias that will tolerate stunningly dry conditions, a few choices with which to console themselves.

Salvia dorrii (purple sage, as in Zane Grey's riders) is the most drought-resistant hardy sage. Native to much of the Intermountain region (eastern Washington to California and northern Arizona, Idaho to western Utah), this is a two-foot-tall (60 cm) deciduous shrub, spreading twice as wide, with oblanceolate silver leaves about an inch (2.5 cm) long, and blue flowers lacking the upper hood (galea) common in *Salvia*,

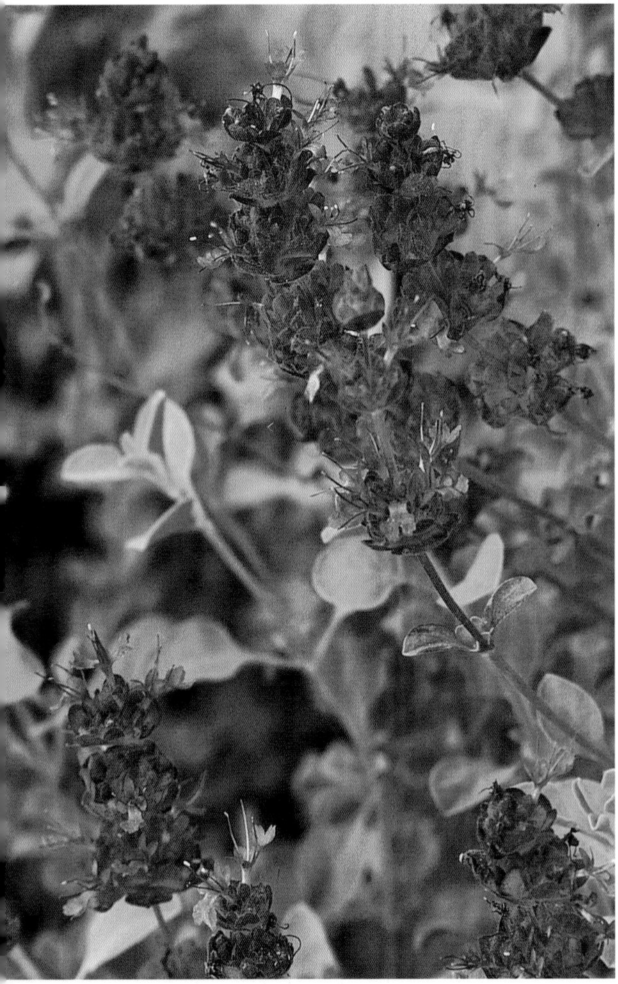

Salvia dorrii

in May or June. This very pretty plant is bizarrely absent from the nursery trade, though seed is occasionally available and can be germinated by sowing it outdoors in winter.

I suppose I have to mention *Salvia greggii* just to prove that I'm paying attention, but this native of central and western Texas (the Big Bend region) and adjacent Coahuila is problematic to me. Ordinary *S. greggii* will overwinter in the garden here if there is snow cover during extremely cold spells, but it always dies some time during the next year. Named selections, including those introduced by Plant Select®, have successfully overwintered when planted out as small plants, and occasionally flowered, but will not return for a second spring unless there is snow cover. Larger plants, from gallon (3-liter) containers, seem to have more promise: all the larger plants made it through the bizarre winter of 2006–07, with six feet (1.8m) of snow lying on the ground for two months, but all the smaller plants died.

Salvia lemmonii, native to southern Arizona, and at least adjacent Sonora, is a remarkable, and gorgeous, addition to the native plant garden, opening its pink-rose-purple sage flowers as early as July in some years, and continuing until frost with an ever-increasing display. *Salvia lemmonii* is probably more of a herbaceous plant than a shrub, though it has a woody base. It makes a plant about three feet (90cm) tall, sprawling, with green, rounded leaves about half an inch (1.25cm) long. The flowers are also about half an inch (1.25cm) long, but borne in such profusion that it hardly makes a difference. Southwestern Native Seed sells seed of a darker-flowered form that is worth acquiring (the plant is easy to grow from seed). It does appreciate a little extra water during very dry summers. Some botanists would have us call it *S. microphylla* var. *wislizeni*, suggesting that it is not much different from that Mexican species (which incidentally is not hardy), but the name change has not caught on.

Salvia pachyphylla is somewhat similar to *S. dorrii* in general appearance, though it has obovate silver-gray leaves and never seems to want to get up off the ground. If it did, it would be about two feet (60cm) tall; the clusters of papery bracts in the inflorescence are the principal distinction between it and *S. dorrii*. There is more violet in the flowers of *S. pachyphylla*, too. It is also less drought-tolerant and less hardy than *S. dorrii*; a plant grown from seed in the garden here is still only six inches (15cm) tall after eight years. Another plant in a raised bed here that gets a little supplemental irrigation is much larger. *Salvia pachyphylla* is native to northern Arizona, southern Nevada, southern California, and Baja California.

Salvia pachyphylla at Kendrick Lake

Sarcobatus. *Sarcobatus vermiculatus* (greasewood) is found throughout western North America, from southern Canada to northern Mexico, but probably not found in very many gardens. This is a deciduous shrub to ten feet (3m) with yellow-green linear leaves less than an inch (2.5cm) long on stiff, spiny branches, and tiny upright pinecones for flowers, in May or June. I've never grown greasewood, partly because the plant is never available in nurseries (no one seems to like it) and partly because growing greasewood might be considered too extreme an expression even in a native plant garden.

Shepherdia. A genus of three species confined to North America, related to silverberry (*Elaeagnus* spp.) but dioecious and with opposite leaves. *Shepherdia canadensis* is a slow-growing shrub, with beautiful silvery brown scales on the undersides of the leaves, that prefers cool conditions and plenty of moisture; a plant in our shade garden is about five feet (1.5 m) tall after fifteen years.

Shepherdia argentea (buffalo berry) is a deciduous shrub or small tree to twenty feet (6 m), with spiny branches and oblanceolate, silvery green leaves one to two inches (2.5 to 5 cm) long, and tiny yellow flowers in April, May, or June. Juicy, edible red (rarely yellow) fruits follow in July or August, but only if you have both male and female plants, naturally. Barr dismissed buffalo berry because of its suckering habit, but its tendency to travel is curtailed if grown in dry soil. *Shepherdia argentea* is a common plant of the northern Great Plains, native to southern Alberta, Saskatchewan, and Manitoba to South Dakota, also in scattered locations from Nebraska south to central New Mexico and west to California and eastern Oregon.

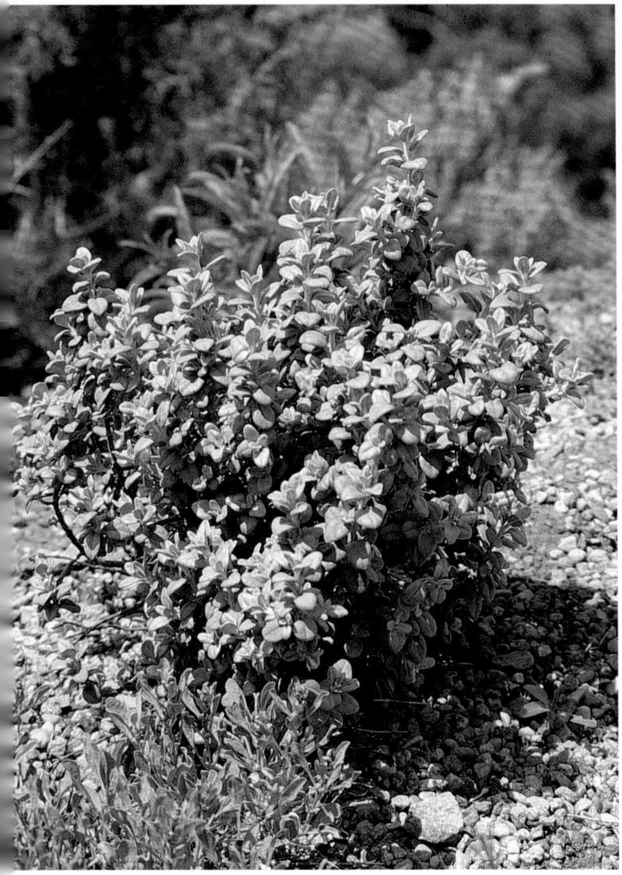
Shepherdia rotundifolia, Kelaidis garden

Shepherdia rotundifolia, native to southern Utah and northern Arizona, is the best of the three. This is an evergreen shrub to six feet (1.8 m), growing twice as wide, with fuzzy white branches, round silver leaves an inch (2.5 cm) long, more or less, and tiny yellow flowers in March, April, or May, followed by dry, insignificant fruit. This is a stunning foliage plant, easily grown from seed soaked overnight in warm water (with a drop of soap added) and then sown under lights. Our largish plant was killed when a rabbit burrowed underneath it; it has not been replaced owing to the almost complete unavailability of the plant in nurseries. Small plants are sometimes offered for sale, but growing them requires patience.

Symphoricarpos (snowberry). These honeysuckle relatives are fairly frequently found in nurseries; the eastern *Symphoricarpos orbiculatus* (coralberry) and some hybrids are especially common in the trade.

Symphoricarpos albus is native to a wide region east of the Continental Divide, its exact distribution being uncertain (to me, anyway) because of the disagreement between botanists as to which plant is which. This is a shrub three feet (90 cm) tall and wide, with bluish green oval leaves about an inch (2.5 cm) long, with tiny white bell-shaped flowers in May or June, followed by clusters of large, very attractive marble-sized white berries. The berries last all winter and are nice for indoor flower arrangements.

Symphoricarpos longiflorus, a western dryland species (California to eastern Oregon to western Colorado to western Texas), is a five-foot (1.5 m) deciduous shrub with half-inch (1.25 cm) intensely fragrant pink bells, bizarrely unavailable in the nursery trade.

Tetradymia (horsebrush). A group of moderately interesting low shrubs related to, and sometimes hybridizing with, rabbitbrush (*Chrysothamnus* spp.). Only the common horsebrush, *Tetradymia canescens*, is occasionally available from native plant nurseries. This is a shrub growing to two feet (60 cm) or a little more, with white-woolly linear inch-long (2.5 cm) leaves, and tiny whitish shaving brushes for flowers in June, July, or August.

CHAPTER NINE

Trees

Gardening under a canopy of deciduous shade trees in a dry climate is a joyless pursuit. I would rather plant a garden on asphalt. Nothing spoils a garden faster than trees, and if you must plant shade trees, grow grass or ivy beneath them, and plant your garden in the sun, if you still have any left after a few years.

I do think that a few well-placed conifers enhance the dry garden to a degree that no deciduous tree can. Mixing them in with scrub oaks, possibly with buffalograss or blue grama as a ground cover, creates an effective imitation of a chaparral of considerable beauty. You can plant perennials and bulbs in the grass, too.

The conifers mentioned here, my personal choices, are extremely drought-tolerant and are fine in heavy clay soils. Despite what you may hear or read, none of these trees is adversely affected by regular irrigation (as for a lawn).

There are of course many other native conifers. I would like to be able to recommend trees like incense cedar (*Calocedrus decurrens*) or white fir (*Abies concolor*), but I believe these are happier with more or less regular irrigation. I definitely do not recommend Colorado blue spruce (*Picea pungens*): a more unhappy tree outside its native moist montane habitat you could not find. I have yet to see a single tree, out of millions

Pinus monophylla

upon millions planted, not infected with spruce gall. Any plant that tempts people to spray poisons up into the air should not be planted in the first place.

Failure to overwinter conifers is a common problem whose cause is almost always attributable to the difference in moisture between the nursery root ball and the surrounding soil. The root ball can dry out in a day, so it should be well watered at planting time and adequately mulched (pine needles and shredded bark are both good). With a good mulch in place, it should not be necessary to water the plant during the winter.

My comments about snow damage should not be construed as a warning against trying some of these trees. Snow damage affects a lot of plants, especially yuccas, so being prepared, especially in spring, is simply part of gardening in our region. I find that a push-broom, pushed against the trunk so that the tree can be gently shaken, is effective, as well as just whacking away at the branches. Snow damage with conifers is in fact fairly rare here, but given the choice between having to go out in the middle of the night with a broom and losing a valued tree, I stay up late.

Cupressus (cypress). The true cypresses are very fast-growing and among the best trees for adding a distinctive blue coloring to the garden picture. They're certainly my favorites. Two species seem to be completely hardy, to at least −25F (−32C), with some reservations.

Cupressus arizonica, the Arizona cypress, is barely a plant of Arizona, being found in scattered localities in the mountains from southeastern Arizona through southwestern New Mexico and western Texas south to Nuevo León. (Californian plants bearing this name are sometimes considered separate species, *C. nevadensis* and *C. stephensonii.*) Mexican cypress would be a more accurate name, but of course it was discovered in southeastern Arizona, hence the name. (The type locality is the same as *Penstemon pinifolius.*) Arizona cypress makes a beautiful blue upright tree with leaf scales tightly clasping the twigs. It can grow to fifty feet (15m) or more, though I think this height has yet to be achieved in cold-winter climates.

Plants of *Cupressus arizonica* grown from seed collected from a population on Cookes Peak in southwestern New Mexico have proven com-

Cupressus arizonica

pletely hardy in Denver-area gardens over a period of years. Young plants may need to be wrapped with burlap for the first two winters, partly as a protection from desiccating winds, which they need anyway, and partly to help acclimatize the plants to hot winter sun. Any winter damage is quickly repaired by new growth the following spring.

Arizona cypresses are, or can be, extremely susceptible to damage by heavy, wet spring snows. In other words you'll need to stay up all night knocking snow off the branches if you want to save your trees. In the blizzard of March 2003, when Denver received almost *five feet* (1.5m) of wet snow in a two-day period, some of the large specimens (18-inch, 45cm caliper) of *Cupressus arizonica* at Denver Botanic Gardens were broken right off at the base. Staying up all night would not have helped.

Cupressus bakeri (Modoc or Baker cypress) is found in a few localities in the Siskiyou Mountains of southwestern Oregon and northern California, down to northern Plumas County in northeastern California. It is probably the most cold-tolerant of all species of cypress, experiencing temperatures well below 0F (−18C) in the wild.

Cupressus bakeri makes a tree up to forty feet (12m) or higher, slightly less blue than Arizona cypress, with smaller leaf scales on more numerous twigs. The thickly clustered copper-colored pollen cones are a beautiful contrast to the blue-green foliage.

Modoc cypress needs a little extra attention in winter for its first few years in the garden. Maybe the lava fields of northeastern California have less hot winter sun than Denver; wrapping with burlap seems to be an essential ingredient in the formula for overwintering young plants. Eventually the cypresses abandon the desire to fry to a crisp in the winter sun, and just grow upward like normal plants. Both the Modoc and Arizona cypresses will produce a sticky, resinous, aromatic ooze when exposed to temperatures below about −10F (−23C); this is not a problem and, again, the plants will quickly recover once spring returns.

Speaking of scents, Modoc cypress exudes a pleasant aroma of cedar, throughout the summer, especially after rain. In winter the scent changes to that of a fine cigar (Romeo y Julieta, Havana, if you must know).

Juniperus (juniper). Anyone who has lived in the Rocky Mountain region as long as I have may have a difficult time talking about junipers without gagging, let alone recommending any for the garden. There are junipers everywhere, in every yard; sometimes whole neighborhoods are populated with topiary poodle bushes. I can't imagine a more nightmarish horticulture.

Still, where the cypresses are either not available or not hardy, a few native upright junipers can be an important and beautiful addition to the dry garden.

Junipers can be fatally susceptible to heavy, wet spring snow and need the same attention to knocking snow off the branches at midnight. In the March 2003 blizzard, many of the 100-year-old junipers throughout the city were reduced to piles of mulch.

Juniperus monosperma (one-seed or cherrystone juniper; Oklahoma west to Colorado and Utah, south to Arizona and Sonora, Chihuahua, and western Texas) is a branching, raggedy-looking thing, sometimes a shrub, sometimes a tree to ten or fifteen feet (3 to 4.5m), with yellow-tinged leaf scales on fairly thick twigs. It can also be quite a tall tree, comparatively speaking: "Cherrystone juniper grows up to 60 feet [18m] or more, but generally it is much shorter; often the tree is as broad as it is high, and usually there are several forks from the base; in any case the trunk, however thick and old, is always short, sometimes with branches coming out close to the ground and resting their tips upon it, or, again, the trunk is bare of branches below, revealing its picturesque contortions" (Peattie 1963). Obviously, then, its appearance fairly reeks of "the old west" and as such it is desirable, and once established, which takes time, it will survive on very little water.

Juniperus osteosperma (Utah or bone-seed juniper) also has yellowish green leaf scales and thick twigs but lacks the resin gland present on *J. monosperma*; it is usually a tree but can be a tree-like shrub as well, growing to twenty feet (6 m) or so, with attractive white bark on older trees. Native from Montana south along the western side of the Rocky Mountains to New Mexico, Arizona, Utah, Nevada, and California. It is the most common tree in Utah and Nevada, the juniper of pinyon-juniper communities. *Juniperus osteosperma* is unbelievably slow-growing. I would recommend regular watering of small plants until they reach six feet (1.8 m) or so; a plant in my front yard has grown about six inches (15 cm) in twenty years with no supplemental irrigation.

Juniperus scopulorum (Rocky Mountain juniper) is found throughout western North America, from British Columbia and Washington to Arizona, New Mexico, and Alberta south to western Texas (apparently not in Mexico). This is a highly variable tree to twenty-five feet (7.5 m), or much taller in favorable locations, with slender twigs and a sometimes droopy appearance. The leaf scales, when pinched or when the sun hits them, tend to smell like a house with too many cats.

The variability of Rocky Mountain juniper has led to a large number of named selections based on color, growth habit, and so forth. You can probably safely plant these in the garden without worrying about introducing foreign genetic material into a purely native plant garden. *Juniperus scopulorum* is the only juniper native to our area carried by garden centers as large plants, and these only with cultivar names. I find some of the nursery-grown plants need tender loving care to get through their first winter (extra helpings of mulch, wrapping with burlap, and so forth).

A couple of other junipers are reportedly hardy. One is *Juniperus deppeana* (alligator juniper; Arizona and Sonora to Coahuila and western Texas); a tree has been at Denver Botanic Gardens for many years. This is an attractive juniper to sixty feet (18m) with bark covered in plates. "The chequered bark is unique," writes Peattie (1963), "and its resemblance to a saurian hide has well earned for it the name of Alligator Juniper. So apt is the description that if you ever heard of the existence of such a tree you identify it upon your first sight of it." I know of no source for large plants, which is the reason why visitors will look for one in our garden in vain. I have never succeeded in keeping seed-grown plants alive for more than a couple of months.

Pinus (pine). Dozens of pines in western North America and northern Mexico are more than worth growing, especially if your garden is blessed with mild winters. I take the easy way out and recommend only two.

Pinus edulis (pinyon, or piñon). Though the tree is always called simply pinyon, maybe two-needled pinyon is more accurate in light of the second species I recommend. Pinyon (southwestern Wyoming to northern Arizona, Colorado south to western Texas and Chihuahua) makes a tree about twenty-five feet (7.5m) high, sometimes higher, with gray-green needles two inches (5cm) long in pairs. *Pinus edulis* is the state tree of New Mexico, where it grows in the greatest abundance. "In youth the Pinyon has a short, thick trunk, giving off branches from the very base; the crown of the tree is flattish or a low dome, and all the branches are twisted and bent low, so that the whole aspect of the tree resembles that of some dwarfed but ancient Apple tree" (Peattie 1963).

Garden performance of *Pinus edulis* is rather different, since even a dry garden in Denver is a gentler environment than barren slopes in southern New Mexico. Maybe it's the "gardener's shadow" that some people speak of; or maybe a wet year, like 2004 in Denver, is vastly wetter than the wettest year a pinyon might experience in its native habitat. A twenty-year-old tree in our garden is as many feet (6m) tall, though it is visited by monstrously large black aphids from time to time. It has produced about two dozen pinyon nuts so far, unless the squirrels know more than I do.

Pinus edulis is a very beautiful addition to the dry garden, but large trees are only rarely available in local nurseries.

Pinus monophylla is the single-leaf pinyon, though every now and then it produces two needles. Native to the Great Basin (Idaho to northern Arizona, through Nevada, where it is the state tree, to southern California), it grows to about forty feet (12m) in the wild and makes a rangy tree, usually with more than one main branch. The single needles, two inches (5cm) long, are gray-green—much more on the gray side of the spectrum than *P. edulis*. Young plants can be mistaken for *Abies concolor* (white fir).

In the garden *Pinus monophylla* makes an elegant tree, tolerating drought to an impressive degree, yet accepting considerable summer rainfall too.

I don't believe a single nursery in the Rocky Mountain region carries single-leaf pinyon; this is such a bizarre situation, I must just have overlooked the plants in my wanderings through local nurseries.

Bibliography

This bibliography barely hints at the rich literature available to anyone who wants to evoke the smell of sagebrush after a summer thunderstorm. I am indebted to numberless articles by Panayoti Kelaidis in almost equally numberless publications, and to many articles in the Cactus and Succulent Journal of the U.S. Cactus and Succulent Society, and also to the British Cactus and Succulent Journal (now *Cactus World*) of the British Cactus and Succulent Society, simply for stimulating my appetite for more of some of my favorite plants, and also for evocations of the dry landscapes throughout western North America.

I would also draw your attention to *Rocky Mountain Alpines* (Williams 1986; now out of print)—and especially "Rocky Mountain drought-hardy shrubs," an article by Allan R. Taylor included therein—as a good source of inspiration.

Donald Culross Peattie's *A Natural History of Western Trees* is one of those books before which I am speechless. If you find anything at all of interest in western trees, then this amazingly well-written book should be on your bookshelf.

Anderson, Edward F. 2001. *The Cactus Family*. Portland, Ore.: Timber Press.

Barkley, T. M. 1986. *Flora of the Great Plains*. Lawrence: University Press of Kansas.

Mahonia fremontii

Barr, Claude A. 1983. *Jewels of the Plains*. Minneapolis: University of Minnesota Press.

Beaman, John H. 1957. The systematics and evolution of *Townsendia* (Compositae). Cambridge, Mass.: The Gray Herbarium of Harvard University.

Bean, W. J. 1970. *Trees and Shrubs Hardy in the British Isles*. 8th ed. London: John Murray.

Benson, Lyman. 1982. *The Cacti of the United States and Canada*. Stanford, Calif.: Stanford University Press.

Bravo-Hollis, Helia, and Hernando Sánchez-Mejorada. 1991. *Las Cactáceas de México*. 3 vols. Mexico City: Universidad Nacional Autónoma de México.

Clay, Sampson. 1937. *The Present-Day Rock Garden*. London: T. C. & E. C. Jack, Ltd.

Cronquist, Arthur, Arthur H. Holmgren, Noel H. Holmgren, R. C. Barneby, James L. Reveal, and Patricia K. Holmgren. 1972–97. *Intermountain Flora*. 6 vols. Bronx: The New York Botanical Garden.

Davis, Ray J. 1952. *Flora of Idaho*. Provo, Utah: Brigham Young University Press.

Dorn, Robert D. 1984. *Vascular Plants of Montana*. Cheyenne: Mountain West Publishing.

———. 1988. *Vascular Plants of Wyoming*. Cheyenne: Mountain West Publishing.

Farrer, Reginald. 1948. *The English Rock Garden*. London: Thomas Nelson and Sons.

Flora of North America Editorial Committee, eds. 1993–. *Flora of North America North of Mexico*. 12 vols. New York and Oxford.

Gabrielson, Ira N. 1932. *Western American Alpines*. New York: Macmillan.

Gentry, Howard Scott. 1982. *Agaves of Continental North America*. Tucson: The University of Arizona Press.

Harrington, H. D. 1954. *Manual of the Plants of Colorado*. Denver: Sage Books.

Hickman, James C., ed. 1993. *The Jepson Manual: Higher Plants of California*. Berkeley and Los Angeles: University of California Press.

Hitchcock, C. Leo, and Arthur Cronquist. 1973. *Flora of the Pacific Northwest*. Seattle: University of Washington Press.

Kearney, Thomas H., and Robert H. Peebles. 1951. *Arizona Flora*. Berkeley and Los Angeles: University of California Press.

Lanner, Ronald M. 1999. *Conifers of California*. Los Olivos, Calif.: Cachuma Press.

Munz, Philip A., and David D. Keck. 1959. *A California Flora*. Berkeley and Los Angeles: University of California Press.

Payson, Edwin Blake. 1927. A monograph of the section Oreocarya of *Cryptantha*. *Annals of the Missouri Botanical Garden* 14. St. Louis: Missouri Botanical Garden Press.

Peattie, Donald Culross. 1963. *A Natural History of Western Trees*. New York: Bonanza Books.

Rowntree, Lester, 1936. *Hardy Californians*. New York: Macmillan.

———. 1939. *Flowering Shrubs of California*. Stanford, Calif.: Stanford University Press.

Snyder, Gary. 1977. *The Old Ways*. San Francisco: City Lights Books.

Taylor, Ronald J. 1992. *Sagebrush Country: A Wildflower Sanctuary*. Missoula, Mont.: Mountain Press.

United States Department of Agriculture, Forestry Division. 1937. *Range Plant Handbook*. Mineola, N.Y.: Dover Publications. Reprinted 1988.

Wagner, Warren L., Robert E. Stackouse, and William M. Klein. 1985. The systematics and evolution of the *Oenothera caespitosa* species complex (Onagraceae). *Monographs in Systematic Botany* 12. St. Louis: Missouri Botanical Garden Press.

Weber, William A. 1987. *Colorado Flora: Western Slope*. Boulder: Colorado Associated University Press.

———. 1990. *Colorado Flora: Eastern Slope*. Niwot: University Press of Colorado.

Welsh, Stanley L., N. Duane Atwood, Sherel Goodrich, and Larry C. Higgins. 1987. *A Utah Flora*. Provo, Utah: Brigham Young University.

Wherry, Edgar T. 1955. *The Genus Phlox*. Philadelphia: Associates of the Morris Arboretum.

Williams, Jean, ed. 1986. *Rocky Mountain Alpines*. Portland, Ore.: Timber Press.

Wooton, E. O., and Paul C. Standley. 1915. Flora of New Mexico. *Contributions from the United States National Herbarium* 19. Washington, D.C.: Government Printing Office.

Index